Watch Ruparanganda

Genitals Are Assets?

Sexual and Reproductive Behaviors of "Street Children" of Harare, Zimbabwe, in the era of the HIV and AIDS Pandemic

LAP LAMBERT Academic Publishing

Impressum/Imprint (nur für Deutschland/ only for Germany)
Bibliografische Information der Deutschen Nationalbibliothek: Die Deutsche Nationalbibliothek verzeichnet diese Publikation in der Deutschen Nationalbibliografie; detaillierte bibliografische Daten sind im Internet über http://dnb.d-nb.de abrufbar.
Alle in diesem Buch genannten Marken und Produktnamen unterliegen warenzeichen-, marken- oder patentrechtlichem Schutz bzw. sind Warenzeichen oder eingetragene Warenzeichen der jeweiligen Inhaber. Die Wiedergabe von Marken, Produktnamen, Gebrauchsnamen, Handelsnamen, Warenbezeichnungen u.s.w. in diesem Werk berechtigt auch ohne besondere Kennzeichnung nicht zu der Annahme, dass solche Namen im Sinne der Warenzeichen- und Markenschutzgesetzgebung als frei zu betrachten wären und daher von jedermann benutzt werden dürften.

Coverbild: www.ingimage.com

Verlag: LAP LAMBERT Academic Publishing GmbH & Co. KG
Dudweiler Landstr. 99, 66123 Saarbrücken, Deutschland
Telefon +49 681 3720-310, Telefax +49 681 3720-3109
Email: info@lap-publishing.com

Herstellung in Deutschland:
Schaltungsdienst Lange o.H.G., Berlin
Books on Demand GmbH, Norderstedt
Reha GmbH, Saarbrücken
Amazon Distribution GmbH, Leipzig
ISBN: 978-3-8443-3080-9

Imprint (only for USA, GB)
Bibliographic information published by the Deutsche Nationalbibliothek: The Deutsche Nationalbibliothek lists this publication in the Deutsche Nationalbibliografie; detailed bibliographic data are available in the Internet at http://dnb.d-nb.de.
Any brand names and product names mentioned in this book are subject to trademark, brand or patent protection and are trademarks or registered trademarks of their respective holders. The use of brand names, product names, common names, trade names, product descriptions etc. even without a particular marking in this works is in no way to be construed to mean that such names may be regarded as unrestricted in respect of trademark and brand protection legislation and could thus be used by anyone.

Cover image: www.ingimage.com

Publisher: LAP LAMBERT Academic Publishing GmbH & Co. KG
Dudweiler Landstr. 99, 66123 Saarbrücken, Germany
Phone +49 681 3720-310, Fax +49 681 3720-3109
Email: info@lap-publishing.com

Printed in the U.S.A.
Printed in the U.K. by (see last page)
ISBN: 978-3-8443-3080-9

Preface

With the HIV and AIDS scourge impacting so heavily on developing nations, more so in sub-Saharan Africa, Zimbabwe is at the epicentre of the pandemic, (Johnson 2006). This has meant an unprecedented increase in the numbers of orphans and vulnerable children, who become destitute. The extended family networks have collapsed due to the debilitating impact of AIDS and the new ways of life. As Sauve (2003) observes, reports from both the developed and developing countries show that homeless youth, are increasingly finding the street safer for economic and social reasons.

The book explores the sexual and economic relations amongst these youth of the streets. This was done through fieldwork spanning over fifteen months, where I used in the main, semi-participant observation, life-story narratives and the conversational style. Apart from in-depth intensive interviews with both boys and girls, found through snowball sampling, informal interviews and direct observation to gain insights into the social and economic activities of the youth were also used. I cannot claim though, to have an exhaustive narrative of these youth's world, but I can confidently present a convincing story of the youths lived experiences.

Cases of the construction of masculinities were quite evident on the streets which made one discover that sexual matters were power issues, which in a big way simulated relations in our predominantly patriarchal society. My social constructionist paradigm was thus justified by the politics of survival on the streets and the unequal gender relations in a striking way and discredited essentialist explanations of the power relations between men and women in society. Also, scholars such as Freud (2001) who believed that "sex was destiny", were discredited by my findings. To the contrary one found that the domination of the girls sexually and socially, was more to do with their economic dependence on the boys who then otherised, objectified and sexually abused them. The girls have no option but to engage in risky sex in order to survive and to have a sense of security on the streets.

The sexual networking that prevails on the streets must be seen as a factor in the spread of the HIVandAIDS pandemic. Not only are the boys of the street involved but also men and women from mainstream society. Those from mainstream society do it for fun or satisfaction of their

i

biological desires but for the street girls and boys it is for survival. My argument is therefore that as long as the material conditions of these youth do not improve, behaviour change in light of HIVandAIDS is not possible despite exposure to knowledge of the pandemic. The youth are quite aware of the devastating nature of the scourge but they said they were not going to stop engaging in multiple sexual relations. They justified why they were not going to use condoms as, will be detailed in the following narrative. The girls have no power to demand safe sex or the use of condoms by the boys. Sexual encounters are controlled by the boys and men in general and thus girls have no autonomy. A real socio-cultural "tragedy" is fomenting on the streets, in that the anti-social behaviour of the children as evidenced by their sexual immorality, sexual violence and physical abuse especially of the girls, points to the collapse of our traditional forms of social control.

ACKNOWLEDGEMENTS

I owe a particular debt to my PhD supervisors from where this book originates, Professor Victor N. Muzvidziwa and Professor M. Bourdillon, for the many hours we spent in discussions as demanded by a project of this nature. Thank you my supervisors for helping me to develop some life skills; of economy in expression, being concise and focussed and being particular with technical issues relating to descriptive narratives. I thoroughly enjoyed all the discussions we had, even without appointment, with regards the progress of my project. You were always available for me.

To the street youth, due to the promise of total confidentiality, I can't mention them by names, I want to say, thank you very much. I know during the first days you seemed apprehensive because so many other people had approached you, as they researched about your lives, but never came back, after such studies and your living conditions did not improve. I want to assure you, your cause has become mine and I promise to be your advocate and I know that, you will soon realize how partisan I had become for your cause. I hope this study will conscientise society about your plight and that policy formulators as well as city council authorities will, realize that any further procrastinating on their part, will be disastrous for society. To those of you who might end up in this University and will read this book, I hope you will be able to realize that I made sure, your voices and your views were heard. It is however unfortunate that, I had to translate your views from Shona to English thereby distorting your world view somewhat.

I wish to acknowledge the generous advice, scholarly discussions and encouragement with regards to this book by colleagues in the Department of Sociology of the University of Zimbabwe. Some of my colleagues read my drafts and gave me important insights into my project. Also, I wish to thank all those who assisted with the typing of this book, who on many occasions worked under extreme pressure.

I am also indebted to a number of church elders from various denominations, as well as some members of the Zimbabwe Traditional Healers' Association, whom I consulted on several issues like totemism, "ritual sex" and the possible implications spiritually, of the phenomenon of street dwelling and the dangers of a generation that continues to grow on the streets. I also want to thank elders from my home village in Watch's Kraal, Chitsa area in Gutu, for the interesting views they gave me in relation to the cultural implications of street dwelling.

I also would like to thank the City of Harare officials who made my study possible. I especially appreciated all the assistance from Mr Magwenjere who was then the Acting City of Harare spokesperson.

I owe a special place in this acknowledgement for my immediate family members. I realize that sometimes, I failed to meaningfully respond to your needs because of the immense pressure this research project put upon me, which made me wish most times, I had had the opportunity to go away from my family for the write - up. Thank you so much guys for all your support, despite my emotional outbursts sometimes, due to academic labour pains. I am now normal as some of you have started to acknowledge.

DEDICATIONS

This book is dedicated to both my late father, *WATCH MUCHINERIPI (HOMWE)* who despite his ailing health in August 2002, encouraged me to go back to the University to *"ramba uchidzidza mwanangu."* (Keep on with University Education...). He passed on in November 2002 and my late mother *Selina Muchineripi* who used to brew traditional beer so the sales could enable me become educated. I remember *"maitsva nomoto, muchisekwa."* (You got blisters and wounds from the fire used when brewing traditional beer.). Rest in peace my mother now that I have made it. To my late sister *Nonny Muchineripi*, who supported me so much in my educational endeavours, I say rest in peace. To all street children and to all philanthropists of the world.

ACRONYMS

C.RC of 1989	:	Convention on the Rights of the Child
ESAP	:	Economic Structural Adjustment Programme
GALZ	:	Gays and Lesbians Association of Zimbabwe
HIV and AIDS:		Human Immune Deficiency Virus/Acquired Immune Deficiency Syndrome
LAMZ of 1982:		Legal Age of Majority Act of Zimbabwe (1982)
NGOs	:	Non-Governmental Organisations
OVCs	:	Orphans and Vulnerable Children
STIs	:	Sexually Transmitted Infections
UN	:	United Nations
UNAIDS	:	United Nations Aids
UNFPA	:	United Nations Population Fund
UNICEF	:	United Nations International Children's Emergency Fund
UZ	:	University of Zimbabwe
ZHDR	:	Zimbabwe Human Development Report
ZRP	:	Zimbabwe Republic Police
ZANU P.F.	:	Zimbabwe African National Union - Patriotic Front

CONTENTS

TITLE   **PAGE**

Preface   *i*

Acknowledgements   *iii*

Dedications   *v*

Acronyms   *vi*

Contents   *vii*

CHAPTER ONE   1

Introduction   1

1.0   *Problematisation of the Study*   *1*

1.1   *Objectives of the Study*   *3*

1.2   *The Socio-Historical Context of the Research*   *3*

1.2.1 *Otherisation and colonisation; as the root causes of*
       Street dwelling and poverty   *3*

1.2.2 *Pre-colonial Zimbabwe;-caring for orphans and*
       vulnerable children; the case of the Shona and the Ndebele   *8*

1.2.3 *The Colonization of Zimbabwe and the Institutionalization of*
       Individualism and Destitution   *11*

1.2.4 *Post-Colonial Zimbabwe: Short-lived economic boom; Social*
       problems of abject poverty and squalor, visible orphans and
       vulnerable children   *13*

1.3   *Defining and Explaining Key Concepts*   *17*

1.3.1 *Culture*   *17*

1.4   *Explaining the Sexual, Sexual behaviour, Sex, Gender,*
       Sexuality and Multiple sexualities in the context of
       the definition of culture   *18*

1.4.1 *Sexual behaviour*   *19*

1.4.2 *Sex, gender and sexuality*   *19*

1.5   *Organisation of the book*   *23*

1.6   *Conclusion*   *25*

CHAPTER TWO   **26**

The State of the HIV and AIDS Pandemic; Orphanhood and   26

Vulnerability - the Case of Street Youth,- A Global to Local View

2.0   *Introduction*   *26*

2.1   *Debates on Origin of the Pandemic*   *28*

2.2   *HIV AND AIDS: A Global Perspective*   *30*

2.2.1 *The State of the Pandemic in Zimbabwe*   *31*

2.3   *Drivers of the Pandemic*   *32*

2.3.1 *Poverty and Sexual Behaviour*   *34*

2.4   *Global, Regional and Local responses to HIV and AIDS* *36*

2.5   *Sexual Behaviour and HIV/AIDS*   *39*

2.6   *Youth, Orphanhood and Vulnerability to HIV and AIDS*

      - Global to local view   *40*

2.7   *Youth in Dominant Society's perception of sex and HIV and AIDS -*

      a global to local view   *44*

2.8   *Mainstream Society's Youth Empowerment Initiatives*

      and Interventions   *46*

2.9   *Street Youth and HIV and AIDS - A Global to Local View* *49*

2.10 *Cases of HIV Intervention Programs for Street Children/Youth -*

      a global to local view   *53*

2.11 *Conclusion*   *62*

CHAPTER THREE   **63**

Theoretical Underpinnings of the Study in Relation to Sexual

and Reproductive Health Issues- A Global to Local View   63

3.0   *Introduction*   *63*

3.1   *Social Constructionists conceptualisation of Sexuality* *65*

3.2	*Sexuality and Essentialist Propositions*	*66*
3.3	*Social Constructionism in Practice-Global to Local Views*	*69*
3.3.1	*The Institutionalisation of Masculinities and femininities in the Western Societies - A good case for social constructionism*	*69*
3.3.2	*Western Perception of African Sexuality As another good case of Social Constructionism*	*71*
3.4	*Use of Sexual Metaphors as an Area of Convergence between Western and African men's psyche: a case in favour of Essentialist propositions*	*75*
3.5	*Sexual Behaviours and Risk to Reproductive health*	*77*
3.5.1	*Abortion*	*77*
3.5.2	*STIs*	*78*
3.5.3	*Prostitution*	*79*
3.6	*Sexual Networking*	*79*
3.7	*Sexual Violence, Sexual Assault and Sexual Abuse*	*80*
3.7.1	*Rape as Sexual Violence*	*81*
3.8	*Sexual Identity; Women Empowerment; The case of Zimbabwean Women*	*83*
3.9	*Perception of reproductive health technologies as a case of social Constructionism*	*85*
3.10	*The Family and the Construction of Sexuality*	*86*
3.11	*The Sexual Act, Variations in techniques in heterosexual relations.*	*90*
3.12	*Homosexuality: A general perspective: The dialectic between the global and the local*	*93*
3.13	*Masturbation*	*94*
3.14	*Other sexual behaviours*	*94*
3.15	*Child care and social constructionism*	*94*
3.16	*Conclusion*	*95*

CHAPTER FOUR   **96**

Methodological Debates and the Organization of the Study   96

4.0   *Introduction*   *96*

4.1   *Objectivity and the search for truth*   *96*

4.2   *Ethnography and Qualitative Research*   *100*

4.3   *Debates around the status of the researcher either*

    as outsider or insider   *104*

4.4   *Research and morality*   *106*

4.5   *Gaining Entry*   *107*

4.6   *Use of Incentives in Research as a way to gain Trust of*

    the Respondents   *109*

4.7   *The Problematics of Investigating Sexual Issues*   *112*

4.8   *Information Gathering Techniques*   *113*

4.9   *Ethical Considerations*   *115*

4.10 *Hazards of the Field*   *117*

4.11 *Organization and conduct of the Study*   *119*

4.12 *Unlocking into the youth's world*   *119*

4.13 *Sampling and Data Collection Techniques*   *123*

4.14 *Data Analysis*   *126*

4.15 *Conclusion*   *126*

CHAPTER FIVE   **128**

The Street as a Resource and a Gendered Terrain; Power and   128

Autonomy in Social and Sexual Encounters on the Streets

5.0   *Introduction*   *128*

5.1   *Accounting for the street dwelling by the youth*   *129*

5.2   *The Cases*   *129*

    CASE ONE   129

    CASE TWO   130

    CASE THREE   131

CASE FOUR   131

5.3   Sub-themes from the cases   131

5.3.1 Visible Orphanhood and Vulnerability   131

5.3.2 Poverty as another Push factor and Peer pressure   132

5.4   The Street Youth's Identity   133

5.4.1 Society owes us an apology   133

5.4.2 Street youth condone their anti-social behaviour   134

5.4.3 Justifying anti-social behaviour on the streets   135

5.4.4 We are the Magundurus   135

5.4.5 The Language of the Streets   136

5.5   Official perception of the street involved youth   137

5.6   Surviving on the Streets; Focussing on issues of power

       and autonomy on the Streets   138

5.6.1 The street as a battlefield   138

5.6.2 Conflicts of street involved boys   141

5.6.3 The Street as a source of livelihood   142

       A case of corruption I witnessed on a Wednesday afternoon

       mid month in June 2006   143

5.6.4 Street Youth Interfacing with the Formal Sector   144

5.6.5 The City fathers perception of the Street as a resource   145

5.7   Power and Autonomy in Social Relations - Boys versus Girls   146

5.7.1 Food Resources and the construction of masculinities   148

5.7.2 Control of "kitchens" as a good case of the construction

       of masculinities   149

5.8   Aspirations of the street youth and their leisure activities   151

5.8.1 The Youth Condemn Streets Ahead - Biting the hand that fed them 152

5.8.2 Caring for one another on the streets   153

5.8.3 Fun and Entertainment on the Streets   155

5.9   Conclusion   156

CHAPTER SIX   157

       Sexual Behaviour Patterns of Street Youth of Harare   157

6.0   Introduction   157

6.1   Nightmarish Sexual Experiences of The First Days On The Streets   158

6.2   Anatomy as destiny on the streets and the "otherisation" of girls   160

6.3   Dating and Courtship on the Streets   161

6.4   Of Romance and the ideal woman   162

6.5   Sources of Sexual knowledge   163

6.6   Initiating consensual heterosexual sex   165

6.7   Heterosexual relations on the streets as - "sex the invisible"   166

6.8   Virginity status of street girls and boys   167

6.9   The notion of "Forced sex" amongst the youth   168

6.10 Gang-rape on the streets   169

6.11 Lovers discourses under the blankets on the streets   170

6.12 Sexual Networking by the Girls   172

6.13 The "Genitals" as assets for survival and a way to climb out
      of poverty. A good Case of intergenerational sex and
      climbing-out-of-poverty" and sexual networking   174

6.14 Homosexuality and some bestiality amongst street girls   176

6.14.1 Sexual Networking by the boys - The Case of the
       "Sexual poacher"   178

6.14.2 Interfacing with mainstream society in Sexual encounters-
       A case of Intergenerational sex involving boys, as evidence of
       sexual networking   179

       One key Informant's sexual Experiences with a 'Sugar Gogo'   180

6.14.3 "Ritual Sex "by boys as a case of sexual networking   181

6.15 Sexual positions and sexual techniques amongst street youth   182

6.16 Enhancing excitement in sexual encounters: -
      Interfacing with "Street Pharmacists"   183

6.17 Masturbation as some form of managing celibacy and a good
      case of sexual abstinence   184

6.18 Boys perception of sex as more of "fucking" or "patriarchal sex"
      - as indicated by the sexual metaphors they use   184

6.19 *Conclusion*   185

CHAPTER SEVEN   **187**
       Reproductive Health Experiences of Street Youth   187
7.0   *Introduction*   *187*
7.1   *Boys appropriation of resources and girls bodies on the streets*   *188*
7.2   *Street Youth Knowledge of the HIV and AIDS Pandemic*   *189*
7.3   *Street youth perception of reproductive health technologies*

       and their uses   *191*
7.4   *Use of herbs to enhance sexual excitement*   *194*
7.4.1 *Dry Sex - A good Case of dangers to reproductive health*

       of the Street girls   *197*
7.5   *Street youth views on circumcision*   *200*
7.6   *Sexually transmitted diseases amongst street youth*   *202*
7.7   *Abortion as a threat to the girls reproductive health*   *204*
7.8   *Pregnancy management on the streets*   *207*
7.9   *Midwives of the streets*   *208*
7.10   *Breast feeding on the Streets*   *209*
7.11   *Conclusion*   *210*

CHAPTER EIGHT   213
       The "Street Family" - A Deconstruction of the Conventional   213
       Parsonian Notion of a Family
8.0   *Introduction*   *213*
8.1   *Dating and Courtship on the Streets*   *214*
8.2   *The Street Marriage*   *216*
8.3   *Marriage, totemism and virginity on the streets*   *218*
8.4   *Patriarchal tendencies in street families*   *222*

A Visit To A Street Family's "Home"   222

8.5 Marriage and Lovers discourses under the blankets   225

8.6 Polygynous relations and Love Portions   227

8.7 Conflicts in Street Families   229

8.7.1 Caring for children on the Streets and parental

    Great expectations   231

8.8 Today's Parents, Tomorrow's Grandfathers and Grandmothers   235

8.9 Conclusion   236

CHAPTER NINE   **238**

Sexual Violence and Physical Abuse of the Street Girls: A Classic   238

Case of the Construction of Masculinities

9.0   *Introduction*   238

9.1   *Power differentials as an indicator that, on the streets "anatomy*

    is destiny"   239

9.2   *Use of Sexual Metaphors as evidence of sadistic tendencies - a*

    form of violence   241

9.3   *"Patriarchal Sex" as objectification of girls - a classic case of*

    sexual violence   243

9.4   *Forced Sex or coercive sex a form of "rape"- A typical case*   245

9.5   *Gang-Rape, an Disgusting Form of Sexual Violence*   247

9.6   *Statutory Rape on the streets*   249

9.7   *Sodomy as a form of Sexual Violence*   250

9.8   *Physical abuse - Cases of domestic Violence on the streets*   251

    Physical Abuse   251

    Sexual abuse   252

    Psychological/Emotional Abuse   252

    Economic Deprivation   252

9.9   *Putting the Cart before the Horse: No Freedom without Resources*   256

    Notable legislation that enhances the legal status of women   256

9.10 *Conclusion*   259

CHAPTER TEN 261

Research Findings, Recommendations and Concluding Remarks 261

10.0 *Summary of Findings* 261

10.1 *Recommendations* 266

10.2 *Contributions to Theory, Methodology and Social Science Research* 271

10.3 *Some possible research areas for the future* 273

Bibliography 274

CHAPTER ONE

INTRODUCTION

1.0 *Problematisation of the Study*

Street Youth seem to be a neglected category in Zimbabwe. A lot of research has been on street children, that is those below 18 years. There is poverty of information with regard to the sexual and reproductive health experiences or private lives of the youth who are between 18 and 24 years of age which is the concern of this anthropological study, in light of the HIV and AIDS pandemic.

Some of the research done on street children locally have been by Bourdillon (1994); Rurevo and Bourdillon (2003); Dube (1997; 1999) and Chirwa (2002). Regionally and globally, international organisations like UNICEF and scholars such as Swart Kruger and Richter (1997 and 1994), Jones (1993), Anarfi (1997) and Tadele (2003) have interesting findings with regard to the survival strategies of these children. These studies tend to be similar in focus, being general and mainly concerned with how these children survived on the streets. Tadele (2003) focussed on the sexual experiences of male street children only. These and other studies are discussed in the literature review chapter below. What is striking from the review of these studies is the lack of an in-depth study of the private lives of these children in Zimbabwe, especially their sexual behaviour patterns. A lot has been said about their sexual networking as discussed below and the forces that push them into it but no serious exploration of their sexual relations on the streets had been done, especially in light of the HIV and AIDS pandemic and the need to have intervention programmes specifically targeting these marginalized groups. Issues of power; that is of masculinity, gender and femininities were not explored by previous researchers. Issues of sexual abuse, rape and sexual violence are quite topical in Zimbabwe today culminating in the enactment of the Domestic Violence Act of 2006. A lot of education targeting the youth in dominant society is done through the various media, workshops and Youth conferences and yet the Street Youth are never involved. I feel this category needs the limelight too, when it comes to issues of sexuality and HIV and AIDS.

1

Most, if not all local studies, have been on "street children" and not "street youth". Street youth in this study, refers to those who are in Zimbabwean legal terms above 18 years but below 24 years old. This group is no longer cared for by non governmental organisations or what are called "drop - in centres", like Streets Ahead of Harare. Government has no programmes for this group hence my concern for their welfare, in the era of the HIV and AIDS pandemic.

The girls of the streets, from their various narratives in the unfolding story, need societal protection, just like all women and girls in dominant society. It's a real tragic - comedy on the streets in that, the city fathers left the problem to develop into a bigger problem from that of small Street Children; to that of Street men and women. Most researchers in Zimbabwe wrote about street children literally meaning those below eighteen years of age, but I had to look at street men and women who went onto the streets at tender ages. This is why sometimes; I refer to the youth as children. Now there are street families, there are marital unions and prostitutes and yet little research work has been done to explore these issues and their implications in light of the HIV and AIDS pandemic.

One finds that even though no "*lobola*" is paid on the streets, there is no equality in the marital unions (*lobola* refers to the bride prize). One girl was right to say that people, must look at the issue of genitals seriously, as the cause of inequality. Because, though women in dominant society have also become empowered educationally, and in terms of playing key roles in society, yet even with the enactment of the Legal Age of Majority Act of 1982, men in Zimbabwe still dominate women. She was protesting in light of the physical and sexual abuse girls suffer on the streets, as will be shown below.

Another street girl actually felt it was no longer necessary for women to adopt a husband's surname at marriage, because this tended to perpetuate patriarchal traditions, making it seem as if women's names were not important. Even the legal age of Majority Act, which sought to empower women to make their own decisions and own property, has failed to bring about equality in marital unions, such that one could argue that unless men start putting on dresses, we might be far from achieving a state of equality in society. It does not matter whether women become Presidents of Nations or referee at the World soccer showcases like the World Cup. It would appear as if the issue revolves around genitals. The women from the developed world

2

acknowledged that the vagina, despite all their efforts to ensure equality, was still considered inferior to the penis and a shameful part of the body to mention (Machera, 2004).

1.1 *Objectives of the Study*

The objectives of this study were:

1. To explore the issues of power and autonomy in sexual relations on the streets and thus contribute to the gender debate.

2. To shed more light on the sexual behaviour patterns of street youth in the era of the HIV and AIDS pandemic so that appropriate intervention strategies can be formulated.

3. To determine the level of street youth awareness of the prevalence of the HIV and AIDS pandemic and their attitudes in light of this.

1.2 *The Socio-Historical Context of the Research*

1.2.1 *"Otherisation" and colonisation; as the root causes of Street dwelling and poverty.*

The story of the Street youth below, is firmly rooted in the social, economic and political history of Zimbabwe; from pre-colonial times to post-colonial socio-political relations. The notion of "otherisation", permeates the thesis like a ribbon, as the main contention is that, reality is a social construction (Berger and Luckmann, 1966). I argue in this story that girls are an otherised and objectified category. There is need therefore to make society aware of this. "Otherisation", in the context of this project, has its origins in the Enlightenment, in which we see the rationalization, universalisation and hierachisation of knowledge. Miller (1986) says that, the concept focuses on how experiences, beliefs and existence in general of other members of society or other groups of people in society (women for example, the youth or street children, Africans, Asians etc), are often stereotyped and marginalized, giving them a feeling of being the "unknown".

From literature review, one discovers that the Western discourse of the eighteenth century - the philosophical and scientific thinking, was embedded in the principle of rationality and universalism and critical of the influences of tradition and religion. Society and knowledge became hierarchised, as well as people within those societies. Men were associated with reasoning and women with emotion and nature, such that some writers on gender see the institutionalisation of masculinities and femininities as rooted in Enlightenment philosophy

3

(Caplan, 1987; Jackson, 1987; Jaggar, 1992).

In order for one to understand the power dynamics between boys and girls on the streets, one needs to have a brief history of the possible explanations of inequality between men and women in general - a global to local view. Wollstonecraft, cited in Gould and Wartofsky (1980), argued that, the connection between reason and morals which lies at the root of Locke's political philosophy and which enjoyed popular acceptance, was for women, both a means of their oppression, and a rallying point for the assertion of political equality. On the basis of the writings of Western philosophers women were denied education and inculcated with the idea that they were frivolous and irrational creatures, such that women constituted and were produced as a category of "the other". Seidler (1985); Carrigan et al (2002) and Jaggar (1992) say that women, were relegated to the domestic sphere, where under the guidance and direction of her rationally superior husband, she tended the house, raised children and gave her family comfort and pleasure. Correspondingly, her 'virtues' were an outgrowth of her sensitive, yielding nature; kindness, humility, gentleness etc. These qualities are expected of girls on the streets by their male counterparts. The boys of the streets behaviour, is as condescending to their female counterparts, as was that of patriarchs described here.

According to Wollstonecraft in Gould and Wartofsky (1980), female nature and feminine virtues were often touted as the complement of male nature and masculine virtues, the two together, making a perfect whole of human behaviour. This western conception of the sexes, some have argued, was imposed on the colonised, which helps one understand how women, who had played an important role in social affairs in our societies, became otherised, in most colonized lands. Bhebhe, (2000), sees the customary law for example, as an oppressive piece of legislation, emanating from this kind of Western philosophy. To Rousseau, women were like children, weak and passive, while men had to be strong and active. Women were deficient in reasoning ability and according to Locke; it was reasoning, which enabled one to discover the laws of nature, thus qualifying one as a participating member of society. Rousseau believed as will be evident in Chapter 3 that, women were for men's pleasure and such an attitude seems to have become so implanted in the man's psyche, he thinks himself to be superior to the woman. This was quite evident on the streets, where the boys felt more superior to the street girls, as will be discussed extensively later, in the discussion chapters.

4

Kolibre (2005) says that, the term 'Other', is used to categorise those who are not part of the dominant culture and the other is often assumed to be inferior. For example, in this book, the street boys regard the girls as inferior to them. In order for one to understand the following narrative, this background is critical, and the realization that colonization of other societies by European countries disrupted the social, political and cultural processes in those countries. In the case of Zimbabwe, one of the problems of colonization, I will argue, is the "Street Kids", Street Children and "Street youth" phenomenon, (the expressions are used interchangeably here). To members of the public, the terms mean the same but in this study, I will mainly use the term street youth that is those above 18 years of age.

Early researchers, and anthropologists, the likes of Malinowski have been accused of having been influenced by these diseases of otherisation, (Jackson 1998). Women too, the feminists, become critical of studies especially by men, as having led to the "Otherisation" of women, (Stanley and Wise, 1983). Colonization of Africa, was a result of "Otherisation" as evidenced by the "Dark Continent" discourse of the 18th century, with regard Africa (Arnfred, 2004). Europeans believed Africans were primitive, backward and uncivilized and believed, their mission was to penetrate the virgin lands of Africa, on a civilizing mission. Chiwome et al (2000) and Ayisi (1979) also argue that, to say that Africans were uncivilized, is a gross assumption emanating from a Eurocentric perception of things, resulting in otherisation of peoples of other cultures. Those, who are critical of the 'Dark Continent discourse, argue that Africans had their well-established religions, social, political, medical and economic institutions which were destroyed by colonization, as a result of the "Otherisation" process. Adleman and Enguidanos (1996), regard this as cultural imperialism, which involves the paradox of experiencing oneself as invisible at the same time that, one is marked out as different,- characterised by the universalising of a dominant group's way of life, disregarding the local including the language of the locals.

Donald and Rattansi (1992), observe that, in colonies for example, the colonial masters imposed their own language and thus even the thinking of the natives changed. This confirms Berger and

5

Luckmann's (1966) view that, language is a critical aspect in the social construction of reality as will be evident below. Wa Thiongo (2005), analyses how colonial administrators, planted their memory on the intellect of the natives. This was achieved by imposing European language on the conquered. In Africa this meant raising European languages to the level of an ideal, whose achievement was the pinnacle of pure enlightenment. This language comes with culture, and the erosion of communalism in most instances on which the Africans-well being rested. The extended family and the kin group, all valued caring for one another. For example, in recruiting new servants of the empire from among the colonized, Lord Macaulay believed that teaching English in India, would produce a class of natives; Indian in blood and colour, but English in taste, opinions, morals, and intellect, who would stand as interpreters between them and the people they governed - buffer between the real owners of the empire and the vast masses of the owned (Boyd, 2000). This is the kind of thinking the western colonisers had and this destroyed the African social fabric.

Language is a means of organizing and conceptualising reality, (Berger and Luckmann 1966) , and it is also a bank of the memory generated by human interaction with the natural social environment. Each language, no matter how small, carries its memory of the world. Suppressing and diminishing the language of the colonized, also meant marginalizing the memory they carried and elevating, to a desirable universality, the memory carried by the language of the conqueror, as evidenced in the various statutes enacted in colonies. The marriage institution was strongly influenced by western ways. The new ways of life that led to the separation of husband and wife for a long time resulted in increased divorce rates. The extended family was also weakened such that one can claim that destitution, orphanhood and poverty have their roots in colonisation.

The concept of race, as of sex, according to Bo'Strath (2000) emerged as a branch of the process of "otherisation". In this instance biology was linked to the concept of progress and anthropology was supplanted by biology as the trendsetter. The discourse shifted from the beauty of race to the priority of blood and the elevation of ethics in the place of science and the notions of white supremacy, led to the hierachisation of races into Whites, Asians, and Blacks. Peil (1997) says that, according to the Europeans, the Whiteman's burden, was to rule and the African's duty was to obey. The Europeans needed to believe that they were innately superior to

6

the Africans, in order to legitimate their continued rule over them. The myth of racial superiority, was a creation of the 18th century discourses and indicates, the manifestation of the notion of otherisation in terms of defining other races as inferior. Beattie (1994) says that, ethnocentric views, were predominant and identifies for example, Hume, Adam Smith and Ferguson among others, who wrote about primitive institutions, and yet, they were not empirical scientists, such that she observes that, their conclusions were speculative and ethnocentric. Kolibrie (2005), argues that, otherisation, created the illusion that, there was one dominant culture and one "other culture". Bo' Strath (2000) asserts that, the image of a European identity, created in the 19th century, necessarily contains a demarcation of the non-European and it is the 'Janus head' of every distinction which is both inclusive and exclusive. Europe was seen in the mirror of the other, a projection that might in fact, have said more about Europe than about the other. In Bo' Strath's conceptualisation of the 'janus head' of Europe, the other incorporates in itself identification, the xenostereotype imposed upon it. This xenostereotype, becomes an autostereotype and hence, constituting the other as a category of analysis. Bo'Strath (2000) goes on to argue that, in the wake of the Enlightenment, the quest for absolute knowledge was followed by a European obsession with classification.

This classification was the wedge that divided and organized hierarchically the empirical world. The practical manifestation of the other and its perpetual reproduction was expressly evidenced by imperialism and it is the argument of Bhebhe (2000), for example that, colonisation inaugurated a general amnesia on some of the Africans' spectacular scientific achievements and deliberately slowed down, the scientification of Africans by teaching them, to forget their past achievements. The Egyptians he alleges, were taught to forget their role as inventors of civilization. Chiwome et al (2000), argue that, the foundation of African experimental knowledge systems that was embodied by traditional healers, spirit mediums and other important personages were seen as an impediment in efforts to universalise Western civilization. The subsistence of African knowledge, cannot be divorced from their culture and the emphasis of Western discourses of rationality and scientific reasoning, actually produced African ways of knowing as the "other". Chavunduka (1994), condemns this otherisation evident in the medical field, as was evidenced by the vilification of the traditional healers and their designation as "witchdoctors".

Western philosophy, not only otherised knowledge, gender and race, but also otherised sexual differences as detailed below in Chapter 3 and 4. Whites were seen as possessing the ideal sexual endowment and blacks could only be defined against the ideal. Gilman (1992), argues that, in the course of the 19th century, the female Hottentot, comes to represent the black female and the prostitute, to represent the sexualised woman. Both the categories, are created to represent classes of people, with specific qualities. The Hottentot, remained representative of the essence of the black female in Europe, although most groups of African blacks were known to Europe, (Arnfred, 2004). The otherisation, climaxed with the abduction of Hottentot, Sarah Bartman, who was showcased in the museums in Europe, as a model of Africanness, which was supposedly very distinct from European concepts and characteristics with Africans being seen as generously endowed in their genitalia compared to the Europeans. African sexuality was created as the 'other'. It's important to highlight here again, that the notion of otherisation, implies the social construction of reality, a perspective that pervades the book.

1.2.2 *Pre-colonial Zimbabwe;-caring for orphans and vulnerable children; the case of the Shona and the Ndebele*

Pre-colonial Zimbabwean social organization was basically communal, with the nuclear family not as the important unit of society, but the extended family. Other kin played a very important role in the social, cultural and economic affairs of the members of a family. Marriage, for example, was the concern of members of the clan, not just the individual intending to marry (Nyathi, 2001; Mutsvairo, 1996; Aschwanden, 1982; Bourdillon, 1993). As Berger and Luckmann (1966), have observed with regards socialization, integration into mainstream society was of critical importance and behaviour almost predictable, because these were simple societies, where knowledge was transmitted manually maybe approximating what Durkheim called, "mechanical solidarity" (Ritzer, 1992). Sexual education of the young, was done through the *dare* (camp for men), and for girls it was done by women for example the aunts, (Shire, 1994). Marriage arrangements, involved the aunts and uncles, from dating and courtship. This is quite the opposite of today's dating, which is done even through the Internet or newspapers, with either men or women initiating the courtship process. This was unheard of; it was always the man, who initiated the process himself or through a relative. Individuals were thus to some extent, products of their social groups, hence the notion of "being" or *UNHU* or *UBUNTU*, being

8

an easy quality to develop, in an individual as identity was quite "immobile," i.e. one could easily be identified with a particular age group or group of people either Shona or Ndebele. My argument is that, to those who today claim the unenviable role to educate people, so that they show qualities and skills of "*UNHU*", are like the Catholic Counter Revolutionaries of the 19th century, who were yearning for a return to the medieval times, (Ritzer, 1992; Zeitlin, 1968). After colonization, traditional systems were just broken down, as the aim of the colonialists, as well evidenced by what Lord Macaulay said in India about Indians cited above, was to teach English in India to produce a class of natives, Indian in blood and colour but English in taste, opinions, morals and intellect. This also happened in Zimbabwe.

Family life in pre-colonial society was characterized by equity. Men and women had their spaces and property, (Shire 1994; Nyathi 2001; Bhebhe 2000; Aschwanden 1982). With colonization, this set up was destroyed, dismantled and men and women were eventually to spend most of their time in the same house. The extended family, provided a social safety net for the bereaved children in traditional society. There were no children who would roam in the forests in search of food in pre-colonial society as destitutes. There were no streets; these were a creation of the colonialists. Divorce was very rare and even widowhood, because the extended family system was the "social-shock-absorber". Children were prized as Mbigi (2000), observes and their care and control was the responsibility of the extended family. With colonisation, as Kaseke (1993), discusses, control of deviant and delinquent children was now the responsibility of the state. He says," There are two main legal instruments which deal with young offenders in Zimbabwe, namely the Children's Protection and Adoption Act (Chapter 33) and the Criminal Procedure and Evidence Act (Chapter 57). The courts have taken over the functions of the extended family (Kaseke, 1993:11).

The wife did not belong to the husband alone, but to the rest of the kin group and *lobola* was the kin group's responsibility. Individualism, was a creation of the colonial system as pastures, common watering holes for livestock and food, were communally shared and thus individualism is well evidenced as the creation of the whites. The "enclosure" system, was imported from England. The Whiteman's cattle would graze on their own, he would live alone and share no resource with anyone and as Lord Macaulay put it correctly, these were the norms and values to be inculcated into the natives and true to their aspirations, they achieved this, the effects of which

9

are permanent, and for all who care, to see. The African's "BEING" or *"UNHU"* or *"UBUNTU"* is no more, and hoping to revive pre-colonial society is like having an "Alice in Wonderland" mentality. The effects of colonization are permanent and the problems of destitution will actually increase.

There were in traditional Shona society, strict religious codes and the African's belief system was very powerful. The colonialists realized this and when they came, they denigrated all sacred places distorting the African spirituality as a way of destroying the base of their being. For example a foreigner's grave Rhodes, was put in one of the most important shrines of the Africans, Matopo Hills. In the Chinhoyi caves, they went there to swim, which was not allowed, taking photographs and videos. One sees, these developments as having brought us into the state of cultural decay we find ourselves in today. A state of *anomie*' as described by Durkheim in relation to the effects of the Industrial Revolution in Europe, was repeated in the colonies and in our case, I see the process as leading to the institutionalisation of *individualism*, and the emergence of *destitution*. The increase in divorce rates, meant the increase in prostitution and the occurrence of "baby dumping," a phenomenon unheard of in pre-colonial societies. Visible orphanhood and destitution were a result of colonization, leading to the state we see today in the urban areas of "street involved" children. Social security systems of the Shona and Ndebele people, gradually collapsed, as the state took over most social responsibilities but with not much success. Kaseke (2003), details some of these schemes.

The urban areas they created are characterized by a high degree of anonymity and the organization of residences in the white's suburbs also adopted by blacks, of having security walls around their premises, destroyed the communal spirit of pre-colonial times. One sees the entrenchment of the attitude, "Each man for himself and God for us all". *The Herald* of Saturday, 20 January, 2006, captures well the institutionalisation of the spirit of individualism in an article titled, "Security Walls kill Spirit of Social interaction", i.e. the durawalls or precast walls put around residential areas, kill the spirit of communalism and togetherness, that prevailed in traditional, pre-colonial societies. Mazrui (2004:42), has rightly pointed out that, "Most of the present day Africa, could be traced to Western interlopers; from the missionaries and slave traders of early days, through to the European colonialists, who curved up the continent with arbitrary national borders, to capitalists, who have plundered its natural resources, often bequeathing decay rather than development".

1.2.3 *The Colonization of Zimbabwe and the Institutionalization of Individualism and Destitution*

Harare is the capital city of Zimbabwe. Its former colonial name is Salisbury, named after one of the Prime Ministers of the colonial masters - the British. It was established as a fort in 1890. Fort, has military connotations as a bulwark against attacking and marauding elements. In this case, the marauding elements were the natives i.e. the Shona and the Ndebeles. The colonialists hoisted the British flag, the Union Jack and this was symbolic of their quest to conquer and subdue the natives. This, they eventually managed to do, despite all the resistance as detailed in history books by for example, Bhebhe, 2004; Herbst, 1990 etc. British superiority was also evidently implied by this process and anyone British had a superiority complex, as was to be evident in the settlement arrangements. The black natives had to be forced into subservience.

The colonization process brought with it the disintegration of the traditional ways of doing things and knowledge systems, with the family as an institution experiencing the most severe negative impact. There was no more *"rooranai vematongo"*, (marry one from within your locality), obviously from those you knew their ways. The education system and the Christian teachings, helped to destroy traditional ways in the spirit of the mission of colonization, to Westernize the natives; such that, one is reminded of Walter Rodney's *"How Europe underdeveloped Africa"*. The growth of towns and cities led to the separation, sometimes for long periods of time, of husbands, from wives and children and this institution that had been associated with ancestral spirits, (Bourdillon, 1993; Kayongo-Male, 1984's) role, began to be marginalized, as new socializing agents emerged like the school and the church and the factory. The colonial strategies to create labour power for the factories, mines and farms like the forced dispossessions of land, (Bhebhe 2004), pushed Africans to seek employment to get cash to pay taxes, the forced reduction of their livestock and the effects of forced labour, (Van Onselen 1976).This led to impoverishment in that, some were left landless. A repeat of the English enclosure systems soon many Africans found their way into the growing towns and at the same time learnt new ways, values and norms different from those of the closed, bounded, pre-colonial society or community. The emergence of poverty, as a result of the colonization of Africans, became an irreversible process and culminated into what contemporary post-colonial society, has to content

11

with - poverty and destitution. This is why Drakakis (1986:9), makes reference to, what a former President of the World Bank McNamara once said, that, "If cities do not begin to deal more destructively with poverty, poverty may begin to deal more destructively with cities."

Harare, whose colonial name was Salisbury, is my focal point in this project; but the preceding socio-historical context is of critical importance, if the reader is to understand the nature and origins of the Street Youth phenomenon. The colonialists in Zimbabwe, created conditions that would force people off their natural habitat, - "push factors". Soon the Africans were to embrace the Western ways of life, as well as the food and leisure activities within the urban areas. Eventually, "push factors" were unnecessary, as the "pull factors" to urban areas like Harare, became very strong to the extent that today, some people no longer want to be associated with the rural areas. With these developments came, the 'death' of the kin group economically and socially, only existing today nominally, to fulfil some social obligations like at funerals. Individualism, became the order of things and people no longer consult elders in times of crisis. Social vices like prostitution, have increased since then, as well as '*mapoto* marriages," as discussed by Chavunduka (1979), which are now called "Small houses", in contemporary society. Divorce rates increased, as men divorced their rural wives, to get new women in the growing cities.

The colonialists, had strategies of controlling the influx of the natives, into the cities then like the "Pass laws," a system legalized by Pass Laws, whereby one had to be employed in order for them to be in an urban area and this was written on the "*chitikinyani*" or (paper identity card) of the 1970's. There was such legislation as the Vagrants Act, which together with a plethora of urban by-laws, were meant to control the movement of people into Harare, and these were strictly implemented and worked so well, in as far as they helped in the entrenchment of an apartheid system, in the then Rhodesia, (Godwin and Hancock 1993). Bourdillon (1994:518), describes them; as low density suburbs comprising, "for the most part, large bungalows, on large plots of ground (half an acre is small), situated along tree-lined avenues", for whites only and the high density suburbs for Africans. "The high density suburbs have small plots, crammed together, with little space for gardens and trees. Houses are typically simple four-room buildings, but there is variation of size and type. Families may rent a single room or a rough wooden shack outside the main house, or perhaps even have a room, in the more densely populated areas,

(Mbare or Epworth). There are around thirty persons living on each plot, with only one official dwelling unit and normally only one toilet", (Bourdillon, 1994:518).

This is Harare, the capital city in post-independent Zimbabwe. Typically, there was even before independence, a medium density suburb meant for the coloured population, again a creation of colonialism and these are popularly known as *"vazukuru"* (nephews and nieces by the Shona), because they were born out of white man's sexual relationships with African women. In colonial times, most of the accommodation for Africans, was for men only, as is evidenced by the Mbare hostels built then, only to accommodate men whilst women, were to live in the rural areas, thus creating prostitution and baby dumping and a new breed of the "totemless". Beerhalls were built, to provide entertainment so the men would not think of going back home, as a labour control strategy and prostitutes, were free to patronize these places to provide sexual relief to the men and thus the emergence of an African with no sexual morals. The city in Harare, then Salisbury, was a no go area for Africans, who were also not allowed to drink clear beer, which was reserved for whites only, a few who consorted with the whites, as Lord Macaulay said of India, and had adopted the taste and norms of the whites, were allowed in such places. This meant designation of spaces as white areas and black areas. Marriage and divorce were now done through the western style, as dictated by the courts and the churches. Aunts and uncles, who had resolved disputes in most marriages, were slowly marginalized but with serious negative repercussions on the African family and the children.

1.2.4 *Post-Colonial Zimbabwe: Short-lived economic boom; Social problems of abject poverty and squalor, visible orphans and vulnerable children*

The euphoria of the early 1980's was short lived, for "Rhodesians Never Die", as an expression, and a book title, was fulfilled. The whites sabotaged the Zimbabwean economy, which culminated in the prescription by the World Bank of an Economic Structural Adjustment Programme in the 1990s. This was however too late to produce positive results, and it was like flogging a dead donkey. The programme's implementation required that, the government remove all subsidies on all forms of services like health; education et cetera, to retrench most of its labour power in the civil service, and those in industry had also to downsize their operations. Most workers lost their jobs. For example Maphosa (2007:2) observes that, "Zimbabwe's current economic problems have been largely attributed to the prescriptions of ESAP." Mushipe,

Mafusire and Zhou (2007) also say that this period witnessed phenomenal growth," as formal employment shrunk and people resorted to informal sector activities for survival (Maphosa, 2007:2).

Muzvidziwa (2003:69), quotes from Osrimu (1998), who noted that the adoption in 1999 of the Economic Structural Adjustment Programme (ESAP), by the Zimbabwe Government at the behest of the World Bank and International Monetary Fund, contributed to an unprecedented rise in the number of the very poor in Zimbabwe. Osrimu observes further that, in 1991, 6.6 million people out of an estimated population of 10.3 were living in abject poverty. Masunungure and Chimanikire (2007), and Maphosa (2007), also discuss the negative consequences on society of ESAP. The early 80's had experienced a boom in terms of socio-economic development and this was seen with the increase of people, who were coming to the big city to seek employment. Life was fairly simple then, but this led to overcrowding which was evident by the late 80s, as the previous restrictions imposed by the colonialists in terms of the occupation of space, only existed nominally, but to the peril of the urbanites.

The effects of the influx of migrants, into the city from the rural areas, together with the effects of mass retrenchments, coupled with the rise in cost of living, exacerbated the economic and social problems experienced by the Africans. Poverty became institutionalised. Kaseke (2003:33), of Zimbabwe says," The country is characterised by poverty". A poverty assessment study undertaken by the government in 1995 revealed that, 62 percent of the population were from poor households, that is, households, which were unable to meet their basic needs (Government of Zimbabwe 1996). In the following book my basic contention is that, poverty and destitution were a creation of colonialism. The prevalence of social vices like prostitution, crime, destitution and squatting, as well as street dwelling, must be analysed within such a socio-historical context.

Poverty, is explained by Gadir Ali (1992:1), who was quoted from the 1990 Development Report (SDR) thus; "Poverty is not the same as inequality - whereas poverty is concerned with the absolute standard of living of a part of society, inequality refers to relative standards of living across the whole society. This report defines poverty as the inability to attain a minimal standard of living". The economic problems bedevilling Zimbabwe are like a 'flue-bug', that swept across most of sub-Saharan Africa in the 90's, with most countries having the SAPS (Structural Adjustment Programmes), prescribed on them by the World Bank, but it was found out that SAPS, did not improve the living standards of people. Instead they became worse-off such that as an economic prescription it wasn't a 'drug' for recovery or of economic recuperation (Gadir Ali, 1992). Muzvidziwa (2005:4), also says that, "Poverty is neither an economic, nor purely social problem, but is multifaceted, with economic, social, political, cultural, and demographic dimensions. It is a condition as well as a process. It has income dimensions (earnings in cash and kind, but in urban areas, it can also be about lack or limited access to basic services such as housing, education, health care, sewer system, water etc." He goes on to observe that, poverty "can also be qualitative in nature where issues of social exclusion, lack of political voice and being invisible and powerless are noted (Jones 1999; Nara, 2001) (*as is the case with street youth*). Others see poverty as ideological degradation, (Sen, 1995) where the poor are not theorized adequately and therefore not well understood" (Muzvidziwa, 2005:5).

The above views need to be seen within the socio-political context characterized by conflict and a liberation war and then a proclaimed programme of reconciliation, which the defeated party, (The colonial government), accepted but not whole-heartedly. They, I argue, undermined the new Black government, in the spirit of maybe, "Rhodesians Never Die." The poverty and squalor, destitution and crowded conditions, were a creation of the colonial government and to some extent, I agree with Herbst (1990:13), who observes thus, "A new era did begin in Zimbabwe with independence in 1980, but the political and economic inheritance of the past, determines many of the constraints and opportunities facing the new leaders - -. To a great extent the politics of Zimbabwe centre on coming to terms with the vestiges of the past."

It is the colonial system that destroyed the African social fabric. New problems arose such as poverty and destitution, with thousands rendered homeless (Bourdillon, 1994, and 1976). There was an increase in the numbers of vulnerable children and the youth, and these became some of the challenges the government has had to contend with, from the mid-1990s. They tried to clear the streets of prostitutes which was also another problem created by the colonial regime, by way of rounding-up or arresting prostitutes in bars and hotels, (Magaisa, 1999). But, the problems seemed to increase. The homeless went into squatter camps and unlike Bourdillon's observations of the 1990s with regard to high density accommodation, in the years after 2000, those numbers seemed to have doubled per household, with a seven roomed house accommodating not less than six families each, comprised on average of five members. There would be in addition outside lodgings with another forty people to make it about 60 in places like Mbare, Epworth, Highfield etc. This put a strain on the provision of social services like water, electricity and sewerage systems, which are always bursting due to pressure. Many "tuck shops" were built, where a variety of services were provided, apart from groceries with some operating shebeens.

The city centre by 2005 became very crowded by vendors, selling fruits and clothes in what were popularly known as "flea markets". Faeces and all kinds of filth were all over, mainly as a result of the increasing numbers of the homeless and the street involved children. The government found itself embarking on a clean-up programme code-named, "Operation Restore Order", (Operation Murambatsvina) but, also known as "Operation Murambavanhu" by the street youth, (Operation Condemn your Own People). Informal shelters were destroyed and thousands left homeless and the children were the most affected, with some reported to have died due to exposure to cold as it was in winter, (May 2005). The clean - up programme, was severely castigated locally and internationally, and did not produce the desired results anyway, but created a lot of animosity for the government, from both the poor and the well to do, who were against the manner in which it was carried out. Generally, one can see a repeat of what happened in England during the early years of the Industrial Revolution, as described by the likes of Charles Dickens in his book "Hard Times".

During the Industrial Revolution in England, there was rapid urbanization of the population, as people had been left landless and homeless by the 'enclosure system', (Aronson, 1995). In the growing towns, the conditions of the working classes deteriorated because of exploitation (Gorz, 1982). The general living and working conditions of the working class were appalling with Mulpars and Murie (1999), citing the general deterioration of sanitation and housing standards of England's major cities like London and Leeds. Just like the living conditions, the working conditions were inhumane, there was inadequate ventilation and lighting. In the factories and shops, child and female labour was rampant across England as is the case in Zimbabwe today, where child labour including of those on the streets is out of control. These street children sometimes work for long hours as the case was in England and it was from these harsh working

16

conditions that the writings of the likes of Charles Dickens emanated. Midwinter (1968), shows that through such writings as "Hard Times", Dickens by implication, lobbied for the improvement of the conditions of the poor in England. "Hard Times", showcased the extent of poverty among the working class of England.

Just like Dickens, Marx and Engels, were also concerned about the deterioration of the living and working conditions of the workers in Europe and condemned the capitalist system for breeding such conditions. It was against this background that, Marx and Engels, proposed an emancipatory project that hailed egalitarianism as its central virtue, (Ashford, 1988). The conditions in our capital city of Harare, are not far from these descriptions, as poverty and destitution, homelessness and various vices associated with such living conditions, are also evident, like crime and prostitution. The main purpose of this background is to enable the reader, to be able to visualize and contextualise the street youth and their sexual behaviour. One must quickly realize and appreciate the fact that, this is a harassed and marginalized group, living in abject poverty on the streets. At the same time, one has to acknowledge that ignoring the historical past, would be like visualising social phenomenon ahistorically, thus theorising in a vacuum.

1.3 *Defining and Explaining Key Concepts*
1.3.1 *Culture*
The project is conceptualised within the context of the notions of dominant culture versus the street youth's own "sub-culture." It's imperative for one to define, explain and critically give an explanation of the concept of culture, and issues of "otherisation" and, thus the social construction of objective experience is implied and that people may not present themselves as they might have desired, (Goffman, 1969).

The conception of culture is contested and yet critical to the understanding of human behaviour in this case, sexual behaviour of the people under scrutiny (Akuffo, 1999:86). I will be elaborate in my definition not just seeing culture as the way of life of a group of people. Different definitions of culture are evident in the literature and this reflects different theoretical bases for understanding, or criteria for evaluating human activity. Culture, can be regarded as a hierarchical concept with some connotations of civilization and as a differential concept, which

17

showcase the distinctive identities of social groups and individuals. Culture can also be regarded as a worldview that guides behaviour. Giddens (1990), establishes a typology of traditional (pre-modern) and post-traditional (modern culture). Modern culture is the one characterized by rationality while the traditional one, is regarded as irrational. Culture is also viewed by neo-Marxists as an ideology, which helps to promote reproduction of the social relations of production, and as enhancing the hegemony of the ruling classes over the masses. Post-modernists like Foucault, deconstruct the whole notion of culture, alluding to its fluidity, relativism and multiculralism and thus the need to tolerate difference. Otherisation as discussed above, could be viewed as exclusive and as a result of intolerance of other cultures. The subculture of the street youth must be understood as meaningful to them even if we do not agree with their behaviour and actions.

1.4 *Explaining the Sexual, Sexual behaviour, Sex, Gender, Sexuality and Multiple sexualities in the context of the definition of culture*

Masters et al (1995:3), observe rightly that, "One would certainly think that there could be no doubt about what is to be understood by the term sexual. First and foremost, of course, it means the "improper", that which must not be mentioned, (Freud, 1943:266), cited by Masters et al (1995:3). Sexual matters, it would seem, have been regarded as taboo in most human societies since time immemorial, hence the notion of "private parts" in English. As observed in this book, even today in developed societies, it is shameful to mention the vagina and many a fight have occurred in my society, especially from the use of this word, as an insult unlike if someone is scolded thus, "*Mboro yako*", (your penis). They laugh but not when the word vagina is used.

The street youth use such jest always like "*mhata yako*," without taking any offence. People laugh but if one scolds you thus, "*Beche ramai vako*" (Your mother's vagina), there will be war. Machera (2004) says, the same when writing on the behaviour of Kenyan students towards the use of words referring to a woman's genitals. No one seems to know when all this mystification started but in my society as recent as the 1950s and part of the 60s, boys and girls in their twenties, well advanced in puberty, would swim in the rivers together, without any awareness that these parts were associated with shame. But from the 1970s, swimming of boys and girls in our rivers disappeared, as either sex became very aware of the notion of "private parts". Culturally, however, sexual education had been done separately in pre-colonial society, (Shire,

1994). It's also interesting to observe that, of all the animal species, only human beings cover their genitals.

1.4.1 *Sexual behaviour*

Sexual behaviour according to Huygens et al (1996), is said to be a configuration made up of a collection of sexual practices, scenarios and meanings, which are socially and culturally defined. In the context of the above definition of culture, it is important to appreciate variability in sexual behaviour and be tolerant because the modification of sexual behaviours conducive to HIV susceptibility, first require an understanding of the socio-cultural forces, which influence the practice of those behaviours in general. It's critical, to realise that isolating the meanings, beliefs, values, gendered ideologies, cultural constructions and social expressions of sexual behaviour, has illuminated why certain prevention efforts have failed while others are more appropriate methods of behaviour modification for HIV prevention. It's of paramount importance to realize that, there are social forces leading to the sexual behaviour that is prevalent on the streets and possibly not in mainstream society, disregarding what could be social malpractice to the mainstream behaviour patterns.

Hyde (1986), points out that, a biologist might define sexual behaviour as any behaviour that increases the likelihood of gametic union (union of sperm and egg), thus emphasising the reproductive function of sex. The problem is that people have sex many times and not for reproductive purposes. Sexual behaviour, to another American researcher was seen as the behaviour that "leads to orgasm, yet this still has problems because a wife might not have an orgasm and yet she experienced sexual behaviour", (Hyde, 1986:4). He goes on to define sexual behaviour as that, which produces arousal and increases the chance of orgasm. Put together with Huygens et al (1996)'s observations, it makes meaning within a cultural context. Pattern, emanates maybe from the fact that there could be evidently, commonly practiced sexual acts, styles and positions in coitus.

1.4.2 *Sex, gender and sexuality*

Sex itself needs to be explained. Many writers express their views but for the purpose of this project, just like the concept of gender was defined and explained in most of the books reviewed, Hyde (1986:7), aptly defines sex as referring to, "sexual anatomy and sexual behaviour". Sex

19

will be used in this sense, in the story of the street youth below, depending on the context. Gender is well defined by Chiroro (2003: x) as referring to, "the socially constructed roles as ascribed to women and men, as opposed to biological and physical characteristics. Gender roles vary according to socio-economic, political and cultural contexts, and are affected by other factors such as age, race, class and ethnicity. Gender roles are learned and are changeable." If the roles are learned and changeable, social constructionism rather than biological/evolutionary (essentialist) explanations, become important in understanding the nature of power relations between the sexes. As Foucault (1998) observes; the sexual resonates with issues of power, as will be discussed below in chapter three and this will be quite evident amongst the street youth with regards the control of the street as a resource and in relation to decision making with regards to sexual and reproductive health issues.

It is important here also to point out that sexuality is not the same as sex. Halperin (1998:413), arguing like Foucault (1998) says, "Sex has no history. It is a natural fact, grounded in the functioning of the body, and, as such, it lies outside of history and culture. Sexuality, by contrast, does not properly refer to some aspect or attribute of bodies. Unlike sex, sexuality is a cultural production: it represents the appropriation of the human body and of its physiological capacities by an ideological discourse. Sexuality, is not a somatic fact, it is a cultural effect." Halperin (1998), demonstrates his admiration of Foucault saying, with regard to his definition that, "The plausibility of such a claim (definition), might seem to rest on nothing more substantial than the prestige of the brilliant, pioneering, but largely theoretical work of the late French philosopher Michel Foucault," (Halperin, 1998:413). This is important if one is to understand the whole notion of social construction in Chapter 3.

Halperin (1998:414), goes on to say, "I think we understand 'sexuality' to refer to a positive, distinct, and constitutive feature of the human personality, to the character-logical seat within the individual of sexual acts, desires and pleasures - the determinant source from which all sexual experience proceeds. Sexuality in this sense is not a purely descriptive term, a neutral representation of some object state of affairs or a simple recognition of some familiar facts about us; rather, it is a distinctive way of constructing, organizing, and interpreting those "facts" and it performs quite a lot of conceptual work." In Domain, Foucault, (1998), argues in a similar fashion and relates sexuality to issues of power.

20

In my book, I am not going to be referring to power as Lukes (1986) does so exhaustively, as acknowledged by Vianello (2004), but, I shall be confined to what Bjornberg (2004:35), has aptly called "normative power", which he explains as "a form of discipline through social agency and language. It works at a cultural level through understandings about what is normal and feasible behaviour." He goes on to observe rightly that, at an individual level, it is possible to manage some degree of autonomy and transgress a normative order and as such individuals as on the streets, can develop their own practices beyond the socially constructed identities that are provided for by hegemonic discourses, leading to what some have called multiple sexualities.

Power as observed above, is a central concept to Foucault's analysis of sexuality and I briefly capture some of his sentiments here, before I look at the notion of autonomy. Foucault looks at power and the family. In Domain, Foucault (1998:405) says that, "Sexuality must not be described as a stubborn drive, by nature alien and of necessity disobedient to a power which exhausts itself trying to subdue it and often fails to control it entirely. It appears rather as an especially dense transfer point for relations of power, between men and women, young people and old people, parents and offspring, teachers and students, priests and laity --." Foucault sees sexuality, as an important factor in understanding relations between men and women and says sexuality is not the most intractable element in power relations, "but rather those endowed with the greatest number of manoeuvres and capable of serving as a point of support, as a linchpin, for the most varied strategies."

All sexual relations are inherently power laden and I think this is evident on the streets, especially between boys and girls and even between boys and those who sponsor them to engage in what I refer to as 'ritual sex'. This is evident in the marital unions also. Foucault (1998:405), says that the family in its contemporary form, must not be understood as a social, economic, and political structure of alliance, that excludes or at least restrains sexuality, that diminishes it as much as possible, preserving only its useful functions. On the contrary, Foucault says, its role is to anchor sexuality and provide it with a permanent support. It ensures the production of sexuality that is not homogeneous with the privileges of alliance, while making it possible for the systems of alliance to be imbued with a new tactic of power which they would otherwise be impervious to. The family is the interchange of sexuality and alliance, it conveys the law and the

21

traditional dimension in the development of sexuality; and it conveys the economy of pleasures and the sensation in the regime of alliance", (Foucault, 1998: 405).

Power, in the context of my project relates to what Bjornberg (2004:35), describes as the capacity to make others do what they would not do by their own will, and in this sense power is understood as "control of others and a capacity to govern other people's behaviour." As noted above, in this book its mainly normative power deriving from the cultural arrangements of a given group. Bjornberg (2004:36) goes on to say that, this way of understanding power is inspired by Foucault's analysis, where power is developed through a process of normalization - -. Through discourses, definitions of what is normal and expected as well as what is deviant, creating knowledge and truth about individuals. However, normative power through discourses does not carry a determining character. Individuals adopt the "normative guidelines" communicated through discourses to their circumstances and social relationships - -. Thus, in practice discourses on norms and 'truths are open for negotiations at local and interpersonal levels." (Bjornberb, 2004:36).

Boys on the streets, were found to borrow quite a lot from dominant culture, when they wanted to subdue the girls by saying that certain activities and arrangements were for them. The definition of autonomy comes out clear when Bjornberg goes on to say that "-power can be understood (also) as 'power over self' or 'self-governance', where the individual is able to make decisions on their own terms without being constrained by a lack of alternatives, or is able to get their own way despite the opposition of others. On the streets, it is important that one realizes the interplay between understanding of the dominant cultural values and those of the sub-culture, to understand the sexual relations that prevail and the management of conflict in such unions, where the traditional systems of managing conflict are non-existent.

The notion of multiple sexualities, evident in the unfolding story, challenges the heteronormativity of sexual behaviour, with "plastic sexuality" freed from the needs of reproduction, (Roseneil and Budgeon, 2004). Alluding to prevalence of multiple sexualities they note that, the sociologies of family and gender, in which the study of intimacy and care has largely been conducted, are under girded by heteronormative assumptions; in other words by institutions, structures of understanding, and practical orientations that make heterosexuality

22

seem not only coherent-that is organized as a sexuality-but also privileged.

In terms of sexuality in Africa, Helle-Valle (2004:195), seems aware of the dangers of regarding heterosexuality as the only form of sexual relations and says, "My argument, therefore, is that sexuality, both as practice and as a discursive theme, is (in Africa as elsewhere), many different things depending on the context it is part of, and must hence always be analysed as part of such communicative contexts." Helle-Valle (2004), talks of different sexualities. Caplan (1985:2) says, "In our society, heterosexual relations are seen as the norm, and homosexual relations are stigmatised. These are issues discussed in chapter 3 and chapter 4 where sexuality is theorized.

1.5 *Organisation of the book.*
Below, one finds that there is a chapter on literature review, in which I look at the state of the HIV and AIDS pandemic globally and locally as well as issues of orphan-hood and vulnerability and some cases of street children from Africa and the rest of the world. One then finds it necessary in the third chapter to theorise issues of sexuality like masculinities and femininities, gender, the family and marriage. I focus at how sexuality is conceptualised, especially, European conceptualisations of African sexuality and its implications in terms of possible HIV and AIDS intervention programmes. One had to theorise issues relating to sexual behaviour patterns and reproductive health issues and reproductive technologies and the attitudes of men versus women.

The purpose of the study was not to expose the Street youth for condemnation, but to conscientise society about their plight and to argue that they are as human as all of us and hence the need to channel resources towards their well-being in light of the HIV and AIDS pandemic. The Ministry of Youth, Gender and Employment Creation, The Ministry of Health and specifically the National AIDS Council, need to realize that this marginalized group, is a high risk group in terms of their sexual behaviour and thus need societal attention. NGOs also need to assist here, by looking at how to help those on the streets who are over 18 years of age. No organization including government ministries and departments has any programme for these street youth, and yet the group poses a health disaster.

One finds an interesting link between the behaviour of the boys on the streets and what goes on in dominant society in that, although most of their behaviour and acts are anti-social, when it comes to sexual and reproductive health issues, they want to borrow conduct from the dominant culture in which women are oppressed. The boys, as is evident below, always make reference to tradition and culture whenever it suits them and this is not in the interest of the girls on the streets.

Chapter four highlights important debates in qualitative research methodology, which I considered before I went to the field. This knowledge helped me to plan for the field work comprehensively. I then show how I organised my study and some of my experiences. Chapter 5 gives the lived experiences of the street youths, showing, what factors pushed them onto the streets. The street is discussed as a gendered terrain, where people of different interests clash- the city fathers and mothers versus street children, as well as the conflicts amongst the street youth. Of interest in this chapter are the power dynamics between the boys and the girls of the streets, in relation to the street as a resource - as a source of their sustenance. Issues of identity are also discussed mainly with regards the lifestyle and survival strategies which tend to be anti-social.

Chapter six explicitly explores the sexual relations prevalent amongst the street youth. Sources of sexual knowledge, as well as sexual techniques and perceptions of sex including the various sexual metaphors used by the youth are investigated. In chapter seven I then explore issues relating to reproductive health of the youth. This includes the youth perception of the various reproductive health technologies in light of their promiscuous behaviour and the HIV and AIDS pandemic and the role of what I call "streets pharmacists". Issues of power relations and decision making are of critical importance in this chapter as in chapter five. The domination of the girls is quite evident as well as the patriarchal tendencies of the boys.

In chapter eight I look at the street family, a unique marital union which Parsons never visualised when he conceptualised the notion of a nuclear family. Issues of gender, power and autonomy that pervade the discussion chapters and are evidently the thread running through all the chapters from the beginning of the book, are also discussed. In chapter nine, I then discuss issues of violence and domestic disputes in street unions and within street sexual relations where the boys otherise and objectify the girls. Chapter ten is the concluding discussion where I highlight my findings and make recommendations, and point to areas for further research.

1.6 *Conclusion*

The purpose of this chapter is mainly to discuss briefly the reasons for carrying out this kind of study of the marginalized. It is because, there is need to theorise the lived experiences of such groups especially their sexual and reproductive health issues, for much has been said concerning their survival strategies. The notion of otherisation is introduced, which implies social construction of reality, for it is not based on biogrammers but on culture and culture has a history, hence it is a social construct. This is important in understanding the institutionalization of masculinities which is an important aspect of this study, as one explores issues of power and autonomy in sexual and reproductive health matters of the street youth.

The socio-historical context of the problem of orphan hood and destitution, leading to some people living on the streets of Harare today, has been discussed. It would be a big anomaly to regard orphan hood, vulnerability and destitution as problems emanating from post-colonial mismanagement of social and economic affairs by the Zimbabwean government, though to some extent they must take the blame, but rather mainly emanating from the negative impact of colonisation.

CHAPTER TWO

HIV AND AIDS, ORPHANHOOD AND VULNERABILITY – A GLOBAL TO LOCAL PERSPECTIVE

2.0 *Introduction*

This chapter is mainly about the state of the HIV and AIDS pandemic as a global scourge. The project was supposed to look at the possible intervention strategies in helping the street involved youth or boys and girls of the street in, coping with the impact of this disease, as a marginalized group. Issues relating to global as well as local effects of the disease are discussed, as well as issues concerning orphan hood and vulnerability. Efforts by the Zimbabwean government to cater for the well being of vulnerable groups, are discussed as the country is a signatory to the Convention on The Rights of the Child of 1989. The chapter will then highlight the fact that poverty and the problems faced by vulnerable groups like the street youth, will affect government's efforts in meeting the Millennium Development Goals (MDGs). I then look at the youth perception of sex in general and their sexual behaviour, including the various governmental initiatives to counter the effects of the disease globally and in Zimbabwe. It becomes imperative to focus at various cases relating to the sexual behaviour of street youth in other countries and what programmes they have put in place, to help the youth cope with the devastating scourge. Statistics relating to sub-Saharan Africa will reveal why I found this to be a necessary study, as this marginalized group of street youth seems to have been neglected by all stakeholders, in the fight against the pandemic, and yet the sexual networking the youth engage in amongst themselves and with members from mainstream society, demands that they become involved in the fight against the pandemic. The reader will find that I adopted totally anthropological techniques as opposed to the sociological survey methods used by most researchers referred to in this book. I realised that my social constructionist theoretical framework required that I gather detailed qualitative data.

By all accounts, Africa is the hardest hit continent, with HIV and AIDS now topping the league table of killer diseases, particularly among the youth (Johnson, 2006). Unlike brain drain that could always be harnessed into brain gain, losing African brains to HIV and AIDS is invariably always about going down the drain, (Olukoshi & Nyamnjoh, 2003). They point out that the youth in Africa, are facing many challenges that could actually deny them the opportunity of taking over the buttons of scholarship and leadership to ensure and enhance the achievements of the older generations. Amongst these challenges, the most lethal, the most devastating, the most crippling, the most insidious, the most dehumanizing, the most threatening to scholarships, society and life in Africa, they say is the HIV and AIDS pandemic, (Olukoshi and Nyamnjoh 2003). Zamberia (2004), alludes to this increase in HIV and AIDS status from the 1980s also.

On Africa, Sessay (2003:42), paints a grim picture saying; "It is not an exaggeration to say that the HIV and AIDS pandemic threatens the very future of Africans and the African continent. Available Statistics are staggering; many more people die of HIV and AIDS in Africa than in the world's wars. The population of adults and children with the HIV and AIDS number 28 million in sub-Saharan Africa, compared with 7 million in Asia, 2 million in Latin America and the Caribbean --- although Africa accounts for only 11 percent of total world population, 70 percent of all HIV and AIDS infections in the world, are in the continent. Even if we query the veracity of these mind-boggling statistics, the fact remains that HIV and AIDS is real and continues to have devastating impacts on communities, families and individuals in sundry ways." Similar sentiments are echoed by Mufune (2003:44) who says that, the African continent has been the hardest hit by the pandemic and that the 'HIV infection profile in sub-Saharan Africa is very different from the HIV infection profile in the developed North. Mufune (2003:44) identifies heterosexual intercourse, as "the principal mode of transmission". Mwikisa (2003:59), also points out that, by the beginning of the new millennium more than thirty-six million people were estimated to be living with HIV and AIDS worldwide and that 95 percent of these people lived in the developing world, mainly in sub-Saharan Africa. Mwikisa goes on to say that, in the year 2000 alone, there were about 5.3 million new infections worldwide and that almost four million of these were in sub-Saharan Africa. By the end of 2001, it was estimated that twenty million were living with HIV and AIDS, 71 percent of them in sub-Saharan Africa. Sub-Saharan Africa accounted for about 70 percent of all adults living with the virus, including 81 percent of women and 87 percent of children. Moreover, 78 percent of the children orphaned by HIV and AIDS were in sub-Saharan Africa.

With regards to deaths in 2001, 73 percent of the global total was in sub-Saharan Africa. Clearly the distribution of the HIV and AIDS epidemic in the world is highly skewed towards sub-Saharan Africa, (Mufune, 2003). The state of the pandemic is also highlighted by Ezeilo (2003:65), who says that in the 2002 UNAIDS report on HIV and AIDS; indications were that the pandemic had reached unprecedented levels in sub-Saharan Africa estimating that 28, 5 million out of the 40 million adults and children with HIV and AIDS around the world, lived in sub-Saharan Africa. Ezeilo (2003:66), warns Africa thus; "These alarming figures clearly demand a multi-faceted approach towards prevention and control of the HIV and AIDS pandemic problem. It has important moral, political and legal dimensions that need to be dealt with, if the pandemic is to be brought under control in Africa." The picture becomes even more terrifying with projections as of Kirunga and Ntozi (1997:175), who say that, "Way and Stanecki (1991) using the long AIDS model, projected that by the year 2015, 13, 8 million people will have died of AIDS in sub-Saharan Africa while Piel (1994) estimates that 200 million will be infected by the year 2010." This has made researchers advocate for "worldwide basic and applied research especially in the area of human sexual behaviour. Most available studies show that transmission of HIV is mainly the result of multiple sexual partners, in both heterosexual and homosexual relationships," (Twa-Twa et al, 1997:83.) In Zimbabwe, the street dwelling people have been completely left out in the programmes to fight the pandemic, hence the need to sensitise society and policy makers on the importance of involving all people in this war.

2.1 Debates on Origin of the Pandemic

Kelly (2004), has a brief history of the origins of the disease pointing out that, from genetic studies, indications were that, HIV might have started by infecting animals for a long time and then diversified and began to infect humans sometime around 1930 according to Korber et al (2000). He goes on to say that the disease could have arrived in North America in the mid 1970s. The predominant theory according to Kelly (2004), was that the virus infected Chimpanzees perhaps for thousands of years. The virus eventually mutated into a form that could infect humans and it may well have been transmitted to humans in Central Africa during the butchering of Chimpanzees for food.

The theory goes on to say that, the virus may have remained isolated, in small, remote societies for decades until changing ways of African life brought it to urban centres, from which it was

28

then transported to the rest of the world by infected persons, (Kelly, 2004:509.) He quotes Hills (2000), who also says that, changing life styles such as increased international travel had had profound effects on the spread of such epidemics. Jackson (2002:2), also says that, "Despite extensive research, the origins of HIV itself remains incompletely understood. HIV belongs to an unusual group of viruses in humans, cats, cattle and some other animals. Retroviruses, including HIV, also belong to the lent viruses being slow to cause disease." She goes on to say that, HIV was related to Simian (monkey) immunodeficiency virus and that, "As viruses easily multiply, HIV has probably mutated from viruses found, in monkeys and apes. Even within one human being during the progress of the infection, HIV mutates significantly and the person develops many slightly different strains of virus over the years," (Jackson, 2002:3). As she goes on to point out, it's not known when exactly this Simian Immunodeficiency virus infected humans. Another interesting observation she makes is that, a few people do fight off new infection effectively, and some cannot clear the virus from their bodies but can live the rest of their lives with HIV and never develop AIDS. These are those we refer to as *makeriya* (virus carriers). She captures on the total perspective of the HIV discourse, saying that, "debates continue as to how, where, when and even why HIV has affected humans. Some have attributed AIDS to God as punishment for sexual promiscuity (Boylies and Bujra, 2000). Others have blamed biological warfare experiments that released the virus into the global population, either deliberately or accidentally (Kelly, 2004). Another line of thought is that polio vaccines, widely given in Central Africa in the 1950s and 1960s using monkey serum could have been contaminated with HIVs (Jackson 2003). Masters, Johnson and Kologny (1995), also point out to similar debates.

In Ghana Awusabo-Asare and Ariati (1997:357), point out that before the first case of HIV Seropositivity was reported in March 1986, most Ghanaians thought that AIDS was a disease that affected white Americans and their high flying Ghanaian counterparts and the disease was believed to be far removed from the daily lives of ordinary Ghanaians. Such a belief according to the two cost Ghanaians heavily, as the disease proved to affect and kill anyone in society. Nakanaabi et al (1997:207), in a paper titled "AIDS mortality in Uganda: circumstances, factors and impact of death", "point out that the epidemic seems to have appeared "in the late 1970s or early 1980s among homosexuals and male bisexuals and intravenous drug users in the USA and among men and women with multiple sexual partners, in some regions of the Caribbean and in

Central Africa. Dube (1997:61), says that, in the early stages, in the quest to understand the disease, "AIDS has been seen as affecting some culturally defined groups of people like homosexuals, black people, foreigners, prostitutes, and drug addicts. For example early suggestions for a name indicate the prejudice so easily associated with the disease. It was referred to as GRIDS - for Gay Related Immune Sexual Syndrome, referring specifically to homosexual men, (Barnette Blackie 1992:1). Dube (1997), goes on to say that, most countries had by then, reported cases of AIDS showing that the implications of the disease were international and transcultural. He observes thus; "AIDS is not a disease of a particular people; gay, black, prostitutes and others; it is a disease of people" (Dube, 1997:42).

2.2 HIV and AIDS: A Global Perspective

Evidence from the International Research Centre (2002), suggests that in the last 15 years HIV and AIDS has evolved into a global pandemic and it is sub-Saharan Africa that has borne the brunt of the scourge. This is because, as will be discussed below, due to the socio-economic, political and cultural factors that provides fertile grounds for an explosion of the disease, in this region.

Its imperative for one to take a global to local approach to the study of any phenomena relating to HIV and AIDS, as lessons can be drawn from experiences from elsewhere. Mann et al (1992:2), pointed out that, a global vision of AIDS is as important to the local, national and international future, as is global thinking about the earth's physical environments. "Indeed, if we were unaware how interdependent our world has become in the past 25 years in political, economic and social terms, - AIDS would have taught us this great lesson." As one tries to explore the issue of street youths' sexual behaviour and HIV and AIDS, it is essential to understand the global context and Sauve (2003:61), captures well the tone of my book, when she observes that, as urbanization makes its way across the globe, many of the world's poorest youths, make their way into the city streets, searching for money, friends and sometimes a future and financial prosperity. The greatest surge of urban migration in the upcoming years will occur in developing countries with the biggest populations in the world, as pointed out by the Population Reference Bureau (2003), quoted by Sauve (2003). It estimates that the ten largest urban centres in 2015, will include Mumbai, Lagos, Dhaka, Sao Paulo, Karachi, Mexico City, Jakarta, and Calcutta, which not surprisingly are some of the cities with the largest and fastest growing Youth population and the United Nations states that 40 percent of young people in the least developed countries live on less than US$1 per day (UNICEF 2000). HIV and AIDS, is a social reality that scholars in Africa can hardly afford to ignore, especially as nearly two thirds of the 40 million infected globally are right here on our continent.

2.2.1 *The State of the pandemic in Zimbabwe*

It is logical for one to place Zimbabwe into the above global and regional picture with regards the state of the HIV and AIDS pandemic. Felsman (2006:6), as does Maphosa (2003) and also Chomutare (2007), observes that, "It is well established that Zimbabwe is at the epicentre of the HIV and AIDS pandemic, with one of the highest HIV rates in the world. Nearly one in four adults between the ages of 19-45 years is living with HIV and AIDS. In 2003, there were some 45 000 deaths of HIV-infected children and currently, more than 165 000 Zimbabwean children are living with HIV infection." From her observations more than 40 000 children are infected through mother to child transmission and life expectancy in Zimbabwe is said to have dropped from 61 years, "during the early 1990s to 35 years by the end of 2004. Out of the estimated 3 million orphans in Zimbabwe, about 980 000 have been orphaned by AIDS." Felsman (2006), then points out that, "despite the positive news that the HIV infection rate in Zimbabwe is declining from 24% in 2003 to 21% in 2005, all reliable field reports from Zimbabwean communities made clear that the number of OVCs continue to climb." The issues of orphans and vulnerable children will be elaborated below, because it is very much linked to the issue under exploration of "street children" or "street kids" or "street youth".

Dhlembeu and Mayanga (2006:36), concur with Felsman's (2006) observations on HIV and AIDS statistics in Zimbabwe and they go on to point out that, "More than half of all new infections occur among young people, and almost 80% of these are among girls." Johnson (2006:50), also says that, well over one million Zimbabwean children, have lost a parent to AIDS and, "as a result face heightened risks of contracting HIV. Malnutrition, sexual exploitation and abuse as well as new pressures and premature adult responsibilities, all contribute to the increased likelihood that the country's orphans and vulnerable children may be infected". Street youth, are amongst the vulnerable children, as the majority of them were found to be either single or double orphans and hence the reason for their being the focus of this research project, because according to the Human Development Report of (2003:8); "There is evidence in many countries that HIV and AIDS thrives under conditions of general developmental vulnerabilities, including poverty and general socio-economic deprivation. This explains why developed countries are not so vulnerable to the epidemic and its impacts." Maphosa (2006:56), also highlights the impact of the pandemic in an article on Corporate response to the HIV and AIDS pandemic in Zimbabwe, observing like the others above that, "Zimbabwe has one of the highest HIV infection rates in the world, and they continue to increase --- Chitiyo (1990) quoted by Jackson 1992 states that, 90 percent of people infected with HIV are employed." This should make society realize that fighting the disease must involve all in society, rich and poor, employed, destitute and vulnerable children.

Mann et al (1992:7), provide a good summary of this section when they observe that, as people confront HIV and AIDS at the individual, community and national levels, a clear global picture, a sense of how each part fits into the whole is critical. At the local level, in Zimbabwe for example, it becomes imperative for society to look at all categories of people, that is, including the marginalized groups when trying to control the scourge, because if left out of the control programmes, they can cause or pose a real threat to the rest of society. Mann et al (1992:7), emphasise their perspective thus, "This global perspective, this capacity to sustain both a local and worldwide vision, is not an abstraction. First, local creativity and actions, inspire and motivate, even as we learn by observing others. Each affected community, each community responding to AIDS, is a laboratory of discovery in HIV and AIDS prevention and care. The capacity for accelerated global learning among communities is central to progress against AIDS, just as international sharing of "scientific information from different research centres is fundamental to scientific advances."

2.3 *Drivers of the Pandemic*
As to the prevalence of the disease in Africa, Mufune (2003:44), makes interesting analysis when he points out that there are three main possible explanations for such trends. These are the cultural explanations, the dependency explanation and the rational choice explanation. Mufune makes reference to Caldwell et al 1989's findings that polygamy and the having of longer-term girlfriends and mistresses and outside wives, fuelled the spread of the disease in Africa. On the other hand other researchers like Odebiyi and Vive Kaunda (1991), also quoted by Mufune (2003:44), observe that, sub-Saharan African infection profile, could be attributed to such

cultural factors as polygamy which drove "women to seek sexual fulfilment outside marriage, and the high value placed on children in African cultures, which drives people into indiscriminate sexual activities". Mufune, however disputes the Caldwells' assumption of putting the blame on the sexual promiscuity of women whose sexuality they claimed, was not controlled. Mufune (2003:44), says that, it is his view that, in fact, the sexual behaviour of women is subject to a great deal of social regulation and that norms are highly variable from one African Society to another.

The cultural aspect in the spread of HIV and AIDS as described by the Caldwells, has been severely criticized for their information was based on unrepresentative documentary methods. The documents written during the period of colonialism were biased and of limited reliability, since they represented stereotypical views of African sex prevailing at the time. In the nineteenth century, there were a number of highly ethnocentric, sensational, moralizing accounts of native sexual behaviour, written by explorers as will be discussed in Chapter three, adventurers, missionaries and amateur anthropologists, whose intention was to shock and perhaps to tilitate the reader or to show that Africans were oversexed or lacking in moral restraint as observed by Green (1994:95) quoted by (Mufune, 2003).

On the other hand, according to Mufune (2003:44), "in opposition to the cultural explanation of Caldwell and others, the dependency model argues that HIV and AIDS in Africa, can only be understood in the wider context of national, regional and global economic inequalities. Other researchers and writers including Schoepf (1988), and Hunt (1989), also subscribe to this school of thought, arguing that, "the spread of HIV is determined by the international political economy and social structures as well as by the actions of individuals and groups, variously situated within this historically constructed system", (Mufune, 2003:45). He goes on to refer to Hunt (1989) using Dependency and World Systems theory which explained the spread of HIV, by starting from the premises that, cities are the places where most jobs in Africa are to be found. People are forced into urban areas by poverty as discussed in the introductory chapter. The spread of HIV follows this pattern, whereby those who go to urban areas end up having other sexual relationships there. Their wives are in rural areas who also end up being infected by STIs and eventually HIV, but they also have to go to their wives where they spread the disease. According to Philipson and Positer (1995:836) quoted by Mufune (2003:45), it is no accident that especially in large cities and along major transportation routes, AIDS is far more prevalent than in comparable settings in Europe and North America. One of the proponents of the dependency view is President Thabo Mbeki of South Africa. He believes AIDS has to do with poverty. This explains why South Africa has responded slowly to the pandemic compared to other sub-Saharan countries.

2.3.1 *Poverty and Sexual Behaviour*

"Poverty, which inordinately affects African women, also limits choice in terms of fertility and sexual activity. Women have less access to cattle and land (the two traditional sources of wealth), as well as to education and the labour market," (Mufune, 2003:45; Orubuloye, 1997; Orubuloye et al, 1995; Caldwell, 1995; Amuyunzu-Nyamongo, 1999; Ntozi and Kiringa, 1997) also make similar observations. Issues of poverty have generally been linked to global developments beginning with colonization in Africa and the accompanying urbanization process. Africa, according to Sahili (2000:20), is not new to globalization and its influences, for its relationship with the Roman Empire, Arabia and later on Portugal and Spain, the first European slave traders during the turn of the 15th century, is well known. He observed that, the slave trade and the partition of Africa amongst the colonial powers, at the Berlin Conference (November 1885), were unfortunate landmarks in the African history. These early encounters with globalization, presented Africa as subdued partner in the global production and trade of goods and services, although Africa contributed the slave labour which produced the bulk of the wealth of the Americas". One needs to have this background in order to understand the whole issue of poverty in Africa and Zimbabwe in particular as discussed in the introductory chapter above, in order for one to realize that the socio-cultural processes and experiences of the peoples of these societies, including the subordination of women and the growing problem of orphans and vulnerable children and Street children, together with the prevalence of the deadly HIV and AIDS pandemic, need be placed in a broader, global scenario, if effective solutions are to be developed. It's imperative that one realizes the fact that, it would be naive to separate the local from the global and to understand issues of poverty; issues of inequality between men and women, which obviously affect sexual relations. There is need to be aware of the history of the African society in question in relation to global influences. It becomes important for one to "establish the various competing cultures in Africa", as Fokwang (1999:47) puts it, also being critical of globalization, arguing that, it "claims a growing interdependence between states, cultures and economies which in essence is an illusion."

Global influences and the attitude of the Europeans had much to do with the creation of inequality in African societies, Fokwang alleges. The otherisation of the African, meant that, the coming Europeans had no intention whatsoever of making better the Africans life, for they were influenced by European philosophical thinking and the rationality of the Enlightenment project. According to Fokwang (1999:48), Hegel had believed that, "the African is not part of humanity, only slavery to Europe can raise him, possibly to the lower ranks of humanity", cited by (Ngugi, 1986:32). On his part, David Hume, a Scottish philosopher maintained that, "Negroes are naturally inferior to the whites because there scarcely ever was a civilized nation of that complexion, nor ever any individual eminent in action or speculation, (cited in Eze, 1997). This otherisation extended on to issues of sexuality, hence the Caldwells much criticized book on African sexuality and the general otherisation of African sexuality to be discussed later. The introduction to the book briefly discussed these issues.

If the above were attitudes of Europeans, one can argue that their mission as is then amply demonstrated by their rampant plundering of African resources and the creation of urban communities, led to the problems being experienced today including HIV and AIDS, as the South African President Thabo Mbeki has tended to argue. Fokwang (1999), goes on to elaborate saying that, the application of such ideologies in the treatment of Africans as those cited above, provoked a sense of inferiority for many in Africa, who began to reject themselves and the products of their minds and hands and began to identify with their oppressors. This is also mentioned by Bhebhe (2000), and Arnfred (2004), who link this western ideology, to the institutionalization of masculinities, again an issue to be discussed later but here relevant, because the African family relations, were broken as new European ways of life were adopted culminating in the generation of homeless, destitute peoples, which had never been the case in pre-colonial societies in Africa.

This is how global issues become important in this project. Yes, today, it is the African governments bearing the brunt of condemnation from within these countries and from outsiders, for the general squalor and poverty in African cities, and the terrible moral decadence being witnessed today, which eventually drives the HIV and AIDS pandemic. As discussed in the introduction, most African countries have experienced revolutions similar to that of England during the Industrial Revolution, in terms of societal breakdown and the emergence of urban areas characterized by poverty and destitution, as described vividly by the likes of Charles Dickens in his book, "Hard Times", or even in the writings of Marx and Engels. These social problems experienced in Europe as a result of the industrial revolution, are even worse in Africa because those responsible for the degeneration of society are not part of it, but are multinational corporations, whose owners are in the developed capitalist world.

In the introductory chapter issues of poverty and ESAP were discussed in relation to the Zimbabwean situation but again one needs to refer to these aspects and relate or connect them to the whole discussion on globalization and its negative impact in Africa. One is forced to agree with Fokwang's (1999:51) observation that, "Looked at from an economic perspective one can argue that globalization, is the culmination of the historical process of capitalist expansion and the effects of its economic laws". The process increases polarization between the rich North and the poor South, and exacerbates unequal development. "This is because wealth so far has been concentrated in the central countries while poverty has concentrated in the peripheries. This implies that the centre and the periphery will continue to exist as counterweights of accumulation, one self-centred, dynamic and dominant and the other marginal stagnant and dependent," (Fokwang, 1999:51). This is critical for the reader to understanding from the beginning, because when in later discussions one talks of empowerment of marginalized groups and women to fight the HIV and AIDS scourge, it should seem to be a pipedream because of the poverty in which these groups find themselves, which makes it difficult for them to change their behaviour. Most of the African countries are surviving at the mercy of donor countries of the North. Rather than see globalization as guaranteeing the improved well being of all countries, Fokwang (1999:51) points out that, globalization could also be seen as a kind of offensive, which knows no frontiers, (interdependence) and is deemed to have world-wide validity, seen also as a process of capitalist expansion, championed by America, aimed at ideological rehabilitation of the absolute superiority of Western Modes of seeing and doing. This kind of analysis puts the whole concept of Millennium Development Goals into question, as to their attainment, in situations of poverty in Africa, where there are no adequate resources.

2.4 *Global, Regional and Local responses to HIV and AIDS*

"The Zimbabwe Human Development Report of (2003) titled, "Redirecting our responses to HIV and AIDS", points out that, the current efforts around HIV and AIDS, stand supported by numerous declarations of commitments by heads of state and government, at the international, regional and national levels. It makes reference to the United Nations Millennium Declaration of 2000, marking an important milestone in the development discourse the world over. "This is because a set of eight development goals, referred to as the Millennium Development Goals (MDGs), emanated from the declaration, committing countries, both rich and poor, to doing all they can to eradicate poverty and hunger, combat and reverse the spread of the HIV and AIDS epidemic, promote gender equality, ensure universal access to education, health care, safe water and sanitation and ensure environmentally sustained development," (ZHD Report, 2003:2). The report goes on to point out that the most challenging goal is the eradication of the HIV and AIDS scourge, because it means the reversal of progress made in attaining all other goals, for example, gender issues as will be seen later, women and girls who are poor, cannot determine with who to have sex, and how and where. They are at the mercy of the man who has the money, which they need in order to survive, to feel protected and secure, mores as is evident on the streets.

Already, as observed in this report there are problems in most developing countries in that, they seem to have lost control of the spread of the disease. "For example, in June 2001, a declaration of Commitment on HIV and AIDS; Global Crisis-global Action was made at a UN General Assembly Special Session on HIV and AIDS. Part of this declaration pointed out that developing countries had expressed pessimism that the continuing spread of HIV and AIDS, would constitute a serious obstacle to the realization of the global development goals, which they adopted at the Millennium Summit of the United Nations. One really wonders whether the summit's declarations had been made with differences amongst states in terms of wealth and poverty levels in perspective.

The above discussion on colonisation, urbanization, and globalization becomes relevant especially in light of the fact that sub-Saharan Africa, mainly formerly colonized, has been the hardest hit by the pandemic as evidenced by the following UN declaration; "Noting with grave concern that Africa, in particular sub-Saharan Africa, is currently the worst affected region, where HIV and AIDS threatens development, social cohesion (the breakdown of families, extended family networks and all social safety nets for example, *resulting in destitution and*

37

children of the streets - own addition), political stability, food security and life expectancy and imposes a devastating economic burden, and that the dramatic situation on the continent needs urgent and exceptional regional and international action, (ZHDR 2003:3). The same UN declaration on HIV and AIDS, further acknowledges the complex interaction between poverty, underdevelopment and AIDS in the following way: - "Recognising that poverty, underdevelopment and illiteracy are amongst the principal contributing factors to the spread of HIV and AIDS, and noting with grave concern that, HIV and AIDS is compounding poverty and is now reversing or impeding development in many countries and should therefore be addressed in an integrated manner." Commitment to the eradication of the disease was well demonstrated by the heads of State and government of the Organisation of African Unity (OAU) now AU (African Union), at the "Abuja African Summit on HIV, tuberculosis (TB) and other diseases" in April 2001, according to the ZHDR (2003).

In Zimbabwe, at country level, the report says that the gravity of the HIV and AIDS challenge, is well articulated in the HIV and AIDS National Policy and Strategic Framework of 1999 as follows; "Since the identification of the first HIV and AIDS Case in 1985, the response to the disease has been very much driven by the health sector. This is because the problem initially presented itself as a medical problem. However, as time passed, it has become very evident that apart from the medical consequences of the disease, there is many more social and economic problem resulting from this disease. "Later the strategic framework adopts a holistic approach to the problem, saying that there was need to put in place of a multi-sectoral participatory mechanism --. "In this way, it is hoped that the impression that AIDS is a health sector issue, will be replaced with an appreciation that AIDS is a threat to Zimbabwe's development and this demands an all encompassing and strategic national response," (ZHDR 2003:4). It was also realized that failure to adjust development parameters, and programming responses could result in the intensification of the social and economic costs of the epidemic which were to increasingly undermine all attempts and efforts to achieve sustainable human development. It was recognized that poverty was "a major factor leading to risky sexual behaviour which increases the chances of HIV transmission, conversely, the incidence and severity of poverty, worsen under the direct and indirect impacts of the epidemic.

The gender dimension to poverty, HIV and AIDS, in which women are disproportionately affected by all the three, is an issue of major concern. For several reasons, women largely constitute the infected, affected, poorest and natural caregivers under the epidemic. The plight of women requires special attention in the design of intervention strategies to combat the HIV and AIDS epidemic. This is why it is also a focal issue in this book to really understand how the girls behave sexually in the streets, in light of issues relating to power and autonomy, in relation to the boys as they also work on the streets and interact on a day to day basis.

The effects of the pandemic are so serious that in February 2003, the UN Secretary General, had to send a joint mission of the special Envoys for Humanitarian Needs in Southern Africa and one for HIV and AIDS in Africa, to visit Southern African Countries, including Zimbabwe and in their report they pointed out thus; "HIV and AIDS, is the most fundamental underlying cause of the Southern African crisis. Combined with food shortages and chronic poverty, HIV and AIDS becomes even more deadly. The link between food security and HIV and AIDS, must be fully recognized in all governments, United Nations, international and non-governmental organizations (NGOs), efforts to address food emergencies and in their support of HIV and AIDS affected populations", (ZHDR 2003:5).

2.5 *Sexual Behaviour and HIV* and *AIDS*
Ogbuagu and Charles (1995:11), from their studies in West Africa, point out that, "In order to understand the spread of AIDS in particular regions, it is necessary that the sexual behavioural factors of the people of such regions are known. When these factors are known, it will be possible to gauge the magnitude of behavioural change over time. The major force behind change argues Caldwell (1990), may well be a knowledge of the risk potential of present levels of sexual behaviour and the greater safety achieved by behavioural change. Many authors have pointed out as does Roy et al (2002), and Gordon and Kanstrup (1992) that, in sub-Saharan Africa, HIV spreads predominantly through heterosexual intercourse. They observe that ten years ago, women were more at risk of becoming infected with HIV if they were, single, widowed or divorced, rather than in a stable marriage. Women who earned their living through selling sex or had several sexual partners were also at high risk of getting HIV. They say that the situation has now changed because in countries with high HIV prevalence, as in most of Southern Africa, where 1 in 4 adults is HIV-positive, trying to identify subgroups at high risk is less meaningful. Women are being infected more and more by their regular partners who may

have other sexual partners, past and present.

Roy et al (2002:5), then go on to point out that researchers from one study in rural Zimbabwe cautioned that, individuals could be more at risk in marriage, for the tendency is just to have unprotected sex. "Before marriage, they either abstained or used condoms. Only if both partners in marriage know their HIV status to be negative, and stay faithful in marriage, are they both protected from infection," (Roy et al, 2002:5). It is important to realize that, a multi-sectoral approach at educating society, rather than particular categories, seems to be a popular strategy (Bujra, 2000; Baylies, 2000; Bujra and Mokake, 2000; Baylies and Bujra, 2000; Sikwibele et al, 2000).

Most researchers feel, it is important to understand the context, that is, socio-economic, in which sexual behaviour is exhibited in order to understand the power relations between men and women. Cultural practices are important in understanding sexual behaviour of men and women. Mbilinyi, and Kaihula, (2000; 182) from their study in Rungwe, Zambia show that, it is culture and gender relations that are important in understating sexual behaviour. The main constraint noted by most writers on African sexual behaviour, is patriarchal tendencies of dominating women, naturally justifying their behaviour, what Ratele, (2004:143) refers to as, "Kinky politics." But as Haram (2004:213) observes, women, in much of Africa, "are asserting themselves sexually by postponing marriage". These are mainly the educated whilst the majority still remain at the mercy of men. Even the educated from her findings are sexually dominated in that, an uneducated man prizes his manhood and does not care whether a woman is educated or not. Such women, though, have the power to move out of a relationship as and when they feel like because of their economic well-being, which the majority of the women cannot do.

Evidence of the disease is there in societies once believed to strictly adhere to tradition, as sexual permissiveness increases amongst the youth. China, as Bo Wang et al (2005), point out and India from studies by the likes of Nag (1995), are good cases in point. As has been noted above, my focus on the street youth does not imply that the disease is for certain categories, more so those labelled as deviants, for even the police are not spared as Akinnawo (1995) shows. It is a people's disease, as Dube (1997:61), remarks above.

2.6 *Youth, Orphanhood and Vulnerability to HIV and AIDS - Global to local view*

Anarfi and Antwi (1995:147), talk of young adults as those from 15 years to 30 years. For example, the term youth will be used most of the time but one must bear in mind that these street youth are the ones also known as, street children by the general public regardless of their age. For example Dube (1997), talks of street children and street youth as being "regarded amongst adolescents generally", or what he refers to as the older boys and older girls." Dube (1999), as also noted by Twa-twa (1997:67), in a study on sexual activity of school students in Tororo and Palhisa districts of Uganda, says that, young people are those aged 10 - 24 years whilst Newton (2000:1), asks the question "How Old is a Youth?", and goes on to give the definition by the World Health Organisation which considers adolescence, to be the period from 10 to 19 years. The United Nations defines youth as including those from 15 to 24 years. Newton (2000), says that, each country they studied used a locally established definition of youth, young people and young adults. For example in Cambodia, from their sub project they aimed to reach young people of 12 to 25; in Eritrea, the target population was youth of 14 to 35, and in Zambia, the goal was to provide improved reproductive health information and services for young people of 10 to 24. In Zimbabwe there are also political dimensions to the definition, as members of the youth league of the Ruling Party, ZANU (PF), could be those from 14 to 50 years. Fokwang (1999:55), also asks thus, "But who are the youth?".

Many argue that it should be defined from a situational perspective because the concept of youth, can be stretched to cover not only the young in terms of the demographer's classification but should cover the psychological realm, since a youth could also be what a person feels and thinks he or she is, in comparison to the agility and vigour of youth". (Fokwang, 1999:55). He goes on to illustrate by way of an example that, a man of sixty years, "could be considered a youth, if he considers himself to be so". He elaborates by pointing out that his definition of a youth, was going to take an eclectic approach where certain cultural indicators were to serve as indicators for the term youth in African societies. For the purpose of this study, youth shall refer to those from 18 to 30 years. My research focused as already mentioned on those above 20 years of age.

An estimated 15 million children worldwide, have been orphaned by AIDS and 98% of these live in sub-Saharan Africa. Greg Powell (2006:131) says that, one of the most tragic and widely publicized consequences of the HIV and AIDS pandemic in Africa, is what has become known as the orphans crisis. Similar sentiments are expressed by a number of UNAIDS reports of 2002;

UNICEF reports of 2003, Muzvidziwa (2002) and Fox (2001) to mention a few, authorities.

As discussed in the first sections of this chapter the HIV and AIDS pandemic is wrecking havoc globally and in sub-Saharan Africa in particular. Let me make reference to an Editorial comment in the Journal of Social Development volume 21, Number 1, 2006 by Mupedziswa, in which he observes that, The Convention on the rights of the Child adopted in 1989 by the UN system, says that every child has the inherent Right to life and states, shall ensure to the maximum child survival and development. The convention further states that humankind owes the child the best it has to give. Despite this noble declaration, millions of children the world over Mupedziswa observes, are suffering as a consequence of neglect by the wider community.

As pointed out earlier, although my focus is on the street youth who are above twenty years of age and also orphaned, one must bear in mind that they were on the streets at tender ages of even below ten yeas and some were on the streets as toddlers in the mid eighties and as such, there is need to briefly review societal role in light of the UN declaration. As Mupedziswa (2006) rightly observes, in many instances, widespread neglect and blatant disregard for the welfare of children is the rule rather than the exception and whenever there is a crisis, be it economic, political or otherwise, it is the livelihoods and general welfare of children that have been most threatened. Mushunje (2006), also observes that children have since time immemorial been viewed as central to Shona society, hence their protection has been rendered an issue of particular importance or concern to the whole community, and yet contemporary Zimbabwean experience reveals the opposite to be true. As Chanda, (1998) notes, the issue of Human Rights violations of any form must now be seriously exposed.

Globally, as Dhlembeu and Mayanga (2006) point out, the HIV and AIDS pandemic is causing problems because there is as yet no cure for the disease. They say that according to the World Health Organisation (WHO) HIV and AIDS, has become a leading cause of death accounting for 22, 6% of total death in 2000 among all the major medical conditions. Because it is people in the reproductive ages of 15 - 49 that mostly succumb to the pandemic, the number is fast increasing. And this culminated in Zimbabwe, in the formulation of a National Plan of Action for OVCs (NPA). Johnson (2006:50), points to some of the problems of OVCs when she says that, well over one million Zimbabwean children have lost a parent to AIDS and as a result face heightened risks of contracting HIV. Malnutrition, sexual exploitation and abuse, as well as new pressures and premature adult responsibilities, all contribute to the increased likelihood that the country's orphans and vulnerable children may be infected. This is quite important for all of us to realize that, those on the streets are equally vulnerable or even in worse circumstances than those OVCs living in some home and yet the tendency, has been to marginalize street youth especially when it comes to protection. Johnson (2006:58), is right to emphasise thus, "Protecting Zimbabwe's vulnerable children must be prioritized, as the future of the country rests on the welfare of its youth."

In terms of commitment, in Zimbabwe theoretically, there is ample evidence on paper as demonstrated by the convening of conferences and meetings but practically there is a yawning gap in these policies, as long as street children remain uncatered for, because they are "our children", they are Zimbabwean children and one wonders why they are not part of the intervention programmes. In a UNICEF Report titled, "Situational Assessment and Analysis of children in Zimbabwe; Hope Never Dries Up: Facing the challenges" of 2002, the plight of vulnerable children is highlighted. The report observes that, socio-economic and HIV and AIDS related difficulties, have compromised children's and women's rights as these groups fail to access essential medical supplies, quality education, safe water and sanitation. The report goes on to also observe that, the crisis has generated factors that make children more vulnerable and thus in need of special protection. Children are being made to work to complement family incomes; such children are withdrawn from schools and put in high risk environments with detrimental consequences for their overall survival, growth and development. These are some of the push factors, forcing children onto the streets because in situations where the government had schemes to assist the affected families, we would not have had an influx of destitute children onto the streets. If the economy was healthy, able to sustain its citizens, then even the extended family networks, would have remained intact as already discussed. The report goes on to say that, increasingly children are also being exposed to unhealthy sexual encounters in order to survive, what can be described as transactional sex. When one looks at the street youth, one discovers that in many ways, the sexual and reproductive behaviour of these youth, is a mirror image of what is happening in mainstream society.

Of Zimbabwean youth sexual behaviour, Kim et al (2001) point out that, it is evident that a lot of

43

work is going on in society targeting the youth and not the street youth. They say that from research, it was evident that in Zimbabwe, 38 percent of the population was aged 10 - 24, with the average age at first intercourse being 18 for both men and women. As was the case, in other countries I looked at, pre-marital sex, seemed to be prevalent and to have become the norm rather than the exception. It was also found out that the Youth in Zimbabwe, were quite aware of HIV and AIDS and the risk of pregnancy, but still engage in unprotected sex. Kethy's (2005) report shows that, the youth in dominant society get into sexual debut at a very early age. To those who subscribe to the Human Factor Approach like Sutherland and Sawatsky (1996), these are signs of human factor decay. The reader must not be shocked by the findings of my study with regard to street youth sexual behaviour, for such behaviour is not unique to street youth. The same report observed that in Zimbabwe as in other countries around the world, gender roles and social norms - along with a host of economic and legal factors, contributed to risky sexual behaviour. It found that stereotyped sexual norms and peers encouraged young males to prove their manhood and enhance their social status by having sex.

2.7 *Youth in Dominant Society's perception of sex and HIV and AIDS - a Global to local view*
The signatories to the Convention on the rights of the child, Zimbabwe included, would have been expected to know that street children who are now the youth, also were at risk of contracting the HIV and AIDS disease. These governments generally, have like in the case of Zimbabwe, completely ignored the street youth. In this section I briefly look at a number of countries and the youth perceptions of sex and HIV and AIDS and the intervention programmes targeted at the youth in dominant society. IKamba Ouedraogo (2003:1), say that, "An estimated 1, 7 million people aged 10 - 24 years are infected with HIV annually in Africa. Globally, more than half of the new HIV cases occur among young men and women aged 15 to 24 years." One major problem confronting the youth in general according to Newton (2000:3), is that, "Despite global calls for action, the barriers to young people's access to information, counselling skills and services are many. Adult discomfort with young people's sexuality is almost universal". She observes further that, many policy makers, programme planners and parents mistakenly believe that information and education about sexuality and reproduction, encourages sexual activity among unmarried teens. "Numerous studies show that young people are poorly informed about basic sexual and reproductive health matters; yet parents, teachers and health care providers, are often unprepared to discuss sexuality with youth", (Newton, 2003:3).

44

Sessay (2003:42), makes reference to the problems of the youth pointing out that, "-many of the continent's youth, face what can be described as a double jeopardy, for not only are they themselves infected with the deadly HIV and AIDS virus, but they are also losing their parents and close family members to the disease. Also the adoption of the Western style of life, has affected the moral rectitude of the youth of contemporary African societies, as they have become sexually loose and despise those among them for example, who still cherish being virgins. Virginity was prized in pre-colonial societies. Ogubuagu and Charles (1993:105), point out for example that, in Nigeria being a virgin is regarded as anti-social behaviour. The youth see some sexually transmitted diseases as some form of rite of passage into full manhood, with some from the city of Calaba, seeing gonorrhoea metaphorically as GCE (General Certificate of Education). Among the young people and even the old in Calabar the researchers found out that, "a person who has not contracted this disease is said not to have earnestly started sexual exploration yet." Symptoms of this disease, were seen as signs of sexual awakening or potency. Oloko and Omoboloye (1993:151), in another study of the sexual networking amongst adolescents in Lagos, made similar observations to those above. Virginity was no longer prized. Half of the adolescents already in secondary school had partners with some having more than one sexual partner. Renne (1993), in another study in a rural Ekiti Yoruba village, found out that virginity, was negatively perceived and associated with anti-social behaviour by many young women. Fertility was more important than virginity. This was the direct opposite of the perception of sexuality and marriage in pre-colonial societies, where according to Anarfi and Awusabo - Asare (1993:37), "Sexual relations and pregnancy occurred in socially recognized relationships".

Anarfi and Awusabo - Asare (1993:37) and also Adegbola and Oni (1993) found out that, in urban areas, boys reported engaging in premarital sex for enjoyment or curiosity or to emulate siblings. Awusabo - Asare et al (1993:69), reported that, among the Akan of Ghana, women lost rights over their sexuality due to economic dependency on men in a society where traditionally they had power over their sexuality. The point to note is that of economic dependency, as this will be evident among the street youth. Of interest also, are the cases of early motherhood in sub-Saharan Africa. Adeokun et al (1995:12), from studies in Ghana observe that, according to the World Federation of Health Agencies (1987:4), 10 countries of sub-Saharan Africa, were found to have the highest levels of early child bearing in the world. Some girls reported having their first child by the age of 14, and yet this might have negative consequences on their reproductive health, their pelvis will be small and could lead to pregnancy complications. From their research they found out that, a number of girls had sex before their menstruation which was against the norm. Kishindo (1995:153)'s study of bar girls in Malawi, like all the other studies above, shows that poverty leads to risky sexual behaviour. As was also found by Twa-twa (1997) and Konde-Luke et al (1997), Kishindo reports that girls would not have the power in sexual encounters, to propose and force their male partners to use the various reproductive health technologies like condoms for safety.

Konde-Lule et al (1997:14), in a study of sexual behaviour of adolescents from 13 - 19 years, found out that, despite having knowledge of the HIV and AIDS pandemic, the youth engaged in sexual networking. This background is important to ensure the reader realizes that, what happens amongst the street youth, is a mirror image of the sexual behaviours prevalent in dominant society. Owuamanam (1995:65), from a study in Western Nigeria says that, "Young people in South western Nigeria, are engaged in risky sexual behaviour patterns. Unfortunately, they are not quick at taking actions that would prevent or reduce the risk of STD and HIV and AIDS transmission. In these days of the AIDS epidemic, sexual networking should be associated with condom use and immediate report of infection to medical personnel or to one's partner so that he or she can seek medication."

In India (Nag 1997), observes that although premarital sex is not as prevalent as in Western societies, it is not as rare as perceived widely. He goes on to point out that statistics are not as high as in the USA where a 1991 census, - The USA National Survey of Family Growth, showed that 76 percent of young men and 66 percent of young women, had had experience of sexual intercourse by their final year of high school. Verna et al (1997:48) from their studies in India, like Nag, feel that despite the low statistics of premarital sex in that country, urgent measures are needed to curb such sexual activities. They say, "Given the magnitude of the problem of AIDS and the rapidity with which it is believed to be spreading, it is essential that youth, which is the most vulnerable group, is given appropriate knowledge as quickly as possible". One might argue though, as will be evident in this book that, knowledge of the disease, will not guarantee behaviour change.

2.8 *Mainstream Society's Youth Empowerment Initiatives and Interventions*

Youth have responded positively to the need to fight the HIV and AIDS scourge and on a global scale, the mainstream society's youths, are lobbying their governments and international society, for resources to fight the HIV and AIDS pandemic. A good case in point, is the convening of the "World's Youths Conference, to lead an Anti-AIDS Crusade in Dakar" - Senegal of 2001, where the youths from the global village, adopted the Dakar Youths Empowerment Strategy. One of the resolutions of this strategy according to the Secretary General of the World Assembly of Youth, a Charumbira of Zimbabwe, was to practise and promote sexual responsibility, including the right not to have sex and use of condoms in the event they chose to indulge. The youths resolved to create and support programs and projects to prevent the spread of HIV and AIDS, reduce stigma and discrimination related to HIV and AIDS and seek treatment, care and support of people living with HIV and AIDS. What struck me though, is the apparent lack of care for their marginalized brothers and sisters, living on the streets, who obviously were never represented at such a forum. The youths forum asked governments and international institutions to implement appropriate policies to effectively combat HIV and AIDS.

An article by Thon (2002), on South Africa titled, "We are changing our behaviour", in the *Mercury* of 6 December, 2002, reports that, youths had modified their sexual behaviour in the face of the HIV and AIDS pandemic as detailed in the Nelson Mandela Avenue Human Science Research Council Study on HIV and AIDS. The survey also found that the average age at which young South Africans became sexually active was 16 years. These findings were similar to trends in Uganda, where the country had managed to reverse the steep upward curve of the epidemic by encouraging people to be faithful or to abstain. Other surveys from South Africa however, reject the above findings as detailed in a LOVELIFE survey report of 2001 which, found out that 31 percent of 12 to 17 year olds, were already sexually active, while 13 percent of 12 to 14 year olds and 42 percent of 15 to 17 year olds were reported to be sexually active.

In Angola, according to UNAIDS (2003), the Angola project aimed to improve adolescent reproductive health, by using behavioural change strategies developed and implemented by youth for youth, which is consonant with the propositions of the competence paradigm on children as propounded by the likes of Bourdillon (1993), and Jones (1986), to mention but a few. The project aimed to introduce life skills training for out of school youths, increasing

47

access to information and education, through a multi-channelled communication strategy targeting youths, and increasing the provision of youth friendly health services. The target groups were aged 10 to 24 years. Of Swaziland, Zamberia (2007:268) says that, as is the case in Zimbabwe, people generally are not willing to be tested. Anti-retroviral therapy might not benefit many. It's however important to note that this is a welcome development in the fight against the scourge.

Sexual debut as early as nine years was reported in Zimbabwe (Mugabe 2001), and at the age of 10 years in Tanzania (Population Reference Bureau 2000), which contradicts the 16 years for Zimbabwe given above, showing definitely that the youth are becoming sexually active at tender ages, and it was found that adolescents who tended to have sexual debuts early, were at a greater risk of HIV and AIDS and STD infection, as they often had sex with some older people who usually had multiple partners. Again as pointed out by Ikamba et al (2003), among sexually active primary school boys of Lendi and Dar-es-Salaam in Tanzania, only 15 percent respectively, reported having a single sexual partner. These are primary school children already involved in sexual networking. Its really frightening statistics for those who grew up in traditional rural society of the 50s and earlier. The participants pointed out that social and economic inequalities, dependency imposed on women and sexual subordination to men, were major reasons for the HIV and AIDS and STD infection among girls. Due to poverty "girls cannot insist upon condom use or the fidelity of their partners" (Ikamba and Ouedraogo, 2003:3).

In all the countries referred to above, it was quite evident that governments were doing a lot of work about the reproductive health issues of the youths. There was information both in the electronic and print media on issues relating to HIV and STIs. The churches had also taken over the role of aunts and uncles to educate the youth about sex. In Zimbabwe for example there are now programmes on radio like; "Bvunza Tete" (Ask aunt Chinóno), about your marriage plans as well as your anxieties with regards the nature of your bodies. The youth who are not married are encouraged to participate in these programmes as a way of empowering them with knowledge on sexual and marital matters. There is also nowadays, a lot of education on sexual abuse for both the school-leaver and those who are in schools and colleges, through the various forms of media as detailed in one report of the Centre for Reproductive Law and Policy Foundation titled, "State of Denial, Adolescent Reproductive Rights in Zimbabwe (1998). The

48

report is the product of collaboration between the Centre for Reproductive Law and Policy (CRLP) and the Child and Law Foundation (CLF), CRLP, a United States based non-profit Legal Advocacy organization, dedicated to promoting and defending women's reproductive rights worldwide.

CLF is a private voluntary organisation in Zimbabwe, working on information and prevention of child sexual abuse and its primary objective, is to document the extent, causes and issues surrounding child sexual abuse, in both urban and rural communities, as well as to review legal provisions and judicial systems relating to sexually abused children. The report's findings regarding the positive attitude of the adolescents to giving information, contradicts many studies assertions that, youth are apprehensive when it comes to sexual matters. The report confirms my general argument that, most studies have sidelined the street youth as the report acknowledges that, "We are indebted to the school-going and out-of school adolescents who courageously agreed o speak candidly to us. Without their openness and cooperation this report would not have been possible". The report goes on to make reference to the empowerment of the youth through legislation pointing out that the reproductive rights of adolescents are protected under international human rights law. It goes on to say that, as stated at the 1994 International conference on Population and Development (ICPD), the human rights that comprise reproductive rights, rest on the recognition that, everyone has the right to attain the highest standard of reproductive and sexual health; - "the right to make decisions concerning reproduction, free of discrimination, coercion and violence and the right to decide when and whether to bear --." (CRLP 1998:3). The street population needs this kind of empowerment also.

2.9   *Street Youth and HIV and AIDS - A Global to Local View*
General studies abound on the lifestyle of street involved children. I will refer to them as youth for my focus was on those above twenty years of age. Few such studies though have explored the sexual behaviour patterns of these youth, and issues of power amongst them. Interesting studies globally have been done by Butler and Rizzim, 2003; Dachner and Tarasuk, 2002; Ennew and Kruger, 2003; Glauser, 1997; Hecht, 1997; Higgit et al, 2003; Huggins and Rodriguez, 2004; Marima, 1993; Richter and Swart, 1996; and Swart, 1990. Agnelli (1986), actually regards the development as a tragedy. I am also tempted to borrow the expression, "a tragedy of lives" from Musengezi and Staunton (2003), in light of the risky sexual behaviour patterns of these youths

49

and the sexual abuse street girls endure.

Tadele's (2003), observation with regards to Ethiopian street youths, points to the general trend, when he says that, almost all studies of adolescent sexuality and HIV and AIDS, have been conducted among high school and college students and as such, less accessible young people (out-of school and street children), have been neglected. He says that, little is known about the sexuality of street children and youth, how HIV affects this group, whether they have access to AIDS prevention information and if so to what extent, (Tadele, 2003). As discussed above, a lot is happening in mainstream society, but before I focus at this group's general lifestyle and survival strategies briefly, I need to define the concept of "Street Youth".

It seems most researchers are agreed that "Street Kids" or Street Children" as they are generally known are not a homogenous group. There are a number of categories which constitute street children and these terms are used interchangeably in this project (Bourdillon, 1994; Dube, 1997; Tadele, 2003; Sauve, 2003). Sauve, of Street Kids International, describes the phenomenon saying that, the United Nations estimates that there are 100 million Street youth across the globe and that these are products of poverty, urbanization, political instability, family break-down and HIV and AIDS, among others. Many are not homeless, but primary income earners for their extended families. Many participate in the sex and drug trade because of limited income generation alternatives. As urbanization makes its way across the globe, many of the world's poorest youth make their way into the streets, searching for money, friends and sometimes a future. The greatest surge of urban migration in the upcoming years will occur in developing countries, (Sauve, 2003).

For the definition of street children Anarfi (1997:284), has a comprehensive description observing that, in Ghana a Street child was seen as a person below the age of 18 years, who spend a significant amount of time living or working on the streets, and that it was difficult to have one precise definition for all children working on the streets. As in other developing countries, two categories of street children have been identified in Ghana, as "children of the street" and "children on the street" (Apt et al, 1991), quoted by (Anarfi 1997:285). Bourdillon (1994:519), also makes similar observations that, this is an armorphous category as also does Swart-Kruger and Richter (1997). According to Kaume-Atterhog (1996:28), quoted by Anarfi

(1997:284), "Children of the street consist of boys and girls, who see the street as their home. They may still have some family ties but seek shelter, food and a sense of family among their companions on the streets or, they may have completely broken ties with their families and literally live on the streets.

(The Second group of children on the street) - includes those who still have family connections, they live at home, often in no more than shacks, sometimes even attend school, but are sent to the streets by parents or go of their own accord to supplement the family income. Anarfi goes on to say that, street children were often referred to as "runaways" or "throwaways," reinforcing the notion that most of them could be running away from domestic crises. "In the case of the runaway, the child gets to the street without a parent's permission, while the 'throwaways are overtly rejected by their parents. Street children, therefore, could have been abandoned by their parent, could be orphaned, or runaways from neglectful or abusive families. Street children are however not a homogeneous group but are members of smaller sub-groups or subcultures. On the basis of choices made while on the streets, children can be placed into broad categories for purposes of analysis", (Anarfi, 1997:184). Anarfi and Antwi (1995:134), had observed that, "Street youth can be difficult to quantify, for they range on a continuum from those who live at home but spend a great deal of time 'hanging out', to those who actually live on the street, (often in abandoned buildings and underground parking lots), and whose financial and personal support comes from street life.

Street youth can be as varied as the general population Muir (1991:139), quoted by Anarfi and Antwi (1995:134). They also point out that in Accra, young people trying to sell their petty goods to people in passing vehicles along some of the major streets, were a common sight. This is the case in Harare, Zimbabwe, where they not only sell but also beg from pedestrians and motorists and yet these ones might not necessarily be homeless. "Some may even be learning pupils and students who sell full-time, during vacations or part time when school is in session, some may still live at home but spend most of their time on the streets, possibly working for their parents", (Anarfi and Antwi, 1995:134). Simasiku (2004:23), gives another definition thus, "Street children are defined as those children for whom the street is the home and the family ties are non existent, ineffective. They are aged 18 years and below and spend most of the day and/or night on the streets. These children are normally located in urban areas and in Kampala, they are commonly found in the high-density of Kirenyi, Katwe, Nateefe, Bwaise and Makerere

Kikoni. They live in groups and scavenge in garbage dumps and disguise their ways by performing petty work like selling "Buveera". Despite seemingly limited in scope, by not identifying different categories, the definition also reinforces the descriptions above.

In Harare, Zimbabwe, as mentioned already, studies by the likes of Bourdillon, Dube, Chirwa and Wakatama, Rurevo and Bourdillon, have also pointed to similar categories and work activities. Most of the studies in Zimbabwe relating to street children, have mainly been on the youths or children's survival strategies. In Zimbabwe, an attempt was made by Dube (1997) in an article titled, "AIDS risk patterns and knowledge of the Disease Among Street Children in Harare," in which again one finds that the researcher, did well in making society aware of risky sexual behaviour amongst these youth. This was however a study based on survey methods and obviously would be just a cursory study of the sexual experiences of the children. He also did not focus on those above eighteen years of age which is a neglected category. My study further explores the nature of sexual relations on the streets, power relations and issues of autonomy in sexual encounters on the streets. Issues of rape and sexual abuse and violence are also unravelled, which have not been studied before.

Before one delves into the discussion on street youth programmes (HIV and AIDS) in other societies or countries, its imperative to again highlight the push and pull factors as it were, with regards the phenomena. Anarfi's (1997:284), conceptual framework as borrowed from Kaume-Atterhog (1996) is used here also. The framework presents the phenomena on a kind of continuum. At one end are causal factors, which are complex and inter-linked factors that push children onto the street. At the other end are aggravating factors, which are the high-risk behaviour of children who remain on the street and the resulting problems. Linking the two are intervening factors which influence the children to either stay or leave the streets. This framework is a comprehensive caption of what happens and is supported by global evidence, in that all who will be referred to below, and those already cited above, do acknowledge that there are push and pull factors, which tend to be the same wherever the phenomena prevails.

Anarfi (1997), observes that, among the causal factors, the child's personality plays a major role in determining whether he or she will run onto the street, especially in societies where nuclear families predominate, for there obviously, are fewer relatives to provide support in times of

52

crisis. The nuclear family itself, as will be discussed in chapter three, is losing grip of things. The other factor according to Anarfi is mistreatment of children by adults and institutions charged with their protection which are on the increase. According to Korbin (1983) quoted by Anarfi (1997:285), "these children are victims of idiosyncratic behaviour, that departs from what is normal or acceptable within their community." Children thus become most vulnerable when the people responsible for their care and safety, betray that function becoming instead, direct threats to their health development or even their life, (UNICEF 1986). As discussed in the introduction, societies undergoing rapid social and economic changes as was the case during the enclosure system in England or the case in colonies, experience a lot of social problems. Korbin (1983) observed that, the incidence of child maltreatment was higher in urban than in rural communities, as the consequences of such change, included increased stress on adults and the isolation of nuclear families. Korbin (1983) quoted by Anarfi (1997) goes on to make reference to a UNICEF report of 1986, which said that where extended families or other support networks were strong, abuse was far rarer.

2.10 *Cases of HIV Intervention Programmes for Street Children/Youth - a Global to local view*

I now try to give examples of what has been happening globally, to cater for street youths in light of the HIV and AIDS pandemic. Street youth perceptions of sex and HIV and AIDS are also briefly discussed. Empowerment programmes or attempts at educating and counselling street youth are evident, as discussed by Baker 2000; DeVenanci 2003; Liebel et al 2001; Moran and Castro, 1997; Panter-Brick 2003 and Rizzim 1996 to mention a few authorities. Several cases are discussed below beginning with that of Ruiz (1994).

In the cited countries, attempts have been made to involve street youth in the fight against the pandemic. Ruiz (1994), writes about the 'Gamines' of Bogota, Colombia, who are youths who live on the streets, sometimes keeping loose family ties. These youths belong to informal groups and use drugs and survive by doing itinerant informal sector work, begging as well as stealing. An organization called The New Life Program (NLP), of the Corporation SOS Aldea de Ninos in Colombia, worked with three other agencies to carry out an investigation, into the activities of these street youths. Ruiz discovered that although some of the street youth sexual lives were influenced by their family origin, institutions in which they had resided and peers and other daily lifestyles had much influence. Ruiz (1994:2), observed from his study that, steady partners were sought for affection and romance, while sexual intercourse was for pleasure and to satisfy biological need. Some homosexuality and prostitution were tolerated. Groups also gang-raped and expelled members who were thought to be traitors. The idea of birth control existed among the girls, but the boys overwhelmingly rejected condom use. From theses findings by Ruiz it would be plausible to argue that, power relations are asymmetrical on the streets with boys dominating and girls seem not to have much say in sexual encounters. His observation that, "The boys got information on sex from prostitutes, erotic magazines and adults but girls rarely talked about sex," also speaks volumes with regard to the effects of culture on attitude towards the acquisition of certain knowledge. As to the boys' attitude towards the HIV and AIDS pandemic, Ruiz (1994), says that many had STDs and were generally aware of the disease, but were misinformed about transmission modes, symptoms and treatment. The boys were particularly negative about meeting someone with the disease, and Ruiz found out that overall, the youths did not perceive themselves as being at risk from HIV infection. The street boys strongly distrusted the health system because they had witnessed some of them being ill-treated by hospital staff for being dirty or received only callous treatment.

Ruiz (1994), further observes that, from the study, it was evident the street youth often continued to engage in high-risk behaviours even though they knew the potential negative consequences. He believed there was need to help them find substitutes for the income, pleasure, power, and communication, stemming from sex and to convince them of their personal risk through participatory activities. As to the intervention programmes, he advocated for the use of a multifaceted approach to promote the use of condoms; to use an integrated approach and integrated prevention activities with other services, designed to meet their basic needs regarding health, education and income. At least in Colombo something organized was in place by 1994 to cater for the sexual and reproductive health needs of the street children. This is why a study of this nature was of critical importance in Zimbabwe today, where the street youths are a neglected category, when it comes to the HIV and AIDS pandemic.

Another interesting case of street youths and their sexual behaviour is documented by Barker (1993:2) in his article titled, "Research on AIDS: Knowledge, attitudes and practices among street youths", which involved studies in four countries, namely Philippines, Thailand, Colombia and Kenya. The studies were done by an organization called CHILDHOPE and they wanted to determine the youth's knowledge, attitudes and practices, with regards to sex and the prevention of human immunodeficiency virus (HIV) infections and other sexually transmitted diseases (STDs). The youth were then involved in AIDS prevention and sex education activities. Findings from the four countries revealed that the street youths engaged in early sexual activity and had multiple partners, and sex was used in all four cases to obtain pleasure (recreation), income (Prostitution), food or shelter (survival sex), and power (gang-rape), (Barker, 1993). Philippine youth reported prostitution and survival sex including homosexual sex, with foreigners and locals.

Kenyan girls reported both prostitution (their main occupation), and survival sex. Kenya boys reported prostitution with foreigners and locals and rapes of girls. In Bogota, males engaged in rape of girls and gang-rapes of girls for punishment or initiation. They also reported using sex workers and exchanging sex with men or women for food and shelter. Females also reported survival sex in order to support children on the streets. "Sexual abuse was common in Kenya and the Philippines; some youths in Manila were abused at shelters," (Barker, 1993:2). It was also found out that in all the four countries, there was a high awareness of AIDS and STDs, but information was often incorrect, especially in regard to transmission of HIV. Those from the Philippines and Colombia, did not have a personal realization or fear that they could contract it, while those from Kenya and Thailand believed they were at high risk and wanted assistance. Barker (1993:2), like Ruiz (1994), points out that, "Without changing the conditions that create a need for survival sex among youths, little can be done about promoting safe sex and healthy lifestyles."

According to Goicochea (1990:1), in an article titled, "Peru: reaching boys who sell sex", like in the cases above, sexual encounters began at a tender age of 13 - 15 years, and often involved a prostitute and the media played an important role, as they found out. They discovered that, "Magazines and other media forms, are utilized by males to obtain sex information. These young boys are often misinformed about healthy sexual practices and contraception. Sexually transmitted diseases (STDs), are a problem for male adolescents ...", (Goicochea, 1990:1). It was found in this case again that, "Poor economic conditions have contributed to young boys engaging in sex for money such as prostitution", such that in Peru private institutes have

55

improved sex education, by training educators to provide information on adolescent sexuality, :and by working directly with street children, who sell sex. These outreach programmes, are concerned with emotional, economic and sexual issues, (Goicochea, 1990:1). Generally adolescents, are seen to have problems with accepting that they are at risk, just as youth in mainstream society, as Molina (1988:2), found from her studies in an article titled, "Is there risk of AIDS among adolescents?" Molina (1988:2) points out that, "A survey of 800 adolescents aged 16 - 19 in Massachusetts, US, indicated that 29% had no knowledge of AIDS, 10% were sexually active and 15% would not change their sex habits to avoid AIDS. A study in Santiago, Chile, showed that young people with the least information on sex and reproduction, had the earliest initiation of sexual activity and the most frequent relations. Surveys throughout Latin America have, indicated that a significant proportion of adolescents have active sex lives, leaving them potentially vulnerable to risk of sexually transmitted diseases, (Molina 1988:2). Still in a general sense in terms of attitude, Margolis (1993:1), found out that in Brazil, the people, "had been reluctant to shed the notion that AIDS is the problem of only discrete risk groups such as homosexual and drug addicts. Few had changed their sexual behaviour, and used condoms regularly. BEMFAM which is a major non profit family planning agency in Brazil, realized the importance of also educating street people, and it sent "psychologists and social workers to plazas, alleys and subway stations, where street youths congregate to distribute condoms, counsel male and female prostitutes, educate them about their rights as minors", (Margolis, 1993:2).

Yet another interesting case study is that of Roy (2003), which was his doctoral thesis titled, "Desire on the street; same sex behaviour and perception of sexuality among street youths of Calcutta," in which he identified poverty as the main factor that drove children onto the streets. As the case in Zimbabwe, Roy (2003:1) says, "Here in the city these children have few political or social rights and face a life of deprivation and suppression, in the form of poverty, hunger, violence and abuse. The prevalence of sexual activity among street children or youth, is well evidenced and they engage in sexual activities, from a very early age. They do so for various reasons, including as a survival strategy." Parsons (2004), of Streets Ahead in Zimbabwe, also points out that, poverty is the main cause for the 'street children' phenomenon and their engaging in scavenging for survival. Her views are in an article titled, 'Bleak future for Zimbabwe's street children", in (*The Standard* of 20, June, 2004:2). Roy (2003:1), observes that, once on the

56

streets these children, as Dube (1999), also found out in Harare, Zimbabwe; constitute their own society. Roy says, "These youths being impulsive in nature and not bound by the social parameters, indulge in promiscuous behaviour, leading to unsafe sex practices and prevalence of sexually transmitted diseases and cases of HIV infection could be traced". On attitude, Roy (2003:1), says that, "also social insecurity and lack of affection results in low self esteem and other psychological problems, including caring least about the consequences of their actions." These youths, as pointed out by Kidd et al (2002), in their article, "Suicide and prostitution among street youths: a qualitative analysis", also end up committing suicide especially due to sexual abuse, as they struggle to eke a living. Kidd et al (2002:3), say that, "A major stressor in the lives of street youths, is finding a source of income. Research has indicated that 16 - 46% of street youths become involved in prostitution".

Close home in South Africa, Swart-Kruger and Richter (1997), made interesting observations relating to my theoretical framework and the social construction of sexuality, in their paper titled, "AIDS - Related knowledge, Attitude and Behaviour among South African Street youth; Reflections on Power, Sexuality and the autonomous self". They say, "AIDS and street children, independently, are topics seemingly predisposed to misperceptions, stereotyping and magical thinking ... these misconstructions, arising as they do from the reflective nature of social problems, which involve both subject and objectified other, influence how we believe we can and should deal, with these problems," (Swart-Kruger and Richter, 1997:957). Seemingly confirming the observations of the feminists and writers like Foucault, (Standing 1992), points out that, "An examination of HIV infection and AIDS issues among street children illustrates most vividly, the fallacy that sex is an activity that takes place between consenting adults, quoted by (Swart-Kruger and Richter, 1997:957). Kruger (1993), quoted by Swart-Kruger and Richter (1997:957) again, also observes that these misconstructions of HIV and AIDS and street children by society, expose also, "the persistent denial of social inequalities in sex and health, which currently frustrate efforts to prevent the spread of HIV infection". At the time of their Study Swart-Kruger and Richter (1997), found that street children in South Africa, were in the main between the ages of 11 and 17 years.Today they are adults of more than twenty-five years of age.

They discovered that rape, prostitution, sexual bartering and exchange, casual sex and romantic sexual relationships, all occurred in the experiences of young people who, lived and worked on

57

the streets. They say that in their study, "The AIDS related knowledge, attitudes and behaviour of 141 street youth, living in seven large cities in South Africa, were elicited in focus group discussions. The results, both qualitative and quantitative, indicated that the AIDS knowledge of South Africa street children, was comparable to levels reported for groups of hard-to-reach' youth in other parts of the world. "Fear of HIV infection did not appear in a list of day priorities constructed by the children, a list dominated by survival concerns, also with food, money and clothes. However more than half of the boys conceded that they engaged in transactional sex", (Swart-Kruger and Richter, 1997:957). The findings are quite similar to those in the cases already discussed above. To note also, is the fact that findings were, "interpreted in terms of the relationships between power dynamics surrounding race and age and how they affect self initiated controls, over sexuality and sexual protection", (Swart-Kruger and Richter, 1997:957).

In Accra city, Anarfi and Antwi (1995), also carried out a study titled, "Street youth in Accra city: Sexual networking in a high risk environment and its implications for the spread of HIV and AIDS". They found out that the need to survive was the prime driving force behind the promiscuity of the street involved youth, such that, in their recommendations, they point out that, given that most of the behaviour of the street involved youth, helps them cope and survive in their adverse environment, AIDS intervention programmes must be innovative and follow an integrated approach. They also say that in addition to mass awareness campaigns, an office must be set up preferably at the centre of activity of the youth to cater specifically for their needs. This will make certain medical and educational facilities more accessible to this category of people who feel cut off from the main society. The young people should be able to visit the office for advice and counselling or even treatment without the fear of being tagged. Social marketing could be put to good use in such an office. These are interesting observations, and these views made me feel Zimbabwe, was really lagging behind in terms of educating the marginalized street population, for there is no program to talk about at the moment. They also recommended for the quick treatment of STIs, as evidence had shown that there was lack of proper treatment of such diseases amongst the Street youth, and yet untreated STIs, were known to facilitate the spread of HIV. Such treatment could be subsidized. They also noted that there was need, "to improve the social and economic conditions of the youth and reduce their dependence on practices such as the peddling and abuse of drugs and prostitution. "Those who require training in certain skills, must be given the opportunity to upgrade themselves," (Anarfi and Antwi, 1995:148). They also noted that, lessons could be drawn from similar programs elsewhere to improve the effectiveness of the AIDS education, which had to be specifically designed to help individuals, build decision making, communications, and assertiveness skills. It was acknowledged that all programs, would not be effective unless the socio-economic conditions of the youth had been addressed, including dysfunctional family relationships.

Anarfi (1997:287), in another study titled, "Vulnerability to STD: Street children in Accra", shows that socio-economic factors are the main driving forces, as discussed earlier. About three-quarters of the children interviewed, gave as their reason for leaving home to 'work and get money - in addition, about six percent said they want 'money', to learn a trade --- Poverty turned out to be the main factor pushing Ghanaian children, into city streets.' According to the children in the focus groups, the main problem for Ghanaian children now, is how to cater for themselves since their parents cannot shoulder all their responsibilities towards them. One outcome is for the children to go to the street, to look for their daily bread as parents are unable to put them, or retain them, in school."

Anarfi on the interventions, points out that education had been carried out then in Ghana, for about a decade and yet it could not be said with certainty that all societies had had equal access to such education, given the unequal access to sources of information in a developing country. Anarfi (1997:302), makes recommendations thus, "It is agreed that the phenomenon of street children is part of the process of rapid urbanization and general economic hardships. Nevertheless, efforts must be made to provide specialist services for such children, such as education and vocational training and in cases of family breakdown, substitute care." Our Zimbabwean approach of 'wishing away' the problem, by just regarding it as a misnomer, needs to be discarded quickly. This is evidenced by the behaviour of city authorities. They, from their procrastinating behaviour seem to believe harassment will make these children eventually disappear from the streets. These children have nowhere to go. We have to realize that, the "Otherisation" and colonisation process, as discussed in the introduction, has changed our traditional societies, such that the new problems, like this of Street children, needs us to be ruled by reason rather than emotion.

Anarfi (1997:302), was quite critical of Ghanaian government attitude, observing that, "The life of the children in the streets is hazardous, but government's response so far is poor. There is need for more co-ordination between the various agencies of government responsible for children. Government needs to evaluate the efficiency of public sector spending as it affects children." In our case, there is really nothing to talk about, as government has virtually no resources even for the training of youth in mainstream society. See Mupedziswa's (2006) observations above. Of importance however, despite the many agencies seemingly interested in the plight of these children like NGOs without much success, "More attention must be paid to the views and feelings of the children involved. We must see them as the subjects not objects of our interventions and policies. The participation of children in decisions, which affect their lives, must be given priority, in accordance with the UN Convention on the Rights of the Child. They also require a voice in the political forums which crucially affect their lives," (Anarfi, 1997:302). Anarfi also pointed out that, prostitution was an integral part of the phenomenon of street dwelling and yet the UN Convention on the Rights of The Child, specifically emphasized the need to protect the child from all forms of sexual exploitation and sexual abuse, such as inducement and coercion of a child into unlawful sexual activity, prostitution and pornography. Attempts must be made to break the 'system' behind street child prostitution and other sexual exploitation of children. Existing law, on such abuse of children must be enforced. Both those who organize child prostitution and their clients must be held criminally responsible. He found that the street children were aware of the HIV and AIDS disease and that, such knowledge the children had, needed to be reinforced.

One of the latest studies is that by Tadele (2003), for his doctoral book titled, "Surviving on the streets, "Sexuality and HIV and AIDS among Male Street Youth in Dessie, Ethiopia." Again like Anarfi, he emphasizes the need to provide lasting solutions to the street dwelling problem because he found out that, the "street children and youth in Dessie are living in a precarious environment and are at high risk of contracting HIV and AIDS, partly because they do not know how to avoid infection. They expressed feelings of helplessness and frustration, about protecting themselves from HIV and AIDS", (Tadele 2003:105). He also pointed out that, the children were recommending that people with HIV and AIDS, be involved in the AIDS prevention campaigns and that, "More vigorous and more personal face to face approaches, should be adopted. In other words, educational programs should not be limited to television, radio and newspapers", (Tadele, 2003:105). Like Anarfi, and others cited earlier on, Tadele believed, after the study that, using peer educators to spread awareness about the disease and involving street children in program planning, "may be the most effective ways to reduce the risk of HIV infection among street children and youth", (Tadele, 2003:105). Tadele, mainly focused on the male youth. I looked at both boys and girls because of the need to explore, the sexual behaviour patterns prevalent on the streets and the nature of the relationships. My study went further to look at the emerging street family and issues of rape and sexual abuse, as well as use of herbs as curatives for STIs and for abortion.

Locally, some cursory studies have been done on street children in general and how they are vulnerable to infection by HIV and AIDS on the streets, as Dube (1997), explains in his article titled, "AIDS - Risk Patterns and Knowledge of the Disease among Street children in Harare". Magaisa (1999), specifically focused at prostitution, which I found not related to the main concerns of my study, although he refers to youth as also involved in prostitution but these are not street youths. Rurevo and Bourdillon (2003:1), in an abstract to their article, say that, their study looks at the background of poverty and family disintegration that resulted in the children being in the street and comment on public perceptions of street girls. The girls were found to develop coping mechanisms, as those living on the streets generally relied on at least occasionally, the trade of sex. They go on to say, "Opportunities for girls to make a living on the streets are limited and our case studies indicate that most of them use sex at some time to sustain their lives. In the assumed context of the AIDS epidemic, this sustenance is "short-term", Rurevo and Bourdillon (2003:2). From my findings below, these observations by Bourdillon and Ruvero were confirmed. I however went further to look at issues of power and autonomy in sexual encounters. I feel in Zimbabwe this study will help shed more light on the health plight of this peripheral group. It will be shown that failure to deal with the HIV and AIDS pandemic on the streets, has disastrous consequences for society as a whole, for these youths also mix and interact with those in mainstream society. Some of them live in the high density suburbs of Epworth, Mbare etc like the "Gamines" of Colombia, cited above.

This book focused at the issue of sexuality on the streets of Harare involving street youths. Main interest was with the possible intervention strategies in the era of the HIV and AIDS pandemic. Not much is being done to specifically involve this group in intervention programs. The views of Hazel Parsons, who chairs "Streets Ahead" Board of Directors, an organization that looks after the interests and welfare of street children in Harare, a Drop In Centre, captures the tome of my study well, when she says that most of the kids they deal with, were abused while sleeping on the streets. She is quoted in *The Standard* of 20 June (2004:2), in an article titled "Bleak future for Zimbabwe' street children", in which she said, "We have more than 150 street children coming in on a monthly basis to get letters for them to receive free treatment for sexually transmitted diseases, with a doctor we have identified in Harare. We are also working in conjunction with UNICEF and the police and we are taking the children to victim friendly clinics. The age groups of the children is worrying, as most are below the age of 16 years. They come from impoverished families and none of them likes scavenging for food." In *The Herald* article, "Abstain from premarital sex, Girl Child Network, urges youths," the Director of Girl Child Network, Ms Betty Makoni, speaking at the commemoration of the day of the African Child in Chitungwiza said, "Society was disturbed by the moral decadence, particularly among the youths, with some as young as 12 years old, already engaging in sex", (*The Herald* 18 June 2004:4). Makoni's organization has so far not done anything about the children on the streets, and one can only assume that her definition of children, is that of those in mainstream society, which is quite a parochial approach. One becomes worried by the seeming lack of concern for the well being of the street children in Zimbabwe.

2.11 *Conclusion*

This chapter highlights the alarming effects of the pandemic globally and especially in sub-Saharan Africa. Unfortunately, the statistics cited here might not include the impact of the scourge among the marginalized youth of the streets. This is why this study becomes imperative especially in light of the state of abject poverty in which these youth live. The plight of the girl child was of much concern to me, in view of the fact that research findings from Africa especially, show that women have no say about their sexual and reproductive health, even in dominant society. If those women in dominant society are sexually objectified and abused, what more of those on the streets, where there is no protection for them at all. The chapter discussed the plight of orphans and vulnerable children, of which street involved youth, are some of them, pointing out that despite bureaucrats rhetoric on ameliorating youth's plight, nothing practical has been forthcoming. Youth in the mainstream society are to some extent catered for, in terms of education about the HIV and AIDS pandemic. Those of the street are just ignored completely. There are no intervention programs, meant for them. In other countries as discussed above, there have been efforts to reach these youth and educate them and give them condoms. In our case, my argument will be that, such programmes will be ineffective, unless the material conditions of the youth improve, especially those of the girl child, who is dependent on the street boys and men from dominant society, for survival.

CHAPTER THREE

THEORETICAL UNDERPINNINGS OF THE STUDY IN RELATION TO SEXUAL AND REPRODUCTIVE HEALTH ISSUES: A GLOBAL TO LOCAL VIEW

3.0 *Introduction*

Much debate has been raging with regard to the sexual behaviour of human beings, (Oakley 1985). It is important for one to contextualise the sexual relations of the street youth within this bio-cultural discourse, in order to confirm or reject some of the propositions of social constructionist and essentialist theories. Main concern, is to uncover the basis of the sexual behaviour of the boys and the girls, in light of the debates surrounding such issues as, masculinities and femininities, gender, power relations and autonomy in sexual encounters and what possibly could be the explanations, for the risky sexual behaviour of the street youth. A global to local perspective is adopted, that is, examples will be drawn from both the developed and the developing countries. The assumption here is that the behaviour of both boys and girls can best be explained within an anthropological, cultural constructionist model rather than a positivist, objectivist, sociological model. As such this is a totally qualitative study.

Silberschmidt (2004:233), underscores the concerns of this project by pointing out that, the AIDS epidemic in sub-Saharan Africa has thrust sexuality, sexual practices and sexual behaviour into the spotlight, as a major public health issue. He says that, although sexual and reproductive health behaviour in sub-Saharan Africa is attracting increasing attention, there is an inadequate understanding of the structures and processes influencing sexuality and sexual behaviour in general and male sexuality and male sexual behaviour in particular. Issues of sexuality have been considered too private and not, a public matter to be discussed. The fact that sexuality is vested with symbols with often opposite meanings for men and women, has not been considered, as well as the complex and changing social and economic contexts and how they interact with sexual conducts, in particular those of men, which have not been addressed by these efforts. Miller (1993); Harris (1993) and Rapp (1993), all show the importance of knowledge of gender in sexuality discourses and point out that the connection between reproduction and gender hierarchy, is central to anthropological theory. Issues of gender and the construction of masculinity are quite important in this study as they will help shed light on the sexual relations between boys and girls, as highlighted by, Adams and Savran (2002:28).

According to Wood and Jewkes (2001; 133), in the past decade, sexuality has become an important area of research and development intervention, in response to concern about reproductive health, notably the spread of HIV and AIDS. The predominant focus has been on educating women, through sexual health programmes, to use contraceptives and particularly condoms, as ways of controlling their fertility and protecting their reproductive health, and yet research results have consistently shown that despite women's awareness of the dangers associated with unprotected sex, little success has been made in changing women sexual practices. In an anthropological study, they carried out in an African township in Cape Town; they found out that men's behaviour was key in understanding the sexual behaviour of women. Owunamanam (1995), also points to the importance of this subject, highlighting that Freud's discussion of infantile sexuality, triggered considerable interest in sexual attitudes of boys and girls, particularly those at the age of adolescence. Also prominent in the development of knowledge of sexual behaviour and in the attempt to make sexuality a scholarly topic for academic and public discussions, are the works of Alfred Kinsey the American, as before Kinsey's research, sexuality was an indecent subject that had to be discussed only in privacy and yet today a lot of research efforts on sexuality are evident from different perspectives.

Ahlberg (1994), has pointed out that, the anthropological analysis of the AIDS pandemic, had contributed to the growth in scope of the study of issues related to reproductive health, by integrating factors relative to the culture of social relationships and to the political and economic context as the case with the circumstances of the street youth in this study. As Whitehead and Barrett (2001), have observed, the sociology of masculinity which concerns the critical study of men, their behavioural practices, values and perspectives, is of paramount importance in our understanding of sexual behaviour.

64

3.1 *Social Constructionists conceptualisation of Sexuality*

At minimum, all social construction approaches adopt the view that, physically identical sexual acts, may have varying social significance and subjective meaning, depending on how they are defined and understood, in different cultures and historical periods. Because a sexual act does not carry with it a universal social meaning, it follows that the relationship between sexual acts and sexual identities is not a fixed one, and it is projected from the observer's time and place to others at great peril. Vance here, is criticising the idea of judging peoples of other cultures sexual behaviour as discussed in the introduction and as will later be shown. (Vance, 1995; Vance, 1992; Whitehead and Barrett, 2001; Berger and Luckmann, 1966).

Vance, further observes that cultures provide widely differing categories, schemata and labels for framing sexual and affective experiences and the relationships of sexual act and identity to sexual community, is equally variable and complex. Vance (1995:129) points out that, "A further step in social construction theory posits that even the direction of sexual desire itself, for example, an object choice or hetero/homosexuality, is not intrinsic or inherent in the individual but is constructed." Not all constructionists agree with this, because some believe the direction of desire and erotic interest are fixed although the behavioural form this interest will take, is constructed by prevailing cultural frames, "as will the subjective experience of the individual and the social significance attached to it by others," (Vance, 1995:29). Vance (1995:29), then goes on to note that, the most radical form of construction theory entertains the idea that, there is no essential, undifferential sexual impulse, "sex drive' or 'lust', which resides in the body due to physiological functioning and sensation. This is confirmed by my findings in that, the sexual behaviour of the street youth, even of the same age, was quite different, with some not interested in girls at all because they feared to contract the dreaded HIV and AIDS virus, whilst some seemed not to care and had multiple partners. "In this case, an important constructionist question concerns the origins of these impulses, since they are no longer assumed to be intrinsic or, perhaps even necessary. This position, contrasts sharply with more middle-grounded constructionist theory, which implicitly accepts an inherent sexual impulse, is then constructed in terms of acts, identity, community and object choice. Other writers who subscribe to a social constructionist paradigm are Crawford (1994); Foxhall (1994); Porter (1994) and Seidler (1985).

Social construction approaches according to Vance (1992:133), call attention to the paradox between the historically variable ways in which culture and society construct seemingly stable reality and experience, such that the prevailing sexual system seems natural and inevitable to its natives, and for many individuals the expressions of some deeply felt essence. On the other hand, it is important to briefly explain the essentialist, evolutionary or biological explanation of sexuality. It is critical for one to have this background so as to understand the debates surrounding issues of masculinity and femininities to be discussed later, issues of gender and reproductive health; as well as the sexual behaviour patterns of street youth and power dynamics in such relationships.

3.2 *Sexuality and Essentialist Propositions*

Zihlman (1993) points out that, the search for understanding contemporary human patterns of behaviour often delves into, the ancient human past, as long as three to four million years ago, soon after our earliest ancestors separated from the apes and began their course along the human trajectory. Implicit in such kind of discussions, is the premise that the roots of human patterns of behaviour, lie in the evolutionary, biological rather than in the more recent historical/cultural domain. Therefore, they argue that, "We must look to human evolution and the anatomy and physiology of sex differences in order to explain human gender differences today" (Zihlman, 1993:32). Seidler (1987), seems in agreement, seeing the Enlightenment overemphasis on the association of reasoning with men and emotionalism and nature with women, as the basis of the institutionalisation of masculinities and femininities, and thus the social construction of sexuality. She also observes that essentialist interpretations of the male/female dichotomy are major problems in comparative studies of gender. "In any given setting, gender differences are often presented and perceived as absolute and dichotomous. Moreover, such gender differences when viewed from an historical or cross-cultural perspective often appear stable or repeat themselves as variations on a single theme," (Cornwall and Lindisfarne, 1994:3).

The major problem is that, essentialist explanations cannot explain variation and the fact that cultural forms are never replicated exactly. Any essentialist male/female dichotomy cannot account for the ways people are gendered in different places at different times and once comparative studies expose a diversity of meanings, the idea of being a man, can no longer be

66

treated as fixed or universal. As will be discussed below, the notion of masculinity, "like the notion of gender itself, are fluid and situational, we must understand the various ways people understand masculinity in any particular setting.   And we must explore how various masculinities are defined and redefined in social interaction. Examining how notions of masculinity are created and presented through interaction reveals clearly, the relation between a multiplicity of gendered identities and power," (Cornwall and Lindisfane, 1994:3). Jaggar 1992; Burke, 1992 and Vance, 1992, all are in agreement with Cornwall and Lindisfane's observations pointing out that, biological arguments about women's behaviour and capabilities, range from the notion that, women should not be in positions of responsibility because their raging reproductive hormones, render them incapable of making sensible decisions, to beliefs that something about women's biology, their genetic make-up, ensures that, they are not aggressive whilst by contrast men, naturally, biologically are dominant and aggressive. As will be discussed later, men are said to rape because, as Burke (1992:67) points out, an anti-feminist writer observed that, they raped because men were," victims of an impulse, which left to itself, is one of the most destructive of human urges."

Jackson (1987), still on essentialism points out that, the patriarchalists, drawing heavily from Darwin and evolutionary theory, have pointed to evidence of patriarchal patterns in animal life and argued that patriarchy was natural. Caplan (1987:1) on the other hand says that, this is why it has become necessary to distinguish between sex in the physiological sense, and gender, which is a cultural construct, meaning a lot of learned behaviour patterns. One can clearly see the importance of Berger and Luckmann's propositions. Hause-Schaublin (1993), argues in support of essentialist explanations saying that, members of all cultures, personally or indirectly know about the fundamental conditions of living and dying to which animals and humans are subject ,and goes on to observe thus; "In contrast to current anthropological approaches which maintain that the meaning of these biological facts is determined by social organisation or social structure only, - - I assert that biological facts remain unaltered, no matter what cultural interpretations try to make out of them. Because each generation and each individual is able to observe and to experience them alike, the cultural interpretation of them has to readapt to them. The culturally constructed knowledge and interpretations of these basic experiences have to some extent to be concurrent with the facts themselves. Thus, I consider procreation theories, to be an illuminating concurrence between basic facts of life and death and what a culture tries to make out of them on

67

different levels of its organisation".

Freud, is regarded as one of the essentialists, with Hyde (1986:32) pointing out that, "Essentially, Freud argued that the female is biologically inferior to the male because she lacks a penis. He saw this absence as a key factor in her personality development, and is quoted to have said, "Anatomy is destiny", (Hyde 1986:32). Freud, believed the small girl in her childhood notices, "The penis of a brother or playmate, at once recognises it as the superior counterpart of their own small and inconspicuous organ, and from that time forward, falls victim to envy for the penis", Hyde (1986:32). Of course, feminists have already rejected these assumptions mainly based on the fact that results were based on Freud's interaction with his patients. Rapp (1993), rightly highlights that the connection between reproductive and gender hierarchy, is central to anthropological theory as multiple anthropological discourses, both feminist and anti-feminist, have placed reproduction at the heart of their explanations of female subordination. Oakley (1986:16), also points out that, that people are male or female can usually be judged by referring to the biological evidence and that they are masculine or feminine cannot be judged in the same way as the criteria are cultural, differing with time and place and, "The constancy of sex must be admitted, but so also must the variability of gender," (Oakley 1985:16). She observes also that, "The general controversy about whether sex differences in personality and behaviour are innate or learned will probably rage fiercely for many years to come. As it is, it is obvious that culture plays an important part in the shaping of male and female personality, and nowhere is this more clearly demonstrated than in the cross-cultural evidences", (Oakley, 1985:76). Other critics of essentialist propositions like Whitehead and Barrett (2001:6) point out that, men are not puppets of their hormones.

To gays and lesbians, essentialist explanations are nonsense, for the best paradigm if one is to understand sexual orientation, "is constructionism, a view with roots in the work of Michel Foucault. Constructionist explanations of sexual orientation, emphasise the historical and cultural contingencies of sexual orientation and sexuality, (Stein 1998:39). He goes on to point out that constructionism is in conflict with the reigning scientific approach to sexual orientation, because such scientific research assumes essentialism," the view that our contemporary categories of sexual orientation can be applied to people in any culture and at any point in history", (Stein 1998:383). Padging (1998:437), also rejects essentialism pointing out that, "This is not to deny that human sexuality, like animal sexuality, is deeply involved with physical reproduction and with intercourse and its pleasures. Biological sexuality, is a necessary precondition for human sexuality. But biological sexuality is only a precondition, a set of potentialities, which is never unmediated by human reality and which becomes transformed in qualitatively new ways in human society". By the end of the reading of this book the reader could agree with me that on the streets, essentialist propositions don't find much support.

3.3   Social Constructionism in Practice-Global to Local Views

As pointed out above for one to really understand relations between boys and girls, and the power dynamics, a general theoretical context is imperative. In order to also understand the perceptions of the parties and their attitudes towards sex and reproductive health technologies, it is important to realise the possible explanations for their behaviour. This theoretical framework also relates to my qualitative methodology in this study, requiring one to spend many months with these youth rather than the use of the survey method. The researcher had to go beyond closed-ended responses in order to understand the relations amongst the youths.

3.3.1   The Institutionalisation of Masculinities and femininities in the Western Societies - A good case for social constructionism.

To understand how men become powerful, we need to understand how men learn to be masculine, and how dominant discourses of masculinity connect with other forms of power, around for example class, ethnicity, race, age, religion, culture and nationhood. To understand the power dynamics between boys and girls of the streets this theoretical context is indispensable. Masculinities are those behaviours, languages and practices, existing in specific cultural and organisational locations, which are commonly associated with males and thus culturally defined as not feminine (Whitehead & Barrett, 2001; Wood & Jewkes, 2001; Campbell, 2001). Most writers have attributed the development and institutionalisation of masculinities to the scientific and philosophical thinking of the 18th century, which was basically essentialist. Jaggar (1992:78) observes that, feminists have always been suspicious of talk about biology, - and their suspicion has good historical grounds, because the Western philosophical tradition has always distinguished between the body, being seen as closer to nature and associated with women, and the mind associated with reasoning and men's nature. She observes thus, "Women's bodies are thought to commit them to the biological reproduction of the species, and they are seen as closer to 'nature'. Men, on the other hand are thought to express their creativity through 'culture'. The traditional Western view therefore, is that women, are more closely associated with nature and men with culture, women with the body and men with the mind, (Jaggar, 1992:78). Women become the "other", as Arnfred (2004); Carrigan et al, (2002), observe with regards the development of industrial capitalism and the domination of women by men. Seidler (1985:83), also points to the same period saying, "In Western Europe since the period of the Enlightenment in the seventeenth century, men have assumed a strong connection between their rationality and their sense of masculine identity."

Arguing like Bourdieu, she goes on to say that, men have learned to appropriate rationality" as if it were an exclusively male quality, denied to others, especially women, (Seidler, 1985:82). She points out that, rationality has become a critical basis of male superiority and is associated with reasoning and knowledge, whilst emotions and feelings associated with women, are not seen or associated with knowledge. Rather, they are associated predominantly with weakness and femininity, and so as antithetical to the 'strengths' with which boys learn their sense of masculine identity. Such attitudes had roots in the philosophical writings of Kent and Rousseau, to mention just a few philosophers.

Rousseau, believed that sexuality was part of animality and it was women who were believed to tempt men to succumb to animal behaviour, for he believed that the consequences of her sex were inevitably, much greater for a woman than maleness was for a man. "The male is only male at certain times, the female is female all her life or at least throughout her youth", (Seidler, 1985: 88). The purpose of the woman to Rousseau, was to reproduce and as far as he was concerned, a "woman is made to please and to be subjected to man and it is according to nature for the woman to obey the man", and it was women who aroused men's passions for sex, (Seidler, 1985: 88). A review of literature on sexuality, gives ample evidence of this kind of thinking in Western society. Masters et al 1995; Kelly 2006; Hyde 1986; King 1994, all have enlightening revelations on Western sexuality. Inequality in the expression of sexuality in classical Greek and Roman times, was centred not only in male-female relationships, but also between male partners in homosexual relationships, (Leslie, 1994; Halperin, 1998; Bullough et al, 1994; Kimmel, 2001; Barker, 1998; Jensen, 1998). Victorian relations between men and women also show sexuality to be a "social construct", (Hyde, 1986; Morgan, 1982; Segal, 2001; Wade, 1994).

Evidence of objectification of women in society, are well discussed with reference to England by Foa (1998), Jackson (1985), Mortensen (1994), Crawford (1994). The section shows how women became otherised and dominated by men in Europe. This relationship translates to how those of other races were also otherised like the Africans, with their sexuality being regarded as closer to that of animals, (Arnfred, 2004; Ratele, 2004; Gaussett, 2001; Becker, 2004).

3.3.2 *Western Perception of African Sexuality as Another Good Case of Social Constructionism.*

This section is relevant to this project in as far as it demonstrates that sexuality is a "social construct". We must not condemn the   street boys for objectifying and otherising the street girls and regarding girls as objects of their pleasure.

As discussed in the introduction, most scholars from the South, believe that the European intolerance and exclusive mentality with regards Africa, is rooted in the Enlightenment and the "Dark Continent discourse," (Arnfred, 2004; Ratele, 2004; Gaussett, 2001; Becker, 2004). Arnfred (2004:7) observes thus, "The time has come for re-thinking sexualities in Africa. The thinking beyond the conceptual structure of colonial and even post-colonial European imaginations, which have oscillated between notions of the exotic, the noble and the depraved savage, consistently however constructing Africans and African sexuality as something 'other'. This 'other' thing, is constructed to be not only different from European/western sexualities and self, but also functions to co-construct that which is European/Western, as modern, rational and civilised." Becker (2004), seems to concur with Arnfred's observations and points out that, studies of the gendered constructions of culture and sexuality in post colonial, and this includes post apartheid, South Africa, require an approach that acknowledges that, the colonial society's dynamics continue to shape post colonial society. Sexuality and gender are prominent among a naturality of contested arenas, where it would be inappropriate to assume a break between the colonial past and post colonial present. Becker, goes on to point out that, there were recent publications on "black" and "white" sexualities and colonialism. Anthropologists and historians such as Stoller, Gilan and Vaughan had shown how colonial discourses, "constructed the colonised's sexualities as the opposite to the 'civilised' cultural identity of the colonisers. The notion of 'African Sexuality' as unitary, coherent and different, served as a pivotal point in how Europeans viewed the indigenous "other". African sexuality and indeed Africans themselves

71

allegedly diseased, primitive, uncontrolled and excessive, came to represent the darkness and dangers of the continent" (Becker, 2004:37).

Arnfred (2004), observes that one cannot just jump into talking about sex in Africa, because there is need to be cautious, since the conceptual terrain is carved and cut in all sorts of often invisible ways, such that a thorough work of deconstruction is called for. Arnfred (2004:61) warns us thus, "the Dark Continent discourse' is still alive and kicking, structuring ways of seeing and understanding even today." It is important to have this background, for it definitely would influence the type of HIV and AIDS interventions to be relevant to the Street Youth. Gaussett (2001:509) observes that, the fight against AIDS in Africa, is often presented as a fight against cultural barriers that are seen as promoting the spread of HIV. This attitude is based on a long history of Western prejudices about sexuality in Africa, which focus on its exotic aspects only, (polygamy, adultery, wife-exchange, circumcision; dry sex, sexual pollution, sexual cleansing, - -". According to Gaussett, (2001:509), such an approach is doomed to fail because it might not be acceptable to the particular people and he says, "The major problems of AIDS prevention in Africa, are not specifically African, but are similar to the problems existing in Africa or Europe. Therefore, anti-AIDS projects should not fight against one local African culture in order to impose another (Western,) but should rather try to make behaviour and practices safer, in a way that is culturally acceptable to people', (Gaussett 2001:509). Cohen and Trussell (1996), like Arnfred believe that, wrong attitudes and beliefs about Africans, seeing them as always in copulation, could lead to poorly conceived intervention strategies. Cohen and Trussell (1996:132) actually say that, "It is widely held in sub-Saharan Africa that, men have an all-but insatiable need to copulate, (what Anarfi 1993:47) calls "the repetitive and overpowering nature of the sexual appetite in males), and this need must be satisfied if they are to remain in good health. The idea that retained semen is somehow poisonous and dangerous to health is frequently expressed. Caldwell et al (1993), state that African cultures, hold frequent sex to be healthy and strengthening and some researchers say that men measure their health or virility status by their ability to achieve multiple orgasms. Ratele (2004:137), also shows concern about how African sexuality has been conceptualised by making reference to Fanon 1986's observation thus; and observes thus, "If the sexual superiority of the Negro is not really 'real', what propels or pulls questions about the bodies, skins, buttocks, penises, vaginas, and lips of Africans, as interesting into our presence?" (Ratele, 2004:137). In Africa, the work of the Caldwells on

72

sexuality, needs closer scrutiny as a typical example of social constructionism.

Heald (1995:489) in an article, "The Power of sex: Some reflections on the Caldwells' "African sexuality" book, demonstrates that the observations of the African writers above, like Arnfred and others, are justified by this case. Heald (1995:489) says, "The boldness of the contrast drawn by J. C. Caldwell and his collaborators between a Eurasian sexual system and an African system, has provided the most influential point of departure for recent discussions of sexuality in Africa, particularly those set, as the Caldwells' is, in the context of the debates around AIDS. However, to an anthropologist, their proposed model of an African sexuality is misleading. As they point out, there has been relatively little anthropological literature specifically devoted to sexuality, and unfamiliar, this has to be learned from works largely devoted to other issues - for example, kinship and ritual. The Caldwells objective was the construction of a model of African society, which was capable of generating ideas about the nature of sexual behaviour so as to explain population and fertility patterns as well as those germane to the spread of AIDS.

Caldwell, Caldwell and Ouiggu pointed in (1989), to the existence of a distinct and internally coherent African system of sexuality, embracing sexuality, marriage etc. But the most controversial aspects of their conclusions from their studies are that, Caldwell et al, argue that the touchstone of the contrast between Eurasian and African sexuality, is not male but female sexual freedom. They go on to argue that, the reason for female sexual freedom, is the lack of moral and institutional limitations placed on sexual practices in general. They refer to African women, as having a fair degree of permissiveness towards premarital relations and that surreptitious extramarital relations, are not the high point of sin and thus are not severely punished. They imply that, there is sexual freedom for women. They make the gross assumption that, "permissiveness should not be seen primarily as conducive to the spread of venereal diseases and AIDS, but rather as an integral part of the whole society that has given great freedom," (Caldwell, 1989:222). These observations do not find any supporting evidence on the streets, where the boys are the ones who have freedom just as the Victorian English man had, as is the case with men in dominant society in Zimbabwe.

Heald (1995:490), rejects the Caldwell's observations and conclusions as does Le Blank et al, (1991) and Ahlberg (1994), asserting that in most African societies, "behaviour is not so

73

permissive.' Heald (1995: 491), correctly says, "Sexuality is constituted differently in different cultural orders and, if we are to begin to understand what often appear to be paradoxes in the sexual norms of African societies, some contextualising is in order. Eurasian and African systems do appear to be cut against the bias, so that the two slide past each other. The morality of one is not easily either recognized or grasped by the other. Hence the Caldwells problem in identifying sexual morality in Africa." The writings of Mutswairo et al (1996); Aschwanden (1982); Bourdillon (1997); Nyathi (2001); on Zimbabwean sexuality, do not confirm at all the findings of the Caldwells, but rather, their writings show that female sexuality is strictly controlled and sexual matters were embedded in mystery. Heald (1995:490), is right when she observes thus of relations in East Africa, "Not only is sex emphatically not a topic for open discussion, but, even in the marital situation, the act of coitus, may never be referred to directly. Elsewhere in East Africa, the norms surrounding sexual intercourse prescribe the particular positions to be used, very often only one, and there are widespread taboos on touching the partner's genitals." As in Zimbabwe, Heald (1995) also says that, she found out that in East Africa, the essential power of sex and the need to control it, was evident.

In most parts of sub-Saharan Africa there, is no evidence to confirm the fact that men are always in coitus and the sexual freedom of women referred to by the Caldwells. For example among the Gikuyu, Xhosa, Karanga, Ndebele and Shona, virginity and sexual abstinence especially by girls, were prized. For the Karanga and other Shona people virginity tests were conducted, (Aschwanden, 1982; Gelfand, 1999; Mutswairo et al, 1996; Nyathi, 2000) and upon marriage, a non-virgin bride could be rejected, or if accepted, she fetched low bride wealth. The same was the case among the Ndebele, (Bongwana 2000), where if there was premarital pregnancy and birth, the bride-giving family had to return a beast to the family of the son-in-law, for the woman was not a virgin anymore. Amongst the Karanga, girls were taught sex avoidance tactics and they could only be courted in the presence of adults and were told not to stroll alone in the presence of men. Sexual activity was considered to be a sacred realm, in which ancestors participated and they were believed to punish deviants, (Aschwanden, 1982; Mutswairo et al, 1996). During sexual activity, the couples had to utter each other's totems, so as to invoke the ancestors and this is what Shire (1994) refers to as, "lovers discourses under the blankets." It was mainly women who would praise the men using *mitupo* (totems). For example Shire refers to several and I choose that of the Hungwe or *Shiri* (bird) totem , which to Shire is celebrated in a

74

language which is regarded as shameful in everyday speech, yet under the blankets, when used to praise *Shiri* men for their sexuality, there was nothing shameful. "It is not regarded as obscene or pornographic when these men praise themselves or are praised as, '*Machende eshumba ---Muranda wemheche*'--- (lion's testicles -- - slave to the vagina),' (Shire, 1994; 157.).

3.4 *Use of Sexual Metaphors as an Area of Convergence between Western and African men's psyche: a case in favour of essentialist propositions*

Generally, it would seem as if the otherisation, objectification and denigration of women, is universal, as evidenced by sexual metaphors used in America, Germany, Zimbabwe to mention a few scattered places. This is of interest as one theorises sexuality in relation to street youth, in terms of how boys and girls relate on the streets. This, I must stress, is a strong case in favour of essentialist views, on the sexual relations between men and women. To some extent, biology has an influence, in that having a penis or a vagina, is the distinguishing aspect, although today we find that with homosexuality, women can go into Lesbian relationships and avoid heterosexual relations, where this kind of sexual attitude is prevalent. Jackson's (1985:55) observation is enlightening here, when she says that; "Contemporary feminists were fighting for political, economic and sexual emancipation, which for the majority, was not reducible to 'free love' or a single moral standard on male terms, on the contrary, in demanding an end to the use of male sexuality as a tool of male supremacy, what they were fighting for, was what western feminists today would call, female sexual autonomy; the right to define and control our own sexuality, free from male sexual exploitation and coercion". In most societies, Western and African, women have no control over their sexuality as evidenced by the general observation that, courtship is initiated by men, who determine the coital positions and even the number of sessions the intercourse will take. In most cases men do not worry about whether the woman gets to orgasm or not, as long as they ejaculate, as if to confirm Rousseau already cited above's proposition that, women were made for men's pleasure.

Here are some of the sexual metaphors used to show that men's attitude towards women is the same. Kimmel (2001:266), makes interesting observations about manhood when he says, "We think of manhood as eternal, a timeless essence that resides deep in the heart of every man. We

75

think of manhood as a thing, a quality that one either has or doesn't have. We think of manhood as innate, residing in the particular biological composition of the human male, the result of androgens or the possession of a penis. We think of manhood as a transcendent tangible property, that each man must manifest in the world, the reward presented with great ceremony to a young novice by his elders, for having successfully completed an arduous initiation ritual. In the words of poet Robert Bly (1990), "the structure at the bottom of the male psyche is still as firm as it was twenty thousand years ago." Kimmel, (2001:267) warns society thus, "This idea that manhood is socially constructed and historically shifting, should not be understood as a loss, that something is being taken away from men". Even the sexual metaphors used in the developed countries, for example America and Germany, show that nothing is changing in terms of the male psyche. Women can put on trousers and play soccer like men, but this does not mean they become equal to men.

In Germany, for example Hesse - Lichtenberger, (2006) in an article, "More than a game," shows how a defeated team in soccer, can suffer the humiliation of being likened to a woman who has been "fucked". This is a developed country, where you find that the psyche of the man is still basically the same; with women being seen as objects of pleasure. In the United States, according to Jensen (1998:533), in an article titled "Patriarchal Sex," American men's attitude towards women, is described below thus;

"There is the curriculum for sex education for a normal grammar lesson I received. Man fucks woman; subject verb, object. The specifics varied depending on the instructor. Some people said, fuck as many women as often as you can for as long as you can get away with it. Others said, fuck a lot of women until you get tired of it, and then find one to marry and just fuck her." And some said *"Don't fuck any woman until you find one to marry and then fuck her for the rest of your life and never fuck anyone else. Others said, women are shit, do what you have to do to fuck them, and then get away from them. The basic concepts were clear: sex is fucking. Fucking is penetration. The things you do before penetration are just warm up exercises. If you don't penetrate, you haven't fucked, you haven't had sex."* Frye, cited by Jensen (1998), defines this kind of heterosexual, and heterosexist, intercourse as, male - dominant-female-subordinate-copulation-whose-completion-and-purpose-is-the-male's ejaculation. Some refer to intercourse as screwing or "hitting the thing" and all this, has passionless connotations as an activity. Baker, (1998) says that, it is not possible to talk of women fucking men. When such is implied it might

mean a woman is seen as uncontrollable. One street youth surprised me when he scolded the other saying, "*Mai vanosvira mboro*". (Your mother is capable of fucking). I could not visualise such an act being possible. During Victorian times the coital position with the woman on top was severely condemned and common belief was that children from such encounters would be dwarfs. The man had to be on top all the time, in most human societies, a coital position also castigated by some feminists, as confirming women's subordinate position to men.

In Zimbabwe, men use similar language like "*Ndakachibvarura*" (I tore "it"); *ndakachimamisa* (I fixed her) "*ndakachibaya*" I pierced her" "*ndakachiridza*" *(*I hit the girl), as if the penis was a spear to inflict pain. When one looks at street youth-language with regards coitus, similar trends emerge. In Zimbabwe, especially during and after soccer matches, sexual metaphors are used. For example the use of the word, "*Hure* (prostitute) "in mocking the defeated team, the same word means "prostitute" (Magaisa, 1999). Cornwall and Lindisfarne (1994) also talk of the "macho" rugby men and Segal talks of the Shona man as "a bull". Irgoroy, (1998:549), sees the main explanations as being in terms of the superiority or inferiority attached to the genitals, with the penis being seen as superior as Freud believed, and the vagina being seen as a passive entity to be penetrated and to receive men's sperm only. According to Irigoroy, Freud believed that a woman felt happy to possess the penis in her vagina, even for a while, because it is something she envies all her life.

3.5 *Sexual behaviours and Risk to Reproductive health*
3.5.1 *Abortion*

Men's abuse of women was also evident amongst street youth, as was that of men's denying of responsibility, for a girl's pregnancy. Men tend to accuse the girl they impregnate of being foolish. A striking example of abortion is from China, not that such practices are uncommon in Zimbabwe, but for want of examples from other continents, and countries, so we are not unnecessarily worried by such developments. In an article by Bo Wang et al (2005:63), it is said that, a sexual revolution of sorts is under way in China, particularly among youth, where although a generation ago, prevailing attitudes towards sex were conservative by any standard and premarital sex was almost unheard of, today young people in China are increasingly open to more liberal ideas about dating and relationships.

77

These are the same developments evident in Zimbabwe and the rest of the world, as ideas from the west, are adopted by the young generation with regards sexual activities. This unfortunately cannot be stopped, no matter how much knowledge on patriotism and tradition is pumped into the heads and hearts of these youth as evidence is common place in both the print and electronic media that youths have embraced western youth values. They regard their own traditional values and norms as inhibitive of their development, just as did the 18th century enlightenment thinkers, who castigated all that had been cherished as knowledge for many generations. This reminds one of Lord Macaulay's strategy in India which is detailed in the introductory chapter. Adoption of a Western life-style has meant the denial of the local values and norms by the youth. Sexual freedom seems to be the in-thing, the modern and post-modern life style and yet as Bo Wang et al (2005:63) rightly point out, increased sexual activity brings economic, social and especially health concerns. More and more Chinese youth are grappling with issues related to contraception and pregnancy, sexually transmitted diseases, STI/HIV and sexual coercion. According to the 2001 Almana of China's Health, as many as 10 million induced abortions are performed annually in China, about 20 - 30% are provided to unmarried young women and indeed, teenage pregnancy and premarital abortion have become a main public health issue in China (Bo Wang, 2005).

In Zimbabwe, unlawful termination of pregnancy is a criminal offence according to the Criminal Law Codification and Reform Act No. 23/2004 and yet, it is common knowledge that, many girls abort using traditional medicines given by traditional healers and herbalists, or some aunt with such knowledge, which has led to deaths in some instances due to over dosage or severe complications as the dead foetus could remain in the uterus. Oakley (1985) rightly observes that, in England, the legal system has over the years seen the likely criminal as a man and not a woman, believing where a woman engages in a criminal act, they are influenced by a man to do it. On the streets, there is evidence of abortions through the use of herbs and reports of girls who nearly died after the dead foetus had remained in the uterus. Daughters of the well to do in society, also abort but because they can afford fees and bribes of medical specialists, they are not easily identified. They also can afford to go out of the country to abort in far away countries, such that realistic statistics on the occurrence of abortion will be difficult to get.

3.5.2 *STIs*

Sexually transmitted infections (STIs), are reported to be on the increase (Kelly, 2006; Masters and Johnson, 1995; Anarfi, 1997) to mention but a few authorities. Some of the STIs are said to resist treatment and end up being related to HIV, and one can imagine the problems this can create in a country like Zimbabwe, where drugs for various ailments are hard to come by. It's bad really, especially for the Street youth, who might have been coerced into the sexual act by a member of the public or by some other street youth.

3.5.3 *Prostitution*

This is another aspect of sexual behaviour also evident in most societies and some now talk of child sex workers (Sauve, 2003). Some refer to it as commercial sex, (Cohen and Trussel, 1996; Magaisa, 1999) or just in general as sex work, as Day (1994) refers to it when writing about the activities of prostitutes in London. Hyde (1986) however points out that in England, prostitution was legitimised in 1864. In Zimbabwe as Synman, (1995) observes, it is an offence under the Sexual Offences Act. With regard to child sex workers Lim (1998:170) paints a very grim picture saying that, while in the case of adults it may be possible to make the distinction between voluntary and enforced prostitution, child prostitution, "constitutes a form of coercion and violence against children and amounts to a form of forced labour and a contemporary form of slavery" (World Congress against The Commercial Sexual Exploitation of Children 1996). Muntarbhorn, the former United Nations Special Rapporteur to the Commission of Human Rights on the Sale of Children, Child Prostitution and Child Pornography once said, "I do not pass judgements on the pros and cons of adult prostitution. However, child prostitution is inadmissible - it is tantamount to exploitation and victimisation of the child, because it undermines the child's development. It is detrimental to the child both physically and emotionally, and is in breach of the child's rights. Lim (1998:170) identifies the street children, as the most vulnerable group to child sexual abuse. Street youth respondents revealed that sexual activities began at a tender age of even seven years and the girls said most of it was forced sex, posing a clear danger to their reproductive health.

3.6 *Sexual Networking*

This has been found to be quite rampant in parts of Africa, especially among the young women, and is described as the sexual involvement with multiple partners, in most cases due to poverty and economic hardships, (Cohen and Trussell, 1996; Adeokun, 1995; Oloko and Omoboloye,

1993; Omordiam, 1993; Oyeneye and Kawonise, 1993; Anarfi, and Awusabo-Asare, 1993 Orubuloye and Oguntimelin, 1999 and Konde Lule et al, 1997), to mention a few studies on sexual networking. In an article, *"Street Youth in Accra City: Sexual networking in a high-risk environment and, its implications for the spread of HIV and AIDS"*, Anarfi and Antwi, (1995) like Dube, (1999)'s conference paper on sexual networking of Street Youth in Harare, show that sexual networking is rampant among the street girls. Anarfi and Antwi (1995:14) point out from their study that, sexual behaviour among the study population, could be described as dangerous, with some involved in sex for survival and an appreciable proportion contracting STIs every now and then. Their study participants lives were one of high stress, (in seeking food, shelter and protection), with little money, unemployment and a lack of medical services. Although awareness of AIDS was almost universal among the group, the preventive messages were largely ignored in the drama of meeting their more immediate needs, such as, where to sleep and how to obtain food, or for those who were on drugs, when to get the next dose.

3.7 *Sexual Violence, Sexual Assault and Sexual Abuse*

The social construction of sexuality is evident here, as men and women might tend to interpret actions differently. Kelly (1998), like Kelly (2004), Masters and Johnson (1995) observes that, sexual violence is difficult to define for most attempts to define it are quite limited definitions in both legal codes and legal practice. The dominant male discourse also functions to naturalise and to justify ideologically men's violence towards women and power relations which underpin the use of force in gender relations. She goes on to say that, there are two interlinked aspects of feminist theory, which connect analysis of sexuality with male violence; "first, the proposition that male control of women's sexuality is a key factor in women's oppression; and that sexuality as it is currently constructed, is based on men's experiences and definitions, which legitimate the use of force or coercion within heterosexual encounters," (Kelly, 1998:28). She quotes Diana Gittins who suggests that, "It is in sexual relations that the essence of patriarchy - - becomes manifest", and Adrienne Rich, who has attempted to integrate, "an analysis of sexual violence within a broader framework of the enforcement of compulsory heterosexuality and argues that, heterosexuality must be examined, historically, and cross -culturally, as a social institution within which a variable range of forms of control, coercion and force, are used by men to ensure sexual access to women", (Kelly, 1988:29).

Moore (1994:139) observes that, despite a great mass of writing, research and speculation, the concept of violence in the social sciences, still seems remarkably under-theorised, a situation that is exacerbated by the fact that the causes of violence, are clearly multiple and cannot be explained using a single set of determinants. From an anthropological perspective, there is an obvious need to integrate the sociological and psychological theories of interpersonal violence, with theories about meaning, representation and symbolism. Moore, also talks of the way discourse about sexuality and gender construct women and men as different sorts of persons, as an area of analysis to explain violence between men and women and says that, one obvious example from Western culture, is the way that male sexuality and persons of the male gender, are portrayed as active, aggressive, thrusting and powerful, while female sexuality and persons of the female gender, are seen as essentially passive, powerless, submissive and receptive.

3.7.1 *Rape as Sexual Violence*

This is one typical example of a form of sexual violence, one must briefly define and discuss for the purpose of this book, since it seems to be prevalent amongst the street youth. Day (1994:173), shows how problematic it is to define rape, pointing out that, "Rape is seen or anticipated in the physical marks left after the event. This view according to Day (1994) excludes " (Other), broken contracts. Sex is often seen precisely as that which is not rational, nor explicitly negotiated. Generally, sexual relations are seen to unfold or happen; notions of consensus remain implicit and assured. Therefore it may be difficult to attach legalistic notions of consensus retrospective to a context in which, at the time, they were irrelevant. Different forms of rape have thus been identified, like date rape Kelly (2004); coercive sex, with Brison (1998) observing that in America, rape statistics are startling and, "some researchers claim that only about 10 percent of all rapes get reported. Every fifteen minutes a woman is beaten. The everydayness of sexual violence, as evidenced by these mind-numbing statistics, leads many to think that male violence against women is natural, a given, something not in need of explanation and not amenable to change," Brison (1998:569).

The problematics of the notion of rape are also echoed by Muehlenhard (1998:622), who points out that, some have argued that," Rape is sex to the rapist and violence to the victim", while feminists like Susan Griffin, see rape as a form of social control of women by men, even in dating relationships. She says that, "Rape is an act of aggression in which the victim is denied her self-determination. It is an act of violence which, if not actually followed by beating or murder, nevertheless, always carries with it, the threat of death", quoted by Muehlenhard (1998:623). Jensen (1998); and Foa (1998), also observe that, rape could be culturally encouraged, as is the case in American society where the boys are told that girls are taught to always say No to sex, and so it is the role of the boys to get it by all means, since the girls won't mean that they don't like it. The boys must IGNORE the NO. On the streets the girls also said they had similar problems from boys, who tended to believe that their No was a Yes, as will be shown later.

The other issue of concern to both feminists and non feminists has been the motive for raping behaviour. Foa (1998:548) observes that, rape is the quintessential instance of women being viewed as objects, of women being treated as entities other than and inferior to men and it is implicit in this object view, that if men and therefore society, viewed women as full moral equals, rape would be an assault no different in kind than any other. As observed above, societal expectations could trigger sexual violence. For example, that boys must not accept a girl's NO for Sex. It is patriarchy that is responsible for rape May and Strikwerda (1998:596). Joyce Coral Oates has been quoted by the two also as having described the sport of boxing, where men are encouraged to violate the social rule against harming one another, as a highly organised ritual that violates taboo and makes the connection here between boxing and rape. According to Oates the former boxing heavyweight champion of the world, Mike Tyson epitomises this connection both because he is a convicted rapist and also because, "in his pre-fights, he regularly used the pre-fight taunt; *"I'll make you into my girlfriend"*, clearly the boast "of a rapist", and she goes on to say that after being convicted of rape, Mike Tyson gave a twisted declaration of his innocence thus; *"I didn't rape anyone. I didn't hurt anyone - no black eye, no broken ribs. When I'm in the ring, I break ribs, I break their jaws. To me that's hurting someone,"* quoted by May and Strikwerida (1998:596). In an article titled, *"Why men rape?"*, Bart and Obrian (1993:92), observe that, many men attribute sexual meanings to behaviours that females consider neutral or friendly and these men, "think they have a right to force the woman to have sex because she has led them on. Thus, it makes sense that active resistance, particularly physical resistance, is necessary to convince these men that the woman is not just playing hard to get. The other view is that such perpetrators of sexual violence, are badly socialised elements, Obrian and Bart (1998:93); Muehlenhard (1998).

According to (Kelly, 1989; Foa, 1998; Brison, 1998; Abane, 2000 and Machera, 2000), from research, they say societal response has not been helpful to victims in that, victims in most cases are assumed to have tempted men into raping them, by being sexually suggestive either through their 'skimpy' dressing or sexually suggestive body movements. The same is the case with even domestic violence, where belief is that, women must not challenge what the man says, lest they provoke them to anger and trigger violence. Foa (1998:597), paints a gloomy picture thus; "For the rape victim; the special problem created by the discovery of pleasure in sex is that, now people believe that, every sex act must be pleasurable to some extent, including rape. Thus, it is believed by some that, the victim in a rape must at some level be enjoying herself."

Brison (1998), also talks of the victim who begins by denying that it could have happened to them and also, some even blame themselves, for the rape. The judicial system according to research findings by Brison (1998) showed that, the process through which the victim goes through in the courts and the interrogation, are very dehumanising in some instances. This could lead some victims just deciding to keep the ordeal to themselves, for the courts do not seem to protect such victims of sexual violence. Segal, (2001:109) observes that, it is not true for instance, that male sexuality is irredeemably violent, coercive or connected with emotions of domination; often it is not, - but, that the possibility of men's sexual coerciveness towards women, is socially tolerated, often indeed both expected and encouraged. It is not, that women's experiences of sex are irredeemably linked with danger and sentiments of submission, - often it is not, but that men, through such institutions as marriage, medicine and law, have managed to exert extraordinary levels of control over it.

3.8 *Sexual Identity; Women Empowerment; The case of Zimbabwean Women*
As discussed in the opening page of this chapter, the social constructionist paradigm informs the book and issues of identity as discussed by Berger and Luckmann and the likes of Jenkins; are of critical importance in understanding sexual behaviour of men and women. Sexual identity consciousness, is quite evident amongst Zimbabwean women today, as the government through the Ministry of Gender and Women's Affairs, educates women to fight gender inequality, gender violence and general cultural inhibitions to the realisation of women's full potential, and maybe as Weeks (1985:31) sings thus, *"I am what I am, my own special creation,"* and in saying so,

83

one would ostensibly be speaking of their time essence, of being their real selves. Identity is a political choice of being and as such required that women, regarded as minors to men, be conscious of the need to develop to their full potentials, through participation in the various aspects of social life, more so today in view of the enabling environment in which women find themselves, and in protecting themselves from the HIV and AIDS pandemic.

One can see in Zimbabwe several pieces of legislation to enable women participate as equals to their male counterparts in society, and being able to determine their own destinies. The first important piece of legislation was the 'Legal Age of Majority Act" of 1983, which empowered young women to make even marital decisions on their own, to inherit their parents estates and own property. The sexual Offences Act as explained by Sunman, (1996) also, sought to protect women from sexual abuse and denigration by men. Felton, (2004) also talks of Indecent Assault as a piece of legislation that protects women's space from that of men.

The most contentious issue today in Zimbabwe has been the tabling of the Domestic Violence Bill", as detailed in (*The Standard* of 10 December 2006). This bill seeks to protect women from all forms of violence. Domestic violence has been defined by Mach era (2000:27) as a term that describes a variety of actions that occur in family relationships. Her sentiments seem to be roofed in a United Nations Report of (1990), in which the term is used narrowly to cover incidents of physical attacks. Machera says it may take the form of physical and sexual violations, such as punching, checking, stabbing, scalding and burning with water, and acid or setting ablaze, the results of which can range from bruising to death. Domestic violence also includes psychological or mental violence, which can consist of repeated verbal abuse, harassment, confinement and deprivation of physical, financial and personal resources.

Domestic violence can have a broader meaning, which includes child abuse, violence between siblings etcetera and it was first established as a development issue at the United Nations Decade for Women's meeting in Nairobi in 1988 and since then, "countries as far apart as the United States of America, Zimbabwe, Brazil, France and the Philippines have seen the issue of domestic violence raised on to their political agendas", (Mach era, 2000:28). Women and men though, need education on what constitutes domestic violence, (Kelly, 1988; Harper, 2005; Chirr et al, 2002; Bam eke, 2001 and Pickup, 2001).

3.9 Perception of reproductive health technologies as a case of social Constructionism

Reproductive health, according to Chiroro (2002: x), quoting from the World Health Organisation, is defined as, "-a state of complete physical, mental and social well being and not merely the absence of disease or infirmity, in all matters related to the reproductive system and to its functions and processes." They go on to say that it implies that, people are able to have a satisfying and safe sex life and that they have the capacity to reproduce and the freedom to decide if, when and how often to do so without coercion. Green et al (2000:585), then point out that, women, particularly those in developing countries, occupy a position characterized by social and economic disadvantage and lack of control compared to men and this can have repercussions on their sexual reproductive health in that, their lack of control, reduces their ability, to determine the spacing of their children and to protect themselves from sexually transmitted diseases and the HIV and AIDS pandemic. Wood and Jewkes (2001:136) also observe that, "The degree to which women are able to control various aspects of their sexual lives is clearly a critical question for health promotion." This is more so because of the realities of power dynamics, not least of which are the gender inequalities which structure heterosexual relations, and according to Segal (2001:103) males, strive to control female reproductive behaviour.

As discussed, women do not control their reproductive health, but men (Baylies and Bujra, 2000; Awusabo-Asare, 1993); Awusabo-Asore (1993:69) points out that, "Given the present spread of AIDS, it has become more urgent to examine the extent to which the vulnerability of women to STDs and related diseases, such as AIDS, is reinforced by social values". This is why Caplan (1985:9) says that, much of the debate about sexuality in the west in recent years has arisen out of feminist struggles for autonomy, in the area of sexuality and reproduction, with campaigns being waged in such areas such as contraception, abortion, and child care, and, most recently genetic engineering and the new reproductive technologies. There is overwhelming evidence to show that men, do not want to use condoms and are against the female condom, in other words, are against the use of technologies that ensure safe sex, (Saba et al, 2001; Day, 1994; Rwabukwali, 1989; Mupemba, 1999; Preston-Whyte, 1999; Jenkins, 1999; Bond and Dover, 1997).

85

3.10 *The Family and the Construction of Sexuality*

One finds it imperative to look briefly at the theoretical developments within the concept of the family, as families are also evident amongst the street youth. The family as conceptualized by Parsons, as the basic unit of society, seems to have been deconstructed by a number of factors. The notion of sex - roles has also been eroded, with the increasing movement of women into formerly male dominated fields, to claim equal access to spaces outside the home, (Kayongo - Male and Onyango,1984 ; Gittins, 1993), and as such "mechanistic explanations" lose credibility, (Rios 2004:75). Foucault (1998), captures these changes correctly when he observes that, the family cell, in the form in which it came to be valued in the course of the eighteenth century, made it possible for the development of the main elements of sexuality, (the female body, infantile precocity, the regulation of birth and to a lesser extent no doubt, the specification of the perverted), to develop along its own primary dimensions; the husband-wife axis and the parents-children axis. Foucault (1998:405) goes on to observe that, the family in its contemporary form, must not be understood as a social, economic and political structure of alliance that excludes or at least restrains sexuality, that diminishes it as much as possible, preserving only its useful functions. On the contrary, its role is to anchor sexuality and provide it with a permanent support. It ensures the production of a sexuality, that is not homogeneous with the privileges of alliance, while making it possible for the systems of alliance to be imbued with a new tactic of power, which they would otherwise be impervious to. The family is the interchange of sexuality and alliance; it conveys the law and the juridical dimension in the development of sexuality; and it conveys the economy of pleasure and the intensity of sensations in the regime of alliance, (Foucault, 1998:405). On the streets, a new form of family has developed and it was of interest to me to find out the nature of relations, and roles in sexual, reproductive and economic activities that existed between the husbands and their wives.

The ideal Parsonian nuclear family is no longer fashionable, hence Budgeon and Roseneil's (2004:127) observation in an article titled, *"Beyond the Conventional Family,"* that in the West, at the start of the 21st century, the family is a sociological concept under severe strain. "Processes of individualization are rendering the romantic dyad and the modern family formation it has supported, increasingly unsuitable, and the normative grip of the gender and sexual order which has underpinned the modern family, is ever weakening. As a result, more and more people are spending longer periods of their lives outside the conventional family unit." Recognizing these tendencies, (Beck-Gernsheum (2002:203) has recently, rather provocatively, described the family as a "zombie category" - dead and still alive. "The weight of opinion within the discipline of sociology, might well disagree with Beck on this, given the effort which has been expended researching the ways in which the category lives on, in changed diversified forms - one parent families, step-families, lesbian and gay 'families of choice, (Weston 1991; Morgan, 1996) cited by Budgeon and Roseneil (2004) observe that, the move by family sociologists to pluralise the concept, to speak of families, rather than the 'family', emphasizes the 'still - aliveness' of the category, and seeks to maintain attention on the family practices. Budgeon and Roseneil (2004:127) rightly point out that, "while we would not wish to deny the ways in which the family remains a central, social institution and a key trope in the cultural imaginary, our intention in this issue of *Current Sociology*, is not to inject a further shot of adrenalin into the category, in the hope of restoring it to full and vibrant health. Rather we aim here to address the ways in which the category of the family is increasingly failing to contain the multiplicity of practices of intimacy and care which have traditionally been its prerogative and its raison d'etre." The street family is another type of family Parsons never imagined would exist some day, on the streets of the cities.

Levin (2002:223), talks of a new family form in her article, *"Living apart together: A New Family form"*, in which the spouses don't live under the same roof but apart in different locations only meeting once in a while. This is seen as ideal, where the partners have children from previous marriages, who might be uncomfortable living with a step-parent. She observes thus, "Today the ritual of marriage is less important and feelings are what matters. Married and cohabiting couples have, however, a lot in common. They live in the same household and in everyday life, there is not a lot of difference in their routines. They share 'bed and table", (Levin, 2004:223). She cites changes to the family in the late 20th century, as a result of the emergence of cohabiting and increase in divorce rates. Stacey (2004:183), also talks of the increase in gay marriages as dealing a major blow to the institution of the heterosexual family, pointing out for example that, Los Angeles is home to the second largest and likely the most socially diverse, population of gay men on the planet.

Di Stefano and Pinneli (2004:339) from their studies also, show that most young women are postponing marriage till they are in their mid-30s and economic factors seem to influence their choice of a spouse. Most families are what Bjornberg (2003:33) refers to as 'dual-earner families; where both partners and spouses are bringing an income into the home. In such families issues of "autonomy" or self-governance as aspects of equality are very important, and on female subordination in marriage relationships observes thus; "Female subordination is generated through the economic structure of marriage or marriage-like relationships. The unpaid work women do, is a basic element in subordination within families and society. Through unpaid work, women create surplus values that are exploited by husbands or male partners. Female unpaid work, contributes to the reproduction of inequality regarding economic status and ownership of property in families," (Bjornberg, 2004:334). She goes on to look at the division of labour within the families and points out that, negotiations are related to how power is working within families, where normative power is a form of discipline through social agency and language. "It works at a cultural level through understandings about what is normal and feasible behaviour," but at the individual level it is possible for one to manage some degree of autonomy and transgress a normative order, and individuals can develop their own practices beyond the socially constructed identities that are provided by hegemonic discourses, (Bjornberg, 2004:34). She still emphasizes on the issue of gender inequality, seeing it as an expression of structural conflict and power and inequality in society which is built into family life and has various kinds of social expression, and also to note is the fact that contradictory needs and interests, are elementary aspects of couples 'everyday lives but do not necessarily become spelled out in open conflict.

There has been the appropriation of women's bodies in male controlled structures like marriage, bride wealth and dowry payments, resulting in the sexual objectification of women (McFadden, 1992; Mires, 1997; Nussbaum, 1999 and Barnard, 1973). Marriage is seen as oppressive to women and as stifling their sexual freedom. De Beavours (1988) argues that, patriarchy uses religion and belief systems to justify its oppression of women. Armstrong (1988) cites the case of Mdutshana Dube *versus* The State where a 16-year-old girl was given over to a 40-year-old man in colonial Zimbabwe.

With reference to the youth and families, Lagree (2004:102) also makes an interesting observation that, "Changes in norms related to sexuality, such as increasing permissiveness, may be regarded as one of the most significant hallmarks of the ongoing process of change," and it is like moving from tradition to more modern ways of behaving. Heath (2004:161), notes in relation to youth of a new development thus, "It is widely agued that we are currently experiencing the individualization of young people's transition to adulthood and the emergence of 'young adulthood', of "independence", as a distinct new life phase. This new phase 'drives the youth phase into adulthood phase and eats away a part of life which until a few decades ago, was a part of adult life for the majority of the population. Youth adulthood is characterized by living alone with peers and occasionally going to live with parents, this sounds like the lives of street youth and social commentators have coined phrases such as "kidulthood" or "adultescence", suggestive of the blurring of supposedly 'youthful' and 'adult' roles and responsibilities. They develop a distinct sense of identity over the course of their existence and could be conceptualized as what Maffesoli (1996) has referred to as 'neo-tribalism,' that is, they live in groups sometimes on their own, away from their families. The only major difference from street youth is that they can freely go back to their homes.

The family forms have also changed as evident in Zimbabwe. Cohabiting is quite rampant, (that is marriages that have not been sanctioned by relatives. A man and a woman just live as husband and wife without having performed the necessary marriage rituals) divorce rates and single parenthood are commonplace and the popular, *"small houses"* which some have seen as a form of modern polygyny, are on the increase in Zimbabwe. "Small house," refers to the informal union between an older married man and a young woman. A man who is already married can have several of such informal marriages. Men from all classes are involved. Some argue that such unions are nowadays being formulated by way of paying bride prizes though most cases do not go through the courts for recognition.

Courtship in Zimbabwe, is no longer only through the traditional forms of arranged relations by aunts or direct proposal or courtship but also through newspapers, the electronic media like the radio and the internet which have also become sources of sexual knowledge. *The Sunday Mail* (Zimbabwe) of 23-29 December 2007: 10 had an article titled "Searching for love through dateline" written by Susan Tokore. She highlighted the point that more and more Zimbabweans are turning to dating agencies to find partners. Sexuality in the traditional sense has been deconstructed as a variety of sexual positions in coitus are now evident. The frontal position, for a long time thought to be the only socially approved coital position, has been ignored by today's youth. They prefer other positions such as rear penetration as will be discussed later. Economic factors, are now important and most educated young men and women, are postponing marriage until they have completed their educational programmes.

Women are now initiating the courtship process also, in that they place their advertisements for male partners of their liking in the various media. I don't know about the initiation of the sexual intercourse process, where power has been skewed in favour of men. Men have been determining the timing of intercourse, positions and the number of times or 'rawunzi' as some call them in Zimbabwe, the intercourse session will have. Issues of power and autonomy in sexual encounters must be seen in the context of the discussion above, for relations have also changed in this area in Zimbabwe, as also is evident on the streets. *Lobola (bride prize)* is no longer the basis for a claim to be married. With regard to extra marital affairs, evidence points to an increase as already discussed due mainly to poverty, (Cohen and Trussel 1996; Ahlberg, Jensen and Perez 1997; Meekirs and Calves 1997; Kimmuna and Djamba 2005; Chiroro 2002).

3.11 *The Sexual Act, Variations in techniques in heterosexual relations*
Friedl (1989) in an article titled, *"Sex the invisible"*, discusses the privacy, associated with human sexual intimacy, as also evident on the streets among street youth. Foa (1998:587) is quite explicit and observes that, though it is now recognized that sexual pleasure exists for all stages of life and is in its own right, a morally permissible goal, Victorian influences still are evident. "It remains the common feeling that, it is a kind of pleasure which should be experienced only in private and only between people who are and intend to be otherwise intimate", (Foa, 1998:587). He goes on to point out that, genital pleasure is still private not only in the description of its physical location, but also in people's conception of its occurrence.

As to the ability of individuals to control themselves sexually, according to Ryan (1992:170), sexuality is seen as subject to quite "a degree of conscious control." Attraction in social encounters that is, how boys and girls become attracted to each other, men and women, can be controlled according to her trend of argument. She observes thus, "What is the scope for our understanding the source of sexual attraction in a way that allows us some possibility of change and control in our lives, - - what constitutes the reality of our emotions. Are they as absolute and irreducible as it is often assumed? Or is the common assumptions of their fixity another way in which we construct ourselves and are constructed?" Hyde (1986) points out that, in all human societies, physical characteristics are important in determining whom one chooses as a sex partner, more so for the choice of a female partner than a male partner.

In America preference, she says, is for the slim, large eyed woman with shapely long legs. The ideal man, she says would be one who is tall, and trim with broad shoulders, narrow hips and a firm jaw. "The region of the body that is judged for attractiveness, varies considerably from one culture to the next. For some people, the shape and colour of the eyes are especially significant. For others the shape of the ears is most important. Some societies go directly to the heart of the matter and judge attractiveness, by the appearance of the external genitals," (Hyde, 1986:14). In some societies elongated labia majora, that is the pads of fat on either side of the vaginal opening in women, (what the street boys call "*tumabhemba*" (that used to cut grass), are considered sexually attractive and it is common practice for women, (especially those of Malawian origin in Zimbabwe), to pull them to make them long. 'Elongated labia majora among the Nawa women of Africa are considered a mark of beauty and are quite prominent", (Hyde, 1986:14). Some men in some societies prefer plump women than slim ones and, "One standard does seem to be a general rule, a poor complexion is considered unattractive in the majority of human societies", (Hyde, 1986:14). The issue of attraction in sexual encounters was of interest to the street youth.

Yet another aspect of sexuality related to the issue of the sexual act are sexual techniques, (Hyde, 1986; Masters and Johnson, 1995, 1986). As discussed earlier on, some positions in coitus were associated with the misfortune of bearing dwarfs especially if the woman was assumed to have been on top of the man during sexual intercourse. Hyde (1986) makes reference to several societies. One is that of the behaviour of people of the Island called Iris Beag, off the coast of Ireland. This is one of the most naïve and sexually repressive societies in the world as she points out. Kissing and various ways of stimulating are unknown and sexual matters are considered to be embarrassing and the men believe intercourse is hard on one's health and will desist from sex the night before they are to do a job that takes great energy. During menstruation and after birth women are considered dangerous to the men and the husbands invariably initiate the activity. The man has orgasm quickly and falls asleep almost immediately and female orgasm is unknown and considered to be deviant. It was difficult to establish if the girls on the streets experienced orgasm as will be discussed later.

Another island in the South of the Pacific, is home to the Mangaians, who are quite sexually liberal, with young boys of seven being encouraged to masturbate and there is organised sexual education, (Hyde, 1986; Masters et al, 1995). Two weeks after a boy has been initiated into manhood, he is expected to have intercourse with an experienced woman. "She provides him with practices in various acts and positions and trains him to hold back until he has a simultaneous orgasm with his partner. After this the Mangaian boy, aggressively seeks out girls or they seek him out; soon he has coitus every night. The girl who has received sexual instruction from an older woman expects demonstrations of his virility as proof of his desire for her. What is valued is the ability of the male to continue vigorously the in-and-out action of coitus, over long periods of time, while the female moves her hips "like a washing machine". Nothing is despised more than a 'dead partner' who does not move. A good man is expected to continue his actions for 15 to 30 minutes or more", (Hyde, 1986:11, Mitterauer, 1994: 234).

Hyde (1986) says that, mouth kissing to some people is sexually arousing. Another particularly exotic variation is reported on the Island of Panape, where the man places a fish in the woman's vulva and then gradually licks it out prior to coitus. 'Inflicting pain on the partner is also a part of the sexual technique in some societies. The Apinaye woman of South America, may bite off bits of her partner's eye- brows noisily, spitting them aside - - men usually tug at the woman's eye-brows - - women of the South Pacific poke a finger into the men's ear when they are highly aroused. People of various societies bite their partners to the point of draining blood and leaving scars; most commonly, it is the woman who inflicts the pain on the man", (Hyde, 1986:13).

From Kinsey et al's (1998) surveys, it was found that, as has been found even in England, among the poor that, "Sex is a man's pleasure and a woman's duty," according to Hyde (1986:15), and she goes on to say that, little is known about sex in the Soviet Union where there is no sex research officially, and Russians regard any such studies as of Kinsey and others, as evidence of moral decadence. However from Stern's book titled, *"Sex in the USSR"*, who was a physician there, "Sex is a rather grim business." Intercourse is typically accomplished in the "doggy" position called "crayfish" by the Soviet. There is little sophistication in techniques. The woman is relatively inexperienced and passive, while the man uses little foreplay and may even be brutal. Most men are unaware that the clitoris exists or has a sexual function. For men, sex is mainly of strength and masculinity. Further, it is believed that the man should not delay his orgasm - indeed "holding back," is regarded as perversion, (Hyde, 1986:17). Use of aphrodisiacs is also noted as a way of enhancing excitement in sexual encounters in many societies, (Hyde, 1986; Cohen and Trussell, 1996; Kelly 2004; Masters and Johnson 1995; Hyo-Je-Cho, 2000). Cohen and Trussell, (1996), found out from research that, dry sex was also considered very vital for excitement in parts of sub-Saharan Africa. This is where women use herbs, put in their vulvas to keep them dry.

3.12 Homosexuality; A general perspective: The dialectic between the global and the local

This aspect of sexual behaviour also clearly demonstrates that sexual behaviour is a social construct and culturally relative and brings out clearly the notion of the "Other". Cohen and Trussell (1996:184) observe that, although very little sound research appears to have been done on homosexuality in sub-Saharan Africa, its existence is overwhelmingly denied in academic publications. "This claim may result because homosexuality, as a lifelong sexual identity, is rare or unknown, rather than because men never have sex with men", (Cohen and Trussell, 1996:134).

Evidence of homosexuality they say, was there in Nigeria and among mineworkers in South Africa. Arnfred (2004:21) observes as does Louw (2001:288), thus; "Amazingly, until recently, same sex relations have been understood as largely none-existent in Africa, the official (and widespread) opinion being that same-sex is decadence, imposed on Africa from the outside. Zimbabwe's President, Robert Mugabe, made that clear in his speech, at the opening of the Zimbabwe International Book Fair in 1995." Arnfred (2004:21) quotes the Zimbabwean President as having said, *"I find it extremely outrageous and repugnant to my human conscience, that such immoral and repulsive organisations, like those of homosexuals'; who offend both against the law of nature and the morals of religious beliefs espoused by our society, should have any advocates among our midst and even elsewhere in the world"*. Kenyan President Daniel Arap Moi, is quoted by Arnfred (2004:21) as having said, *"Words like lesbianism and homosexuality do not exist in African languages"*. Arnfred (2004:21); Marck J (1997:383), like many others not cited here due to limits in terms of length of the book, point out that, Moi might

93

have had a point, "but the point is different from what he thinks; same-sex practices did and do exist in Africa, in remarkable quantity and diversity, but not necessarily as identities."

Although in some African countries like South Africa same-sex marriages are now legally recognised, in most African societies, lesbianism is very much condemned, (Morgan and Wieringa, 2004; Wieringa, 2004; Kheswa and Wieringa, 2004; Nkunzi and Morgan, 2004). These researchers argue though, like the rest above, that same sex relations have been in Africa since time immemorial and this was never an import. As one looks at street youth sexual behaviour, it also becomes evident that homosexual activities are taking place on the streets.

3.13   *Masturbation*
Other sexual behaviours are masturbation, also known as one person sex, (Hyde, 1986:228) or solitary sex, (Kelly 2004; Masters and Johnson 1995; and McCormack 1985). Hyde says that, it does not necessarily take two to have sex, and that one can produce one's own sexual stimulation. Sexual-self stimulation is called autoeroticism and the best examples are masturbation and fantasy. Research by Kinsey et al (1988), showed that masturbation was a very common sexual behaviour and almost all men and the majority of women masturbated to orgasm, at least a few times during their lives and men did so frequently, with women manipulating their clitoris and their inner lips or by inserting objects into their vaginas.

3.14   *Other sexual behaviours*
There is also oral sex, which is non-coital, where the woman can put the penis in their mouth and Kelly (2006) says, some man can ejaculate into the mouth or some women can just stimulate the man's genitals. Sodomy and bestiality are sexual behaviours regarded as criminal behaviours, in Zimbabwe, (Synman, 1995; and Feltore, 2004) and in the Criminal Law (Codification and Reform) No. 23/2004).

3.15   *Child Care and Social Constructionism*
On the streets are children in street families or of single parents. Theoretically one finds that in most societies, children have been prized, but it has been the role of women mainly to look after and care for children in most societies. More so, in countries characterised by male migrant

labour practices like South Africa, (Morrell and Ritcher, 2006; Rabe, 2006; Ritcher and Ramphele, 2006; Wilson, 2006). Fatherhood has become important today, with some Scandinavian countries now having what is called paternity leave, to ensure fathers also care for their children (Morrell and Ritcher, 2006). I briefly looked at this because on the streets I discovered that some of the boys, would spent some time with their children, though mainly it would be the mothers who were responsible for childcare. When it came to parental expectations of such children, both the street mother and street father, showed a lot of concern and worry about these issues.

3.16 *Conclusion*

Chapter three theorises sexuality and privileges the social constructionist paradigm as the most useful in explaining the sexual and reproductive health behaviour of men and women in society. Basically from the discussion, one realizes that men, whether in mainstream society or on the streets as will be evident below, have an evident "convergence of their psyche". They all objectify women and consider them as less human than themselves and equate womanhood with childhood. Men believe women behave like small children and thus cannot do without men. Men tend to naturalise the low status position of women in society and thus their perception of women can best be analysed from an essentialist prospective. To the likes of Freud, Rousseau, Van Kraft Ebbing to mention but a few, sex is destiny and women are natural commodities, consumables. Objectification of women is evident, especially in the language men use when referring to sexual encounters, the most notorious being the word, "Fuck," as Jensen (1998) observes above, with regard to American men's patriarchal attitude to sexual intercourse and the otherisation of women. The chapter is relevant in that my basic premise is that the study is not about exposing the street youth for condemnation, for worse things are happening in mainstream society. Rather the project is about shedding light on street youth so resources are channelled towards these marginalized youth, in this era of the HIV and AIDS pandemic. Various sexual behaviours have been discussed as well as the forces that operate, forcing women to submit to unsafe sex. This will be quite evident on the streets where the girls' bodies are "owned" by the boys'.

CHAPTER FOUR

METHODOLOGICAL DEBATES AND THE ORGANISATION OF THE STUDY

4.0 *Introduction*

Below, first I focus on the various theoretical debates on which my study was premised. Issues of objectivity and truth are discussed as well as matters relating to the status of the researcher. I show that this is not very important for all anthropologists whether insider or outsider, must take cognisance of certain basics, like the rigour expected of them, honesty and truthfulness in their research endeavours. I also point out the hazards and limitations researchers generally encounter. Care must be taken to ensure that the voices of the subjects of study are heard. The notion of participant observer is explained in the context of this study, where my concern was not to actually witness the street youth engaged in the various sexual acts on the streets. The chapter also discusses, justification for researchers interference in the lives of the poor, they normally study. Ethical issues, are also discussed and the various research methods that were employed. I then put my own study within this general framework, discussing how I gained entry and the various strategies, like giving the youth some goodies and driving them to the University to create rapport and trust.

4.1 *Objectivity and the search for truth*

One of the issues grappled with from the beginning was that of objectivity. How I was to obtain truth and representative data from the field. Data that could be useful, what Ennew (1976:43) refers to as, "the theoretical status of ethnographic data." Llobera (1976:20) also, acknowledges that, there is the question of objectivity which has caused the proliferation of theories", to explain the nature of social science research. Smith (1993:83), points to the possibility of different perceptions of the same social phenomenon by different researchers who could be studying it simultaneously. Smith (1993:83) actually says, "Human beings do and say things for reasons. The cluster of theories one holds at various levels about human nature, the nature of society, the nature of particular social setting or context within which an expression occurs, are crucial to the interpretations one offers, of these reasons." To understand the street youth for example, I had to interpret their expressions in terms of an already existing web of background meanings or theories, I had about them. Esner (1993) like Bourdieu (1977), says that the theoretical constructs with which a researcher works, define in large measure the features of the universe they are likely to see.

Bourdieu (1977:2), is right when he observes that, "The anthropologist's particular relation to the objects of his study contains the making of a theoretical distortion, in as much as this situation as an observer, excluded from the real play of social activities by the fact that, he has no place (except by choice or by way of a game) in the system observed." Bourdieu, goes on to say that, because of being an outsider to those engaged in social action to be studied, inclines the researcher as observer to, "a hermeneutic representation of practices, leading him to reduce all social relations to communicative relations and more precisely, to decoding operations." The researcher becomes preoccupied by what he anticipated to see, that could answer his or her questions at the expense of what will be happening on the ground. Social constructionism is thus an inherent aspect of all ethnographic write-ups. Social constructionism, as Berger and Luckmann, (1966) also observe, is evident in the conduct of research by anthropologists, especially with regard to the relations between the observed and the observer. Like Esner (1993), Bourdieu (1977:2) then says, "Hence, it is not sufficient for anthropology to break with native experience and the native representation of that experience, it has to make a second break and question, the presuppositions inherent in the position of an outside observer, who, in his pre-occupation with interpreting practices, is inclined to introduce into the object, the principles of his relation to the object, as is attested by the special importance he assigns to communicative functions (whether in language, myth or marriage)". Bourdieu further points out that, knowledge does not merely depend on the particular standpoint an observer situated in space and time takes up on the object, because the "knowing subject" inflicts on practice, "a much more fundamental and pernicious alteration which, being a constituent condition of the cognitive operation, is bound to pass unnoticed, in taking up a point of view on the action, withdrawing from it, in order to observe it from above and from a distance, he constitutes practically, activity as an object of observation and analysis, a representation, (Bourdieau, 1977:2). This is what makes me feel that being an outsider, is of no consequence but rather, strict observance of anthropological principles of rigour, objectivity and neutrality, in other words, I felt I had to be honest in everything I was going to do with the youth.

It is important to realize that, early social science research was premised on enlightenment, scientific and philosophical thinking of the 18th Century. The early social scientists believed in the positivist thinking of the sociologist Auguste Comte and later Durkheim, who believed objective studies were possible in the social sciences. Christians (2000:134), observes rightly that, "Typically, debates over the character of the social sciences, revolved around the theory and methodology of the natural sciences. However, the argument here, is not how they resemble natural science, but their inscription into the dominant, enlightenment worldview." But then, with time, it became evident as observed above by Esner and Bourdieau and others that, objective findings, were not possible where *"Knowing subjects,"* were involved. It emerged from the propositions of the early sociologists, that a quantitative methodology was possible and later evolved the qualitative research methodology premised on an opposing view, that since humans' behaviour could not be controlled and the context of human behaviour not controllable by the researcher, procedures of the natural science research and those of the social, could not be seen as similar because replicability, though possible, would not produce same results. For example, no one can go to the streets and study the youth as I did, under the same circumstances because these will have changed. Attitudes and a whole host of circumstances, will have changed although the same youth, could still be there.

Stredwick (2001:5) as does Prah (1989:35), rightly points to the debate surrounding qualitative research methodology saying that, there are numerous methodologies which constitute the field of qualitative research, "and which are often subject to epistemological ambiguities, ontological disputes and paradigmatic ambivalence. The lack of clarity and cohesion within the qualitative discipline can be seen in part as the result of the historical development of epistemological thinking and also as arising out of philosophical contest over objectivism and subjectivism." He rightly observes that in the social sciences, a dichotomous relationship has evolved between these philosophical traditions whereby objectivism, is associated with quantitative methods, and subjectivism with interpretive or humanistic models of enquiry. I opted for the latter in this study.

Morris (1977:330), sees the research process as a knowledge generating endeavour. He emphasizes the need for truth and representation, which I found to be key qualities in the organization and in conducting of my field research. He says that, "The classical theory of truth as correspondence or representation has been taken for granted by ordinary people of all cultures and by most philosophers from Aristotle to Davidson. Knowledge consists for the search of truth. Both Arndt and Popper insist that knowledge involved a search for truth, and truth consists of the correspondence of knowledge with its object." The problem though, as Morris (1977) notes, is that, human life is an essential paradox, for there is an inherent dualism in existence, in that humans are contemplative creatures - and through their conscious experience, see themselves as separate from the world - while at the same time being active participants in the world.

Strathern (1987:252) quotes Lubbock, who observed that, to understand people different from us, "it is necessary to be aware of their particular premises and values." These were issues I had to grapple with in an endeavour to gain entry into the world of the street youth, as will be elaborated below. Strathern then, goes on to refer to Malinowski, who believed that, to each culture, the values were slightly different as people aspire after different aims, follow different impulses and he believed the goal in field research, was to grasp the native's point of view. Early anthropologists were mainly studying peoples of other cultures; they referred to as the natives. This is a situation where, an outsider studies a particular group different from his, not only in terms of being geographically and politically in different societies, but even within the same society as I argue below; the whole status of being an "insider" anthropologist is critiqued. For example I feel I was both an "insider and an outsider" to the street youth world and thus were to me the "natives." Lubbock (1875), observations remained in my mind all the time, as I did my study that, "The whole mental condition of the savage is indeed, dissimilar from ours, that, it is often very difficult for us to follow, what is passing in his mind... Many things appear natural and almost self-evident to him, which produce a very different effect on us. ...Thus though savages always have a reason such as it is, for what they do and what they think, these reasons often seem to us irrelevant or absurd", (Strathern (1987:252). As will be evident in the discussion it would be utter misrepresentation of the situation for me, to claim that I understood the world of the street youth, because it is only a partial view, I did gain.

In this instance then, it becomes clear that quantitative approaches become difficult to employ successfully; with the subjective methodologies being more useful in getting representative data on the subject. To conclude this section on the broad parameters dividing ethnographic studies from quantitative studies, Stredwick (2001:6) says, "Commonly epistemological disputes arise from the deeply entrenched antipathy between those with positivist orientations, who privilege,

99

formulated, scientific approaches, and interpretivists, who emphasize the importance of meaning and situational context." He goes on to say that often the two orientations are presented as though diametrically opposed with naturalistically oriented paradigms, being seen as an attack on reason and truth and positivistic ones being perceived as inadequate for unravelling the meanings attached to social action. According to Denzin and Lincolin (2000:3), multiple methodologies characterize qualitative studies which makes "the field of qualitative research one of the most controversial and complex areas in which to operate, these separate and multiple uses and meanings of the methods of qualitative research, make it difficult for researchers, to agree on any essential definition of the field, for it is never just one thing." This is evident in my fieldwork, which if one was to replicate, would not claim to have the same experiences as mine. Perceptions of situations and activities, would be different, due to a lot of other factors, relating to the researcher and his motives and the social phenomena under study.

4.2 *Ethnography and Qualitative Research*

As I prepared to go to the field, on my mind were issues pertaining to the meaning of ethnography and the problems of employing qualitative methodologies. Chambers (2000) explains that, ethnography is principally defined by the subject matter, which is 'ethnos', or culture, and not by its methodology. It is often but not invariably qualitative. The word culture, Chambers acknowledges, is difficult to define but the reader might be reminded of my efforts to define it in the introduction. It is important to explain the origin of ethnography with the likes of Malinowski, who advocated for ethnographic methodologies saying, this enabled the researcher or ethnographer, "…to observe behaviours and to explain their significance, in relation to their functions in an institutional and cultural context," (Chambers, 2000:853). Green (1993) and Henstrand (1993) also, discuss the importance of an ethnographer to have an interest, "…in the meaning and function of theory, in the conduct of qualitative research "…as an advancement in methodological issues," (Green, 1993: vii).

In my study, though initially I had thought I could do some survey during the preliminary stages of the study, I later abandoned this going for a totally qualitative study, as will be elaborated later. Denzin and Lincoln (2000:2), succinctly describe qualitative research saying that, "Qualitative research in sociology and anthropology was born out of concern to understand the "other". Furthermore, this other, was the exotic other, a primitive, non-white person from a foreign culture, judged to be less civilized than the researcher. This is the attitude, which then created problems for such studies from a post-modernist perspective, as Angrosno and de-Perez (2000:675) try to explain. Post-modernism has critiqued modern ethnographers, especially for maintaining distance from the subjects of their study, claiming to be the sole arbiters of knowledge about those societies and cultures they study, "because today they are in a position to have their analyses read and contested by those for whom they presume to speak." Postmodernists have critiqued traditional assumptions of even using insiders to verify their findings. William Foot Whyte used Doc, to read some of his texts to see if he had captured what was going on. This practice, postmodernists feel is no longer justifiable, due to differences for example, in perceptions and they say, "Ethnographic truth, has come to be seen as a thing of many parts, and no one perspective, can claim exclusive privilege in the representation thereof. Indeed the result of ethnographic research is reducible to a form of knowledge that can be packaged in the monologic voice of the ethnographer alone," (Marcuse, 1997:92) quoted by Angrosno and de Perez (2000:675).

Reflexivity becomes an important issue all ethnographers need to be aware of, (Pool, 1999; Beal, 1995; Davies, 1999). Postmodernists also point out that, the fact that researchers eventually write up some texts, still has problems of representation in that, it's claimed rather than evident. What I found out about the street youth, is not what another ethnographer might report, and my key informants being semi-literate, I found out that giving anyone of them the scripts to read, would have just been an academic exercise. I believe in honest reporting and truthfulness, to be important principles to be cherished by all anthropologists.

Issues of relations of observer-observed alluded to above, become very important with Weis et al (2000:169) pointing out that, the tradition has been for the researcher to be removed form the context. They quote Ruth Behar (1993) who was critical of such a relationship and observed thus of ethnographers; "We ask for revelations from others, but we reveal little or nothing of ourselves; we make others vulnerable, but we ourselves remain invulnerable. Our informants are then left carrying the burden of representations as we hide behind the cloak of alleged neutrality." Postmodernists have been associated with the concept of reflexivity in research, which requires that the researcher, becomes part of the research process and text. In my case, though I use the term informant when referring to those who gave me information, I also regarded them as research participants. They were involved in the research process. Rosaldo (1989) quoted by Weis et all (2000:109), however cautions ethnographers thus; "if classic ethnography's vice was the slippage from the idea of detachment, to actual indifference, that of present day reflexivity, is the tendency for the self-absorbed self, to lose sight altogether of the culturally different "other". This could be evidenced by for example, playing the role of an advocate for the group under study. Emotionally, the researcher might be aligned to the group. I cannot deny that I felt strongly at times, to condemn the city authorities and the media and other stakeholders, for perceiving the street children negatively.

Another issue of importance pertaining to qualitative research, I also observed in my study as will be evident below is that of using a number of methods, as a strategy that adds to rigour. Flick (1989) quoted by Denzin and Lincoln (2000) and Rener and Hunter quoted by Weis et al (2000) all point out that, qualitative research is inherently multi-method in nature. The use of multiple methods or triangulation, "reflects an attempt to secure an in-depth understanding of phenomenon in question, objective reality can never be captured... The combination of multiple methods, empirical materials, perspectives and observations, in a single study is best understood then, as a strategy that adds to rigour, breadth and depth to any investigation," (Denzin and Lincoln, 2000:119).

My study used triangulation definitely; such techniques as observation, conversations and discussions, in-depth interviews as well as semi-participant observation, were found to be effective in capturing the various behaviours and activities of the street youth. Leeds (1987:91) says that, it is important to "go to the field, try to put your presumptions to one side, and 'bathe' in it." Leeds says that, through ethnographic studies, new discoveries, new perceptions, new visions, new themes, new hypobook keep flowing, and goes on to point out that, he who does not do fieldwork "can rarely have such experiences... He who does not directly, intimately, intensely experience another culture,... does not discover the Westerness of his own thought from his own thought and the impositions of categories rectified from his own ethnic (and ethnocentric) history on other people, (Leeds, 1987:91).

Evans-Pritchard also, as observed by Ennew (1976:5), believed that the ethnographer or anthropologist, had to come into direct contact with the object of study. That one had to conduct research in the language, concepts and values of a strange society, such that a great deal depends on the character and temperament and ability, of the anthropologist to make a transference from one language and values to those of a strange society. This means for example that, I had to be part of the street youth community, in order to claim some fair knowledge of their lived experiences and activities, rather than depend on a survey study, of questionnaires, maybe administered by some research assistants whilst I, as researcher, was just there directing their activities from my office and then claim to have studied the street youth sexual behaviour. Evans-Pritchard, according to Ennew (1976:5), actually rightly observed that, "The native society has to be in the anthropologist himself and not merely in his notebooks, what comes out of a study of a primitive people derives not merely from intellectual impressions of native life but from its impacts on the entire personality of the observer as a total human being".

I need to point out here that some of the above issues made me prefer to go it alone into the field, without an assistant, because I did not want to have reports of what was going on, coming from another person. I had to do it alone, for it would be difficult to verify data presented to me by a research assistant.

Of course there are problems with qualitative research findings. Denzin and Lincoln (2000:8), point to some of the suspicions associated with qualitative studies, which make researchers findings suspect. They point out that, "The academic and disciplinary resistances to qualitative research, illustrate the politics embedded in this field of discourse. The challenges to qualitative research are many. Qualitative researchers are called journalists or soft scientists. Their work is termed unscientific or" only exploratory, or subjective." An example of the problems of these qualitative studies is that of Stoller with regard to his study among the Songhay of Niger, where he later learned that, "Everyone had lied to me and …the data I had so painstakingly collected were worthless. I learned a lesson; informants routinely lie to their anthropologists," (Denzin and Lincoln 2000:16). These observations, I must point out, really made me alert and aware of some of the shortcomings of ethnographic studies. As observed already, triangulation could help to check untruths as in my case, apart from general discussions from where I picked important clues pointing to my desired themes. I then had to do some observations and had to then select several cases from the youths, who were living in different bases so I could verify the information I was getting, checking against what the others would have said.

Stake (2000:436), explains the nature and usefulness of cases saying that, a case is a form of research defined by interest in individual cases not by the methods of inquiring used. Interest of the research is focused on a case at a time for some time. Stake (2000:436) says, "Functional or dysfunctional, rational or irrational, the case is a system, its behaviour is patterned. Coherence and sequence are prominent... bounded ness and behaviour patterns are useful concepts for specifying the case." He goes on to emphasize that one might simultaneously carry studies on one or more than one case study but each case study is a concentrated inquiry into a single case.

4.3 Debates around the status of the researcher either as outsider or insider

Much has been said about this by other researchers but here I review some of the views in relation to my study. Today there is a proliferation of anthropological studies by 'native' anthropologists also called "insider anthropologists" or "citizen anthropologists" mainly of the South. Morouta (1979:562) talks of the decolonization of anthropology making an interesting observation that, "I am aware of the view that anthropology cannot be done in one's own society, (Levi-Strauss 1966) - However, I have chosen to use "anthropology" rather than "sociology" because I believe with Merson (1972:136), that outsiders (foreign anthropologists), insiders (national social scientists), can play distinctive and interactive roles in the process of truth seeking." Bruce (1997:54) and Geertz (1984), also note the evident changes in the field of anthropology saying that, classical anthropological studies, mainly characterized by the study of other peoples and participant observation as a method of gathering information, are today critiqued severely by postmodernists.

Foreign anthropologists, are criticized as a way to demonstrate that one cannot claim to have more objective studies to those of citizen anthropologists' hence Jojoga's (1973:454) observation that, foreign anthropologists' studies, were usually an attempt, "to study the people for the benefit of the colonial government, and thus talks of the political nature of anthropology", (Morouta, 1979:563). Morouta's study is a good case in point of Papua New Guineans, who have criticized the content of the writings of foreign anthropologists, as full of distortions' and, "The plea of Papua New Guineans, for insider research, is not always for research in any Papua New Guinean Society, but often specifically for research in one's own small community of origin," (Morouta, 179:563). Again one sees the fear that, if one studies another ethnic group as a citizen anthropologist, there could be distortions. I had to realize I was not of the streets and hence, had to be aware of the pitfalls of studying "other" people.

Krotz (1997:244) also observes rightly that, "One of the characteristics which, at first glance distinguished 'classical' anthropology from the one practised at the present time in the South is that, in the latter, those studying and those being studied are citizens of the same country. It is more fundamentally important that, today, even relatively distant indigenous and peasant communities can have access to the results of anthropological studies generated about them in another part of the country and that they can establish several types of interaction with the authors of those studies." Anne-Marie Fortier (1996:307) also points out that, "Conducting field research 'at home', differs from the traditional 'exotic' anthropological fieldwork in many respects, one of which is the closeness of one's principal home." In my case, I studied street youth of Harare, where my home is and that is where I work as a lecturer at the University of Zimbabwe, and yet our world experiences are remotely related. The advantages to a citizen researcher are quite obvious. In terms of costs of the study, I was at a big advantage because I had my own accommodation and my own food, as well as my own car. I drove to and from the field as and when I liked, both during the day and at night.

The problematics associated with being a citizen anthropologist which apply to my study are that, even in one's own culture, objectivity is an elusive ideal, worse in communities like that of the street people, whom Dube (1999), had described as an "organized society" on its own. Morouta (1979:503) quotes Enos (1972:43) a Papua New Guinean who observes that, although he is a Niugunean, he is "at the same time a stranger, an outsider in other cultures but my own, no matter how hard I try." These native researchers are aware of their problems but what is important is to realize also that, "implicit in this preference, is not simply the desire to counter-balance foreign with indigenous view points but sometimes what Merton (1972) has called, "the extreme form of the doctrine of the insider." In this form, the belief is that outsiders, are excluded in principle from knowing the truth about society - that foreign anthropologists can only write half truths…in addition, some writers, e.g. Talyaga (1974) imply that, regardless of the objective quality of their research work, outsiders do not have the right to publish their findings against the wishes of their subjects. This kind of attitude, might not be good for anthropology, because the question of objectivity, must not be premised on the origin of the anthropologist, which could lead to the ultimate balkanization of social science, as Merton has pointed out. The whole development of a localized anthropology, may be a result of lack of funding rather than anything to do with objectivity. If one thoroughly observes the rigours of anthropological study or research, they may produce useful research findings whether they are foreigners or insiders. Narayan (1995:672), Krotz (1997:244) query the notion of being an insider asking how native a native anthropologist could be.

4.4 *Research and morality*

As a researcher one finds that we are emotionally involved, in the lived experiences of those we study and we tend to sympathize with their plight, as in the case of the street youth. Cole (1995:446) observes that, anthropologists have never had to look far to see violations of human rights, and that substantial evidence of systems of inequality and the denial of basic human rights can be found at the sites of anthropologists fieldwork, and where they do their excavations and as they study the various physical characteristics and languages of various peoples. He goes on to say, "My colleagues; while there is no question of widespread violations of human rights wherever we anthropologists work and wherever we live, there is a question about what if anything, we as anthropologists, should do and can do about it all. In the past and no less today, there have been intense debates on the appropriate role of anthropologists in world affairs, including responses to oppressive circumstances," (Cole, 1995:446). The question on my mind was; whether it was justifiable that I study the street youths' sexual life and leave it there. I thought about this after one of my supervisors had asked me whether it was justifiable for me to interfere with the lives of the street youth. Answers come from some of the views discussed here. Cole (1995:447) says with regard the role of anthropologists that, at one end of a continuum are those who argue that our role is to understand the human condition with objectivity, describing what is the nature and content of human culture. "At the other end of the continuum are those who insist that the role of the anthropologists, is indeed to understand the world, but in addition, we have the responsibility to help make it a better place." I found myself agreeing with this latter school of thought, as also noted by Muzvidziwa (2004:310) from his study, who says that, "It is important to take into account the political context of fieldwork at every stage of the research process. I sometimes faced tension between the need to intervene by publicizing police harassment of women vendors and the need to maintain a distanced position, enabling one to complete the study. I reasoned that any such active interventions needed to be on a sustained basis and since I was going to withdraw for sometime after my fieldwork, my activism would not work in the best long term interests of the participants." Cohen (1995), actually wonders how anthropologists are to make such a contribution and raises questions like; "Are we to join in direct actions, with people whose rights are being trampled upon? Or is our role to write articles and books, that describe oppressive situations and which therefore sound an alarm on what is taking place?" For the purpose of completing my study I found myself agreeing with Muzvidziwa, hoping that after completing my doctoral book, I could then write a book about my findings. Erwing (1996); Albert (1997); Sanadjian (1990); Bongo (2002) and Magaisa (1999), are some researchers, who discuss the problems associated with being a researcher among harassed subjects of one's study.

4.5 *Gaining Entry*

I am far older than these youth I studied. I am also male and yet I had girls as participants and all these factors, definitely impacted on my relationships with the street youths apart from the fact that I am from the University and from the middle-class as it were. I am also a born-again Christian used to "normal" language not the obscene language that I was to hear from the street youths. This, as Hutnyk (1998:342) observes, has impact on the field of study. The issue of sexuality is quite a sensitive one and is regarded as taboo in our society. How to introduce the topic and to freely discuss it with the street youths was a big challenge.

Researchers like Magaisa (1999); Bongo (2003), Muzvidziwa (2004) and Bourdillon (1994), all show that it is not easy to gain entry into the world of marginalized groups, who are harassed from time to time by state officials, as they are very suspicious of strangers. Magaisa (1999:7), refers to some of the problems saying that, when he first went into the field to research on prostitution, he faced a dilemma because when he introduced himself as a researcher, most of his respondents were "disinterested and never bothered to pay attention and when I pretended to be a potential client, matters did not change much because real clients did not ask silly questions." He had eventually to buy them beer and dance with them and then to confide in some waitress who then helped him gain entry into the world of the prostitutes. Bongo (2003:46) also says that, he had problems of gaining entry during his study and that, "in fact, in almost 10 out of the total 170 interviews I carried out, the informants were very suspicious of me when I started probing about the impact of craft on trees. Some people thought I was some government detective out to identify tree cutters so that they could be arrested and fined."

Sanadjian (1990:129), also makes reference to problems during his study of the Lurs. He had to win the sympathy of the educated as a way to gain entry into the field, in a politically volatile environment. He says, "It was not accidental that I could secure, in this depressing period, a significant contribution from the politically educated Lurs, who supported various political groups, to my research. These locals volunteered, for example, to make detailed surveys of the socio-economic factors of the area, with which they were most familiar." The street children as a harassed group, are quite suspicious of strangers. To be honest, I would have found it difficult to introduce myself to them. I was lucky to get in contact with one former employee of Streets Ahead, which is a drop -in centre for such children. He introduced me to the youth in one of the "bases". The youth themselves, eventually introduced me to their colleagues after some time, something similar to snowballing.

With regard to such factors like age, sex, and class background, Fortier (1996:315), doing a study on activities of Italian women's clubs, points out that, age difference can affect the researcher. She was far younger than the women involved in club activities and says whenever she was involved in the women's conversations, she often, "felt incapable of engaging in immediate conversations with many of the women at the Ladies Club. Most of the women from the Women's Club are in their 50s, married, mothers, some even grandmothers. At first, I felt awkward with these women. They shared experiences (although she was also Italian), which I knew nothing of, which were not part of my daily life. I did not act like they did. I did not act like a woman, with a home, family etc." To some extent, a researcher must realize that, age differences will mean different experiences, expectations and perceptions of life and thus the researcher has to be very sensitive to questions indicating such differences. This also shows that being a citizen anthropologist, does not mean you will get information easily; rather, as I also found out from the streets, you have to overcome a number of barriers, one being that of age.

On the issue of sex differences Gregory (1984:19), makes an interesting reference to the debate on this subject when he says that, there is need for more attention to gender balance in field research because he says, "The myth of the male ethnographer and the woman's world, is not false in the sense of being untrue - there are real and serious problems in cross-sex data collection. But the myth's function as a charter and explanation has predisposed (many of) us to respond to it in ways that transform this basic truth, into what is in effect a false statement." Gregory, elaborates by pointing out that, it has generally been accepted as a truism that, male ethnographers more often than not, encounter problems in getting information about the world of women in the communities they study. For example Oakley (1981), has interesting observations with regards gendered interviews as quoted by Fontana and Fray (200:655). She says gaining trust, is essential to the success of the interviews and once gained, trust can still be very fragile. Oakley then points out that, with regard to gendered interviews, both the interviewers and the respondents are considered faceless and invisible and they must be, if the paradigmatic assumption of gathering value free data is to be maintained. Yet as Denzin (1989) also observes, "gender filters knowledge," that is the sex of the interviewer and that of the respondent, do make a difference, as the interview takes place within the cultural boundaries of a paternalistic social system in which masculine identities are differentiated from feminine ones, (Fontana and Fray 2000). I need to point out here that, once I got accepted by the boys, gaining the trust of the girls was not a problem for me, such that the above views, which sound quite practicable, were not confirmed by my field experiences among street girls. On the streets as the reader will learn later, once the boys accept you, the girls will not be a problem. The researcher only has to establish rapport. Being accepted is easy once the "gate-keepers," who are the boys agree to work with a researcher.

4.6 *Use of Incentives in Research as a way to gain Trust of the Respondents*
Use of incentives might not be tantamount to deceit or fraud, as other researchers have used monetary and other material resources to sustain their respondents' interests. Sometimes it might be counselling required by the respondents during times of crises. Magaisa (1999) researching on prostitutes, had to buy them beer and dance with them and at one time he was caught up in the net of the police when he was required to testify as the "brother" of one of the prostitutes. He says he was careful not to sleep with them; well who can doubt or query this? Muzvidziwa (2004:306), also says that, "There were times, when I felt obliged to give gifts in kind to some participants, especially those who became part of the extended observation study. I interrelated with them as a friend and a classificatory relative. This made me realize that a researcher should have resources at his/her disposal so as to participate in gift exchange transactions." As already

discussed earlier on, with regards the status of the anthropologist as either insider or outsider, Muzvidziwa (2004) notes that, "Being a citizen anthropologist as such, does not in itself guarantee that one would assimilate with ease. Commitment to the well being of the respondents is likely to be higher, when the researcher is a citizen or a permanent member of the community he or she is studying. Research should in many ways be regarded as a moral endeavour. Central to the research process is the need for integrity and responsibility for one's actions, with regard to other fellow human beings." These observations were confirmed by my field experiences. Sometimes, I gave the youth money to buy food. I had to make sure I was not seen by members of the public, because the government does not want people to give these children anything, Authorities believe it encourages them to remain on the streets. If anyone is found giving the street youth anything, they can be arrested by Municipal Police.

Respondents as Magaisa (1999) observes, can make demands. He was referred to as "my darling" by one of the drunken prostitutes, who demanded for "a beer," and he had to buy her, during his study of prostitution in Harare. This is what Muzvidziwa calls friendships and notes that, "Friendship creates obligations and expectations. Yet it is inevitable that a researcher engaged in fieldwork with time came to be regarded as a friend and in turn develops friendship networks with respondents. However, one need to always balance the research interests to friendship networks", (Muzvidziwa, 2004:314). He goes further to make another important observation that, "It would be naïve on my part to suggest that relations with respondents were based on true equality, considering the amount of resources at my disposal and my job as a University Lecturer. Yet in many ways that status differential, did not go in the way of research as an interactive process. Ethical conduct in research settings requires, that a researcher is fully aware at every stage, of the potential distortions in terms of research outcomes due to unequal power balances", (Muzvidziwa, 2004:316).

Muzvidziwa's experiences are quoted extensively because I found them quite practicable and a reality one had to contend with. He makes another interesting observation on researcher vulnerability as a result of relations with respondents. He says, "Researcher vulnerability is a factor rarely discussed in research manuals. This is something real. Friendship can create a state of vulnerability for both researcher and respondents. During fieldwork a number of respondents began to confide in me, regarding their personal lives as well as family life. These intricate and delicate issues regarding people's lives weigh heavily on the researcher, who must act at times as counsellor and confidant. Increasingly during fieldwork I came to play this role often, despite my limited training in interpersonal relations and conflict reduction and coping strategies", (Muzvidziwa, 2004:314). As detailed below, the street youth made a lot of demands from me. I find Muzvidziwa's experiences quite relevant especially his humble observation that, "Sometimes, I felt inadequately prepared to handle respondents problems. I gave my respondents an ear; I suggest that a researcher should avoid appearing to be in a hurry as this is demeaning to the respondents", (Muzvidziwa, 2004:316). The street youth had many questions relating to the various themes. I had to be honest and avoid giving half truths as answers.

It is important to gain trust of the respondents. As Bongo (2003) notes, respondents may be suspicious of a researcher's intentions. For example, there are big girls on the streets. I made sure all interviews involving the youth, girls or boys were not done in secluded places far way from the other youth on the streets, or my personal driver. Muzvidziwa (2004:315) says that, "...there is need for one to be morally upright and principled, as faltering in this regard might ruin the whole research process".

Fontana and Frey (2000:656) also advise on how to gather data. They point out that in most cases, note taking has to be done discreetly, and tape recorders whenever used, be used inconspicuously. They also talk of taking "mental notes and then rushing to the privacy of a bathroom to jot notes down, on toilet papers at times... write everything down no matter how unimportant it may seem at the time - try to be as inconspicuous as possible in the note taking; and analyze the notes frequently." I had nowhere to quickly dash to, on the streets. I had to capture everything mentally, and then when I got home, I would write everything down, sometimes verbatim. I would sometimes go to sleep at night and then wake up, having remembered some aspect I had forgotten to write down, and do it. I never wrote anything on the streets. All information was captured in a friendly informal setting, without any behaviour that could raise suspicion.

Bongo (2003:43), quotes Selltiz et al's (1961:210) observations when one is a participant observer, with regard to two issues - "When should the observer take notes? How should notes be kept?". Bongo goes on to say that, the best time for recording is on the spot and during the event. "However, there were many situations in which note taking on the spot was not feasible, as it would arouse the suspicion of the craft workers being observed, especially those in debarking trees," (Bongo, 2003:43). My field experiences confirm Bongo's findings in that, I realised that, writing anything could have raised a lot of suspicion as to the purpose of such information.

Bourdillon (1994) observes that street children, seemed reluctant to be researched on, pointing out that, "All fieldworkers have commented on the fact that street children have very limited concentration span and constantly flirt from one topic to another. This is probably partly due to the lack of any need to concentrate in street life, exacerbated by continuous glue-sniffing," (Bourdillon, 1994:524). Maybe it depends on the circumstances. I found the youth to be involved and attentive. It is important to be sure the youths are not under the influence of drugs lest one records wrong information - thus timing is very important as Stoller found out above. Bourdillon (1994:529), goes on to point out that, "The limited concentration span by street children affects their ability to take part in any form of institutionalized life, including the life of schools." Gregory's (1984) observations with regard to, the research context is very important. For example when dealing with girls' sexuality, I had to discuss in the absence of the boys. Gregory's (1984:321)'s observations with regards the truthfulness of the responses of the respondents, are important because the respondents, can give researchers responses to questions, that please the researcher and yet may not be a true reflection of the situation.

4.7 *The Problematics of Investigating Sexual Issues*
In this section I briefly make reference to the problems associated with investigating sensitive issues and the various techniques like participant observation, interviews, and focus group discussions. I also note contributions by the various debates surrounding these techniques. Some of the issues have already been referred to above and hence I will just summarize. Magaisa (1999:9) observes that discussing sexual issues in Zimbabwe is taboo. Gregory (1984), also agrees with this observation. Ondimu (2004) of Kenya, also notes that researching on sexual matters is not easy due to normative factors constraining women respondents. According to Trussell et al (1996), men are free to express themselves on sexual matters than women and they may even exaggerate their sexual exploits whilst women as Ondimu (2004) discovered, tend to be conservative with information. My personal experiences point to the contrary, as I have

already observed. This could be so because; in the world of the street youth sexual issues are not taboo at all. Girls mentioned any part of their bodies without any problems just as boys. They however seemed conservative as Ondimu (2004) says, when it came to their sexual exploits; they were not as enthusiastic to elaborate as the boys. Girls also used lighter vulgar words to mention their vagina like *"mhata"* rather than *"beche"*, which the boys did. Verification of sexual experiences was easy, for those issues relevant to the study tended to be general knowledge amongst the street youth.

4.8 *Information Gathering Techniques*

Trussel et al (1996:106), point out that, "The principal sources of information about sexual behaviour are ethnographic accounts and survey methods. Ethnographic accounts, typically focus on sexual behaviour only in so far as it relates to family, marriage and kinship." One research endeavour that seriously delved into sexuality amongst street youths was done by Tadele (2004), in Ethiopia. He used participant observation and interviewing as the principal sources of data. As Trussell et al (1996:106) point out, "Anthropological research uses primarily qualitative methods and participant observation for data collection. The goal usually is not to quantify the behaviours, but to understand their intent and meanings. The principal danger with using survey methodology, to collect data on sexual behaviour, is that respondents, may simply say what they think researchers want to hear and that without elaborate probing, such methods may lead to a serious undercount of the true situation." In my case, I mainly used what Field (2001:211) has referred to as "life story interviews," mainly.

It is not easy to use participant observation when studying street youth as Swart (1990) found out, let alone to investigate sexual matters, which occurred in private places most of the time, hence the need to define the nature of my participation. Rock and Downes (1982:29) observe thus, quoted by Magaisa (1999:6), "There is a general difficulty in trying to know groups who have nothing to gain from becoming known". Magaisa (1999:6) also says, "Generally sex is a sensitive and delicate issue and therefore not many people, may be interested in narrating their sexual lives to strangers." Now, when it comes to gaining insight through participant observation, the term ceases to have its Malinowskian meaning, of observer as a participant as Magaisa points out. The researcher rather participates, as observer. Magaisa studying prostitution, justifies his participant observer status by referring to Punch (1989)'s research on police deviance, who says that he never witnessed the bribery and corrupt practices he was studying but, "Nevertheless, he was a participant observer in the day to day world of these activities. This means that the researcher doesn't actually involve himself in the deviant or criminal behaviour, but sees what people do and say in his/her presence", (Magaisa ,1999:7). It is in the latter sense that one can claim to have been a participant observer as Magaisa claims saying that, "In this research I observed and talked to sex workers, without having to engage in a sexual relationship with them. I shared space with prostitutes in bars, night clubs and shebeens in Harare. I moved with them, bought beer and drank together, and I shared with them numerous stories and conversations. It is in this sense that, I consider myself to have been participating," (Magaisa 1999:7).

The other information gathering technique is the semi-structured interview, which according to Bongo (2003:44), is referred to by Mersan et al (1956) as the, "focused interview." I used this method to supplement my observations. Bongo (2003:44), elaborates on the relevance of this method saying, "The main function of the interviewer in this type of interview, is to focus attention upon a given experience and its effects. He has a list that constitutes a framework of topics to be covered, but the manner in which questions are asked and their timing are left largely to the interviewer's discretion. Although the interviewee is free to express completely his line of thought, the direction of the interview is clearly in the hands of the interviewer. He wants definite types of information, and part of his task is to confine the respondent to discussion of issues about which he wants knowledge. The flexibility of the semi-structured interview if properly used, helps to bring out the affective and value in certain aspects of the subject's responses, and to determine the personal significance of his/her attitudes." All the time, during such sessions, the researcher must watch out for questions indicating uneasiness on the part of the respondents.

Gregory (1984:32) observes that, we must recognize the problem moments, which are often signalled by "such things as shifts in tone of voice, informant uneasiness, evasiveness, irritable response to questions, attempts to change the subject, or the cessation of conversation when other persons approach." Gregory (1984:320), goes on then to note that, "Simplistically put then, our research efforts will yield two types of material - one body of material that is reasonably reliable and another that is not; and with time we will be able to make the distinction between the two, -

114

that is a major aspect of our job as ethnographers. The reliable material is readily usable and requires no comment, but what of the unreliable material? Buried within the latter will be a great deal of useful information. The distortions, omissions and half truths, as well as the signals, that these are occurring and the context in which they occur, become themselves a wealth of valuable information from which, much else can be inferred." These are true observations and as already noted, in my case, involvement of the youth, in different locations of the city, enabled me to verify given information.

To conclude this section, it is important for the reader to note Frotz's (1997:833) observations that, "There are some exceptions in the ethnographic and historical literature, but they are so few that hidden coitus may safely be declared a near universal." As already pointed out earlier, my aim was not to witness the youth in an actual sexual encounter, but to learn from their conversations, their narratives and responses to my questions during the in-depth interviews. Friedl (1994:834) also says that, "The scant attention paid to sexual privacy in cultural and social anthropology is all the more puzzling and intriguing because all ethnographers, know that wherever in the world they go, they will not be permitted to observe or film actual sexual intercourse among the people with whom they work." He goes on, as I have already pointed out above to say that, still one can learn about the subject pointing out thus; "On the other hand, we can expect to learn about the enormous variety of cultural values and attitudes associated with sex and sexuality, values that are verbalized and symbolized in myriad, emotionally charged forms. Apart from rare instances of personal dalliance, not for ethnographic purposes, anthropologists cannot check by direct observation, any stories informants tell about their current sexual activities." This is to ensure the reader realizes that, this study was not meant to gain insight of the sexual behaviour of the youth, by practically witnessing them in coitus.

4.9 Ethical Considerations

This was a very important aspect of my study, which needed a lot of attention up to the presentation of data. Some of the issues have been referred to in earlier discussions but here, I briefly focus at ethical issues in my research more so because of Fabian (1991) quoted by Muzvidziwa (2004:310), who points out that, "There is no way of knowing in advance what kind of consequences our projects will bring about." Muzvidziwa says, he for confidentiality purposes, ensured that there were no names and addresses on interview schedules and no one had access to research information, except himself, as a way to ensure complete anonymity of participants. I chose to refer to my respondents just as respondents, or participants, to ensure absolute anonymity, except for one called "*Sekuru Gudo*" (Uncle Baboon), for I learnt later that, there were several with such a nick name later, in other parts of the city, amongst the street involved youth.

The question or rather issue of protection of respondents' identities must be of paramount importance to any researcher. Magaisa (1999:10) also points out that, "The first moral problem that confronted me in the course of this research, was how to protect the identity of my respondents. I discovered that prostitutes in Harare, used pseudonyms and never revealed their true identities to clients, other women or researchers. I only got to know their real names by chance, from their close friends and relatives." I found out that, though street youths do not have any form of identification, their anonymity in research reports was of critical importance. Magaisa (1999:17) emphasizes thus, "Regardless of the fact that, I worked with false identities, I have further protected their anonymity by giving them my own names." In my case, to ensure complete anonymity, I chose to refer to my respondents just as respondents, or participants or just to use numerals like 1;2;etc.

The youths do engage in some socially unacceptable activities and the purpose of my study was not to expose them to the police or any authorities. This is why I maintain their complete anonymity. Magaisa (1999:7), actually supports this view saying that, "Prostitutes often showed me men and women who were involved in criminal activities of various kinds but I have ignored this information, so that future researchers are not accused of being sell-outs." To Bongo (2003), issues of confidentiality, were also quite central to his study.

Ethically, the next important question I had to ask was whether the researchers or anthropologists had a right to interfere in the lives of others. As already discussed earlier, the purpose must be to improve the well being of our respondents. Bourdillon (1994:529), points out in the form of a caution thus; "As academics we need to be sensitive to the accusations from some officials that, we are using street children simply to further our own careers, a sophisticated form of exploitation." Magaisa (1999:17) also observes thus, "The research also raised questions as to whether researchers have the right to invade people's privacy, simply because they are doing research. It can be argued that every social research does invade the privacy of someone in order to bring out the unknown in the form of knowledge." He goes on to quote from Rock and Downes (1982:38), who observe that, "The role of anthropologists or sociologists, may easily become that of sneak-spy and false confidant." Maybe this could be simply put as deceit and fraud in research, which is tantamount to exploitation as Bourdillon puts it, in that, the researcher is the only one who benefits. Muzvidziwa (2004:310), also makes reference to the negative consequences of research by quoting Fabian (1991:189), who refers to the potential unintended consequences research findings may have on those we study saying, "Are we not blocking with our ethnographies. What may have been routes of escape from oppression, in situations where resistance is not (yet) possible?," he asked and to some extent, maybe implying that, we may end up being accused of being sell-outs by our respondents.

4.10 *Hazards of the Field*

There are hazards associated with being in the field of research, (Torry, 1979). In my case, I was dealing with youngsters some of whom abuse drugs and are most of the time feeling high due to effects of such drugs and possibilities of being harassed were there. Bourdillon (1994:522), points to the drunkenness of the youths, saying car minders are, "regularly high and often exceedingly aggressive as a result." Bourdillon (1994:522), also refers to an incident when Maxwell, his assistant researcher, was challenged in the following quotation, "When Maxwell started to spend time with the boys on the street, he found he was welcome to join them on a drinking spree at the weekend. But when he refused to smoke marijuana, he was immediately made to feel as an intruding outsider and had to go elsewhere." Fights and squabbles over sex were said to be common and Bourdillon says, "*(Monyas,* street lingo for the physically powerful), often have homosexual partners from among their young clients and sometimes arrange for their clients to serve more wealthy homosexuals for a good fee, only part of which goes to the child concerned. Sex is everyday language among the children and sexual relations are a common cause of squabbles and fights." Violence is evidently prevalent on the streets. Swart-Kruger and Richter (1997), doing studies of street youths in South Africa also discuss the issue of violence as well as Tadele (2004) from his doctoral research in Ethiopia. The researcher can also be caught up and be accused of being an intruder and a sell-out and be beaten up. For example Fontana and Frey (2005:655), make reference to a case thus, "At times, what the researcher may feel is good rapport turns out not to be as Thompson (1985), found out in a

117

nightmarish way, when he was subjected to a brutal beating by the Hell's Angels just as his study of them was coming to a close..."

There are big girls on the streets and I had feared this could cause problems for me, especially on night visits should I be seen by the boys. Fortunately, there was no problem whenever I was seen in the company of the girls. Bunja (1975:555) quoted by Gregory (1984:323) points out that, "The female ethnographer working with men, may incur the jealousy and suspicion of local women concerning her motives. We might add that the male ethnographer working with women may similarly arouse the suspicion of local men concerning his motives." Magaisa (1999), refers to an incident in which the police caught him together with the prostitutes he was studying. I really feared to go to some of the bases along the Mukuvisi River where those who were believed to be ill were said to live. This was because some of the street youth whom I was shown and were said to live there, were real alcoholics and I feared them. They looked ruthless and brutish. I thought these were some of the limits of ethnographic studies. One has also to consider the risks. It's like going to sleep with the street youth in their bases, would have been going too far. Different characters live in those bases and some of them just come occasionally and such are the characters I feared most.

I want to quote from Sperber (1985:34), as I conclude this part, quoted by Morris (1997:337) who says that, "The task of ethnographic studies is interpretation, making intelligible the experiences of a particular social domain, and that the task of anthropology as a generalizing science, is to describe the causal mechanisms that account for cultural phenomenon." He sees these as two autonomous tasks, which are best initially divorced from each other. But ethnographic texts themselves, often incorporate different research strategies and thus include historical and comparative studies and causal explanations as well as hermeneutic understating. But an anthropology worthy of the name, seems to me to embrace what Adam Kuper (1994), has described as, "the cosmopolitan project - linking with other social sciences, (as well as with the humanities), to contribute towards the comparative understanding of human life. It thus affirms realist ontology, and acknowledges that anthropological understanding, is a search for truth. It also affirms the salience of human subjectivity, and combines hermeneutics (the descriptive understanding of human life), with the advocacy of an empirical social science." This is why, as already discussed, I subscribe to what I might call "activist" anthropology. The purpose of the ethnographic studies, being to influence, the policy formulation process, especially in favour of the marginalized vulnerable groups. I definitely will not disengage from the field of study, as even today almost after seventeen months, I have been on the streets from time to time, I feel I have "bathed in street life; in the field of study," and I am indebted to the street youth for life, as long as their material conditions are not improved.

4.11 *Organization and conduct of my Study*

With the theoretical background above, one feels the reader finds logic, in the researcher's detailed narrative of how and what transpired in the field of research and why. It becomes easy for one to contextualize the researcher's explanation, of how he conducted and organized the study, bearing in mind that we always must acknowledge, what has been found out by others before us, we find useful, rather than pretending that all my methods and techniques, were new and unique. It is the information I found that was unique.

4.12 *Unlocking into the youth's world*

This is just an elaboration of what was said earlier. This was in two parts. Part one, I had to ensure the research project was feasible by finding out if the street children were still there on the streets. And then, I had to seek permission from the city fathers to do the research. This was granted on 6 December 2005 (see letter in Appendix). This was after I was satisfied that the conditions on the streets were conducive to the conducting of the study. As already discussed, this is one of the challenging aspects of fieldwork. Initially, I intended to use Streets Ahead (the drop-in centre for street children in the city centre), as my point of entry. I had hoped the officials at this Non-Governmental Organization, were going to introduce me to the street youth. Just as well, I did not go to therm, I would have blown up the opportunity to carry out the study. The youth would have associated me with this organization which they say they have a bone to chew with. They harbour a lot of bitterness against this institution because they said, they were suffering because Streets Ahead had neglected them. I then decided to go it alone, and initially, that was in September 2005, I decided to just loiter on the streets and locate the street youth on the various streets. At first, it seemed like a wild goose chase, because they seemed not to be in the streets in the city centre. I almost gave it up, thinking that there were no more street children or "Street Kids" or "Street Youth." I will use these terms interchangeably as the ordinary person in the street refers to them as such, despite the fact that some are over eighteen years and some have children and some are married. They are still regarded as street children or street kids by members of the public and the city fathers.

One of the days, as I was walking in the city I met Mr X. He is a former employee of Streets Ahead and I had known him in 2001 when I had been engaged together with a Mr S. Matindike to do some peer training programme for Streets Ahead. I explained to him my predicament, that I was failing to locate the Street Children. He is the one who then educated me on the movements of the children from the time of Murambatsvina (Operation Restore Order of 2005, May). He actually said, some time after June 2005 up to August the same year, the street children were very difficult to locate, since they were still being hunted by the city authorities. Some of them had been rounded up and taken to far away places. He however, advised me that the best time to find them on the streets, on the outskirts of the city centre was from 12 noon usually. The problem was that, I was getting into town at around 9.00a.m on my way to the University where I work. I would then try to locate them and yet they were still in their resting bases. I learned that they also used some sentinels (*vasori*) who would be sent into the city, to find out, whether it would be safe to move onto the streets or not.

Mr X then waited for me the next day. He had the time because he was no longer employed, because I learnt later that, he had been implicated in a case of sexually abusing some street girls. He then took me to one of the children's bases on the western side of the city. It was around 12 noon and only a few were there playing cards popularly known as crazy 8. After about an hour as he engaged in conversations with the youth, more and more came from the western direction and some were moving right into the city centre. They were coming from what I leant later was one of the boys' "kitchens." They would have prepared their food there and eaten, because they spend the whole day on the streets. Mr X then, having met a number of boys, he knew, then introduced me to the street children, and also mentioned that, I was going to explain the purpose of my study to them. That day I did not remain with the children, I left, only to return after 3 days, as I had to plan how best to win them over despite having been introduced. Initially, not much interest had been shown though, and I suppose, it was because none of the children knew exactly where I was coming from.

On the third day, I must say, every working day I was passing through town to the University and so now, with the project in the city, I found it quite conveniently located. In terms of transport costs, it proved quite a big advantage unlike if the study was located way out of my way to work. I went to this base only, because when Mr X introduced me, not much was said about other locations. I was going to use snow-balling as already discussed above. My problem was that when I got to the boys, they regarded me as "*Big Dhara reku* Streets Ahead." (The old men from Streets Ahead).*Big dhara* is street lingo for generally a well off men. He could be as young as twenty but if he is deemed to have money, he earns the status of "*Big Dhara*". It is a salutation that makes the person feel like doing something for someone. I realized there was a problem, as one of them said this, as I approached them. I did not want to be associated with Streets Ahead. Mr X had however told them in my presence, that, I was from the University. I found out that some who saw me in the company of Mr X the first day and were busy on the streets with selling of parking discs, did not hear this and assumed I was also from Streets Ahead. There were some big rocks, where they were playing cards and others were busy talking to motorists and never noticed my arrival. They welcomed me saluting me as "*Big Dhara,*" I thought that was quick, I already had been given a nickname, I did not show any signs of resistance because obviously I did not want to start the relationship by showing that, I didn't like such labels. One of the big boys then said:

> We expected you the other day as you had promised. We had planned to gather all the street youth so you could talk to them at once about HIV and AIDS as we heard from Mr X, you are an expert on that. We are going to help you if you want to educate us about this. We are dying from the disease *Big Dhara*."

This was again another distortion, I thought, which needed to be put right. They seemed to listen when I apologized for not coming. As I was talking to them, a vendor selling salted nuts came to where we were and I told them I was buying them the nuts. They were so happy and some clapped their hands.

> "*Big Dhara maita henyu, munemoyo wakanaka*"

(Big Dhara thank you so much, you are so kind), one small boy said with a smile. I won their hearts. I then explained to them that I was from the University of Zimbabwe, and was not to be associated with Streets Ahead. I only knew Mr X in his individual capacity. I then told them the purpose of the study, as I was to explain to a number of other groups in other bases later. One boy actually, said;

"*Pa University mudhara pane vanhu vanopisa musoro. Vamwe vacho vaimbouya vachitaura nesu.*" (At the University are hot heads, some of the lectures used to come to talk to us). He did not go further as one rebuked him. "*Rega mudhara apedze kutaura*" (leave the old man to finish what he has to say to us).

I must say this was the most challenging part. To try to gain entry and establish a relationship, I then went on to explain to them that I was a registered doctorate student, and that if they accepted to take part in my study on their sexual behaviour and the HIV and AIDS pandemic, I would be very happy. There was much interest expressed by the boys. I then told them that, the study was initially going to be for about one year three months or, five months but then the relationship was going to continue. I virtually explained everything including the fact that, I was going to write a long report, which would be marked, and that I could show them the reports when I had compiled it. There seemed to be no problem. I then told them that, there was no need to gather their colleagues as yet, because I was actually going to select a few at a time for the detailed study apart from the general conversations I was going to have with them, as they did their work. I told them I would only listen, sit amongst them and discuss when they were not busy working. Most of the time I was going to be observing their activities on the streets.

The following day, two of them took me to a base located close to one of the popular nightclubs in Harare, where they introduced me to their colleagues. Again the salutation "*Big Dhara*" was used and they expressed willingness to take part in the study. I had never hoped they would quickly understand me and my intentions. The two who had accompanied me then, promised to take me to other bases some time which they later did, taking me to a base for girls. Because of the joy they had, when they introduced me to the girls, the girls also had no problem with my request for their involvement in my study. The youth were told that their real names were not going to be used and that their participation was voluntary and they were free to withdraw from the study at any time. Before leaving the girls, I bought each of the four children there a banana. The girls were quite touched by this gesture of affection for their young ones. Thus snowballing was basically used in the process to find out who were to be included in the study. I explained to the youth that for their involvement, especially in the long in-depth interviews conducted usually on Saturday afternoons and on Sundays, they were to get some pocket money from me but I did not give the figures. As discussed under theoretical implications of this chapter, the researcher must have some resources, "more so if he is a lecturer." That was the expectation of the youth. It

122

would not have been morally right for the researcher to go to the field on a full stomach and talk to hungry children and so from time to time, I sponsored the buying of food even in their groups like meat and vegetables, they would cook in their "Kitchen." Other researchers as discussed earlier, have also used the same approach to establish bonds and rapport with the participants. Having been accepted, I then began to employ the various qualitative methods to get information that would answer my objectives as outlined in the theoretical discussion above.

4.13 *Sampling and Data Collection Techniques*

I planned everything before going to the field. I was going to carry out a qualitative study. The purpose being to have an in-depth exploration of the sexual experiences of the street youth apart from also learning about their life histories, income earning activities and leisure pursuits and survival strategies. I decided that I was going to employ the multiple method approach as already discussed and this was to include participant observation, the conversational style and key informant narratives. I discovered that initially, I was going to capture issues during informal group discussions as they interacted in their natural setting. I would just pose questions and they would respond in any order in a relaxed atmosphere and yet through triangulation, i.e. employing same methods with several groups and a number of cases, I managed to get useful, complementary narratives from the street youth. After the preliminary group discussions, which were coupled with passive observations and conversations, I then decided to have in-depth interviews from time to time with some of the street youth. I had decided before going to the field that I was only going to involve "Street youth of the streets," in the key participant, in-depth studies. Several were selected as the cases - both male and female. From the start, I also had planned that I was only going to have youth who were above twenty years of age and had been on the streets for more than seven years. I found plenty of them and then, through the general group discussions I had managed to identify those who seemed forthcoming with information, and eventually selected them as my cases.

From the descriptions, its evident I was participating already in the activities of my respondents, not necessarily having to observe the youth having sexual intercourse, but as discussed earlier on, my participant observer status was based on the fact that, I was involved in the activities and conversations of the youth. I was not selling the parking discs or even cleaning cars, but the mere fact that with time, after a month, I would literally be seated on pavements with them and listening to their sexual exploits and what would have happened during my absence, this made me become a participant observer, as claimed by the likes of Muzvidziwa, Magaisa, Bongo, Gregory already discussed.

Data gathering was mainly by way of taking mental notes for reasons already discussed. To confirm my fears of writing notes in their presence, one day there was one of them whose name I would always forget and yet he eventually became one of my key informants. I told him I always forgot his name and I was going to write it somewhere. As I took out a pen and tried to write it at the back of one of my notebooks, he quickly expressed his unwillingness to have his name written because he actually said;

> "*Ah Mudhara zvekunyora zita rangu siyana nazvo, inga vamwe hauna kuvanyora wani,*" with some seriousness, (Old man, it is not right to write my name. Why didn't you write the names of others).

It clicked in my mind that I had made the right decision not to write anything on the streets. I could still reproduce some of the conversations verbatim when I got home, anyway. Sometimes I would forget some of the issues only to remember after having gone to sleep. I would wake up even at any hour of the night and write those views. Sometimes I would even dream being on the streets. I thought I was going native.

I had three note books, with one I used as my diary. In this, initially I would forget for two or so days to write something relating to how I was budgeting my time and how I was prioritizing the various activities that required my attention. After two months, I found use of the diary quite an effective way of instilling discipline in me and enabled me to complete my fieldwork according to my timetable. I had to be disciplined and consistent. Of course as a family man, I also had my small security project to attend to. Eventually, I stopped the security project altogether for it had proved to be a time consuming. Fortunately my children were in boarding school and so I did not ignore them. During the December holidays of 2005 and 2006 they really felt ignored. I was preoccupied with either reading, writing or I would be away in the field. The other notebook was for events taking place on the street or in the field of research where I had to write everything no matter how simple or small as already discussed. I discovered that whatever occurred was important for me to understand the lives of street youth.

I then had a notebook for each of the cases, a boy and a girl per each of my broad themes, for focused interviews. This was meant as a way to verify the type of information I was getting, and true, this worked. It seemed as if the youth had been eavesdropping on my conversations and interviews with their colleagues. I got very similar information confirming that, I was getting the truth about their sexual and reproductive health experiences on the streets. The process of interviewing required a lot of time, as the youths would be busy or sometimes would come late onto the streets. During some weekends, they would not be there. It was really not that easy. I had to be patient and tolerant, qualities I normally did not have before this study. I am one who was used to having things done within a given time limit but on the streets I learnt to be sensitive to constraints of the respondents. I discovered after three months it was no longer uncommon for me to literally dream during my sleep at night whilst being on the streets, having interviews with the street youth. I thought I had really "bathed" in the field.

Towards the end of fourteen months, I had focus group discussions with some of my key participants. Girls were on their own, and the boys on their own to discuss a number of issues. I felt it was a good way of winding up my detailed interviews with them from where I captured a lot of issues. From time to time, I also had casual discussions with members of the city council, some police officers and employees of non-governmental organizations, apart from discussions with some University colleagues, who had done in fieldwork at some point, involving street people. I had discussions with villagers from my rural home, some church elders and members of the traditional healers association including the president of the organisation of traditional healers, Professor Gordon Chavunduka. I am happy I did the study on my own because, I can claim full ownership of what I report, and I can claim full anonymity of my respondents and full confidentiality as these research findings cannot be handled by an assistant researcher. I must also note that during this study, I felt more of an outsider than an insider. The obscene language, the values of the Street Youth and their lifestyle, made me feel like a stranger amongst them and I want to say, I support those who critique the notion of ethnographer status as either insider or outsider as of no importance. I don't think being a citizen anthropologist gave me much advantage if the rigours of doing ethnographic studies were to be followed prodigiously. True ethnography, must not be based on the status of the researcher but on the quality of their research endeavours and reports, as Muzvidziwa points out above.

4.14 *Data Analysis*

As Chikowore (2004:3) observes, data collection and analysis were simultaneous and interwoven activities. Once I had written down almost verbatim, most of the conversations and narratives, I would then engage in coding and the arrangement of the data into the various main themes and sub-themes. I need to point out though that, to some extent I felt the translation of what the youth said from Shona to English, in some way compromised the meanings of what we would have discussed. I tried though to capture their views as objectively as possible, for my narrative to achieve the status of the "good stuff" of social science as described by Denzin and Lincoln (2000:770)

Coding as Ryan and Bernard (2000:780) as well as Chikovore (2004:31) point out, is the heart and soul of whole text analysis. Most researches point out that data management and analysis involves coding, which is the process of sampling and identification of themes. "Themes are abstract constructs that investigators identify before, during and after data collection," (Ryan and Bernard, 2000:780). As they further note, I discovered that my own experiences coupled with the subject knowledge I got from literature review, in a big way, helped me to determine the themes. Obviously the data from the field, enabled me to determine the relevance of the various themes and sub-themes. Denzin and Lincoln (2000:770), also say that coding is the heart and soul of whole-text analysis, as it forces the researcher to determine what chunks of information belong to which theme thus seeing relationships. I found this process quite challenging but exciting.

4.15 *Conclusion*

In this study I completely covered the identities of my participants. Confidentiality, I felt was very important in light of the bruising battles the youth have suffered on the streets, as a result of the raging conflict over control of street space between the city authorities and these children. On the streets two worlds collide, that of the youth and that of the city authorities who represent values of dominant society. The chapter has shown that research must be within some theoretical context, in this case being a qualitative anthropological project, other researchers experiences were of paramount importance. I then relate my experiences in light of other researchers' findings and I either agree or disagree with them in some instances. The study was mainly based on the youth narratives, conversations and discussions, involving youth from three bases for

126

verification of some of the reports I got on sexual and reproductive health behaviour.

I highlight that, in order to create a mutually beneficial relationship, some deceit is inevitable as one has to use material and financial resources to win the youth's hearts, which however raises some moral and ethical questions. To note however, is the fact that there was no coercion whatsoever. Involvement of the youth was very voluntary and they were told from the beginning that at any point they could withdraw from participating. None withdrew. Their involvement was quite encouraging and I had to be honest with them. I told them I did not expect their situation to improve immediately and yet definitely, my study findings were going to get to the tables of the powers that be. As Minta (1998:117), observes with regards his long term relationship with a Puerto Rican cane cutter he had studied, I definitely am in agreement with him, as he observes rightly that, ethnography must not only study people for short term gains like attaining certain academic qualifications, but they should endeavour to continue to keep in touch with such groups. Muzvidziwa (2004) also emphasizes these issues as discussed above.

I wish to point out however that for me, to claim an objective portrayal of the youth sexual and reproductive health experiences, will be an over ambitious projection of events on the streets. To claim to have got the key into the youth's world again, must be seen as a partial possibility, despite efforts to verify whatever information I was getting about the youth's sexual behaviour. Some discussions and meetings could have taken place during my absence of the youth on their own and decisions made on how to conduct themselves or how to ensure certain information was not revealed. I never heard of such meetings though, if they took place, but girls and boys, involved seemed quite dependable and truthful for most of what they told me, was confirmed by their colleagues in the discussions and conversations. A number of methods to collect data were used and certain patterns emerged all the time and I became confident that I had unlocked the door into the youths world.

CHAPTER FIVE

THE STREET AS A RESOURCE AND A GENDERED TERRAIN; "POWER" AND "AUTONOMY" IN SOCIAL AND SEXUAL ENCOUNTERS ON THE STREETS

5.0 *Introduction*

This chapter explores the lived experiences of the street youth of Harare. These are boys and girls who are above twenty years of age. They have been living on the streets for more than seven years. Today on the streets of Harare, are a number of groups of street involved people, as is the case globally, especially in developing countries, (Tadele, 2004, Anarfi, 1997, Bourdillon, 1994, Sauve, 2003). I identified mainly one category for the purpose of my study, that of street people "of the street; amongst whom are the target group of my study, "the youth". These literally live and stay on the streets. The other broad category again is that of street people "on the streets." These are those children, youth and adults who are on the streets during the day mainly to earn a living through vending and other anti-social activities. They retire to a home at the end of the day.

Below, I discuss some of the possible explanations for their coming to live on the streets at very tender ages and also their lifestyle and survival strategies. It is important for the reader to know who these youths are and where they have come from. Case material from in-depth narrative interviews, will be used in addition to my observations and conversations with them. Structure-agency conceptualisations are well demonstrated by the way the youth employ a variety of strategies to remain and survive on the streets, despite some insurmountable structural challenges. The city authorities don't want them there but, they say they will not leave the streets. There are conflicts amongst the street dwelling and street working groups, as well as power struggles between boys and girls. The identity of the youth is also exposed, that is, their lifestyle as well as their anti-social activities. Since the purpose of the study is not to sell them out to the police, I refer to them just as respondents or participants.

The narration will amply show that girls, are an otherised category on the streets, what Fokwang

128

(1999), aptly refers to as "an underclass of an underclass." Exploration of the power dynamics between boys and girls of the street, is one of my key objectives in this study. It will be evident that social relations on the streets simulate the unequal power relations between men and women in mainstream society. This definitely defies essentialist explanations of human behaviour and rather supports overwhelmingly the propositions of the social constructionists, who in summary argue that, men are not puppets of their hormones.

5.1 *Accounting for the Street Dwelling By the Youth*

One finds it imperative to mention from the beginning that, the problem of street dwelling points to the breakdown of the indigenous people's social fabric. In pre-colonial traditional society, that is in both Ndebele and Shona societies, there is no evidence of visible orphanhood, (Nyathi 2001, Mutswairo 1996, Aschwanden, 1983). One could critique their writings as having been influenced by nostalgic memories, but still writings by many researchers, on the extended family system in Africa as a whole, show close knit communities which provided social safety nets for members, in times of crises such as death. Children were prized, (Mbigi, 2000). That there were no streets in such societies is indisputable. Today in Zimbabwe, the phenomenon of destitute, street dwelling, vulnerable children, youth and adults, is no longer confined to big cities, as was the case in the 1980s. They are now seen even in small settlements like Beitbridge and growth points. They are likely to be found even in the villages soon - roaming children, with no one to care for. The cases below are quite revealing, most studies in Zimbabwe have tended to focus on street children, those below the age of 18. My concern was with those above 18 years of age.

5.2 The Cases

CASE ONE

"I am here not because I have no relatives. I am here because my late father's relatives rejected me and my mother. After my Father's death, my mother who was a second wife was accused of causing my father's death at the instigation of my father's first wife, that she had killed my father. My father was a soldier and was on leave when this happened. Actually he drank poisoned beer and came already complaining of feeling dizzy as I heard from my mother. The relatives dispossessed her of everything - no inheritance, and threatened to kill her. She ran away at night. She took me to her widowed mother and dumped me there. There was no food and I was being scolded all the time. My mother's brother who worked at a nearby farm would whenever he came, be told I was naughty by my grandmother and he would beat me. One day, he actually used a log (he showed me a scar at the back of his head). I decided to run away at a tender age of ten years in 1993."

He said with a quaky voice due to emotion. Witchcraft accusations tend to mystify the real causes of conflict, (Bourdillon, 1993). It is common knowledge that, most contemporary polygamous relations, are characterised by conflict between or amongst the wives. Be that as it may, one thing emerges quite clear; that, relatives abdicated their responsibility of cushioning the bereaved members from the adversities of life. Both mother and child became impoverished and were forced to flee from their home. The boy actually revealed thus;-

"My mother left her garden with vegetables, left her chickens and three goats. She left most of our clothes because we were going to walk a long distance"

This is a boy who came from Marange in Mutare district, and is now 24 years old.

CASE TWO

Another case is that of a girl who came from Zvishavane, at the age of fifteen. She is now twenty-three yeas old, and has a husband on the streets.

She left home because :-

"I had been raped by my paternal aunt's husband. My father died when I was twelve years old. This man is the one who would provide our needs and plough our fields. When I reported the case to the police at the growth point all hell broke loose. My mother and other relatives accused me of putting the family to shame. They felt it was a family issue. My mother began to hate me. My aunt wanted to tear me apart when her husband returned from the police where he had been taken for questioning. I became an enemy of all relatives and I decided to steal money from my mother and ran away".

Aschwanden (1983) and Shire (1994), explore quite exhaustively the nature of social and sexual relations amongst various parties in traditional society. There was what was called *"Chiramu"*.

This allowed an in-law or the husband of a paternal aunt to have sexually suggestive play and jokes with girls from the wife's side, either younger sisters or her brother's daughters. Most cases today regarded as sexual abuse, were considered to be "normal play", and nothing would happen to the men, even in cases of forced sex.

CASE THREE

Yet another case is that of a girl who came onto the streets from one of the high density suburbs of Harare - Dzivaresekwa. She said:-

> "After my father's death, my mother took care of us. She was not working but would go to the beer hall. I had to sell vegetables by the roadside close to our home. My mother would abuse me. She would scold me and beat me if vegetables were not bought. Sometimes I would not go to school sekuru (she said with tears in her eyes). A friend of mine who is also here, the one who is now pregnant you spoke to yesterday, pressurised me to run away. She was also being abused by her uncle and aunt, because her father and mother died due to HIV and AIDS as she openly tells me."

CASE FOUR

The other case was that of a girl who had literally grown up on the streets of Harare who said,

> "I was born in a squatter camp close to VID (Vehicle Inspection Depot) on the banks of the *Mukuvisi* river. My parents operated a shebeen where even illicit brews like *"chi* one-day and *tototo"* were brewed. Both died within two years of each other due to tuberculosis. I don't know my nationality and I don't have a totem because my parents had no time to discuss such issues. I was sent to beg on the streets at the age of six years. I grew up on the streets. My parents owned nothing."

From the above narratives, I realised that there were prominent sub-themes to my chapter topic that needed to be discussed, as I do below.

5.3   *Sub-themes from the cases*

5.3.1 *Visible Orphanhood and Vulnerability*

As I pointed out earlier on in the introduction to the book, visible orphanhood can only be associated with colonialism. The institutionalisation of individualism and the nuclear family are all aspects of an urban way of life. The introduction of a cash economy and the need for one to work far away from home led to the breakdown of the traditional African family system. With time, destitution in urban areas and orphanhood became quite prevalent. Vulnerability of such orphans is indisputable, in light of the above narratives. Physical abuse was reported by most of my informants, most of whom were either single or double orphans. Sexual abuse was also common place, as the girl from Zvishavane reveals and these factors forced the children onto the streets. Society must take the blame for the prevalence of this problem. City authorities and government officials, who try to remove them from the streets, must be aware of these push factors rather than just propose that those children must go where they came from. One is reminded of the early years of industrialisation in England, where the enclosure system led to the forced removal of peasants from their pieces of land. They became impoverished and were pushed onto the growing cities. Charles Dickens's book "Hard Times," captures the social problems that resulted from that development. The same process was imported into the British colonies.

5.3.2 *Poverty as another Push factor and Peer pressure*

Most of my informants pointed to a state of absolute poverty in their former homes which also forced them onto the streets. A number said that they had been pressurised by their peers to run away from their poor circumstances onto the streets. The above cases, had ample evidence of poverty and definitely this must be a factor to consider in addition to abusive home environments. One of the boys actually said;

"When you no longer have a mother and father; who cares nowadays whether you go to school or not or whether you have clothes to wear or whether you have food Big *Dhara*. Those relatives will be having problems to look after their own children and so you will be like a problem. I am happy on the streets. I provide for my own needs without bothering anyone *Mudhara* (old man). The extended family is dead *mudhara*. There is nothing like that. Some of my relatives are here in Harare but I don't bother myself going to them."

The others nodded in agreement. Big *Dhara* (Big Older Men), does not refer to physical stature and chronological age only in street lingo, but also to one perceived to be well off. The youth would use this title as a way to make me realise I had to live up to their expectations by giving them money. I did from time to time anyway.

5.4 *The Street Youth's Identity*

Once on the streets, the child or youth finds out that, they have to conform to the street life. Life on the streets is no bed of roses they soon realise. One day as I observed a group of them play cards popularly known as "crazy eight", I provoked them into a prolonged discussion when I referred to them as "Street children." Actually, I had asked in sympathy to their plight,

"*Imi sama* Street Kids *munodini ku* reporter *varume vano kuitai vakadzi*" (You as Street children, why don't you set traps for these men who sodomise you). One of them had quickly interjected;

"Old man don't call us street children. The street does not become pregnant", the others laughed.

Another had added

"It's not Big *Dhara*'s fault. That is what people call us - street children or young ones of goats - street kids."

They roared into laughter again. I realised that they were aware that society, seemed to reject responsibility for failing a whole lot of its own young generation. Despite the fact that the Zimbabwean government is a signatory to the Convention on the Rights of the Child of 1989, nothing has been done to cater for the welfare needs of these destitute children. It would seem when the government talks of children, youth development and welfare programmes, these are not supposed to benefit those on the streets, including HIV and AIDS programmes.

5.4.1 *Society owes us an apology.*

The street youth by reminding me that the street does not become pregnant, meant to imply that they were products of society. One had to identify them with mainstream society, as evidence of dominant society's failure to take care of its own. They are not offspring of the street but of society. They perceived themselves as a condemned lot, not of the street, but from dominant society. Be that as it may, they have an evident identity for survival purposes, meant to draw society's attention and sympathy to their plight. They are filthy, smelly because they don't bath regularly, of unkempt hair and generally an eye-sore to the city authorities and the government officials and members of the public. Even if you give them new clothes, they will sell them very cheaply and remain in their dirty, greasy clothes. These are mainly the boys who are quite visible on the streets. The girls are "invisible", for they spend most of the day in designated places - bus terminuses referred to as *"danga"* (kraal) by the boys. The girls are smart and one might not know they are of the streets unless shown by the boys. These girls are different from the dirty ones one sees begging on the road in the city at road intersections. These are the ones who come from the high density suburbs to which they retire, at the end of the day, and these were not part of my study.

5.4.2 *Street youth condone their anti-social behaviour*

When one gets onto the streets first time, they go through some initiation process. If it is a boy, they have to quickly look scruffy as observed above. One of the boys said of such an experience;

"Big *Dhara* my first week on the streets was a frightening experience. During those years the boys used to sniff glue. The first time I was forced to take it, I experienced a black out, (The others present, laughed). I felt as if the world was turning upside down. My clothes were torn apart by the boys and my good shoes were sold. The filthy sleeping places made me smell. I was taught that urinating and defecating in public places like pavements was good. A church gave us clothes at some point and the bigger boys took them to *Mbare* (a high density suburb) to sell them and they bought alcoholic spirits *(Chapomba)* in street lingo. We were forced to drink and we ended fighting amongst ourselves. We would scold and harass members of the public. Vulgar language became part of my everyday language *Mudhara*. Life is very rough and you can be sodomised easily by those who have been on the streets for longer periods"

One interjected saying;

"First days on the streets are dangerous *Mudhara* because you can be killed, arrested or sodomised. For girls, we fight sometimes to have sex with them first before any other boy. If boys are drunk they fight over her or have sex with her one after the other. The girls have no option but to have one permanent strong boy who protects them but the first time it's always forced sex".

134

I wondered how one could run away from a home environment into an even harsher environment but my question was answered when one of the boys said, -

"It's exciting though on the streets, after the initial phase, when you get used to the ways of the streets."

5.4.3 *Justifying anti-social behaviour on the streets*

I found out that to the youth, engaging in anti-social activities like illicit sex, rape or forced sex are matters to laugh about and brag to others about, as manly exploits. Stealing and being arrested are not embarrassing incidents at all, as the youth condone stealing as part of their survival strategies. I was really surprised by one boy who came onto the streets from Glen View, one of Harare's high density suburbs. He has both parents and the father is working. He is a naughty character and justified his being on the streets thus:-

"I wanted to steal without causing embarrassment to myself and my family. I decided to come onto the streets. My father is not a lodger. He has his own house but I ran away from school. I am the naughty type Big *Dhara*, on the streets I do what I want."

The youth can urinate anywhere during the night especially. During the day they use sanitary lanes but in the evening because the streets are dark due to the city authorities' failure to replace expired lighting tubes, they even defecate and vomit on pavements and its something to laugh about for the youth. They perceive themselves as waging a war against, the city fathers, government and members of the public. One boy actually said;

"We are your children, Big *Dhara* but people condemn us. We fight back. This is why we are rough sometimes to members of the public. Is it wrong for us to revenge their bad attitude towards us?" I had no answer.

5.4.4 *We are the Magundurus*

Rather than refer to themselves as street children, they say they prefer to be called *Magundurus*. This 'nick name' arose as a result of their sleeping behaviour according to some of them. At night before Operation *Murambatsvina* or Operation Restore Order which the youth call, "Operation *Murambavanhu*" -(Operation Condemn Your People), because it was meant to remove the poor from the urban areas, they would sleep anywhere on the pavements even without blankets. This operation was mainly carried out by government to restore sanity in the day to day operations of members of the public, and in the location of residential and commercial activities. The other explanation of *Mugunduru* was that, because when they scavenged for food from metal bins in the 1990s, they made a rattling sound, people called them by that sound. It was not uncommon to hear them greet each other thus *"Mugunduru uri bhoo?"*, (Are you well *Mugunduru.)* They liked this kind of salutation, not 'Street Kid' or 'Street Child', unless it was meant to provoke.

5.4.5 *The Language of the Streets*
I must say that, this made me feel I was more of an outsider when on the streets. To the youth, both boys and girls vulgar language is the "in-thing", and I learnt that it is usually used to embarrass members of the public, whom the street youth perceive to be enemies as one said;

"Members of the public scorn us. They think we are a nuisance and some of them laugh at us and think we are criminals".

This made me realise the application of symbolic interactionists notion of the self-fulfilling prophecy. An individual ends up behaving as he believes the others perceived him. One day one of the boys infuriated by the other's refusal to give him a cigarette scolded him shouting aloud;

"Mai vanosvira mboro,"

Some members of the public in the busy street who heard this just laughed. I could not believe my ears as the other youth burst into laughter. To the youth, vulgar language is part of their identity and no part of the body is taboo to mention. This was an advantage to me, when it came to exploring sexual matters as both boys and girls were quite forthcoming with information. Before going to the streets I had thought of engaging a female research assistant, believing girls would not be comfortable talking to me as an adult male researcher. I was mistaken, I realised when I got to the streets that vulgar language and street lingo are part of the youth's identity. I was told that one of them was almost shot by a woman security officer, who was in plain clothes, who had refused to give him a meat-pie she was eating. The boy then scolded her by her genitals. This did not go down well with her.

"Beche rako" (Your big vagina)" he had scolded her.

The youth especially the boys use a lot of street lingo or slang. I had to probe all the time making me realise that I was an outsider. For example they referred to the concoction of herbs they used to cure venereal diseases as *"guchu"* and the STIs as *"sikon'o"*. Remand prison which is also considered an important stage in the rights of passage of the street boy, is referred to as "Reeds". The girls referred to the well to do men from members of the public who dated them as *"mhene"* or "big *dhara*".

5.5 *Official perception of the street involved youth*

Official here, refers mainly to the city authorities and the government's views with regards the street dwellers phenomenon. According to one senior officer of the city council;

"The street children (as they are known by members of society, nomatter what their actual ages, or marital status), are a problem we are really worried about. You are aware since the identification of the problem, efforts have been made to remove the street kids but they always come back. Your research topic might be correct. We have procrastinated to our peril. These are now men and women and in light of their anti-social activities a thorn in the flesh. They are vulgar and a hopeless lot of scoundrels. Very rough and dirty with no courtesy or respect for anyone. Definitely after your study come and give us your propositions as to the lasting solutions because they are definitely dying from AIDS. They are also killing members of the public who have sexual relations with these boys or the girls. They mug people, they steal and snatch jewellery, they smoke *mbanje* and defecate anywhere. These are the street kids and they say we must not remove them from the streets because it's their home. In the process they spurn all efforts to restore the sunshine city status of Harare. We are going to remove them as members of the public are quite bitter that as city council we seem to be contented with the state of things on the streets."

This is the manager who gave me the letter of approval to carry out research on the streets of Harare. The letter is in appendix one, but I removed his name for confidential reasons. To the public and society, the above views of the manager, are an apt summary as will be discussed below under struggles for control of street space, street battles, and the social relations between boys and girls. Suffice to say, according to official(s), the street youth are a menace and have to be dealt with. They seem not worried about their origins and circumstances. For sure to the officials, the street youth, have a definite identity and lifestyle.

5.6 *Surviving on the Streets; Focussing on issues of power and autonomy on the Streets*

The street is definitely in this narrative an important resource to the various parties, - the city authorities, members of the public and the street involved youth. A resource in this discussion simply means something that sustains our life. When we talk of the street, we think in terms of space and territoriality and definitely issues of power; as such, use of such space has got to be defined. Amongst the street involved youth, are girls and it becomes important to see how they relate to boys as they try to eke a living from the street.

5.6.1 *The street as a battlefield*

To the street youth "of the streets", the designation of their working areas and sleeping areas as "BASES", signifies the existence of conflict on the streets, and power struggles over the control of this resource. The term "base" is a military metaphor that reminds one of the camps, from which fighters of the Zimbabwean liberation struggle operated from, against the colonial regime and its soldiers. One of my key informants explained thus;

> "We sleep in bases. We work on the streets in bases and in groups. On busy streets you find us. To us it's like we are always in confrontations with the council municipal police. We are always in battles. It's now better these days because some of them are now our friends because we give them 'scubas,' (this is opaque beer popularly known as scuds -scuba is street lingo). We drink with some of them in the beerhalls we showed you in the city here."

During conversations with the girls the issue of bribery had also emerged. They are made aware of pending raids by some municipal police officers and even by members of the Zimbabwe Republic police. One girl revealed thus;

> "*Sekuru* (Uncle), in order to survive on the street you have to be clever or else you will be arrested and harassed all the time. Some of the police officers are our boyfriends. Sometimes it's better to have sex with them in order to know what will be happening. Nothing gets finished"

The other girls laughed as she meant that her vagina would remain intact. The other girls mentioned that they had boyfriends in the Zimbabwe Republic police and Zimbabwe National army. I saw quite a number of such officers in uniform all the time at the bus terminuses. I would

138

see some speaking to the girls and this confirmed the girls' claims, they had friendly relations.

The street is a battlefield in that from time to time there are raids by the council in order to remove these youth. The youth, on the other hand as already shown above, resist. Even if loaded onto lorries and taken to far away places, they come back. They are also a terror unto the members of the public who condemn them as thugs and criminals such that the street becomes **a contested terrain**.

The sources of conflict are evidenced by the following views even from the media by members of the public. One such letter appeared in the *Sunday Mail* of 18-24 March 2007, which referred to a theft case of a cell phone, by a street kid from a female pedestrian, in the presence of the police and yet the latter did nothing. "It made me suspect such officers could be working in cohoots with the street youth," the writer whose name sounds prophetic of the tragedy to happen on our streets, *"Muchaparara"* (You shall perish), of Greencroft, a suburb in Harare said, in his letter titled *"Street Kids have turned into muggers"*

When I saw this letter I realised that procrastination was now proving to be a real thief of time to the city officials, as well as to members of the public. The once small boys and girls of the streets, were now a threat, with news that the city centre and its dark areas were no longer safe areas for members of the public due to the street kids menace. The problem which could have been resolved when these were still young had been left until the children became men and women, who obviously had scores to settle with members of the public. It's a tragic state of affairs on the streets. Muchaparara actually said;

"I watched half-shocked last Thursday, as a street urchin grabbed a cell phone from a woman along First Street in broad daylight and dashed off with it - never to be seen again. (Its like employing guerrilla tactics of attacking and disappearing on the streets)

He continues;

"What disappointed me most was the half-hearted, if not stage-managed, chase by equally filthy youths, while the police stood by at one corner unconcerned. That the police (These are the Zimbabwe Republic Police), officers just stood there basking in the sunshine and let the kids speed off with the woman's cell-phone, left a bad taste in my mouth",

As it also did in mine and I suppose many who read this letter. He makes recommendations to the city authorities thus;-

"One thing I should say, and I believe I represent most, if not all peace-loving residents of Harare, is that action should be taken against these street kids, who should be re-branded street muggers. One solution would be to allocate a farm for them. It would be good to have some productive work done by them instead of letting them mill around the streets and abuse our mothers and sisters. ZRP, please help us! We have had enough of this senseless harassment."

The war-like situation on the streets is also echoed by another writer called Mukondiwa in the *Sunday Mail* of 11-17 February 2007, in an article titled', Deliver us from Street Kids." He described the tragic situation thus;

"Some time ago, the thugs and terrorists known as Street Kids were weeded out of the streets and the city was safe. The programme was not followed up keenly and now they reign supreme again."

I am forced to quote extensively from the media so that the reader, can see that the youths' views and my own assessment of the "war-like" situation are corroborated. What goes on, on the streets is far stranger than fiction and I need supporting evidence like this. The writer uses military metaphors thus;

"There are the thugs at Construction House who harass young ladies and children. Then there are the terrorists who snatch jewellery from women along Sam Nujoma Street opposite the park and the Herald House. There is the main group, however, that causes **mayhem** at the Eastgate food complex and these would probably need a **motor bomb** to deal with them once and for all."

The Public Relations Manager of the City of Harare, a Mr Toriro also had an article in the same newspaper as the above, in which he showed that the authorities were fighting a losing battle against the Street Youth and he titled his article, "Bands of Street Kids Resurface." He appealed for assistance from various stakeholders to get rid of street youths, as the council seemed to have failed. The youth's sentiments as I lived with them confirmed the surrendering attitude of the city authorities. One of them fumed having been harassed by police;

"Big *Dhara*, we are in a war on the streets. Anytime we can be arrested, beaten or even killed. Now it's better, we are grown up because we can resist those invasions. When we were young we suffered a lot because we did not know members of the municipal police and security agents. This time the council will not remove us. They are very rough because they used to take us to places where we would spend up to three days without food or water. They are real murderers. Some of us were injured and some died. We are not going to move this time."

The other youth were much in agreement with one saying;

"There will be war on the streets. Just wait and see Big *Dhara*."

Yet another article which is quite revealing by Alice Mutamaenda in the *Sunday Mail* of 11-17 February 2007 titled, *"Bands of Street Kids Resurface."* She also uses military metaphors.

"Unruly bands of Street Kids have reinvaded some of Harare's major streets, literally making them their homes. The Street Kids are harassing pedestrians, preparing meals on roadsides and disturbing traffic while the more daring ones have resorted to illegal vending. Pedestrians, particularly women, have fallen prey to the marauding street kids especially during evenings."

During my study I witnessed some of this especially during weekends, at some of the popular night spots, I will not mention, due to ethical reasons and because I don't want to expose the "bases" of my informants. Muggings were commonplace as well as thefts, mainly snatching of valuables from the patrons and even pedestrians. Girls would be used to lure some unsuspecting drinkers into dark alleys, from where a number were mugged and their valuables including shoes were taken.

5.6.2 *Conflicts of street involved boys*

Street battles are also amongst the street involved people. As mentioned earlier, there are some who just come onto the streets to earn an income and retire to a home at the end of the day. This group of youth, though dirty are not as filthy as the *Magundurus* and they resist such a label. The conflict over the street space as a resource was evidenced by some of these boys responses when

141

I approached them and enquired as to whether they were also *Magundurus*. One of them said with surprise;

> "Big *dhara*, we are not criminals like those *Magunduru* who defecate anywhere like a dog (I was a bit taken aback). Those are dogs" (Others came to join as he continued).

> "Big Dhara, those are not fit to be humans. They chose a life of animals. They don't wash their clothes or bath themselves. They sleep with one girl in turn and the girls are also like the boys. We have homes and some of us are married and come to work on the streets to fend for our families. They must be removed from the streets. They are criminals."

They complained bitterly that the *Magundurus* were perpetrators of criminal acts. The police would also arrest them and this sometimes caused street brawls between them. They also don't interact on a day to day basis, though their work activities are similar - mainly selling parking discs to motorists as well as directing motorists into parking bays. On the other hand the Street *Magunduru*, put the blame on this group for their arrests by the police from time to time. They claimed they were not criminals but those youth from Mbare and Epworth were the trouble causers. One *Mugunduru* actually said;

> "Big dhara those boys are *Maboora Ngoma* (trouble causers because of anti social behaviour). They can have two sets of clothes, some dirty in order to look like a *Mugunduru* especially when they want to commit crimes. Another set is in a fair state of repair and could show they are different from us. The police always come hard on us when a crime has been committed. These boys must be removed from the streets."

I was reminded of Goffman's dramaturgy from these accusations and counter accusations. I also realised the conflict was over the control of the street as a resource.

5.6.3 *The Street as a source of livelihood*

The street is an important space to the various parties with interest in controlling it. Its value is perceived differently by various parties in it. It is an important source of the street youth's livelihood. It is here that they make their money as one *Mugunduru* said;

> "This is our industry Big *Dhara*. We are not educated and we cannot find employment anywhere. We have no skills to enable us work for any employer"

The street youths are involved in a number of activities. I saw that they get most of their income

142

from selling parking discs and this activity is a preserve of the boys. These are sold to motorists, who usually will be busy and have no time to buy such tickets from municipal selling points. A booklet cost an average $600 during the course of my study and the boys would sell each of the ten 30 minute parking disk for $150. They made quite some profit from the ten leaves in a booklet. This is brisk business especially from the middle of 2004, when the city council introduced heavy fines for parking without these discs. The city council also introduced even more drastic measures of clamping such vehicles, a system of locking the wheels. They also tow away some of these vehicles to their yard along Coventry road. This system has irked most motorists but the street boys are quite happy because the fear of these punitive measures, make motorists buy their parking discs.

A case of corruption I witnessed on a Wednesday afternoon mid month in June 2006.

I had discovered that clamping of cars seemed to be quite prevalent in areas where there were these street youth either "of the street" or those from residential areas. On investigating through curiosity one girl had said to me;

"*Sekuru* (Uncle) don't reveal my identity. I will be killed by these boys, but because you are so kind to us (because I would buy them goodies or give them money). I want you to come today in the evening at the usual night-spot. I will show you some municipal officers who also frequent the streets to clamp cars and drink at the popular night spot. They are the ones who also sleep with us and alert us of pending raids."

I followed her instructions. My suspicions were confirmed as I saw some of the boys in the company of the municipal officers I had seen on the streets in uniform several times. Her revelations had been confirmed that;

"The municipal police network with these boys and are given money. This is why you always see them clamping cars in areas where the boys are."

Whenever there is no clamping, I discovered the boys were very unhappy. The girl had gone on;

"This is why the boys don't want us to be on the streets. They say that we will sell them out to the police in case we are arrested. They say women are not good at keeping secrets. If anyone of us goes there, she will be beaten".

I believed her because girls were quite invisible. One had to go to the bus termini if they wanted to see them.

The street is an important resource to the boys as they earn their livelihood from it. I remember the Blood Transfusion People **camped** in one of the busy roads, on which was a very important working base for the street boys. The Zimbabwe Republic Police officers provided security. They were soliciting for blood from members of the public, unaware that they were "interfering" with the activities of these boys. When I got to this base one morning on a Monday, it was deserted and when I saw the **campers** and their security, I realised why the "base" had been abandoned. One boy complained bitterly;

"Why can't they go to schools and churches Big *Dhara*. They have put us into a drought situation for a whole week. It means we don't get any money. This city council did give them permission to fix us because they know we are working here".

For a whole week there was no activity and coincidentally there was no clamping of cars in that area. The other income generating activities of the youth involve members of the business community.

5.6.4 *Street Youth Interfacing with the Formal Sector*
There was ample evidence to show that the street youth were in some way a necessary evil, especially to members of the business community. They were a source of cheap labour power and readily available. Most businesses that are located in high rise buildings need the services of these boys, to off-load and load vehicles. It could be stationery or furniture or any heavy loads like rolls of clothing material. Most of the lifts in such high rise buildings are out of order. Some reputable supermarkets and food outlets I cannot mention, also use the youth to clean their backyards as well as their rubbish bins and give the youth food leftovers. Food collection and preparation is done by the boys and not the girls or "their wives". Some of the business executives also hire these youth to cut grass and hedge at their homes in the **plush** low density suburbs and give them goodies, clothes and money. One of the boys related a case in which he was engaged as a herdboy by one businessman at his farm in Shamva. He ran away when he lost several head of cattle and just abandoned the rest. One girl also said that she was engaged by one nurse as a baby minder. The husband wanted to sleep with her and she ran away but not without

144

some of their property, as compensation for wasting her time. She was later arrested but released by the police, when she related her ordeal to the police, in the presence of the nurse and her husband who ended up almost on each other's throats.

5.6.5 *The City fathers perception of the Street as a resource*

It is an important resource adding significantly to the image of the city's image. Percy Toriro, the Public Relations Manager of the City Council of Harare's sentiments in *The Sunday Mail* of 11-17 February 2007 are revealing;

> "We need to co-operate with police, non-governmental organisations and other stakeholders to contain the situation. Efforts have been made in the past to take the children off the streets, but they keep coming back. We are looking for a permanent solution to the problem."

He went on to say that the city was striving to become a world class city by 2010 and such a goal, could only be realised if the problem of street kids was permanently dealt with. To the city authorities, the presence of the youth on the streets is a negative factor, that interferes with the business activities of members of the public, who pay rates to the city council and to members of the business community, who also complain of thefts from their patrons and customers, and once in a while from their businesses. Tourists also fear to be in such dangerous environments. According to the Vagrants Act of 1970 and other city by-laws ignored at independence, when the Africans moved **enmasse** into the urban areas at the attainment of independence, urban spaces were designated for specific activities not what was now happening. The by-laws before independence, designated certain spaces as no go areas, especially by Africans who could be prosecuted as trespassers.

The sunshine city status once enjoyed by Harare formerly Salisbury, got eclipsed in the euphoria at independence and now the city is a shadow of its former glorious status. Faeces are a common sight on the streets and even vomit. Litter is all over the place, including empty beer containers especially during weekends. The streets are dark at night and criminals including street youth, lurk in these areas awaiting unsuspecting, innocent pedestrians who are mugged, raped or killed. Cases of corpses being found in the Kopje area are quite common knowledge. A classic case of gang rape also occurred in the late 1990s when a middle-aged woman was victim in Harare on her way from work. The city streets have become dangerous and night window-shopping and even relaxing in the gardens, is no longer possible. For these have become death traps. This is why the street as a resource has now become a battle-field. The city fathers seem to have lost the war against the youth with the latter claiming;-

"Tawindi ndeyedu Big *Dhara*. City Council *yachepa. Hatibve muno"* (The city is ours Big *Dhara*. The city authorities have failed to remove us. We are not leaving the streets.)

5.7 *Power and Autonomy in Social Relations - Boys versus Girls*

On the streets one thing became evident after my first visits - that the girls were invisible and boys quite visible on the streets. I wondered why, only to discover that the street was really a gendered terrain as one of my female key informants observed thus;

Sekuru, we are an oppressed lot *(takadzvanyirirwa zvachose isu vasikana)*. We are living at the mercy of these rough boys. We have no freedom *sekuru*. Think of it *sekuru*, we are not allowed on the street where the money is. The boys scare us off saying that its not a good place for girls because in case of raids we wont be able to evade the Council Police or even run away fast or resist arrest.

Another girl had interjected;

Sekuru, these boys are jealous. They give flimsy reasons why we must not be on the streets *(vanotaura zvamangamanga, zvenhema)* and yet we can also do what they do. To tell you the truth, they want to keep us dependent on them for survival so that they can have sex with us as they please. This is the truth, Girls! (she appealed to the others as yet another interjected).

"Its true *sekuru* the boys don't want us on the streets because they say we are women, we are not courageous which is all lies. Its about making sure we are not exposed to other men. What is manly about selling parking discs *sekuru* or even washing cars? Who does the washing in the houses *sekuru*?" (they laughed and I joined them)

As she continued;

"The real issue is that they are also afraid we will divulge their criminal activities to the police. They engage in criminal activities as you saw for yourself last Saturday night *sekuru Imbavha idzi sekuru dzemakoko*."(These boys are real thieves)

146

I had been at one of the nightspots and witnessed their criminal activities like pick-pocketing and snatching of cell phones. To the boys its part of work as one of them had said it to me thus;

> *"Big Dhara pane mari ndipo pane bhutsu yemupurisa. Ukatya kusungwa unofa nenzara, ndiwo mahazards echibasa chedu"* (If you want to survive don't be afraid of the police. On the streets we are not afraid of arrests because its part of our lifestyle. These are the hazards of our industry).

The girls were quite bitter that they were confined to the *"danga,"* (kraal), their space and yet girl vendors were on the streets just like the boys. (Girl vendors are youth "on the streets," and have a home. There was no reason to deny them such lucrative activities. It was more profitable business to be on the streets than to sell sweets and cigarettes at the bus terminus where there were customers only in the evenings when most people were on their way home.

One of the talkative girls in relation to the jealousy of the boys had said;

> *"Ko ungandifudzire chinhu changu here? Hachina mita ichi. Vanofunga kuti takapusa. Tinoitawo zvavanoita. Tinotsvaga "mhene" dzedu, dzine mari. Iwafa wafa sekuru."* (How can boys restrain us from free movements? This vagina is mine. It has no meter reading to show how much it has been used. We are not fools, we also have well to do men who provide our needs. We are promiscuous as they are also).

It was quite evident that there was conflict over control of the street as an asset or resource. The girls of the street were completely alienated from the only "safe" source of sustenance. They were being forced to engage in multiple sexual relations in order to survive on the streets. On the other hand, the boys used myths and made reference to traditions in mainstream society ,for their attitude towards girls. One of the boys justified the girls confinement thus;

> *"Big Dhara* even at home boys don't spend the day with girls. That would be unmanly. Moreover girls or women are just associated with bad luck especially when they are on the moon (The others burst out into laughter as he continued). With such girls amongst you misfortunes can befall you and arrests become frequent. This is why they live in the *danga."* (kraal).

147

Such thinking reminded me of an article I had read in *The Sunday Mail* of 4 - 11 February 2007, in which a female reporter had been refused permission to get to a workplace of some illegal gold panners in one of their areas of operation. The "*Makorokoza*" boys or men, have the belief that women should not come to where they will be working, because they bring upon them bad luck. She only managed to interview them when she pleaded ignorance of such a rule. I was also reminded of the separate spaces for men and women in traditional pre-colonial societies, as well captured by Shire (1994). Men were associated with the "*dare*" (men's camp) and women with the "*nhanga*." (Women's camp) If a man was found in the *nhanga*, he was mocked and labelled "*jengavakadzi*," (one who is always with women), which was unmanly. It was clear; the street was being associated with the construction of masculinities. The street as a resource had been appropriated by the boys, and the girls were left with nothing except their bodies to be sexually abused by the boys.

5.7.1 *Food Resources and the Construction of Masculinities*

As evident in the above section, the construction of masculinities through some myths definitely define boys and girls spaces on the streets. Though the chores done by boys on the streets are mainly done by girls and women in mainstream society, the boys feel its not the work of girls because of the assumed hazards of working on the streets. Another area which demonstrates, the relevance of my social constructionist framework, is that of the collection, preparation and sharing of food. This shows that social relations between boys and girls of the street, simulate relations of domination and oppression in dominant society.

In dominant society, men, traditionally the breadwinners, would surrender all the food brought in to the home to the women for its preparation and sharing. They believed it was women's work, again this being evidence of the construction of masculinities, for in formal work places like hotels and hospitals and boarding schools, men prepare and share food. On the streets, the boys claim the girls are not allowed to go to supermarkets to collect leftover foods or even to prepare the food. They claim that men at work prepare their own food in industry; they call "*gaba*," (food prepared in tins). This is quite a common practice amongst municipal employees and other men who work in large groups. They prepare their *sadza* (that is maize porridge) by the workplace using fire wood.

Food resources on the streets are made up of left-overs from takeaways and supermarkets. There is no drinking of tea. The boys engage in what they call, "Food for Work Programmes," similar expression used by Government of Zimbabwe to describe the scheme, usually instituted during years of drought, whereby those populations being stalked by hunger, work on some government scheme like road construction and then they are given food. It could be 20kg of mealie-meal, beans, *matemba* (small fish) etc. The same happens on the streets as already discussed where the boys engage in a variety of chores and are given money or food. It is a source of power for the boys in relation to the street girls. The girls depend on the boys for their survival.

5.7.2 *Control of "kitchens" as a good case of the construction of masculinities*

Construction of masculinities, was quite evident on the streets with boys believing they were the breadwinners and girls were their dependants, rather than their equals in all spheres of street life. This was clear in the area of food collection, preparation and sharing and in relation to the space designated as the "kitchen." This is just symbolic in that, there is no physical structure. It is located in a ditch close to one of Harare's posh hotels. The entrance to the hotel is just about one hundred metres away. I remember many times seeing posh cars being parked and being driven away from the hotel as I observed from this kitchen, which is a boys' preserve. Girls are not allowed there.

Men in the latest designer suits as well as ladies some of whom profess to be child rights activists, have been to the posh hotel without realizing the objects of their concern or deliberations, were just a stone's throw from their lavishly furnished venue. They seemed oblivious of the presence of these "street kids." Quite a number of conferences have been convened at this venue also with a number being on orphans and vulnerable children, - all being political rhetoric because on the ground, there is ample evidence of the deteriorating living conditions of the orphans of the streets. What hypocrisy, when the children were languishing with hunger under the bureaucrats' noses.

To the North West of the kitchen, are the prestigious municipal offices about 100 metres away, responsible for licensing activities that must take place within Harare including food vending and cooking. To the North about 160 metres, is the towering, majestic ZANU (PF) Headquarters, where the political party with majority seats in Parliament, often meets to deliberate on socio-economic progress and challenges. To the east of this 'kitchen', is the biggest public library in Harare, the Queen Victoria and these street youth walk past unconcerned, on their way to the 'symbolic kitchen'. To the south of the kitchen are the Harare Magistrates courts (Rotten row), where criminals and those who breach the law are taken to. None from these institutions seems to notice the smoke that billows, slowly into the sky from this open ditch where the street youth gather most mornings, to prepare their *sadza* in the black, filthy tins.

I discovered the spirit of communalism was quite evident, as they put their money together to buy mealie-meal and relish. Relish is mainly vegetables and meat. This usually happened if they did not get enough food from the food outlets. They cooked together and ate the food together, usually before ten in the morning. The silver tins are now black from smoke and no one bothers to wash them. After eating the food which is put on cardboard boxes as well as the relish, the boys, if 'sentinels' tell them its safe on the streets, will then make their way into the city centre, as the kitchen is on the fringes of the city. When I asked why they did not let girls do the cooking they laughed and one said;

> "*Mudhara zvemustreet ndezve varume. Vasikana vanotikanyira zvinhu mudhara. Isu zvedu ndezve boys chete. Hatigare navakadzi vanotiunzira mhepo.*" (Old man, here on the streets we don't allow girls to do this for us lest they bring upon us misfortunes), The others present roared with laughter.

I could not understand this but I did not dare probe lest it antagonised my relations with the boys. I could not visualize what was masculine about food preparation when it is girls and women who do it all the time where I lived. This made me realize that although I was a citizen anthropologist, I was also an "outsider." This was the world of street youth and I had to accept the differences from my world. This, which seemed absurd to me was the normal way of doing things, hence confirming Berger and Luckmann's (1966) observation that, reality was a social construction and made sense to those involved in it. I wondered also whether this "culture shock" I was experiencing, was tolerable or this was just behaviour intolerable to normal humans of any civilized society. Yes, I need to agree with the observations of the Zimbabwe Human Development Report of 2004's claim for the celebration of difference and diversity, but I wondered if this was the kind of difference, that would have made Desmond Tutu "excited", (Zimbabwe Human Development Report 2004:1).

The kitchen is where they also relax before going onto the streets. It is their meeting point, after having slept in different places. It is there where they discuss some of their experiences during the previous day or night including anti-social incidents. I thought this was why they did not want girls there because they would hear of their anti-social activities and if girls were caught by the police, boys believed, they would sell them out to the police. I was reminded of Aschwanden (1982) and Shire (1984)'s writings with regards men and women spaces in Shona society. In the"*dare*" (camp) men would not prepare food but here on the street, the men were collecting, and preparing food. The women's place, called "*nhanga*" rhymes like '*danga,*' (kraal) which the boys prefer using but there is not much activity here. The boys were quite generous - the Shona way. They had always made offers of food to me, which I would politely decline. They laughed one day, when one of them said;

"You think he is a vagabond like you who uses paper as a plate. Don't forget he is a lecturer at the country's biggest University." I did not comment.

The boys had also indicated that once in a while there were raids on the kitchen and girls would not be able to escape arrest. From all this however, I realized that the boys aim was to ensure girls were not in control of any resources that could empower them. They rendered the girls completely dependent upon them, which made their autonomy or self-governance, as observed by Bjornberg (2004) , impossible. Girls live on the streets at the mercy of the boys. The girls are used as sex objects.

5.8 *Aspirations of the street youth and their leisure activities*

Like all humans, the street youth have their own wishes and fears. These were mainly evident during my conversations with them. They also were bitter that society had condemned them to a life of destitution. They had no kind words for the government and non-governmental organizations especially Streets Ahead. I discovered that Streets Ahead, had been very involved in assisting these youth before they turned eighteen years of age. When they became 18 years of age, they asked them to look after themselves as they were no longer welcome at their offices and were no longer eligible for any material assistance.

5.8.1 *The Youth Condemn Streets Ahead - Biting the hand that fed them*

Streets Ahead is a drop-in centre nestled in the avenues of Harare. Its main mandate is to establish a platform to enable dialogue between it and the destitute children. The organization's main interest is reintegrating the children into their families. It is not a home to look after such children like an orphanage, as Professor Bourdillon said to me," It's an NGO with limited resources". They are funded by donors and they had problems getting funding for their activities. They had limited resources.

The youth, especially the boys were quite bitter that the organization was no longer taking care of them. They believed that Streets Ahead had lots of money, given to it by donors, which was meant to benefit the orphaned, vulnerable of the streets, no matter the age. One of my key informants views are revealing;

"These Streets Ahead people have enriched themselves with moneys meant to benefit us. They took videos of destitute children and photographs which they show foreign donors and yet it is just a gimmick meant to woodwink those donors to believe they are a charitable organization."

Another had interjected angrily;

"*VeStreets Ahead imhata dzevanhu* (Steets Ahead Officials are stupid) its painful to know they drive posh cars bought with money meant for us yet they chase us from their premises saying we are above 18years. Where do they want us to go. They did not send us to school. They did not send us for any training even welding."

The boys were quite unhappy, with some threatening to beat officials from the organization should they see them on the streets. The girls were not very bitter as they said that whenever they needed assistance, they were still welcome at the institution. One girl actually made the following revelations when I told them of the way boys condemned Streets Ahead;

"These boys are not grateful. They used to be welcome there but because of their drunkenness and rowdy and rough behaviour they are no longer wanted there."

The other girls felt that was the main reason why they were no longer welcome. To the girls, the organization has assisted them in many ways. They have been given clothes and food. They also have been educated on the dangers of multiple sexual partners on the streets, and HIV and AIDS, though one lamented thus;

> "*Sekuru* though we know the dangers of risky sexual behaviour, we have no power on the streets to say NO to sex lest we be beaten. We just sleep with the boys, its their own fault if they contract HIV and AIDS. They force us. You have seen how rough they can be when drunk."

The girls wished they could be given money to start income generating projects on the streets. They felt the city council could allow them to vend on the streets freely so they can be financially empowered. They believed this could give them power to refuse men's manoeuvres to have sex with them. Difficult circumstances were forcing them to sleep with any men, despite the knowledge of the dreaded HIV and AIDS scourge, they lamented. The boys too, were worried they were becoming old and yet there were no prospects of being formally employed. They wished they could also be given a chance by NGOs or the government to be involved in projects with one boy saying;

> "We read in the papers of the government giving money to youth. These youth are living in homes and are better off even in terms of education. To the government we are non-existent so we are going to steal so they know we are there. Stealing is work for us, they must know. We will steal from them until they realize we are also the youth."

5.8.2 *Caring for one another on the streets*

The story about the lifestyle and survival strategies of street youth would be incomplete if I don't talk about the spirit of communalism that prevails on the streets. This would be evidently associated with small primitive societies described by Durkheim as based on mechanical solidarity. On the streets, I found out that they protect each other from abuse by those not of their own. A brawl between a street youth of the street and one of the "youth on the streets," would draw the attention of all the others. If one of the street youths of the street, had an altercation, it ended up involving other *magunduru* close-by what in Shona is described as "*Chirwirangwe*," signifying group cohesion. Food is for all *magundurus* and they would take turns to collect it from various outlets first thing in the morning like before, seven o'clock. Girls are not allowed, they are just given food as discussed above. There are however no structures in terms of power on the streets as each claims to be independent because they came into the streets on their own. But their lifestyle which is similar is evidence of a common lifestyle.

Girls are not supposed to claim any independence, so they cannot make decisions concerning their sexual and reproductive health. They are completely at the mercy of the boys. In the event of crises such as arrests, and detention in police cells, they would visit such colleagues and bring them food. Most of the girls have "husbands." They would be responsible for taking food to the remand prison or the jail once in a while, as I witnessed on many occasions. They will be given money by the boys especially the "sexual poachers." These are boys who don't want to have permanent female partners but just depend on what they call "hit and run" affairs, or casual sex, just to sexually relieve themselves, and if it means using money, so be it. The word poacher became popularized in Zimbabwe in the late 1980s, when a member of parliament was arrested for possessing rhino horns. In street lingo it means the "streetwise."

If one was not feeling well, they would really show concern. The truth however is that, I never witnessed a serious case of illness on the streets. I however learnt that on a recent visit to the streets (well after my study) on 15 December 2007 that one of the boys, who had been associated in the act of masturbation had died when he was hit by a car along Julius Nyerere way. One of the boys said, "*But Big Dhara takaita mudeme mudeme tikamuviga kuTafara zvakanaka.*" (Big Dhara we pooled our resources as street children and we gave him a decent burial at Tafara cemetery). Most of those with serious ailments were said to retire to a squatter settlement along the Mukuvisi river. Minor ailments meant first buying for example light drugs. If there was a serious case of sickness they also could phone for an ambulance to come and pick their sick colleague although they complained that they tended to delay if it was an anonymous caller of no fixed abode. Sometimes they would go to a Dr X in Sunningdale, who used to work closely with Streets Ahead. They however complained that he was now no longer helping them as he complained of depletion of his medical resources. If it were a sexually transmitted infection, he did not want to treat someone he once treated and so they ended up using the "*guchu*" prepared by herbalists especially at *Mupedzanhamo* People's Market in *Mbare*. I call these herbalists "street pharmacists"

5.8.3 *Fun and Entertainment on the Streets*

Leisure activities relate mainly to the "visible" boys. They mainly patronize drinking places in the city. I used to go with some of them, to these drinking places, which they patronise at night. I saw that when drunk they would also propose those women who patronize drinking places and even pay for casual sexual services. The boys would also buy and smoke "*mbanje*", marijuana quite often. Sometimes they abused alcoholic spirits called in street lingo "*chapomba.*" This is officially known as Chateau. After being drunk they would become vulgar and violent. In most cases I would sneak out of the pubs. Girls would also in the interim, especially during weekends, at night, be having sexual partners from mainstream society, who just need services after a couple of beers in the night clubs. They referred to these as "*mhene,*" that is men who gave them goodies and money.

The boys frequented another filthy restaurant in the avenues to watch television especially soccer matches on Sundays. The boys also went to Mai *Musodzi* hall in Mbare to watch films. At this hall films are shown from 6pm to 6am every night and this has become a rendezvous for criminals. They have somewhere to spend the cold nights. Street youth also pay to watch the films, yet they use the place as their bedroom during very cold nights. I went to some of the "BASES", where they sleep and I realized why most boys prefer to go to Mai *Musodzi* Hall, despite the place being a dangerous place to be at night.

In their resting bases are dirty, greasy blankets which they were given many years ago by well wishers. They are not enough for their needs. The place stinks although they seemed unconcerned. One time I went into one of the disused buildings in the kopje area, they use as their sleeping base. In one corner of this very large, dark room, a young girl of sixteen had given birth the previous night. The place looked like a pig- sty and yet they walked barefooted. I gave the girl who had named her baby son Tawanda (we are now many) - what is called "*makorokoto*" (congratulatory token) in Shona, something to show that you are also happy about the "new arrival". She told me she had a husband on the streets. A street youth "of the streets." The other street girls had played the role of midwives as they often did, she had revealed to me.

155

5.9 *Conclusion*

The above narrative has shed light on the lived experiences of the street youth, showing evidently that there, are in most cases reasons why they are on the streets. Basically, its about the inevitable breakdown of the African communal lifestyle, in which orphanhood and destitution assumably were invisible. Due to colonization and urbanization, the extended family system that used to cushion bereaved members from the adversities of life, now only exists nominally. Most of my informants were either single or double orphans.

The story above also vividly explored the challenges confronting the youth of the streets, especially the city council authorities, which makes the streets a "war-zone" to the street youth. It is interesting to note some of their survival strategies which demonstrate that despite structural constraints the youth have agency.

The power dynamics between boys and girls were also exploited. Girls are an otherised and abused lot on the streets and have been alienated from the street as a space and as a resource. They thus constitute an "underclass of an underclass," as the boys want them to be financially and materially disempowered, so that they can have sex with the girls without any resentment. One can argue, the girls are just sex objects of the boys with no autonomy in those sexual encounters.

Construction of masculinities has been well explored and boys argue girls will bring them misfortune on the streets, which is just a myth. Boys argue in patriarchal terms that, since time immemorial women and men have occupied separate spaces - the "*dare*" or men's camp in traditional society and the "*nhanga*" women's domain. From the above narrative, it was quite evident that, there is no institution, governmental or non governmental organization, that has any programmes to empower the street youth. It would seem as if the government's definition of youth does not include those on the streets, who now pose as a 'Frankenstein monster', to members of the public and government. Despite the adversities the youth have, they have their happy moments and also make the old adage, "if wishes were horses, beggars would ride," sensible in light of their aspirations.

156

CHAPTER SIX

SEXUAL BEHAVIOUR PATTERNS OF STREET YOUTH OF HARARE

6.0 *Introduction*

Much research has been done in Zimbabwe relating to the survival strategies of street children and street youth in general, (Bourdillon, 1994; Dube, 1997; 1999, Chirwa and Wakatama, 2000). The Legal Age of majority Act of (1983), stipulates that an adult is anyone above eighteen years of age. For the purpose of my study, youth, will refer to those above fifteen years of age but below twenty four years as per United Nations definition (Newton 2000:1). To members of the public in Zimbabwe, these street dwelling youngsters, are also referred to as "street kids," irregardless of their age or marital status. Most of the information in this chapter came from conversations with the youth, listening to their discussions and detailed key informant narratives.

This chapter's main focus is on the sexual relations prevalent on the streets. Obviously, one has to look at how sexual encounters are initiated, including cases of dating and courtship as well as romance. One finds it necessary also to look at some considerations in these sexual relationships relating to totemism, and virginity and the sources of sexual knowledge amongst the street youth. Various forms of heterosexual relations, like consensual sex and forced sex, are discussed as well as gang rape of girls by the boys. Sexual relations of those in marital unions, are also explored especially issues relating to behaviour of the parties whilst in coitus. Sexual networking by both boys and girls, is exposed and the possible explanations for such behaviour unravelled, as the story of the youth" of the streets," unfolds.

Homosexuality, bestiality, as well as what I refer to as "ritual sex" by boys, will also be discussed. This kind of behaviour will show that genitals are assets for survival, rather than for sexual gratification only. The story also unravels the various sexual techniques, used in coitus on the streets and how the boys and girls enhance their sexual encounters using herbs. Perceptions of sex by both boys and girls, are an important aspect of the discussion. Boys regard sex as "fucking" or what I term "patriarchal sex," characterized by vigour and sadistic tendencies. The boys want to inflict pain on the girls during sexual intercourse because they give them money and food. It is like fixing the girls as will be evident from the sexual metaphors that boys used to describe sexual encounters with girls. The girls don't like it. They however have no power or autonomy in these encounters and thus just bear the consequences of being materially dependent on boys for their survival. The boys are so jealous they contemplate of using juju, to keep away other boys, as well as "sugar daddies" from mainstream society, from their female partners which reminds one of the "chastity belts" of the Victorian times. This was a locking system, disabling the females from engaging in sexual intercourse, as the belts covered the genital area, only to leave small halls for defecating and urinating.

6.1 *Nightmarish Sexual Experiences of the First Days on the Streets*

The youth generally showed that the worst experiences for any newcomer on the streets whether boy or girl, were the first few days on the streets. Most revealed in the narratives that, if they had had alternative places to go to, they would have left a long time ago. With regards sexual exploitation of the first days on the streets one female key informant or research participant from Zvishavane said;

"*Sekuru*, (uncle), I will never forgive these boys for the sexual abuse I suffered. When I got to Masvingo's Mucheke bus terminus, the second night some boys forced me to sleep with them. I was no longer a virgin though. Two of them forced themselves on me. It was a horrifying, brutish experience. *Imhuka idzi sekuru* (These are beasts uncle).

She went on to explain how she had struggled to lock her legs for the better part of the night, until in the early hours when she got exhausted, and succumbed. Like a dog after a tiring hare, one of the boys forced her off the wall she was resting against, onto the tarmac. She opened her legs, and soon the short and stout street boy was pumping into her with vigour. When she fled to Harare, the same thing happened to her at Mbare Musika. She had not known Harare and she says that, she was easy prey for the street boys. At *Mbare* she said;

"A fight ensued between two boys as to who was to have sex with me first. They did not bother about whether I consented. It was a question of time before one elderly destitute remonstrated them and one of them took me behind a public toilet. I had no alternative *sekuru*. This is the true experience of all the girls. Just talk to them. One would be lying to say they resisted successfully".

158

One boy gave a vivid description of his experiences too saying;

> "*Big dhara* when I came onto the streets ten years ago there were few girls of the streets. One had to fight off other boys, who would try to sodomise you. There is one who is still quite notorious called *Sekuru Gudo*. He forced himself on me in the Kopje and I resisted and hit him in the face. Other boys don't bother at all because it is part of their lives. He ejaculated all the same all over my thighs. This S*ekuru Gudo*, as you must have made your own assessment, is quite close to a real baboon. He steals even from us and he does not care whether it is a boy or a girl, when he wants to have sex. He is always drunk maybe to ensure that he is not ashamed of his animal behaviour

Yet another boy had a very sad story to tell, of how he was sodomised at the age of eleven when he came to live on the streets. He was quite bitter that the boy who molested him had died before he revenged. That culprit as he described him was swept away by stream waters during a heavy storm, whilst sleeping in one of the city centre drainage canals.

> "*Mudhara*, I am not happy at all, yet there was no one to come to my rescue. Life on the streets can be very rough before you become a street-wise yourself. Some of these homosexual boys would have been sodomised in remand prison. That is where they learn the techniques".

One girl emotionally narrated her sexual ordeal on the streets thus;

> "This rough guy, you will not see him because he is now very ill and lives at Mkuvisi. He forced himself on me at the Kopje after having mixed my coke drink with *chapomba*, (An alcoholic drink of refined spirit). He tore my pants despite the fact that I did not resist much. It was deliberate *sekuru*, just to fix me. The next thing sperms were flowing down my legs. I was drunk and I had to use my torn pant to clean the mess. He had disappeared into the night".

None of my informants related of a warm welcome on the streets. Boys had very nasty experiences just as the girls. They would be forced to sniff glue or drink alcoholic spirits and then they would also end up being sodomised. When I showed amazement as to the boys risky sexual behaviour one had educated me thus;

> "*Big dhara* all these boys know of HIV and AIDS. The girls too are well informed because at Streets Ahead they used to show us films and video tapes on the dangers of unprotected sex.

But to tell you the truth *mudhara*, no one will listen to you on the streets. The girls also have no choice. They will be asking for trouble if they resisted sex demands of boys, at all".

6.2 *"Anatomy as destiny" on the streets and the "otherisation" of girls*

I found out that the attitude of boys towards girls on the streets generally, mirrored the unequal relations between men and women in mainstream society. As will be shown below, the boys had low opinion of girls, as one male informant revealed, to me saying;

"These girls are useless. They would not survive on their own on the streets. We look after them and they have to provide sexual favours for us. As you have witnessed *Big Dhara* they just sit all day. We do the work as the men. Ask all the boys, there is no girl who comes to the street and spends a day without having a partner".

When I told him that the girls had complained of sexual abuse, the boy and his colleagues laughed saying;

"*Kusina mai hakuendwe mudhara. Mustreet ndeme varume mudhara. Mukadzi haurarame mustreet unotokwirwa kuti zviite bho-o handizvo here* Jack (not real name). (Don't go where you are not known. The street is for men old man. For a woman to survive on the streets, she has to agree to sexual intercourse for her to last - isn't it Jack?) He appealed to his friend.

Jack revealed the patriarchal attitude of the boys saying, that girls deserved the rough treatment, for they were very loose and slept with any men and yet they were being fed by some of them. The girls always cheated the street boys, he revealed saying;

"These girls are very loose and they don't choose men. They cheat us and sleep anywhere, anytime. This is why they are being beaten all the time".

This reminded me of the Caldwells book on African sexuality, which has provoked much protest from Pan-Africanist academics on sexuality like, Arnfred (2004). The Caldwells from their African studies in West Africa concluded that, a woman was culturally much more independent sexually than the men. Most findings however confirm the opposite. Its men who are free to do as they please. Even on the streets, one girl lamented thus;

"*Sekuru.* I wish I was a boy. Boys are happier than us. For us sexual abuse is always the problem and we cannot run away from it. These boys take us like their objects. We have no power at all to do anything unless allowed by the boys".

She had fumed. She expressed the views I got from most of the girls. Boys treated them like sub-humans. I was interested in finding out how boys and girls, perceived each other, and the sexual relations amongst them. The attitude of the boys towards the girls I realized was not different from that of men towards women in dominant society. Having painted this grim picture, I now refer to issues relating to the initiation of sexual encounters in light of both the *Shona* and *Ndebele* tradition.

6.3 *Dating and Courtship on the Streets*

I asked girls during a general discussion and the girls burst out into laughter, when I enquired from them whether they had love affairs based on courtship. I was making reference especially to some of them who were in marital unions. One of them actually said;

"In the street *sekuru* there is courtship especially when the girls become streetwise. You find that the girl has a lot of boys who protect her from sexual abuse. Some of us are no longer forced into sexual relations. It happened during the first days when we were strangers to the boys".

Another had pointed out:

"But the courtship is not the normal one you know where a boy and a girl exchange love tokens like clothes or handkerchiefs. Food is the love token," (she stopped as the others burst into laughter and yet another quipped)".

"When they have money they might buy you some pants as a sign that he is the only one to have sexual relations with you. *Sekuru Gudo* threatens that he sometimes puts juju he gets from Mbare on those pants that will make a man fail to disengage during sexual intercourse if his lover cheats him".

Again there was laughter, as the girl made reference to *Sekuru Gudo's* threats, which they had proved to be "fake" as his female partner always had other lovers. Whenever he was too drunk or whenever he was in police custody for his criminal behaviour, the girlfriend/wife would sleep with other men. It was clear the girls had knowledge of what used to happen in traditional *Shona* society. Dating and courtship used to be arranged by other kin in pre-colonial *Shona* society, for a love affair was not, between boys and girls alone, but involved other extended family members. It was evident that food and protection from harassment, seemed to be key elements in a love affair leading even to a girl being impregnated. One boy actually said:

"Love token exchange is old fashioned. There is no time for that on the streets *mudhara*. We buy them goodies and that's it. If I buy her food and protect her I have a right to have sex with

161

her. Isn't it *mudhara*. You can't herd cows which will be milked by others" (*Haungafudzi vamwe vachikama*).

Both of us laughed and I went on to find out whether totems were important in these relationships. The boys had laughed again believing this was old fashioned.

"*Iyo haina mutupo. Chero tikave nemutupo umwe mudhara*. (The vagina knows no totem. Even if we be of the same totem, the vagina will still be as sweet).

The boys burst into laughter as they also concentrated on a game of cards - popularly known as "crazy eight", on the streets as well as in mainstream society. Another had also added thus:

"*Zvinopedza nguva izvo mudhara, iyo yamira zvayo. Tungidza chete.*" (It will be wasting time to ask about totems when the penis is already erect).

Girls were also of similar sentiments pointing out that some of them did not even know their totems. One said,

"Don't be cheated *sekuru* many of us don't know our totems. You hear *sekuru Gudo* one time saying he is *Nyamuzihwa* and sometimes he is *soko murehwa*. Those are not his totems. He will just be joking. Girls? -- *Sekuru* is it important?"

She appealed to others and one said:

"*Sekuru*, there is no time to talk about totems on the streets to say the truth. We just sleep with any man who gives us money. This is the truth."

I realized it was possible for a brother and sister dumped by one mother at different times in her lifetime, to impregnate each other on the streets. This was unheard of in traditional *Shona* society and when it happened this was called "*Makunakuna*" (taboo), and would call for some cleansing ceremony lest some misfortune would befall the families of the culprits or the community as a whole. There could be a drought or a devastating contagious disease. Totems were of religious significance in *Shona* society, as they were a link between the living and the dead. Now with a growing population of the totemless, it means the death of the kinship system, of the indigenous people of Zimbabwe slowly. We will end up with a situation similar to that of the black-Americans, who no longer have any totems.

6.4 *"Of Romance and the ideal woman on the streets"*

One afternoon as we sat on the pavement, in a busy street, the boys who had started drinking whistled as a way of drawing each other's attention to the figure of a woman who was passing-by. I must emphasize that, if an attractive woman passed through, even in the company of a man, they would whistle. I realized that this was the case, whenever light complexioned women, who would be on the plump side were seen. One of them said;

"*Big dhara pakadii apo? Ndivo vakadzika avo mudhara vakaita sevepaVhaa-- pamunoticha. Mudhara chimbotidana*". (How about that old man? That's a nice woman; quite attractive as those at the University where you teach old man, why don't you invite us there sometime).

The others laughed and one cautioned him thus;

"*Ziva zve scubha rawanwa. Unofunga kuti ungadiwa iwe, tibvire apa*". (You are now drunk. Don't waste the old man's time, who can love you at the University).

A heated discussion ensued though, as to the ideal woman who was sweet in sexual intercourse. It was generally agreed that the woman had to be light in complexion with firm breasts and;

"*Ane ngoma kushure Big Dhara handizvo here?*" (One with big buttocks, Isn't it mudhara?" he asked for expert advice but another quickly interjected)

"Guys sweetness or no sweetness is in the head. I had sex with a prostitute last week when I was drunk. I wasted my money. I felt nothing. I can't even remember if I ejaculated". The boys roared with laughter. I also joined them.

The girls said that there was nothing like romance with the street boys but with men from dominant society "*mhene*" (those with money, cars and cellphones). One of them said;

"*Sekuru ava havakweshi mazino. Kiss yacho haiite. Havana time yekubatabata mukadzi. Vanonyara futi kana vasina kudhakwa. Vanotoshingiswa nehwahwa*". (These boys don't clean their mouths. They have no time for caressing us. They have no time for love exchanges as they are shy, they only gather courage when drunk). One who had a husband on the streets also concurred saying;

"*Isu kungozvariswa. Kungokwirwa chete. Varume chaivo ndeavo vari kufamba uko*". (They just make us pregnant. Real men are from mainstream society).

6.5 *Sources of Sexual knowledge*

Some boys explained how they had difficulty in knowing how to penetrate a girl on the streets, the first time. They had heard other boys talk of sexual intercourse with girls, but had been shy to reveal to others, that, they did not have sexual experience,. One key informant of Mozambican origin actually said;

"*Mudhara,* I had a problem when I fell in love with a girl on the streets. The first few days, I did not know how to do it and she laughed at me. My first experience she actually had to hold my penis and placed it in her vagina".

He revealed that it was not all the street boys who were keen to sleep with girls and even to sexually abuse them. He pointed to several who were seated at the pavement some distance from us. He said those boys did not want to have any girls. I later interviewed some of them and they confirmed what this Mozambican boy had said to me. I had an opportunity to speak to *Sekuru Gudo* one afternoon. The young man is notorious for abusing drugs and is feared by most of the youth for being very rough. He said to me:

"*Mudhara* some of us have been asked hundred times by people about our way of life on the streets and nothing changed. Why should I spare thirty minutes talking to you when I can be making money. Do you pay me *mudhara* for my time?"

Eventually he apologized for being blunt to my request for a conversation and said;

"Yes some of us know where the vagina is very well and we love it." (The other boys giggled as he continued), "Call us at the university and we will show your girls that we are real men. We are not animals as some people regard us."

He revealed to me that he literally grew up on the streets and he got sexual knowledge from discussions with others. He also said that his first sexual experience, was with a prostitute he paid and told him what to do. The other boys showed that prostitutes were their readily available source of sexual knowledge. Generally, the boys lamented their state of poverty in terms of sexual knowledge, but pointed out that once in a while they got magazines like Cosmopolitan from generous Nigerians, in which there are issues on sexual positions and techniques. One such magazine of February 2000 was shown to me. On page 60 was the title **SEX** and there was an article titled, *"Your Sex Zodiac, Want a skyrocketing sex life? It's in your stars"*.

The girls too expressed a lot of sexual inadequacy in terms of knowledge. They were only used to sexual intercourse on the streets. Some had had romantic affairs before they came onto the streets, like one girl from Dzivarasekwa said;

"I had a boyfriend when I was in Grade Seven. He had just finished form four and he is the one who taught me how to kiss and where to touch before the actual game. He is the one who broke my virginity *sekuru,* but then he later went to work in Bulawayo and the affair ended."

Yet another girl who came from Epworth said;

"Some of us had affairs with boys far older than us and they taught us about sex. From time to time we go out with men from the public. Girls *sekuru* might be shy to say it all but we know even more than boys about sex."

I realized that there was much experimenting by the youth, when it came to sexual encounters. In traditional *Shona* society, sexual education had been done by elders. Girls were taught by the aunts who also taught girls not to be on their own with boys and also not to accept goodies from strangers for they would end up paying through having sex with those men. Because of the social set up then, it was possible to avoid boys but not today. Girls are forced onto the streets to live with boys, in an environment where social controls do not apply anymore, for the youth have their own life-style or sub-culture. This is why defining the word culture now becomes problematic. In simple societies as Berger and Luckmann (1966) point out, behaviour could be predictable but not in complex industrialised societies.

6.6 *Initiating consensual heterosexual sex*

On the streets, I found out that unlike the sexual abuse that characterized girls' first experiences, its mainly consensual heterosexual sex with either boys of the street or men from dominant society. What confused me however was the fact that, both boys and girls indicated that sexual encounters, were always initially characterized by force. Girls do not open their legs easily, if it is the first sexual encounter with that boy. It is the men or the boys who initiate the sexual encounters as one of them informed me thus;

"We have our female partners. We also approach them and court them. It is however not the usual courting because it is a one day thing. No one has time on the streets. It's about survival. Girls want food and money and protection. If the boy can provide these, that is the courtship and the next thing you have sex with the girl."

The girls also confirmed that it was the boys who proposed to girls and not the other way round. One of them said:

"It is not exactly like what used to happen. We hear a man would walk until the soles of his shoes were finished before he was loved. On the streets, it does not take much time because girls are forced to have a male partner by the circumstances we find ourselves in".

Another girl had also pointed out thus;

"*Sekuru*, it's not really courtship. It's threatened. You just succumb to pressure even from other girls, who fear to end up giving you their own food if you don't have a partner. Men from mainstream society also propose but it's like they take us like prostitutes. We agree to sleep with them for a fee."

I told them that in mainstream society, there was a new development with regards to courtship. Girls or women were now initiating courtship through the various media like newspapers and even the radio. Dating was now also even via the internet. One of the girls actually was sceptical of the new developments saying;

"*Sekuru*, it is not proper according to our Shona ways,"

I told them that it was becoming quite common though, for women to initiate courtship, and that this was a result of Western culture impacting on our own.

6.7 *Heterosexual relations on the streets as - "sex the invisible"*

It is true that I had assumed that one day I was going to see some street youth in coitus on the streets. I was mistaken, because for the fifteen months I was with the street youth, I never found any having sexual intercourse. Friedl's (1989) description of sex as the "invisible," was confirmed. I realized that the street youth sexual behaviour was not very different from that of those in mainstream society. They avoided having sex in open places. I found it unethical to go into such places especially on Friday and Saturday nights, when it was highly likely to find some youths in coitus. Moreover those were the places in which there had been several cases of mugging and robbery of members of the public during my might visits to the streets. As a researcher, I felt I was an outsider in as far as I was afraid to go into such places. I could have found some in coitus but I must admit, I felt I could not go that far, in light of the risk to my life.

I observed that girls could be picked up by some well off men especially during weekends. Some of the men were patrons of the night clubs frequented by the street youth. The girls revealed to me that they never went to the homes of their male partners. They feared to be found in some of the houses by those men's wives. Some of their clients also feared to take them to their homes, lest they stole from them. They therefore ended up having sexual intercourse in cars or in some of the dark sanitary lanes of the city centre. Some of the brave men would take them to the Harare gardens, located also in the city, although nowadays according to the girls due to muggings in the past, few dare to go there to have sex.

6.8 Virginity status of street girls and boys

One boy denigrated the girls thus;

> "*Tumagaba utwu. Mudhara hamuna* virgin mustreet. *Tuma hure, takuvara neskon'o.*" (Those are tins - there is no virgin on the streets. These are prostitutes. We are always affected by sexually transmitted diseases).

The other boys laughed and also confirmed his statements. These boys seemed not worried about the status of the girls as one of them lamented thus;

> "Virgins are good but are now hard to come by. Even in society there are no more virgins. It's like a bad omen to come across a virgin *Big Dhara.*"

As the boys showed during this discussion, girls are expected to be virgins and not the boys. It is the girls who get condemned for lack of virginity and are regarded as promiscuous and not the boys. That the boys' prized virginity despite their skepticism as to its existence was shown by the numerous conflicts that ensued, over who was to have sex with new street girls as one revealed to me saying;

> "Just let a girl come onto the streets and the boys are at each other's throats, over who has to sleep with her first. This is why *mudhara* most new girls end up sleeping with several boys even in one night. Sometimes these *magunduru* behave like dogs."

The others seemed unhappy with his likening them to dogs as one, protested thus:-

> "Heh you- don't say that as if you are innocent. You are actually one of the bad guys; always suffering from *skon'o*. Show the old man your penis. *Big Dhara,* he has *skon'o.* He has sores on his penis and yet he pretends to be a good boy."

On the other hand, the girls seemed not worried about their status as one actually said; "Long back it was important because a woman was respected for it. Her parents would be thanked. In the streets why should I worry over being a virgin? After all once you come here, forget about being a virgin if you were one. The boys will just pounce on you."

Another girl had also interjected;

> "*Sekuru* none of these girls was a virgin when they came onto the streets, rather ask how many times most of us had aborted."

The other girls laughed to show that such practice was common amongst them. I did not want to focus on reproductive health issues in this chapter, but the youth's sexual behaviour only. From

167

the conversations and discussions with individual youth I found out that virginity was not prized at all by the youth, but boys still expected to sleep with a virgin.

6.9 The notion of "Forced sex" amongst the youth

I wondered whether to term this kind of sexual behaviour as rape or "normal sexual behaviour in sexual encounters for the first time." As already discussed earlier on, this always occurred whenever there was a new girl. However I learnt that, this also sometimes happened with the "street-wise." The girls did not have kind words for this kind of sexual encounter with one saying;

> "*Sekuru*, the boys believe it is their right to sleep with any girl of the streets. Even if you have your male partner they don't care sometimes. *Sekuru Gudo* is notorious for pushing your male partner from your top and he inserts his penis. Ask the girls how many times this baboon has done it."

The girls laughed but from the non-verbal cues seemed, to concur with what she had said. The girl went on to talk of an aggressive group who lived in a squatter camp along *Mukuvisi* who would be in the company of *Sekuru Gudo*. The boys were also not happy about the behaviour of these boys, who claimed to be the owners of the city, "*Vana* Mr Harare" (The Mr Harares) because they had been on the streets the longest. These boys were notorious for demanding for what is called "protection fee" from the rest of the street youth. I actually witnessed several incidents in which they would go round the working bases and actually put their hands into the others pockets to get money by force.

The girls feel the boys use force, but don't believe they are raped, especially if it is the first time to sleep with a boy as one observed, thus;

> "*Sekuru*, isn't it true that women are not supposed to open their legs that easy because men will think you are loose. We sometimes resist if it is the first time by locking our legs."

The others laughed and I probed by way of a question as to who had said that, that was the right behaviour and one said;

> "Be honest, will you be happy if I just open my legs for you?", the others laughed again as I joined them and I joked with her saying;

> "You wouldn't be so cruel to your uncle *muzukuru* (niece) as to lock your legs."

There was an uproarious burst of laughter.

168

According to the boys, use of force is not rape because;

"Girls don't easily open their legs the first time. We cannot even have rear entry, we like (dog-style in street lingo). They pretend to be virgins these girls' *mudhara* and so "*unotobhevhura makumbo.*" (you force open the legs). They don't cry out as if they were being raped and this shows that its consensual sex. Once *yapinda mudhara* (you penetrate her) she clings to you."

There was much laughter from the others. I found out that generally, forced sex was not rape even from the girls' perspective. There were however instances of rape, as one girl said. I thought this naturalising of aggressive and abusive behaviour by the boys, was a mirror-image of what prevailed in mainstream society, where Victorian sexual tendencies still were evident. Men determined and controlled women's sexual behaviour.

6.10 *Gang-rape on the streets*

It was on a Saturday morning, end of August 2006. Like all month ends this had been characterized by a lot of excitement. I left one of the nightclubs around 9.00p.m. The following morning I learnt that two of my key informants, had been implicated in a case of rape. The other two boys were said to have disappeared into the dark sanitary lanes. According to some of the boys this must have happened around one o'clock in the morning. After having been placed on remand on free bail, I had a detailed discussion with these two boys. One of them actually said;

"This is not a street girl but a vendor. Her problem is that she would accept our money, most boys know her and she is very loose. It just happened that when we got very drunk we decided to fix her and show her that we knew of her cheating us. As she left the night club we pretended to accompany her as a friend. Its one of the guys from Mukuvisi who tripped her to the ground and out of need for fun we had sex with her. She cried out and some plain clothes police officers arrested us. We however told the police the culprits had run away".

I had decided to talk to this girl but I learnt that she had changed to another location of the city. This incident actually was common knowledge amongst the boys as well as the girls. The girls told me that they never went to night clubs on their own. The boys are not afraid of contracting sexually transmitted diseases and they just make fun out of such incidents. I was reminded of a case of gang-rape that occurred on the streets of Harare, in the late 1990s involving a middle - aged working woman by some "street children." The ages of the youth were not given then, as they were said to be at large.

169

6.11 *Lovers discourses under the blankets on the streets*

Shire (1994) refers to the sexually stimulating language used by women during coitus, in praise of their husbands, as some form of special discourse. He refers to it as "lovers discourse under the blankets". Shire, gives an example of the *Hungwe* man's *"chidawo"*, (praise in poetic form linked to one's totem), pointing out that under the blankets vulgar language was acceptable and not embarrassing. After sexual intercourse the woman would praise the men using language not normally said in public. The words like, *"machende eshumba - muranda wemheche"*, are under normal circumstances considered to be obscene and not acceptable. During and after coitus they are said without causing any embarrassment to the parties present.

I was keen to find out from the girls especially the ones in marital unions whether they knew about such praising of their husbands and it caused a lot of debate. One said;

"It's old fashioned *sekuru*. Why should I praise the man when I am the one who is sweet?"

There was a heated discussion amongst the five street girls present as to who was sweeter between the man and the woman during coitus. They appealed to me, but I told them I was not an expert either, and one said;

"Sekuru, you are not being honest, you know the answer, and you don't want to tell us".

However, the discussion went on, when one of them said,

"In our culture then, women were not working and so praised men in everything. It's men who wanted to be praised. Why were men not praising women? Things have changed *sekuru*."

I realized that was not happening on the streets, more so because to the street youth totems were not important. One quickly found out also that the girls were quite informed as to their rights and those of women in general but complained thus;

Sekuru, gone are those days. We are now in modern times. We are equal to men."

The other girls laughed to show they were not in agreement as one said;

"On the streets *shamwari* (my friend), you are fooling yourself. These guys are not educated that's the problem. They are backward *sekuru*. They behave like old people."

Yet another interjected

"But do you praise your husband after sex using his totem."

The other girls shook their heads to show it was not happening on the streets. This showed that in terms of sexual behaviour the girls were not different from the thinking of university third year students, both males and females. For three years from 2005 to 2007, I used to ask my third year social theory classes, whether they put any importance on totems. There was general agreement totems were now irrelevant. When I asked them about the issue of praising each other after sex, which caused some uncontrollable fits of laughter, it was evident, it was no longer happening. The boys of the streets' attitude were no different as some did not even know their totems. One of the boys said;

"*Mudhara mibvunzo yako inonyanya kudhibha*" (Old man your questions are too deep). He had gone on, to say;

"*Mustreet hamuna jira, hamuna gumbeze mudhara,*" (We don't have blankets on the streets).

It was somehow true. When I went to their sleeping bases I had seen blankets which were in tatters. Most of the youth go to *Mai Musodzi* Hall in Mbare, to watch films as well as to sleep there. The street 'kids' don't have blankets. For example in one of the abandoned buildings in the Kopje area I visited during the day and during nights, more than fifty could be there at night and yet there were only a few torn blankets.

The girls were in stitches with laughter when I asked them whether they ever handled their lover's genitals. The same was the reaction amongst the boys. One of the girls in between bursts of laughter managed to say;

"*Ah, sekuru muri svatu imi, mibvunzo yenyu haiite*" (*Sekuru* your questions are too explicit) and went on;

"Girls do you touch your men's penis or testicles?"-

She appealed to the others, who again burst into uncontrollable fits of laughter. I thought it was so much fun because it was coming from an elderly person, who under normal circumstances was not supposed to use such language, when talking to girls and boys far younger. The girls believed it was taboo as one said;

"*Sekuru tinongonzwa yavamo. Aiwa kubata hazviite.* (We leave the men to insert into the vagina. We don't touch the penis).

But one who had just joined the discussion made me laugh when she said;

"What happens during intercourse *sekuru* only the two will know. Some of these boys of the streets don't know where the "*buri*" (vulva) is."

The other girls laughed and seemed to agree that sometimes, they insert the penis into their vaginas. The boys on the other hand, felt the vagina was not to be touched as they burst into fits

171

of laughter,

"*Haribatwe Big dhara - Haritambwe naro zinhu riye, haritariswe futi* (We don't hold that dreadful thing - we don't even look at it).

The boys seemed to agree the vagina was not to be touched, and there was no caressing or foreplay on the streets, as one again caused some laughter when he said;

"We don't have time to waste touching parts that do not matter, like breasts when we know exactly what we want - to penetrate - so go straight for it".

6.12 *Sexual Networking by the Girls*

The girls were open from the beginning about their promiscuity. They justified their sexual escapades financially mainly. The girls of the street referred to what I call their "three types of clients." The first group is that of the street boys. They mainly engage in sex with them for protection. There is a lot of rough play on the streets, if you are not well connected to bullies of the streets. One girl actually summarized the views of most of my female informants;

"We have to sleep with these boys and pretend they are the only ones. Trouble befalls any of us who is caught cheating. Cheating is common because these boys don't behave like normal people when they get money. They squander it in town or in Mbare, even with prostitutes. Meanwhile, if you have a child of his, they don't care, so we are forced to sleep with other men *sekuru*. Can you call us prostitutes in that case?"

She sought for my opinion and before I had responded, one of the girls had interjected saying;

"What is a prostitute Jestina (not real name)? There is nothing like that on the streets, as these boys also must also be called prostitutes. Men want to do what they like whilst oppressing us."

I learnt that in the event that a girl was not happy with a male partner's sexual behaviour, they also sought for other men as a way of hurting or fixing such a partner. The partner however must not know or else the girl will be harmed.

The second group is that of "street youth on the street," the rivals of the "street youth of the street" *(Mugundurus)*. These boys usually have sufficient money to enable them pay for sexual services rendered by the street girls. Most of these boys have wives where they live in high density suburbs. These sexual encounters are called "short-time" in street lingo or casual sex. They just go into a corner and engage in sexual intercourse, and thereafter the girl is given money and they part ways. The girls in this kind of sexual encounter want money, not protection, what one might term as "survival sex".

Apart from the street boys, the girls sleep with municipal police and members of the uniformed forces for protection rather than for money. One girl actually had no kind words for these men.

"*Sekuru*, those men in blue (she said whilst looking in the direction from which some municipal police were coming), can be rough. We have sex with them for protection, but the problem comes if these men are changed to another area of the city and new ones come. Before you sexually spoil them, usually you suffer a lot of harassment. Nowadays however, we know of pending raids whilst the authorities are planning in their offices. Some of the police tell us. Even members of the Zimbabwe Republic Police and the army are our boyfriends."

This was true because I had personally seen a number of these officers spending time talking to these girls at their "base" at the bus terminus. So group one was mainly of men who provided protection. The street boys would also give the girls food and money. Rarely did the officers give them money because one girl lamented thus:-

"*Naavo kurarirwa mahara, havazive kuti zasi kunogezwa nesipo* (with the officers its free sex. They don't know that we need soap to wash our vaginas).

The other girls burst into laughter and I could not control myself too.

The third group is one I aptly regard as of "intergenerational sex and this tended to involve men from the racial divide. At night, coloured men would be at the night clubs. There were white men whose names were mentioned and I saw them on several occasions in parked cars and some girls would go there. Once in a while the cars would be driven away and after some hour or two the girl would be brought back or as the girls put it, they could be left a bit far away so that their boys don't see it. I personally witnessed these incidents at night during weekends a. One girl actually said;

"*Sekuru*, we don't care about the age when it comes to money. "*Mhene*", (street lingo for a man with money), can be three times my age, that is sixty years old; I don't care as long as I survive. Men from all walks of life including whites and coloureds pick us up. They take us to gardens or we have sex in their cars. Some don't even want penetrative sex but just to be caressed..., what we call 'sucking', sekuru".

The others laughed and she went on;

"*Sekuru*, white men are not as excited about penetrative sex as our African men. They are quite generous with money. You can be given up to $500 000, 00 for one hour only."

This was in June 2006, and this would have been a lot of money then. The other girls confirmed as did the boys later that white men also came to have sex with girls or came to sodomise the boys as will be discussed later.

6.13 The "Genitals" as assets for survival and a way "to climb out of poverty". A good Case of intergenerational sex, and sexual networking

I was introduced to one girl by on of my key informants I shall call G and below is my conversation with her;

G's friend (Former street girl now living in Warren Park), one of the high density residential areas of Harare;

It was on a Saturday, at a night club I can't mention, when G one of my key informants called me whilst in the company of a young blonde.

"*Big Dhara*, meet Georgina, (not real name) a former street girl. I think you remember some of the boys telling you there was a girl now living in Warren Park" (Yes, I remember, I assured him and then he went on)

"Georgina, *Mudhara wedu uyu anofundisa paUZ*" (Georgina, this old man is one of us and is a lecturer at the UZ). U.Z. means the University of Zimbabwe.

Georgina stared into my face wondering what the matter could be and then G went on;

"Georgina, *Mudhara*, used to be my first girl, maybe the first I had sex with on the streets", (Both laughed and hugged).

He lamented thus;

"*Mudhara*, she now goes out with "*Mhene*" (men with lots of money from mainstream society). You might want to speak to her, I will be back soon."

Georgina did not resist. It was mid-month in August 2006 and not very busy, by the nightclub. I took her to my car where my driver was standing at the back smoking. The whole place from the nightclub to the street, was well lit and some of the boys and girls were just chitchatting, seemingly unaware of my discussion with Georgina. The city authorities had put new florescent tubes. She had heard a number of them actually welcoming me with their usual salutation of "*Big Dhara*, how are you?" which assured her it was safe for her to be with me.

She narrated her experiences thus -

174

"I will be short because my man will be here in about forty minutes" (Her cell phone rang and she brought it from her bra.

A state of the art handset and she responded thus in my presence);

"I am just meeting my aunt at the club, then I will be at the State Lottery hall" (She seemed to be assuring him she was not up to some mischief. She was also lying for there was no aunt). "Nothing to fear my dear. Don't you trust me? I am waiting for you here as I told you. I am not drinking any beer. I told you I want to stop. You will prove it for yourself. "Where are you yourself (She asked and went on). "OK in forty minutes you find me at the State Lottery Hall".(and hung up) *Sekuru* (she called me just like the others). "What exactly do you want, because I will disappear from here soon?"

(I told her I just wanted to confirm whether she was a former street girl and what had then happened, to enable her to leave the streets. She laughed and said;

"*Sekuru* that will need the whole day. But let me just say, I came onto the streets from VID Squatter camp (VID means Vehicle Inspection Depot). The depot is on the banks of the Mukuvisi river. A squatter camp used to be close-by in the late 1980's. The girls know me after my parents had died from tuberculosis. I think you have heard of VID squatter camp and the shebeens, which mainly sold "*Sikokian*") (very powerful and dangerous brew). I started to live on the streets at the age of eight years and met G three years later. We were friends but at the age of 18 years, a man who used to patronize this night club and was a heavy truck driver, got interested in me and, I became his "small house." He secured lodgings for me in Kambuzuma but six months down the line he went down South. Fortunately he had introduced me to a number of his friends, whom we used to drink with, and this man who has been phoning, used to know my former boyfriend. He found lodgings for me in Warren Park and he does everything for me. He lives in Haig Park with his family but provides everything I need. He allows me to go to the pub only in the company of his relatives who, live in Warren Park and never on my own; because I told him it was difficult for me to stop drinking, though I now want to stop". (She went on), "I will be brief because now I am left with ten minutes to walk."

The man called again to say he was parked by the Hall and yet she was nowhere to be seen.

"Do you want me to bring my aunt?", (She lied). "It has been a long time since we met and so there were many stories (she said as she bid me farewell and went to the State Lottery Hall to join her "husband").

I then went to the Club and thanked G, for affording me such an opportunity and he said,
"*Mudhara,* we told you that these girls are favourites of the big *Madhara* with money. You
should see the merc (Mercedes-Benz) the old man drives. He is about fifty five years of age
so she told us."

G then told me that once in a while Georgina came to the club and that he was going to afford
me another interview but this was not to be. I gave him money to buy two pints of clear beer as a
token of appreciation for his role.

"As we told you she is a prostitute. She is not an honest housewife. You saw she is quite
beautiful and the older men preferred such young and light complexioned girls."

(I asked him what he meant by beautiful. He laughed and said) "It's difficult but I think you
know what beauty is when you see it. We mainly prefer girls like Georgina. Light in complexion
with nice protruding buttocks *Mudhara* (He said laughing). "You wont believe she was very
skinny but from the time we heard that she had aborted, just two months down the line she
started to gain weight and was taken off the streets by these hyenas (He said laughing and I
wondered why he called then hyenas and he said,

"Ah *Mudhara*, they are courageous, to just pick a girl nowadays and start co-habiting with
her. Some people seem not to fear HIV and AIDS. They are just like us, who do not care
whether we live or die. For us it's better even if we die because we don't have children" he
said laughing.

This case sends chills down my spine, as I imagine that the young girl apart from engaging in
intergenerational sex, obviously was sleeping with many other men. The old man with the
Mercedes-Benz was not aware of her past as a sexually promiscuous girl. The risk of spreading
HIV and AIDS to many families was quite high and I felt this was a classic case of sexual
networking. Dominant society, I thought, had to realise that ignoring sexual activities of the
street youth, was actually posing a danger to society as a whole.

6.14 *Homosexuality and some bestiality amongst street girls*

One of the street boys had revealed during one of my numerous conversations with them thus;

"*Big Dhara* these girls are satanic when they want money. This is why we are rough. They
suck the penis of a man, especially whites."

This came during the early months of my study and when I decided to explore it on the street; I had personally seen some girls being driven off in cars from some night spots. The girls were not explicit as to how they did it, because they felt I was going too far except to mention thus, as did several of them;

"*Sekuru* when you have to survive on the streets you even eat a snake
(One of them had said and the others burst into laughter as one said;

"Ah tell him straight, that the penis is the snake. What I can tell you *sekuru* is that once in a while we engage in sucking (street lingo for oral sex). Some men just want you to caress their penis only and not put in the mouth. (The other girls laughed when she said, "One white old man loves this. Haven't you seen that small red car on Fridays by the club (I told them I had seen it and she went on);

"That is a generous old white man very concerned about our welfare. Some of us have been to his house in Belgravia.

This reminded me of a news item that had been on Zimbabwean television that week (November 2006), of some Indian nationals, who had forced their female employees to perform oral sexual acts with them, in one of Harare's suburbs called Milton Park.

The girls agreed oral sex was quite prevalent, especially with white and coloured men. The boys also confirmed it and one naughty key informant had expressed his dislike for kissing the street girls thus;

"*Big Dhara* I can't kiss a girl of the street. I just fuck her. I can't kiss a mouth that eats a penis. These street girls are witches *mudhara*; they can have sex with dogs." Another boy had interjected,

"Haven't you heard that some women were having sex with dogs in Borrowdale in the 1990s? Some of the girls on the streets still do it but its a guarded secret. You just hear some tell you in confidence that it is happening."

There was concern written on the faces of those around me. It was no laughing matter as one boy observed angrily.

"No wonder why some of us contract *sikon'o* that resists drugs. Some have sores that never heal because of these bitches. That is why they are sometimes beaten on the streets. They are very rough."

According to the girls, anal penetration was unheard of on the streets amongst the girls. It was the boys who were the culprits as one key informant lamented thus;

"*Mudhara* some of these boys you see are animals. Didn't you hear of a white businessman who was once in the papers in the early 90s, (I said I had heard about it and he went on). I was still young but when I came to the streets I saw him. He no longer comes here but some boys go to his house.

Another boy had shed more light on the issue;

"We suspect these men in posh cars, who come and pretend that they need us to cut their hedge or do some work at their homes, because some of them will be homosexuals."

The boys told me on many occasions that it was difficult to see it but there were some of them who were homosexuals. Amongst them were the likes of *Sekuru Gudo,* who was notorious for thigh sex with new arrivals on the streets. One boy had actually said;

"If you see *Sekuru Gudo* with small boys who are new on the streets and he buys them food, then know that they will be his wives. He is notorious for that, but penetrative anal sex might not happen."

Some of the boys wanted to inform me in confidence of beastiality. They did not go into details because one of those involved was very violent and they feared for their lives. They did not want me to ask about it, as one of my key informants just said;

"*Big Dhara* whites have fun with us. They take many videos. Some of us are taken having sex with dogs."

This I must say I had heard from girls much earlier, when they angrily accused the boys of being beasts, who molested them on the streets. In confidence the key informant had said;

"*Ndapota mudhara iwe chingoziva kuti magunduru imhuka*" (Please I beg you not to mention it, just know that street boys are animals).

I thought this was another form of sexual networking by both boys and girls - having sexual relations with dogs.

6.14.1 *Sexual Networking by the boys - The Case of the "Sexual poacher"*

Poachers are boys who do not have stable, lasting relations of intimacy with girls. They are a good example of sexual promiscuity by the boys of the streets. They call themselves poachers and take pride in being regarded as such. They regard themselves as the street-wise who can sleep with many girls and prostitutes. One key informant a poacher said;

"*Mudhara*, I only have sex with any woman when I can afford. I don't care whether it is a prostitute or a girl of the street or one who is married on the street. You now know that there are fathers and mothers amongst us? (he asked laughing and I agreed with a broad smile).

He went on;

"On a good Friday if I have enough money I go to Mbare. You have heard of the VITO bar, that's my favourite but it's a dangerous place because that's where most criminals of Mbare meet. I usually manage to pick a prostitute. Sometimes I pay and sometimes I run away after the sexual intercourse (he again laughed showing that it must have happened many times.) The following day I can sleep with a street girl. I have a girl friend in Epworth. It's a long story how I got her but I also sleep with her *mudhara*."

When one talks of love affairs on the streets, most of the boys one discovers, prefer being poachers and this is why some of them were saying;

"*Mudhara*, some of us have wives but whenever you go somewhere there is the problem of the poacher. *Mapocha* are like dogs *mudhara*. They don't want steady affairs. They want other men's wives."

I asked as to how they then accept responsibility for pregnancies on the streets and he said;

"Like mine *mudhara* from the beginning we have never separated. We have always been together but those who get arrested - Ah- it's a pity, the wives will be forced to sleep with the poachers."

Poacher in Zimbabwean terminology refers to one who kills wild animals in prohibited areas such as the rhino, which is regarded as an endangered species. Poacher, one might say also means thief and I decided to call them "sexual poachers," because of their behaviour of having sexual relations with even the married girls.

6.14.2 *Interfacing with mainstream society in Sexual encounters; A case of Intergenerational sex involving boys - as evidence of sexual networking*

One of my key informants related an incident in which he had sex with a "sugar *gogo*" or "sugar *mama*" in street lingo, meaning a woman far older. The girls and boys confirmed that, just like the girls intergenerational sex, such relations with older women were prevalent. It was however evident that girls, were more involved than boys. The youth generally said no condoms were being used in most of the cases, with one boy saying;

"These sugar *mhamhas* come for us knowing we are still hot. They want hot sperms *mudhara.*"

One key Informant's sexual Experience with a 'Sugar Gogo'

He narrated his experiences as follows;

"It was on a Saturday afternoon in April 2004 and we were on the street as usual. We saw a blue car driving into a parking bay and I approached the driver and saw it was a woman, "*Maswera sei mukoma,*" (How has been your day), she asked me and I told her I was fine. My other friend also came since it was mid-month and it was generally quiet in terms of business for us, as he thought it was a prospective client. Then she said to me, if I have some work at my house would you like to go with me, and then I will give you money to catch a kombi back into town (commuter omnibus as they are officially known). What kind of work? I asked. To me she smelt of wine because as you know I drink beer "*Asi unonditya kani?*" (Are you afraid of me?), she asked with a smile and quite a romantic tone *Mudhara* as if she was speaking to her lover. (I laughed and he said), "*Mudhara,* funny and strange things happen on these streets of ours.

I asked my friend who accepted to accompany me because I told her I was afraid to go alone with strangers and in a cool voice she said,

"If you are afraid let your friend accompany you but once we arrive at my house and you are assured of your safety he can come back, the hedge I want you to cut stretches for only 50 meters" I told her she could have come in the morning but she told me not to worry. When we got to Eastlea, *Big Dhara*, I was awe-stricken. She lived all by herself because she said her children had gone to Bulawayo to their aunt for the holidays and her husband was dead. *Mudhara, hapana hedge yakazochekwa, munhu ndiye akazochekwa* because *ndiyo ngoma yangu Mudhara* (No hedge cutting took place as I fucked her). The long and short of it is that, after taking a bath, I was given nice clothes including a pair of socks and shoes which I later sold at Mupedzanhamo and she gave me some wine then some rice - nice rice and chicken *Mudhara.* She then took me to her beautiful bedroom where there was an imposing bedroom suite, the headboard of which I have never seen in these shops. *Mudhara,* I feared at first but ended up having sex with her and there was no condom. The woman who must have been in her late 40s, looked gorgeous. I spent the weekend there and she became my sweet-mama but she left for the UK (United Kingdom) in October the same year. It was an experience of a lifetime and a number of us are hired by these sugar mamas to have sex with them. I never wanted you to know because I was ashamed but now that you ask, I have to confide in you."

I thought this was another good case of intergenerational sex, which is not recommended by reproductive health experts, as it exposes the youth to the dreaded HIV and AIDS pandemic. I imagined on the other hand, what that woman was doing in the U.K, probably sleeping with many more men without condoms.

6.14.3 *"Ritual Sex" by boys, as a good case of sexual networking*

Bizarre occurrences take place on the streets, and I found some of these to be far stranger than fiction. I was told by the boys that sometimes, well to do men driving posh cars came for their **sperms**. I was reminded of an incident involving a popular prophet based in Norton and Kuwadzana suburbs in Harare in the 1990s, whose popularity fizzled, when people discovered he had been using his sperms in his healing sessions. According to one of my key informants, it's true as he revealed thus;

"*Big dhara a mugunduru* is like a soldier. We are prepared for anything. Now some business people come at night to pick some of us. They take them to some hotels in the avenues having given them beer and some new clothes. The old clothes they take with them and we suspect use of these for juju also. They ask them to pick a prostitute from the bar. They pay for everything including food and beers. They give the young men money to give to the "bitches" after they have had sex with them in one of the hotel rooms. The man pays for booking the room and then the *mungunduru* is given a condom. When he ejaculates all sperms are collected in the condom which is then taken by the businessman."

From general discussion with some members of the Zimbabwe National Traditional Healers Association, I learnt that there were many uses sperms could be put to. One obvious one was that, sperms were associated with the generation of life and so could be used to boost one's business in terms of growth, popularity and profits. Another explanation was that "big dealers", that is, those people involved in shady deals and risk arrest, use *juju* mixed with these sperms to make authorities just forget about their existence. Criminals, it was mentioned could put the juju with sperms into water and smear all over the place where a crime will have been committed and the investigating officers will fail to get any leads. There are so many myths associated with the use of sperms. I felt it was an issue worth exploring in future.

181

The dirty clothes taken from the street youth, could be put in water and washed without soap - they are soaked until all dirt and sweat is wrung out into the water and then mixed with *juju*. The street youth seem aware of the possible long term effects on those from whom the sperms are taken as one said;

> "No wonder why big dhara some of us end up mentally disturbed, it could be because of the *juju*."

I decided to call this kind of sexual behaviour "ritual sex", because it seemed shrouded in mystery. In Zimbabwe there is what is called "ritual murder," also explained in terms of the need for human parts like ears, the heart, testicles and the penis or vagina, and blood or even eyes to boost one's business. These are dangerous beliefs which lead to ritual murders.

6.15 *Sexual positions and sexual techniques amongst street youth during sexual intercourse*

I found out that this was mainly an area in which boys showed their domination of girls also, apart from those discussed above. The boys determined the sexual position during coitus. It was revealed that the common position during the first sexual encounter with a boy, was that of a girl sleeping on her back. This required some force as even the girls revealed above. First sexual encounters were characterized by vigour and aggressive behaviour on the part of the boys as the girls resisted penetration, mainly by locking their legs. Sometimes a girl behaved like this because she did not want to sleep with the boy or sometimes just to prove to the boy she was not loose. This position however, was not popular with the boys and I was reminded of Baron and Bryne's (1987:534), discussion of the two main categories of sexual positions i.e. the "Oceanic" position and the "missionary" position in coitus.

The Oceanic style was mainly characterized by vigour and was from the rear or what was called "dog-style" by the boys. The "missionary style the boys called the "hospital-style", which is generally known as the frontal position, and was seen as characterized by passivity; this is where the man is on top. One boy said;

> "*Mudhara* it's hard to get money on the street. When you sleep with a girl you must get your money's worth. The dog style is the most popular with us boys because it sinks right inside."

This confirmed the sadistic attitude of the boys, that is the desire to inflict pain.
Another boy had said;

"The dog style is meant to fix these girls. They must know we are real men", and the others burst into laughter.

On the other hand the girls seemed to prefer the missionary or hospital-style with one of them saying,

"These guys take us for dogs *sekuru*. I personally don't like the "dog-style" because when you kneel on the pavement or ground its painful *sekuru*. These boys will not listen to that. They just want it from the back, maybe because of what we told you last time that, when they are sober, they are so shy to talk about sex." I concluded that these were the two main techniques in coitus. The boys and girls did not talk of any other positions.

6.16 *Enhancing excitement in sexual encounters: - Interfacing with "Street Pharmacists"*
One girl said,

"*Sekuru* if your boyfriend discovers that your vagina is wet, there could be trouble. We use herbs we buy from herbalists in Mbare to dry our vaginas."
Another had interjected

"*Sekuru* it's a problem even if it is urine, they will think you had been having "short-time" (Street lingo for quick sexual encounter with other men) and you may be beaten badly."
The girls revealed that there were some women and men in Mbare, who knew effective herbs to keep the vagina dry. I decided to call these "street pharmacists." Their drugs some will argue, are effective whilst some will doubt their efficacy but to the youth, both boys and girls applauded the role herbalists played in "safeguarding" their health. This leads to dry sex which they said, could be painful and could cause bleeding if the man forced hard, too quickly into her.

The boys also told me that they also used herbs to enhance their virility. These they also bought once in a while from herbalists especially when they want to prove they are better than other boys as one informant said it;

"Boys want to show girls they are the most exciting sexually *sekuru*. We sometimes eat herbs. (" *Kudya mushonga*,") This we do a day or two before the sexual encounter."
Another interjected and there was laughter when he referred to an incident when S*ekuru Gudo* had an erect penis which he would show others.

183

"He took an overdose sekuru and he had problems with his penis. The girls of the street don't like him."

Another said; He went to Mbare to look for a prostitute", There was an uproarious burst of laughter. These aphrodisiacs the boys call "*guchu*" in general. (concoction of herbs in plastic bottles).

6.17 *Masturbation as some form of celibacy and a good case of sexual abstinence*

There was much laughter when one day I asked whether there were some who were afraid of sex with girls as one said;

"*Big dhara mafata aripo* (There are Catholic priests amongst us. These Roman Catholic priests are normally associated with celibacy)

There was much laughter when another said;

"*Varipo vanorarama negwetengwe*" (There are some of us who survive on masturbation) "*Gwetengwe*" is street lingo for masturbation as I discovered when I probed. This I discovered was quite prevalent amongst the boys as was confirmed by one pregnant girl.

"Those boys *sekuru havana kukwana*. Sometimes *vanotideedza kana vachi mastabheta*" (Those boys are naughty because sometimes they call us to watch them as they masturbate).

One of the boys had a ready answer as to why some of them masturbated. He said;

"*Big Dhara* some of us are afraid of HIV and AIDS. The best is to masturbate. It's not expensive".

The others had laughed but also seeming to agree with that view. I however discovered that there were some myths associated with this behaviour when one said;

"*Big Dhara* it's easy to see those who masturbate during the night because in the morning they will be weak and passive. Sometimes they sleep on pavements during the day when others are active."

The others seemed to agree saying that when drunk the boys' behaviour was not like that of one who had masturbated. I could see that some of those involved were present as this topic caused much laughter and they would look at certain individuals.

6.18 *Boys perception of sex as more of "fucking" or "patriarchal sex" - as indicated by the sexual metaphors they use*

The sexual metaphors used by the boys during my conversations and discussions with them reminded me of Jensen's (1998) notion of patriarchal sex among American men. This kind of sex is mainly characterized by "fucking", which to Jensen is more of violent sexual encounters, forced sex based on the belief that girls will always say No for Yes. This is what I found to be prevalent on the streets. The boys have sadistic tendencies, of desiring to cause pain as evidenced by the language they used like;

"Ndakachimamisa" (I made her defecate because of excitement when I had sex with her)

7   *"Ndachibvarura chiye"* (I really tore her vagina apart)

8   *"Ndakachiridza madeko"* (I hit her like a drum last night).

   "Tugaba twusikana utwu. Twumahure" (These girls vaginas are like open tins)

This is denigrating language referring to the girls as tins that their vaginas are like tins and the girls are hopeless prostitutes.

The boys' language is not romantic at all but rather they, objectify girls. They take them as tins into which they pour their sperms as and when they feel like. Shire (1984), Magaisa (1999), Baines (1998), all make reference to such sexual metaphors, used by men in different societies. I felt that the mind of men universally, tended to converge when it came to sexual issues. The word "fuck," "I fucked her." Fuck as a word might mean emotions of anger. It might even mean physically assaulting someone. When used in sexual matters, it might mean fixing the woman rather than it being an enjoyable sexual encounter for the two. The street boys talk of *"Kutsiva mari yangu,"* that is I have to get my money's worth from the sexual encounter. This amply shows that the intercourse encounter, is not based on feelings of love but more of a pain inflicting game.

6.19 *Conclusion*

The above story of the sexual behaviour patterns of street youth, has amply showed how girls of the streets are dominated in sexual encounters. They are an otherised, objectified and denigrated category. They have no other means to sustain themselves on the streets, where there are a hierarchy of opportunities most of which are the preserve of the boys. Not only are girls powerless in sexual encounters, involving the street boys but they are also exploited by men from mainstream society. Some of these men, like security personnel, must, one imagines, have been protecting them from sexual abuse. The above narrative, reads like a tragic - comedy, when one looks at the lived experiences of the street girls. Yes, there are happy moments but from this

185

tale, most of the time the girls are an abused lot, physically, sexually, emotionally and economically.

Boys too are an exploited lot just like the girls in some instances. For example, cases of "ritual sex," homosexuality and beastiality, are also issues that raise tempers in all moral abiding citizens. The youth have no option but to indulge, as those who sponsor such sexual escapades pay them handsomely. Of course, it is also quite interesting to discover that the boys' behaviour, is not different from that of men in mainstream society, who also denigrate women and dictate sexual matters to women in bedrooms. What some aptly refer to as "bedroom power." Women still must demystify this and ensure equality in sexual encounters. They must also determine what sexual positions the two must take during coitus and must have power to say No to sex, rather than be sexual objects of men.

Women are still dominated sexually by men, hence they are forced to abandon their surnames in the event of marriage. It's like losing one's spirituality and identity. Women activists lobbying for equality with their male counterparts, have globally scored successes in many areas of social life; with women being elected to be leaders of their nations - as Presidents. But sexually they remain dominated by men. Men initiate sexual encounters and determine the sexual position and technique during coitus. However nowadays women are also initiating courtship and dating as is the case through the internet and newspapers. Women are not supposed to show that they have sexual experience, as we see amongst the street youth. It is the boys who have freedom to talk of their sexual escapades and not the girls; - bragging that they are "sexual poachers". From this narrative one discovers also that, the youth are fond of unprotected sex. They are aware of the risks of the HIV and AIDS pandemic, but the girls are powerless, to say no to condomless sexual intercourse. This story reveals vividly the sexual experiences of the youth and the unequal power relations that prevail between boys and girls "of the streets".

CHAPTER SEVEN

REPRODUCTIVE HEALTH EXPERIENCES OF STREET YOUTH

7.0 *Introduction*

This chapter explores the power dynamics amongst the street youth in relation to reproductive health issues. To begin with one has to grapple with issues of body ownership on the streets, as well as matters of independence or autonomy in sexual encounters and reproductive health matters. It becomes imperative to focus at the youth's attitude towards the HIV and AIDS pandemic, and whether they believe it exists and that, it is a killer. The youth's knowledge of the various reproductive health technologies will be explored and their attitudes towards the use of such protective technologies. It is the concern of this chapter, to delve into youth's use of herbs and traditional medicines and the possible effects of these on their reproductive health and health in general. Use of modern medicines, will also be examined in light of the variety of drugs now available on the public markets, like the popular Mupedzanhamo in Harare, a typical example of a street pharmacy, with reports in the media of expired drugs, even ARVs (Anti-retrovirals) which are for the suppression of HIV and AIDS, being available on the streets.

One will have to discuss issues relating to sexually transmitted diseases and their prevalence amongst the street involved youth. Of course, I will also focus at abortion as an important issue that can have serious repercussions on a girl or woman's health. It will also be important for one to look at how girls handle pregnancies on the streets and eventually where they go in order to deliver. The discussion will unfold taking cognizance of some of the prevailing views as echoed by, Green et al, (2000:585). They point out that women particularly those in developing countries, occupy a position characterized by social and economic disadvantage. They lack control of their reproductive health, compared to men and this can have a bad effect on their reproductive health. They go on to point out hat women as a disempowered group, lack control of their bodies; they cannot determine the spacing of their children. They cannot protect themselves from sexually transmitted diseases and the HIV and AIDS pandemic, (Green et al, 2000). "Street Pharmacists" refers to herbalist and all unregistered dealers in medical drugs who are also accused of marketing counterfeit medical drugs which could harm people.

7.1 *Boys appropriation of resources including girls bodies on the streets*

In order to get to grips with the power relations on the streets, one needs to realize that the basis of power on the streets is the control of the important resources for the youth's survival. The street is regarded as the main source of the youth's sustenance, and thus, those who control it, the boys in this instance, have power to determine the lifestyle to prevail on the streets. One female key informant actually said in confidence.

"We, *sekuru*, are not seen as humans on the streets by these boys. We are very oppressed. They don't want us to have our own money. They don't want us to be on the streets where the money is. We spend our lives here (at the bus terminus) selling cigarettes and sweets, which does give us very little profit. The boys are on the street where there is a lot of money. We depend on them for survival. They own us like their cows. We are their …"

She did not finish because one girl came to say that plain clothes municipal police popularly known as "*Velicencing*", (those who are tasked with the responsibility of ridding the streets of vendors), were arresting vendors. The girls quickly hid their commodities behind a stinking toilet. On many occasions I had wondered, how they could withstand such a pungent smell for more than twelve hours a day.

Another girl also said;

"Sekuru as we have always told you, these boys are no different from beasts. They should see us as their sisters but alas, to them we are like some piece of furniture, they sit on and do as they please".

I decided that I was going to involve more girls in this discussion, rather than individuals. One Thursday afternoon I had more than five of them around me. They were fuming about the ill treatment from the boys, as well as men in general, who seemed to regard them as rubbish pits.

"Men in general see us (our vaginas) as bins where all rubbish must be thrown. We are not human, we don't have feelings so these boys think"

Another had interjected shouting

> "Wait, wait let met tell sekuru. Sekuru, do you know that these boys sexually abuse us. We are not supposed to say anything concerning our bodies when they want to have sex with us. They say because they give us food and money, we have to avail our vaginas without any say. If you complain about the way they want to have sex with you, you can be beaten"

There was general agreement amongst the girls, that in order not to bring trouble upon themselves as one of them said;

> "Just open the legs and let them have the vagina they want. To be safe, I just say have it".

The others laughed, as she moved her body showing the sexual movements, of one offering herself for the boy's sexual gratification. The boys from general conversations with them showed that they owned the girls bodies with one saying;

> "These girls are ours, we looked after them, from the time they came onto the streets knowing nothing as to how to survive. They cannot teach us anything. We do what we want with them Big Dhora, We have sex with them when we want and they cant say no because we are providing all their needs".

The other boys had indicated they were in full agreement and there was uproarious laughter when one of them said,

> "We boys must be angry because the money we get and give them gets finished but their vaginas don't get finished"

I realized that from the way resources were controlled by the boys, no girl could claim sexual independence. That the girls were completely alienated from the street, had serious implications, when it came to their reproductive health as will be discussed below.

7.2 *Street Youth Knowledge of the HIV and AIDS Pandemic*

From general conversations, I learnt that despite the fact that there was no organisation working with youth in this area, they had some idea about the disease as one had said;

> "Big *Dhara* that diseases is for real. We don't want to pretend that its not there *Mudhara*. It kills"

189

During another discussion one boy had said

"One gets finished. Only the nose and the voice and ears remain Big *Dhara*. That disease kills *mudhara*. Some of us have died over the years. We are dying *mudhara* but *magunduru* will not change his behaviour *mudhara*".

I discovered that those who became very ill, would retire to a squatter camp popularly known as "Kuvarwere", (for the ill), along the *Mukuvisi* river. Actually I found from discussions it was a place where all sorts of vices were taking place and that is, where some of the dangerous street boys dwelt. Very few would be ill there. I thought it was a way of covering up this base, so that the police would not raid them. The ill obviously would not manage to run on the streets, in the event of a raid by the municipal police. I wanted to find out why they were not going to avoid unprotected sex, when they were dying and one had said;

"*Mudhara*, it is painful to feed a woman. You spend all your money on her and then you wear a condom - no (in street lingo they called the condom *"jombo"* which means a safety shoe).

I discovered that there were no myths on the streets about the disease amongst the street boys. They knew the disease was caused by mainly unprotected sex. One of the boys actually said;

"People must never lie that the disease is caused by infections through cuts, or blood from another person, or that those who get it are punished for their adulterous behaviour. That is a disease of the vagina," he said to much laughter from his peers".

In Shona he said, *"Chirwere chemhata mudhara"*.

They boys said that, they had been shown films and videos of people suffering from the disease when they used to go to a drop in centre in the avenues called, "Streets Ahead". The girls too showed that they were aware of the dreaded pandemic with one saying;

"Its not about evil spirits as some people want to hide the truth. Its about having many partners and having unprotected sex. But who listens to you on the streets *sekuru*. These boys will not listen to that, we will be beaten".

Another girl had also said;

"Some of us have seen people with the disease here on the streets. They have since died but a girl does not own her body as we once told you. We are just moving bodies of the boys *sekuru*, Do you understand this *sekuru*. No girl is herself".

The girls said that it was unfortunate no organisation was working with them on the streets, with regards their reproductive health and socially in general.

7.3 *Street youth perception of reproductive health technologies*

The girls showed that their knowledge of various reproductive health technologies was limited. They mainly talked of the visible technology as represented by the male condom. They did not talk of invisible ones such as depo provera, or contraceptives with one girl saying:

"Sekuru on the street we are disadvantaged because of our backgrounds of orphanhood. Also because of little education. We used to be given lessons at Streets Ahead but that was that. They should have made some health workers come to talk to us and listen to any problems we have on the streets".

Another girl had also said;

"People out there just talk about good behaviour and safe sex but they forget that all of us would want things to be like that but circumstances will force you to do what is dangerous"

Yet another interjected saying;

"On the streets its useless to even listen to such lessons. The girls have no say, have no power over their bodies *sekuru*. So maybe you can talk to the Minister of Health that all of us get injections to prevent pregnancy but this must not be known by boys. We will be killed on the streets by these rough boys".

I wanted to maintain relations based on honesty and decided to be assuring of my assistance, but at the same time realizing the need to tell the truth rather than make false promises. I told the girls that as I informed them from the beginning, I was only a university lecturer. I had no access to the minister but after the study, I told them, the report could get to some of the policy markers. One had interjected.

"Girls, even if he cannot see the Minister, he could talk to staff at Streets Ahead to make sure we get tablets especially or injections so that we don't become pregnant. Some of us are tired of aborting".

She said as the others laughed. When I responded by telling her that children were a precious gift from God, they burst into laughter, to show that abortions were the norm on the streets and one said,

"*Sekuru,* not on the streets, Sometimes you sleep with someone just for money and not their child. Its different when you do have someone who will care for both of you. These men just want to have sex only and they disappear".

There was much laughter when I talked about the female condom to show that, it was hard to come by. They had heard about it, but did not know where to get the condom. Again any visible technology could mean thorough beating. There were some misconceptions also. With one saying,

"We have heard of that condom but some were saying, it might be pushed into the stomach by the penis. Some of us fear we might end up being operated on, in order to remove it from inside"

Generally the girls seemed not interested in using this condom because of such a myth, apart from possibilities of victimization by the boys. About the male condom one said;

"Do you think these boys are civilized people, if any girl asks them to use a condom, she must know where to go that day. She can be beaten, The boys don't want to hear of such things," Another talkative one interjected making the rest laugh;

"They want flesh to flesh *sekuru.* One time when I, jokingly told a boy he had wear a condom, he said that he was not going to put on a *"jombo"* (Safety shoe) because the jelly inside the condom causes some rush on his penis".

The others laughed, for it was clear that it was just a way of denying to use a condom. The same girl had gone on to observe thus;

"What's surprising is that they know they sleep with the same girl and can contract an STI but they don't want condoms".

The boys had their reasons for disliking condoms of any kind, whether female or male. One of the key informants summarized the boys feelings thus;

192

"Big *Dhara*, you know that women are like children. If a man is not strong they can be very promiscuous. Women need men to control them. They will sleep all over knowing that they will not become pregnant".

I wondered though, because, they were still being forced to sleep with many boys on the streets. I thought this was not convincing, until he said as the others also confirmed later;

"The truth is that we want our money's worth, having sex with a condom on is like masturbating. When God created man he should have put the plastic on the penis"

Both of us laughed and he continued;

"Isn't it true *mudhara* that God wants it as it is - flesh to flesh?"

I told him that there is a problem of sexually transmitted diseases and the killer HIV and AIDS pandemic to which he responded thus;

"On the streets, we feel death is death. You die when your day to die comes. It can be a car accident, it can be murder, it can be from any other illness, death is death no matter the cause"

I had a group discussion with many more boys and had other discussions, with other key informants. From all these it was evident that boys were adamant they will not use condoms. One interesting response from one of the boys was that;

"I can't feed a girl only to masturbate into her vagina, without getting the real taste of the vagina. The vagina is tasty *mudhara*. You can start with a condom and you end up removing it"

The others had roared with laughter because In Shona he had said;

"Mhata inonaka mudhara. Haidi ma "condom", unopedzisira waribvisa".

The boys generally do not want to hear about condoms or even contraceptive tablets as one of them said.

"Kugaro dunga matablets kuuraya vana vari mudumbu" (Always taking tablets that kill their foetus in the womb is wrong)

He seemed to be condemning all women who use contraceptives and when I probed as to who the girls were, the boys around had laughed with one saying;

"Mudhara are you supporting murder by these girls. We don't allow them to use any such tablets here. Its not good to have sex with one you know will never get pregnant"

It was problematic to really understand what the boys wanted, because when I asked whether they wanted to have children, most of them said they did not want to have children. They preferred being "sexual poachers", that is sleeping with any woman as and when they wanted, even those who are in marital unions, as a way of avoiding being responsible for any children. A "sexual poacher" is one who does not have a stable relationship. Its street lingo to mean those who just have sex and run away as if to say, should the girl become pregnant, I wont be responsible. The problem on the streets is that the boys are very rough with the girls, such that no girl dares to talk about safe sex, more so because they depend on the boys for their survival.

7.4 *Use of herbs to enhance sexual excitement*

There is evidence of the use of various herbs by both boys and girls to enhance sexual excitement. The boys referred to a number of herbalists in the high density suburbs, who operate from a popular market place called *"Mupedzanhamo"*, which literally means, "your problems are finished". *The Sunday Mail* of 5 August (2007 p. m8), has an article on this flea market activities titled, *"Unique one-stop shop attracts customers from all walks of life; Mupedzanhamo a hive of activity".* The *Sunday Mail* reporter said everyone was welcome in this flea market's. All kinds of merchandise are on sale. These would include clothes, herbal medicines and illegal products. He says, "The illegal products include Diproson, Movate and Clear (Lotions probably so on the merchandise range is what the vendors call the best products for African beauty queens, Appetite capsules which are meant to enlarge breasts and bums". I personally went to this flea market on several occasions, just to take stock of the variety of merchandise and I also bought some tennis shoes because the products are cheap. The other time I bought three shirts. Of interest here however, are the other observations made by the reporter, in relation to the sale of various aphrodisiacs, because the street youth were also some of the customers. The reporter describes well these street pharmacists, saying; "At the far end of the market, different kinds of medicines are being advertised to customers," Hey, you! I mean you, wanna! Come here and see what I have for you. This one is good for you and your husband. These are called *mhere pamubhedha* (noise of excitement in bed during sexual intercourse). I will also give you this

194

pink one if your husband or boyfriend does not give you money".

The street youth had their own experiences and names of various aphrodisiacs. They gave some of the names as one key informant put it;

"There is *"mugara gunguwo and mudenhatsindi"*, These are quite good when you want to have several rounds with a girl especially those girls who want to pride themselves for nothing. Boys will want to cheapen them by fucking them too hard, too bad *mudhara* until they cry".

The other boys laughed and another had also said;

"Mudhara nyaya dzekukwira mustreet ndedze makwikwi ekukaurisa vasikana ivava. Ukasanyatso tushwetedza tunokuseka kuti hapana zviripo saka tichizoshandisa mushonga kuti inyatso mira mboro mudhara. Hatijaidze, tinonyatsotungidza zvebasa".

(*Mudhara* on the streets these girls compare you and if you don't fuck her too hard she will tell others that you are not a virile man). There was uncontrollable laughter from his peers. I realized that it was a game of fixing the girls, like the intention was to inflict pain. The boys however lamented the fact that it was difficult to know how much of the herbs they were to take at a time. The herbs were either put in coca-cola, a soft drink or in opaque beer but they were not sure of the quantity to take at a time. This I felt, posed a danger to their health and even to the reproductive organs, because if the penis became too erect they said it became painful. One actually said;

"Some of these herbs *mudhara* require that you immediately have a girl, not to take more than twelve hours or else you will have lots of pain as the penis will be very erect and cause pain. Some people also say too much of the herbs could cause high blood pressure and yet some of us take the herbs quite often".

It was evident from the sexual metaphors used by the boys, that they had sadistic tendencies in sexual encounters. They would say *"Ndakachibaya* too bad" (pierced her too badly).

"Nakachimamisa heavy "(I made her defecate meaning I fixed her)

"Ndakachibvarura" (I tore her vagina apart).

195

I felt such language encouraged the boys to seek for herbs to boost their virility so that they will have something to talk about to their friends. Girls really constituted an otherised, denigrated category. One girl had lamented thus;

> "*Sekuru ndinogaro demba chandakaitira musikana, apa ndiri nherera, Uri mukomana zviri nani*".

(*Sekuru*, I always regret why I am a girl and an orphan at the same time. It would have been better if I were a boy).

Girls use lots of different types of herbs compared to the boys, which I felt could have negative effects on their reproductive health. One of the key informants said;

> "*Sekuru* on the streets we mainly use herbs to avoid pregnancy. There are a variety of effective herbs from herbalists especially at *Mupedzanhamo* in *Mbare*, We buy them cheap from there. Most of us, we told you, are ashamed to go to hospitals to talk to health personnel. Moreso because we are of no fixed abode. They will know we are street girls and they will laugh at us. This is our problem *Sekuru* that people laugh at us and condemn us".

She as was confirmed by other girls, pointed out to some of the problems arising from use of herbs;

> "We have problems knowing if the quantities we take are the right ones. Sometimes you feel weak; sometimes you have stomach pains and headaches or even irregular menstrual cycles, due to these herbs. I personally at one time had several periods in one month lasting three days at a time when the normal one is about five days only. My fear is that these herbs might affect our health negatively".

When I talked to many other girls, it was the same view which seemed to be expressed with one saying;

> "We have real problems on the streets. *Sekuru*, we have the big problems of lack of access to proper reproductive health facilities. These herbs we use in the long run might damage our health. The problem is that no one seems to care to help us on the streets. We are not human beings to the authorities. We are not Zimbabweans. Even the police don't care how we live except to beat and harass us. We are not protected. If you dare go there with a problem they will tell you that street kids are a problem they must solve their own problems".

I did not want to be detracted from the real issue of reproductive health by explaining their relationships with the police, and I went on to ask what other herbs they used apart from those meant to stop pregnancy. We discussed the effectiveness of such herbs in stopping pregnancy and one girl had given her own personal experience thus;

> "*Sekuru* on the streets if you just rely on these herbs you might end up getting an unwanted pregnancy. We also buy tablets from Mbare. These are tablets you can put into the vagina from time to time and are sold by Nigerians. I use them and it is said that this weakens the sperms in the event of having a sexual encounter".

Another girl had made the following observations;

> "Some of us are afraid of using these tablets because no one has explained to us how they work. On the streets sometimes you just get the tablets from another girl's pockets and there is no explanation. Some girls are given these tablets by the men they sleep with. The problem is to know the real purpose of the tablets".

I thought they were right to be afraid, especially if they did not know what kind of tablets these were and their actual purpose, let alone the expiry dates. As will be shown below the boys also use tablets they just buy from the streets, or from Mbare to try and cure their sexually transmitted diseases.

7.4.1 *Dry Sex - A good Case of risking the reproductive health of the Street girls*

Some of the boys had expressed displeasure having sex with a girl whose vagina was just a *"gaba"* (tin). She would be too open and easy to penetrate with no friction. One of the boys had said, denigrating girls generally that;

> "*Tumagaba utwu mudhara. Vamwe vacho haumbonzwi kuti yapinda nokuti unongova mwena*"

(The girls vaginas are now like tins due to sleeping with too many men. You don't feel any friction when you penetrate their vaginas. They are useless)

The girls have found means of ensuring that the boys get excitement. They practise dry sex. This involves inserting herbs, into their vaginas. One girl explained thus;

197

"We buy herbs from *Mupedzanhamo*. Some of it is in powder form and soft, fresh leaves we squash and insert in the vagina. The *mukina* tree's leaves are used for a variety of purposes on the streets even to abort. (I was shown the leaves). We do this when we go to bath. Several hours are enough so that you won't get some itching inside the vagina. The vagina contracts such that when you meet a man he will think you are a virgin".

Another girl had interjected;

"These boys are primitive they don't know that the vagina is always wet, if he finds it wet during intercourse, they are unhappy. They can become violent and say give me back my food and my money. Its not fair *sekuru*, some of them are just cruel. If you use herbs there is a danger of being injured during sexual intercourse as the muscles of the vagina will be tight. There is no foreplay on the streets. They just behave like he goats (*sezvinhongo*). They just force their penis even if you ask them to do it slowly, if you cry out, that is what they want, they become even more vigorous".

I realized that such kind of dry sex was dangerous to the girl in that she could have lacerations on the inside of the vagina due to forced penetration. These cuts could mean the girl becomes vulnerable to contracting a sexually transmitted infection or they could contract the dreaded HIV and AIDS virus. To the girls, it was better if they had been born boys. One said;

"But *sekuru* don't you think from the beginning God had favouritism for boys (*Mwari vaiva nefevha)*", the others laughed and she went on;

"The boys who are rough to us, don't get wet. We are abused and we end up abusing ourselves due to fear. Don't you agree *sekuru*. It is the boy who dictates everything on the streets. They tell you I don't want this sexual position, I want it like this",

she said, with some body movements indicating the "dog style" in street lingo and the girls burst into laughter. I realized the questions were not meant for me as one of them responded thus;

"Iwe unofunga kuti Mwari mukadzi here. Zvanzi mukadzi zvinoreva kuti mutadzi saka tiri kure naMwari. Iye zvino kwave kutaurwa nezve kuti varume vasekamusaizwe kuti vasabate AIDS isu hapana anofunga nezvedu. Vanotoda kuti varume vavate nevakadzi hobho hobho. Handizvo here sekuru?"

(Do you think God is a woman. The word *mukadzi* (woman) means a sinner and so women are

198

in second position. Now you hear some people saying men must be circumcised so that they are not affected by AIDS and no one thinks of protecting women. It means men will sleep with many women without any fear. Isn't it *sekuru?*). I decided this would be an issue requiring some in-depth exploration and brushed it aside. On the streets I discovered that, due to the youth's interaction with people from dominant society in social and sexual networks, they were quite informed about the general feelings of people with regards politics, the economy, religious and health issues. I cannot explore some of these here. I found out that the street lingo used on the streets, was also used by the youth in mainstream society because one day during my study as I listened to the radio, I learnt that the youth in mainstream society, were dating through the radio and non were revealing their totems. I heard in one programme on reproductive health, one young man using the word *"sikon'o "*, street lingo for sexually transmitted diseases, and this made me realize that the street youth's lifestyle in a big way, reflected what was going on socially and morally in mainstream society.

The boys had no kind words for the girls use of herbs to ensure dry virgins. One actually said;

> *"Tunoitira varume vaye vane mari, isu tinongosvirana mudhara. Handisati ndambonzwa ane beche rakaite tight, kunyepa"*

(These girls are liars maybe they dry their vaginas so as to sleep with men with lots of money. Some of us find them to be just open without any tight vaginas)

They roared with laughter as another also came in to say;

> "These girls tell you lies Big *Dhara*, They are not saints. Take what they say to you with a pinch of salt. They bite the hand that feeds them". I probed as to what he meant and he elaborated thus;

> *"Isu tinopiwa mvura dzoga mudhara, topiwa sikon'o, topiwa AIDS. Tumapenzi twusikana utwu"*

(They don't dry their watery vaginas for us, instead they infect us with various STIs and even AIDS).

They laughed again. One of the naughty ones however had different opinions as he said in a braggish manner;

> *"Mudhara vana ava tiri kuva shungurudza. Tiri kuvachemedza especially sesu vamwe*

199

vanoto meka shuwa kuti mhata yakaoma or else they give me back my money. *Vanoshandisa mushonga kuti vave* dry its true Big *Dhara.*

(Old man we are really molesting these girls. We are making them cry and they have to make sure their vaginas are dry lest they give me back my money and food. They normally are dry when I have sex with them). On the streets I learnt that the word *"mhata"* which in some *shona* dialects meant anus was being used to mean *"beche"* which means vagina.

7.5   Street youth views on circumcision

There were conflicting views on this issue and it seemed to be a power ladden notion to the youth.   The boys were not quite sure as to their safety and protection.   One boy said showing some fear of the practice;

"Nyaya yekungo chekwa chekwa unenge warariswa nemushonga kuti usarwadziwe?". (when they cut off the fore skin do they give you herbs or medicines so that you don't feel the pain). Another had answered back;

"Don't you know the *varemba* (circumcision tribe) people who do it. I heard its done whilst you are very awake. You are being taught to be brave"

The others laughed and seemed to say that was not a good practice.   If the pain was not going to be suppressed, they would rather contract AIDS as one put it.

"We are having sex all the time without circumcision and not contracting any AIDS".

Another had also said;

"Vashaya zvekuita madoctors, vapererwa, chirwere cheAIDS chava shupa, vatopusa. Asi kana ndisingazobatwi nesikon'o ini ndingada"

(Doctors no longer know how to stop the HIV and AIDS virus. But if it helps to stop sexually transmitted infections I want to be circumcised).

There was general agreement that the practice was not good.   One who had tried to argue for circumcision was strongly reproved by the boys who were present, with one boy saying to him;

"Doctors want to make money through the circumcision. They will not be for free yet they are not circumcised themselves.   If you sleep with an affected woman, you will definitely die.

200

That doctor will be driving a posh car at your expense and will not even know that you died with a circumcised penis".

There was uproarious laughter and the boys said in chorus;

"What do you think big *dhara*?"

From the beginning of my study I had resolved not to take sides, in the various debates. I only responded if I had a factual answer, to convince all of them. Tot their question, I responded by telling them what they already knew, that there were studies by doctors in Kenya and South Africa, as they had read from the Zimbabwe Herald. These were experiments and what the doctors did during circumcision, I was not aware. I told them it was better to wait for the doctors results.

The girls on the other hand, had no kind words for such a development. I found out that they felt it was to their disadvantage as one said;

"*Iganda here rinondiitisa mimba kana kuti masperms, Ko Ivo wani vanoti AIDS iri muma fluids, neropa saka masperms anenge asisina AIDS here*".

(Is it the foreskin that makes a girl pregnant or is it not sperms. Sperms will still come out. Doctors say fluids including blood and sperms carry the virus and so how can circumcision stop AIDS). I realized there was confusion and that the development was still shrouded in mystery. The girls would have preferred a system in men, that would make them safe or protected them from unwanted pregnancies. Another girl had asked thus;

"But *sekuru*, as they do this to protect the men what are they doing to protect the woman into whom the man vomits *(kurutsira?)*"

The other girls laughed as I skirted the question with no specific answer and another came to my rescue saying.

"*Sekuru* is only trying to find out how we feel. He is a researcher as he told you and a sociologist. Is a sociologist a doctor (meaning medical doctor) the others said "NO" and she went on;

"It is for us to give him our views about what he asks",

The girls seemed to have taken heed of the fact that a sociologist had no answers to some of

201

these questions, and the debate had raged on, but without the sociologist being grilled with questions.

One of the girls had punctuated the debate with some skepticism saying

"Lets wait and see, but we might see the wiping of all women by this disease, whilst men remain, what world will it be like without women?"

I found it difficult to imagine what that meant. On the whole I found out that the girls were not in favour of male circumcision as an intervention strategy.

7.6 *Sexually transmitted diseases amongst street youth*

One of my key informants related to me of an incident in which a soldier who used to have sex with her on the streets, got affected by a sexually transmitted disease.

"*Sekuru* I thought that was the end for me. He was fuming. We had been sleeping together "short-time" for about a month especially on Friday nights whenever he was in town. He took me to a private doctor though as if he knew of my fear to go to a general hospital. He said he wanted both of us to be treated so that he could have sex with me knowing that he was safe. *Sekuru* (she laughed) I wondered how I was going to know I was the one who had infected him. Its difficult to ask these men of their other sexual partners. He also assumed he was my only partner which was wrong because he never paid *lobola* (bride-prize) for me and he only sees me when he likes and yet I eat sadza every day. Those who feed and protect me have to sleep with me. This is the problem. He was eventually transferred to a barrack in Masvingo and the affair died a…….."

The girls had harrowing experiences with one saying;

"I once contracted a painful STI. There were pimple like things on my genitals. These were very painful and caused much itching. It was like a rush but I never stopped sleeping with the boys. After all if you tell them such things they will not believe you, they will sleep with you all the same. *Sekuru* as we told you some of them don't care even if you are menstruating. They just want to ejaculate into the vagina".

202

The girls mentioned gonorrhoea as the most prevalent and easy to detect because of its puss like nature and offensive smell. They also like the boys talked, of that STI mainly characterized by sores or pimples. The boys also, talked of one they called *"Yemajuru"* (of termites) because one feels as if some termites were moving out through the urethra.

Boys had strong words of condemnation for the girls promiscuous behaviour. They really failed to realize that they were the actual culprits, apart from men from mainstream society. One of the male key informants said;

> "You see *sekuru*, these girls are rotten. Their vaginas most of them are stinking. You can smell it sometimes that this girl must be having gonorrhoea. The boys however also believe that a real bull is seen from scars. *(Bhuru rinoonekwa namavanga)* The main problem we have is that we cannot just feed these girls and not sleep with them. We have to sleep with them Big *Dhara*", he said laughing and continued;

> "As you heard the most common *sikon'o* which has affected most of us is gonorrhoea. If you have not suffered from this STI some boys laugh at you saying you are not a real man. And you don't know where the vagina is. This makes all boys want to prove their manhood, and we end up with these problems. The next common kind of *sikon'o* is that one which causes sores. This is also a problem".

From conversation and discussions, I found out that the boys are not going to change their behaviour. Like the girls they believed it was better to use herbs to cure the sexual infections than to go to some public hospitals. I felt this could be harmful as they would not know what quantities to take at a time nor the number of times to take the herbs. The boys called the herbal concoction *"guchu"*. The *"guchu"* I saw in one of the resting bases, was a two-litre plastic container full of water and herbs. That guchu I learnt, could be taken by any boy who suspected that he might have been affected by an STI. I thought that was communalism in practice, unheard of nowadays in dominant society. This had prevailed in pre-colonial shona society;-sharing as evidenced by strong kinship ties which no longer prevail. The spirit of individualism was planted and nurtured by colonization and urbanization. Even in countries where colonization never took place, but urban settlements grew, evidence of Western life styles characterized by individualism, are everywhere for all to see. In sub-Saharan Africa, there is massive literature, pointing to the weakening of the extended family as a good example.

One of the boys made an interesting point with regards their reproductive health saying; "You see *mudhara*, all people must know that as adults we are always mixing with many other people and having sex. If government does not provide us with injections from time to time the whole nation suffers".

I liked his global view of the problem, intimating the rampant sexual networking, they engaged in amongst themselves and with those from mainstream society, thus cutting across the social and racial divide. They pointed out that whites and coloureds too, were involved in sexual activities on the streets, as well as dogs. The youth were very open to say that they took their genitals as assets from which they could sustain themselves. It was not therefore rational for them, to think in terms of safety for the most important consideration to them was survival. This sounds quite stranger than fiction, and yet in dominant society such illicit sexual activities even with dogs also occur. I thought it was another area of specialisation that needed exploration. One could look at sexual behaviour in contemporary "normal society" the case of any of the major tribal groups.

One of the boys showed me a plastic container with about forty capsules and he said;

"These are from Nigerians who bring them from Dubai Big *Dhara*. They kill all viruses in the blood whether AIDS or *sikon'o*. They are used by men and women. We sell to our colleagues who are not clever enough to know where to get them. Some of the boys who had *sikon'o* have told me that after three days symptoms disappear. The problem is that one has to have enough food. You take these with food. You also must not take beer and these are problems"

I got worried when I realized there was no information on how to use those tablets. The youth could not know the expiry dates and the side effects or negative effects of continuous use of such drugs. There was no information about the drugs, not even the name. They just called them capsules. Abuse of drugs on the streets makes intervention, an urgent matter for the reproductive health of these youth is under serious threat.

7.7   *Abortion as a threat to the girls reproductive health*

One of the issues that caused much debate on the streets was that of abortion and who was to blame. I found out from both boys and girls that this was quite prevalent. Obviously, since the boys discouraged girls from using any form of contraceptives, and they did not want to use condoms, unwanted pregnancies were many. The girls were quite vulnerable on the streets in terms of their reproductive health, due to their weak position economically and lack of autonomy, in both social and sexual encounters. One girl narrated how she almost died when she had an unsuccessful abortion - the dead foetus remained in the uterus and actually decayed there;

> "*Sekuru*, these boys are murderers, real murderers, we abort because of these boys. They don't want to use condoms and yet they don't want children. They tell you if you have a child, it will be your own responsibility and they mean it. I can't get enough on the streets in terms of my own needs, and to think of having a child is unbearable. One has to abort"

On this issue I had decided to discuss in confidence with individual girls, but with the boys, it was an open debate. She educated me as to how it was done thus;

> "*Sekuru* we take water and put surf- the surf we use for washing. You mix with tanganda tea leaves - we use for making tea. You also put a bit of cement - the one used for building, it is very necessary for an abortion to be successful, but one has to know the quantity lest it causes some damage. When you have these in water, then you take leaves of the *Mukina* tree, which is found along *Mukuvisi* river. You squash the leaves using a stone on a pavement, so that the juice comes out into the water fast, one has to take this mixture late in the afternoon so the abortion takes place in the early hours of the morning the next day if there are no problems. One has to drink about 750 ml of the mixture at once sekuru. You have to be brave for this also means life or death".

She had told me of how a foetus had remained in her uterus long after it had died. She ended up in one of the referral hospitals to where she was taken by an ambulance, whilst in a critical state, due to complications two months after the failed abortion. Some of the girls confirmed this incident later, as I interviewed them as individuals. The girls also mentioned other herbs girls would buy from the open markets like, *Mupedzanhamo*. The risk to their reproductive health and their lives was quite real. One of them said;

> "*Sekuru*, on the streets aborting is like defecating- (*hazvina kusiyana nekumama*) because it is happening so often one cannot say the exact number of times. You should just know that, it is happening all the time. Luckily there are some amongst us who are now our experts. They help any of us who has an unwanted pregnancy. They are also the mid-wives on the streets.

You see some of us who are pregnant and have husbands on the streets. Those do not abort because the boy accepts responsibility. But they abort to avoid many children also".

The girls had lamented again the lack of health personnel who were keen to educate them on contraception on the streets. They said they would prefer invisible technologies like injections because these boys will not be able to destroy. The boys will not know they were using any contraceptives. One had actually said;

> "*Sekuru* if such injections could be availed to girls on the streets, we would want to be sterilized - never to bear any children"

The boys on the other hand were quite evidently disinterested in having children as one said during a group discussion;

> "*Mudhara* that issue is none of our business. If the girl is not clever she will be impregnated. *Anofanira kuziva zvinhu, hazvidi hope zvemustreet big dhara anoita vana hundred*".

(She must be a street wise or else she will have one hundred children).

Another had said;

> "*Mudhara* some of us don't want any children and that is why we are poachers. We just sleep with any woman and we don't want any stable relations. *Zvevana* (children), No! big Dhara No! (NO big Dhara No to having children in the street), he said emphatically as the others laughed, their lungs out.

I discovered that the boys literally hated having children, but the contradiction in their attitude was also confusing. They did not want girls to use any contraceptives. They did not want "plastic sex", No, big Dhara No, to condoms they always said. They wanted "flesh to flesh", and yet they did not want the girls to become pregnant.

When I told the girls that it was a criminal offence to abort, one of them, enlightened me on the issue thus;

> "*Sekuru*, that law cannot apply to us of the streets, because in all other matters no one cares about our welfare. Even if I am beaten by a boy and go to the charge office (Central police station), they chase me away like a dog even when I am bleeding from the nose, saying you

street kids are a problem, go and solve your problems alone. Amongst us aborting is acceptable behaviour. It is normal, there is nothing embarrassing about it, and we talk amongst ourselves as girls, as to the timing of the abortion."

Another girl had bitterly responded saying;

"Most of the educated women are aborting isn't it *sekuru?* only that no one knows about it because they go to their private doctors. Now if those with the means abort why cant a street girl do it. People are not honest because only the unfortunate are caught and punished but *"vana vemhene vanongo aborta pasina anoziva. Vanogona kuendeswa kunze kwenyika ndiani angaziva* (those girls from well off families can be flown out of the country to abort and who will know.) She went on thus, *"Sekuru nyaya iyi ndeye wapusa wapusa chaiyo"* She burst out into laughter, (*Sekuru* who is fooling who here in this matter of abortion).

7.8 *Pregnance management on the streets*

In traditional *shona* society if a woman got pregnant, elderly women would educate her on how to manage the pregnancy and what herbs to use. There were techniques a woman would be taught, as to how to enlarge her vaginal opening so that she won't have problems at child birth since there were no hospitals and the contemporary caesarean operations associated with the maternity wards. On the streets the girls were quite forth coming with information. One of the mid-wives who was a key informant had this to say;

"*Sekuru*, girls want to avoid the general hospitals by all means for fear they will expose themselves as the poor. At hospitals they will want to know many things, like your residential address. The name of the responsible boy or men, how much they earn, a lot of questions sekuru. We, some of us due to our circumstances, have learnt from some herbalists over the years, what to use as herbs for *"masuwo"* (vaginal opening herbs), and as a result we have not had any complications on the streets).

Complications have only occurred when girls abort. This is still a problem area. As to what herbs they actually used and other items she said;

"We use blue soap mixed with some powdered herbs called *"masvedzu"* (the slippery) from about five month of the pregnancy, to ensure the vagina stretched to the right size. We put in

207

our palms to measure every now and again whilst a colleague sleeps on her back. Usually we do it when we go to bath and wash at the *Mukuvisi* river. You heard from the girls that *sekuru Gudo* is the problem at the river as he wants to get to you whilst you are naked"

She laughed, as I reminisced on what Kelly (2004) had referred to as voyeurism, that is, the practice of watching nude people. She talked of the herbs the pregnant girl would also be given to chew all the time, to make sure the foetus is not affected by diseases whilst in the mother's womb. I thought health officials could exploit such indigenous knowledge systems to enhance health delivery, especially to pregnant women.

7.9 *Midwives of the streets*

Four girls gave birth during the time of my study. I did not witness the actual deliveries for coincidentally all were during the early hours of the morning. It would also have been also difficult to actually witness the mid-wives at work, due to ethical reasons. In our *Shona* culture one has to give something like money or a clothing item to show you rejoice with the one who has just given birth, *"makorokoto."* I happily did this, in all the cases, including one in which the father actually requested *"makorokoto"*, for his two year old son called *"Tanyaradzwa"*, (We have been comforted).

These births took place in a corner in the dark room, which is very filthy and has a bad smell of human waste and urine. To one from the middle -class, the resting base resembles a pig-stye. The place looks uninhabitable by any human standards. This is where they live. When I talked of the need for good hygiene as a way of provoking them to talk one mid-wife said;

"*Sekuru*, look at those two children playing there; {The two boys were about three years old), do you see them sekuru? (There was no way I would have failed to see them for they were just four metres from us). They have never been to a doctor. They have never fallen ill but they were born in that corner we showed you and they spend the nights there," She said laughing and went on;

"Go to any surgery you will find the well to do in long queues with their sick children, isn't it *sekuru*? Why is it like that when they have good food, sleep in nice houses and on beds. It is God *sekuru*. He cannot allow us to suffer more than this. Don't you think *sekuru*".

The youth were fond of asking me questions, not because they expected answers from me, but maybe to ensure I was listening to all they were saying.

Another had explained how exactly they assist their colleagues to deliver;

"We buy gloves from *Mbare' Siyaso or Mupedzanhamo*. Siyaso means leave us alone and it is the name for popular market place where a lot of informal activities take place. Some say the name meant were to stop harassing those who operated there. We know it is important to ensure good hygiene. We quickly wrap our dresses around the new born or even our heavy jackets. We then wash later because we don't have the towels and the dishes on the streets. We wipe off the blood and we also tie the mother's umbilical cord nicely and insert it back into the mother. We also nicely tie the navel of the baby", she smiled and said, "so you see sekuru some of us can work in any maternity hospital, we then give our friend plenty of food".

The midwives however noted that there had been several natural abortions amongst the street girls. They had managed to keep the situation under control, without going to any hospital, and one of them observed thus;

"We know how to stop blood from oozing out, we know a lot of things *sekuru*. We can use herbs."

7.10 *Breast feeding on the Streets*

The suckling mothers revealed it all. One of them actually said;

"*Sekuru* this is a bouncing baby only six months old, I suckle and give her nothing else. I intend to suckle her until she gets to two years because of lack of foods on the streets. No children ever suffer from *kwashiorkor* here on the streets"

Another with a one year old baby however had something to convey as she said;

"Wait, *sekuru*, I am already having problems from my husband who says I must wean this baby because she can eat *sadza* now".

When I asked why they were going to do that, she laughed and then said,

"I haven't been having sex with him because we feared it might affect the child and the child might die"

One of the mid-wives who was close-by actually confirmed that, it was part of their training to abstain from sex as long as they were suckling but had a different reason from the one I had heard since time immemorial that the baby's milk will be polluted and the baby will die,

She actually said;

"The nutrients in the baby's milk will become lessened in the event that the mother becomes pregnant. This will affect the health of the baby".

I thought this was important knowledge just rotting on the streets. Another girl said;

"The problem with our husbands *sekuru* is that they cannot wait not to have sex. *Tanzwa nemabarika* (we are tired of their adulterous ways), *Kune* masmall house *sekuru muMbare umu* and we fear AIDS", (There are other women waiting to take our husbands in *Mbare* and we fear HIV and AIDS).

Small house is a Zimbabwean expression popularized in the early years of the 21st century. It refers to any other woman with, whom a married man has a love affair, as well as sexual relations. The girls I discussed with were quite bitter that some husbands were not prepared to wait as they did when suckling their babies. They would always sleep with other women. The mothers however did not believe, these fathers adulterous behaviour would bring a bad spell upon the suckling baby, as had been the thinking in traditional Shona society. They were more afraid of contracting STI's and the dreaded HIV and AIDS pandemic, and also to lose their husbands to other women. It was generally agreed that once the baby could eat other foods, they could have sexual relations as those foods would act as supplements in the event the mother got pregnant.

The girls with husbands showed that they only wanted at most two children. They were quite assertive with one saying,

"*Tumwe ndinokanda mutoilet sekuru, handidi maproblems*" (Some I will throw into the toilet, I don't want many children they will give me problems).

She literally meant to flush them into the sewerage drainage system. This happens and it reminded me of an incident that happened at the University of Zimbabwe where I teach in 2005. A foetus was found to have blocked a drainage pipe. Obviously, the most likely culprit was one of the female students. Cases of baby dumping are also quite prevalent in the big cities today in Zimbabwe, and one cannot rule out street girls as some of the culprits.

7.11 *Conclusion*

The story about the lived experiences of street youth in relation to their reproductive health above, may be aptly summarized under the sub-theme "appropriated bodies and suppressed souls of the girls". The girls from my research were found to be worse off in terms of threatened reproductive health. On the streets, it was evidently a simulation of the unequal relations between men and women in mainstream society. The boys are an empowered and privileged lot, compared to their girl counterparts, as they control the only resources for survival on the streets, i.e. the street and food. Girls have no say in sexual encounters at all, and cannot negotiate for safe sex which endangers them in terms of their reproductive health. In order to please the abusive boys and men from mainstream society, the girls engage in the dangerous practice of dry sex, which can cause lacerations or cuts inside the vagina due to forced penetration, thus exposing them to the HIV and AIDS pandemic.

The boys don't want to hear about any contraceptives on the streets and yet they don't want to have children. Girls are forced to engage in dangerous practices in order to avoid unwanted pregnancies. They use a variety of herbs without any specialist advice. They can suffer permanent damage to their health from use of such herbs. Some drugs that are brought onto the streets, they use to insert in their vaginas, could affect them negatively. Those drugs I saw in circulation had no names or even instructions as to how to use them, let alone expiry dates. It was difficult to ascertain whether these pills or capsules, were genuine or counterfeit. The girls are forced to abort which can be fatal as evidenced by the case of one girl whose dead foetus remained in the womb for some time.

The boys, who are very promiscuous, are also at risk of damaged health due to abuse of drugs and herbs. They are always suffering from STI's due to sleeping with the same girls as they claim to be vagina "poachers". The youth especially the boys believe the various local drugs can cure any disease including HIV and AIDS as was discovered by Zamberia (2007) when he

211

carried out a study involving university students in Swaziland. The issue of circumcision was criticized by the girls as a strategy to protect the boys and men in general, and as a way to encourage men to be promiscuous knowing fully well that they wont contract HIV and AIDS. It's the girls who become exposed to the virus so circumcision empowers men at the expense of women, they argued.

I learnt that the girls had much knowledge of indigenous ways of managing miscarriages, abortions, pregnancies and even post-partum experiences of the partners. One can only propose that health programmes be designed to incorporate these groups. Doctors could find out why these youth and their children who live in filthy conditions, are quite fit, compared to those from proper homes in the suburbs.

CHAPTER EIGHT

THE "STREET FAMILY" AND THE DECONSTRUCTION OF THE CONVENTIONAL PARSONIAN NOTION OF A FAMILY

8.0 *Introduction*

The tragic aspect of the story of the street children, herein referred to as the street youth, is well evidenced by the emergence of the street family. The establishment of this institution must be a cause of serious concern to the nation as a whole. It follows logically that the street population, which could have been permanently removed from the streets, is going to steadily increase and the street becomes the only known home of the children born on the streets. The ones who are now having families on the streets are better in that, some of them can trace their roots to some rural home and relatives, but it is frightening to imagine human beings without any kinship roots, in our society.

This exposé is meant to conscientise society of the growth of the "street family." I focus at how such families came into being including issues of dating and courtship on the streets, for marriage rather than just for sexual pleasure. It would be interesting to see how such unions contrast with the traditional shona marriages or unions, as well as other sexual relations prevalent on the streets. Religious issues that have tended to be the bedrock of marital unions in traditional marriages, characterised by placing importance on virginity and totems will be explored. The story will go into the details of how men and women or husband and wife, relate during coitus and the role of each. For example, women were expected during and after coitus to praise the man, (*madanha nechidawo*). They would have a special cloth with which to clean his penis after the encounter, as well as to clean their genitals.

I will also look at the sources of conflict in such unions of the streets and some of the strategies for resolving the disputes. Polygynous relations popularly known as "small houses," will be exposed as well as use of love portions in some marital unions. I shall discus the aspirations of the parents for their children and their fear of old age. I will show that marital unions of the streets in a big way, are a simulation of the unequal power relations in families in dominant society. It was evident that sex roles were in existence in these unions, with the husbands being the bread winners, whilst the "wives" cared for children and washed clothes.

8.1 *Dating and Courtship on the Streets*

In traditional shona society marriage was a sacred institution shrouded in mystery, as it was linked to ancestral spirits, (Bourdillon 1976, Shire 1984, Aschwanden 1983). Much literature shows how the process of marriage was not an individual affair but a matter of concern to other kin like uncles and aunts. In such societies they had encouraged marriage to those within one's neighbourhood for very good reasons, *(Rooranai vematongo)*. This would mean fear by either party to engage in any antisocial behaviour that could bring embarrassment to themselves and to other relatives. Such kinds of marriage or families reinforced the existing relations within the social fabric. (Aschwanden 1983, Bourdillon 1979, Nyathi 2000). On the streets it is really a different kettle of fish. Dating and courtship do not take time, as was the case in traditional times, but evidently are always initiated by the men. In traditional society, dating and courtship could be initiated by other kin even without the knowledge of the man, who could then be told by such kin, that they had initiated the courtship process for him. In modern times during colonial times, if he were working in the city, the other relatives could give a photograph of the man to the girl they were proposing and by the time he visited his rural home, a girl could be waiting for him. Dating and courtship were characterised by perseverance as a sign the suitor was serious. A classic Zimbabwean example is that of the late Vice President of Zimbabwe, Simon Vengai Muzenda, who wrote his wife-to-be a proposal letter and she took more than two years to respond, but he says he was determined to win, - eventually he did win her.

On the streets one of my male key informants who is married had this to say;

"Big *Dhara* on the streets, it's about who you are. The girls are told of the boys who are aggressive and notorious like some of us. The girl needs protection from both physical and sexual harassment on the streets and must quickly get a man. She must not fall in love with a coward because what you heard last time could happen to them whilst in coitus. The likes of *Sekuru Gudo* can just come and push off the husband and get on top of the woman" he laughed and said;

"You might not believe this but you can confirm later even with the girls. If they fall in love with a man who is not feared by the other boys the relationship will not last as she will be

214

forced to sleep with the stronger guys"

I thought this really epitomised the rule of the jungle. To the Street Youth however, that was the normal way. It was not about romantic love but a survival strategy. The girl needed protection and a sense of security in terms of material provisions. The dating however had some similarity to traditional ways as one "wife" said;

"When I got to the street, Bridget (not real name) and others, told me after a day or so that they could not continue to feed me. I had to find my own man who could provide my needs. They suggested to me one naughty boy. He became my husband but only for six months as he was arrested and he died in remand prison. (She had gone on) -

"The first days Sekuru for a girl on the streets are very tough because you won't be knowing the boys very well unlike now. The girls encouraged me to love another boy but again after a few weeks he disappeared due to clashes on the streets amongst the boys. He went to Chegutu until I fell in love with *"Baba va Tafara"* (The name of the son is, "We Rejoice".

I discovered that on the streets there was dating, as boys approached the girls, but it was the other girls who helped the girl to know the boy to have a relationship with, one who would be able to protect her. It was not based on love of an individual boy, but the need to have someone who would be able to provide for the girl's needs. One girl said;

"On the streets you have no choice. The boys demand that you love them and if you spurn their proposals they will force you, so you need a strong, feared guy for protection."

I thought this was not different from the arranged marriages in traditional society, although these would be based on the sentiments of the other kin. The need for a sense of security in marriage was also there. With colonisation and urbanisation, girls would prefer men who were now working in the growing towns. On the streets however, the relations are instant, in that if the girl has been told of the boy, she starts sleeping with him. For the girls of the streets no girl experiences any romantic affair.

One girl said;

"Sekuru on the streets it's not like in the village or in the location where you can play hard to get. Here on the streets it is quite rough. You have to sleep with the boy once he starts giving you food or money. If you refuse he will force open your legs and it's not embarrassing at all.

This is how it is done here on the streets. He gives you food, you give him your "vagina", she said laughing. I thought this was not very different from what is now happening in mainstream society. Women were quite vulnerable and were looking for man who could provide   for their needs. Survival sex was also evident in mainstream society.

They would sleep with such man as a way of winning them over. I was reminded of the women who are aptly called "gold diggers". They fall in love for material benefits - they look for the well to do who are even terminally ill, so that if they die they inherit part of such man's estates. In traditional society from literature review, one finds that a boy and a girl could spend years dating each other and when they eventually fell in love, they would wait until the actual marriage process had been finalised, in order to have sexual relations. Of course nowadays things have changed in that one finds that women are also initiating dating through the internet and other forms, for example, through both the print and electronic media.

8.2 *The Street Marriage*

When I tried to find out how the girls distinguish between those who just want to have sex and those who want to marry them on the streets one girl said;

"It is difficult to know in the beginning if the relationship will last. This is because the behaviour of these boys is the same. There are as you heard, mostly "sexual poachers", who just want to have sex with any girl for fun and they disappear. Those who ended having families talk of having children. The problem however is that all the boys hate contraceptives and condoms as if to say we must get pregnant, but the poachers will tell you that if you get pregnant, it's your own fault".

(A "sexual poacher" is street lingo for one who sleeps with any woman, whether they have a husband or not and also prostitutes. "Poacher", in Zimbabwean language, with regards wild life issues, means thief so these boys are "sexual thieves".

I tried to find out why the boys and girls felt their unions were marriages and one boy said, as was confirmed by the girls later;

"There is no payment of *lobola* (bride-prize) but the girl with my child is my wife. She sleeps with me only and we are husband and wife, as the others on the street know. If she sleeps with another man, then she will be inviting death not just trouble" he said laughing.

I wanted to really know why he claimed that she was his wife when he had not done anything

216

apart from impregnating the girl. I was really surprised when he gave me an answer that demonstrated his knowledge of current legal affairs;

"We are above 18 years. You know Big *Dhara* that nowadays we are allowed to live together and be recognised as a family".

He was referring in an expert way to the provisions of the Legal Age of Majority Act, of 1983. This Act was meant to empower women who had been regarded as minors despite being above 18 years of age. They were considered as minors and could not inherit their deceased parents' estates or even to marry without the consent of their parents. The street youth know some of the legal enablements of the Act, despite being semi-literate. Out of interest I had probed the boy as to the source of such knowledge and he said;

"When we were at Streets Ahead, they used to tell us that, after we turned 18 the law said we were adults and the institution was not going to care for adults. They told us we were supposed to look after ourselves and even to marry for the law allowed us"

I talked to his wife who also expressed similar sentiments adding thus;

"Some of us grew on the streets and as I told you I lost both parents when I was about eight years of age. They had lived all their life in squatter camps around the city and survived by brewing illicit beer you know as "chi one day.""

I established that to the youth this was a marital union and each party had specific roles. The wife was to bear children and wash clothes. Those with wives, tended to be the oldest and smartest of the boys. The husbands would provide food and money.

When I tried to find out from some of the "sexual poachers", how they perceived such relationships, the boys demonstrated their knowledge of traditional systems with one saying mockingly;

"*Mahumbwe mudhara*", (that is childish play). Who can claim to have a wife *musango* (in the forest) like this. Big *Dhara* those wives of theirs are also ours, after all they did not pay any *lobola*".

There were several of these boys around and they started laughing and arguing amongst themselves with some saying, "*Vakadzi vevanhu mhani boys*" (They are married), whilst others insisted there were no wives on the streets, because the marriages or unions had not been solemnised by any Pastor. One actually said;

"Those are our girls too. If you have a child with a girl, it does not mean she is your wife.

217

No. We are sleeping with these girls all the time and they have other men, so how can someone say they have a wife"

Another interjected causing uproarious laughter;

"After all it's the "poachers" who impregnate most of those girls. *Hauzivi here mudhara kuti zvekubira, zveganyabvu ndizvo zvinonaka. Ndizvo zvinogutsa vakadzi vemustreet ava.*"

(Don't you know that the rough riders easily impregnate these street women). I was now confused as yet another interjected

"*Mudhara* the children are ours. The ear of the child is mine, the eyes his, the nose John's, the feet *Sekuru Gudo-*",

The boys burst into uncontrollable fits of laughter and I could not restrain myself. I did not want to say biologically that was incorrect, because it would have stifled discussions unnecessarily.

So, these are the street marriages. There is a biological mother and one boy who claims to be the biological father, although from the preceding conversations, I had with the boys, it emerged that the men would rather claim to be social fathers if paternity tests had not been done.

The girls too expressed in confidence the problems of fatherhood on the streets. One key informant who is married said;

"Life on the streets is not like what you know in a proper home, but even in proper homes what husband can be sure of the paternity of the children. *Mai ndivo vanoziva baba vevana sekuru,* (It's the mother who really knows the actual father of a child). It is worse on the streets because sometimes you can be forced by circumstances to sleep with another man when your husband is not there. These husbands of ours sometimes just disappear or go to other women we call "small houses". They are very naughty so you see, it is difficult to know the actual father but we just give to the one who claims to be the husband."

8.3 *Marriage, totemism and virginity on the streets*

In traditional society the three issues were intertwined and inseparable for a happy, recognised marriage, (Shire 1984, Aschwanden 1983). Virginity was prized. If a girl got married and was a virgin the husband gave the in laws an extra beast, as a token of appreciation *(mombe yechimanda)*. But if she was no longer a virgin it was an embarrassment to the girl's family as possibilities of being returned to her parents were high. If not sent back all the same, the husband's family had a way of showing their displeasure. They would cut a hole in a blanket or cloth to show that their daughter was no longer a virgin. On the streets the girls had this to say;

"Virginity is unheard of *sekuru*. I told you I was raped by my paternal aunt's husband. Even though, I was no longer a virgin as I had already slept with a boy I was learning with at primary school when I was in Grade seven. This is the problem *sekuru*, things have changed. Even in society virginity is no longer important because where I come from, I can't remember of cases of virginity tests which was done a long time ago. Girls no longer prize themselves being virgins but otherwise some girls will laugh at you as being backward."

I had a general discussion with a number of "wives" of the streets, for literally all the girls have husbands but some don't have any children because they don't trust the boys will take good care of these children if they were to have them. One of them had made others laugh when she said;

"*Nemagora iwaya ungaite virgin rekwaani mustreet. Sekuru munotamba imi. Vanenge vachadya mhata nemuromo ava vakomana ava.*" (With these vulture like-boys, there is no way one could be a virgin on the streets. The boys like the vagina so much they might eat it).

The girls laughed as another said;

"*Sekuru*, you don't eat your virginity, that is one important thing. You die on the streets. Even if you come as a virgin you would have to quickly choose between death and life."

The others laughed and it became clear that there were no virgins with one arguing like a member of the ruling party in Zimbabwe's league thus;

"*Ko ivo vakomana vacho mavirgin here? Ivo ndivo vakatibvisa uvirgin hwacho*" (Are the boys virgins? They are the ones who broke it and so they can't ask for it).

The women's league refers to women who belong to the ruling party in Zimbabwe. Most are gender activists and very critical of men's traditional behaviour. They always question why women should be expected to behave in some ways to please men and yet the men are not expected to do the same. The other girls laughed and concurred with her views with one again saying;

"Men are the same whether on the streets or in the homes"

There was much debate amongst the boys on the issue of virginity with one saying;

"*Mudhara* that is a difficult question. Someone can just claim and yet he could be lying. You see this is the problem with this act which is between two people and in a hidden place. I myself have never had sex with a virgin and I don't value that". Another had interjected,

219

"Ko iyo mhata isiri virgin hainaki here mudhara. Mukadzi ivirgin kumunhu one, anomuvata first. *Vamwe vose tinongonakirwa wani nemukadzi iyeyo".* (The non virgin is still sweet. Virginity breaking can only be done by one person. The rest of us who have sex with such a girl, also have much fun and enjoyment).

The other boys agreed that on the streets there were no virgins although one cautioned thus;

"You say that because you only get *"magaba".* (those no longer virgins whose vaginas are like empty tins).

There was uproarious laughter and yet despite that observation, the boys seemed in agreement that virginity was not important. Actually one had no kind words for such girls even in dominant society. In street lingo he said;

"Mabhambi ayo asingazive zvinhu, vanobhowa," (They are the backward type who are boring and I wouldn't want to have such a girl).

On the issue of totemism, again I discovered that a new generation of the totemless was emerging on the streets. Slowly totems which had been revered by our ancestors as a linkpin between the dead and the living was being demystified by the emergence of a totemless quasi-tribe of the streets. It was evident amongst both the girls and the boys, when I enquired as to their totems in groups. The girls had shown that totems were not important, for some of them had not been told such things by their deceased parents. In shona traditional society, marriage or sexual relations with one of the same totem was generally discouraged. If for example, one was *Shumba Murambwi* (of the lion totem) then the other had to be *Gumbo* (leg totem) or something else like Tsoko *(monkey totem).* Some could marry of the same totem though, but those of the *Gumbo* totem, would not marry at all, it was taboo. Belief was that, it could bring misfortunes upon the pair. They could bear children who were albinos or who were physically disabled.

One girl actually said;

"I for example grew up on the streets. I was born in a squatter camp. I don't have any living parent. It's meaningless to me".

Yet another said;

"We don't eat totems and we don't even know what they were meant to do. Today these are meaningless".

The boys were not agreed when I had a discussion with them. Two groups emerged one saying totems were important. These were mainly those who had spent some time in the rural areas. One actually said;

"All people belong to an ancestral group *(Dzinza)*. No one can say they don't have a totem although we don't ask each other about that".

He was however cut short when another interjected saying;

"You are a poacher and you are now lying to this old man. Do you ask the prostitutes their totems? Be honest. You don't. We all don't. You don't even know the girls' totems here on the streets; do you? Big *dhara hapana nyaya apa*, he is lying (Big *dhara* there is no issue to waste time discussing)."

It was generally agreed that totems were not important anymore. One boy had gone on to open another pandora's box, when he wondered whether the married wives would accept being called by the man's surname. The boys had generally agreed that it was important for the woman or wife to accept because it was traditional. I wondered at such contradictions. At one time they would condemn tradition; at another they would want tradition and praise it. One of them even appealed to the bible thus;

"Even in the bible God said a woman was to leave her people and join the man's people and change her surname."

The other boys seemed happy with that and I thought it was because it boosted their egos. The girls however had different views. They argued like the feminists who are critical of men's status and domination of women with one of them saying;

"*Sekuru* on the streets I think that should not be. I remember one of us had a quarrel with her former husband who would call her by his name. The girls know of that incident even the boys do, and from that time we call each other by our first names or by our children's names. I don't belong to any man. So why should I change my name. Personally I don't want. Fortunately, my husband is not fussy about that."

The others felt it was unfair for them to be called by a name of a man whose relatives they did not know. They argued that names had nothing to do with sexual relations at all, and were of no consequence for their well being on the streets. I wondered whether society was aware of these developments, where those who claim to be married were now not interested in their husbands' names. One had punctuated the debate thus;

"*Sekuru* some of these traditions were unfair. Why can't men be called by a woman's surname also. Things have changed *Sekuru*, women now become Presidents, women wear trousers, women are in the army, women play soccer. Lets combine surnames of husband and wife into one, Moyo and Shumba would become Mashu.

She made the rest laugh when she said further;

"Women must be on top of men in coitus".

This kind of thinking did not seem weird to me. Even the boys seemed to think along those lines for I remembered what one boy said during my first days on the streets, whilst scolding another on the streets. He said;

"*Mai vanosvira mboro.*" (Your mother fucks the penis).

This was said in my presence and there was much laughter from those around, as the other said;

"I am lucky because I don't have a mother."

Generally, one discovered that, although in my case I was a citizen anthropologist, in many ways I was an outsider, because under normal circumstances such things would not have been mentioned in public, more so in the presence of a father figure.

8.4 *Patriarchal tendencies in street families*

Despite seeing divergence from the norm in many ways especially amongst the girls, the boys who were married tended to exhibit patriarchal tendencies in many ways. One obvious one was that of jealousy, and strict monitoring of the movements of the "wife". That wives were dominated just as in mainstream society was indisputable. The wives were completely controlled and had no freedom to engage in activities that could materially empower them. The husbands were the "bread-winners", who spend the day on the streets, doing a variety of income generating activities. The wives spend the day at the bus termini and were invisible as Dube (1999), also discovered. It is taboo for girls or wives to be on the streets. The street is the preserve of the husbands. It is interesting to note that the wives don't look for food. It is done by the husbands. They are just given the food and at the end of the day they go to their resting bases, where the "wives" are expected to provide sexual services.

A Visit To A Street Family's "Home"

One of my key informants, became my confidante who would even accompany me to my office at the University of Zimbabwe. We became very close although at one time he stole from me.

He tore off about three leaves from my parking discs' booklet and I discovered it. Apart from this incident, he was quite a likable character. The wife also became very close especially as she helped to put me into contact with other girls of the streets. I had given her quite a substantial amount as *"Makorokoto"*, for her two year old baby. I think this made her to like me.

One afternoon my request was granted. I had requested to visit his home. I had some bit of money and had bought him some opaque beer, which he had demanded because he was going to lose income as Friday afternoons tended to be busy. We were however going to be back but not with the wife, who preferred to remain at the home. The home is a shack close to several other shacks on the fringes of the city. He had bragged as we arrived at his shelter thus;

> "Some of us have homes *Mudhara*. We are not just drinking beer without planning for tomorrow. See, this is where I live not in the kopje buildings where they are crowded and they have sex in a crowded place,"

He laughed and I joined him as he went on;

> "Unfortunately you are too big, Big *Dhara*. You won't be comfortable getting inside because it's low and small but you have seen where I live"

It was a plastic shack maybe nine square metres in area. I could see when I bent down some dirty blankets on the ground which served as their bed and a bag of clothes. He boasted about his wife who responded smiling showing the couple got along very well;

> "There are clothes in that bag Big *dhara*. I have property, my wife washes my clothes and I am not as dirty as the others. I don't have a mother. My son is now my brother,"

He said laughing as we sat down on the ground close to the shack. He was preparing to drink his beer. I had given the wife a bottle of fanta which she preferred to drink after we had left.

The shelter is in a secluded, bushy area I can't mention for ethical reasons. This report might be read by people who want to remove these youth from the streets and it would seem as if I will have sold out my respondents. At night I imagined it would be dark and quite a no go area for the weak hearted like myself. There was an anthill with holes and I imagined seeing a big snake coming out of one of the holes and move straight into the shack whilst they were asleep. The husband then summarised it all;

> "I am happy. I have a home Big *Dhara*. I work on the street for my family. They have food

and clothes. You see my bouncing baby son *Mudhara*. He doesn't know a clinic. My wife, doesn't know a clinic and you can see I look after her. *Tarisa figure mudhara* (Look, she has nice buttocks).

We all laughed including the playing small boy who grinned imitating us.

He explained how he had tried to marry on several occasions but alas there had been problems until he got the current street wife. There wasn't much in terms of cutlery because I learnt that nothing was cooked there; he said

"*Hapadiwi chiutsi pano, saka taka survivor Murambatsvina. Ndiwe mudhara wandada kuti uone upenyu hwemugunduru. Vamwe vanhu vanofunga kuti hatifungi, tiri mbavha*" (We don't cook here, no smoke strictly because that will sell us out, that is how we survived the big raid and clean up operation by Government, called *Murambatsvina*-Operation Restore Order which the street youth referred to as Operation *Murambavanhu* (Operation Reject your Own People).

There were several shacks in that bush and he told me they were all deserted during the day. To me it resembled a classic example of an urban village. I thought there was need for one to carry out a study on the real relations in such a settlement. I brushed this aside as my present concern was just to see their home.

The wife told me on another day, that her problem was that the husband sometimes went away to high density suburbs to drink beer and does not come back. In such cases she has no option but to look for other men. She was quite frank saying;

"*Sekuru,* these men of ours who are not known by any relatives *(varume vemudondo)* are a problem. They are used to sleeping with many women as sexual poachers."

I thought these were the likely sentiments of most married women in dominant society. The husbands would be bragging to be the best on earth, only for one to discover the opposite being the truth from the horse's mouth.

I thought of the **Parsonian** notion of the nuclear family and found this one being worlds apart, nuclear yes, it appeared, but members, both husband and wife, had other sexual partners. In legal jargon this was a family in the true sense of Zimbabwean law. But, none of the two parties seemed honest with the other. The expressive function of the **Parsonian** housewife, was not evident as both spend the day on the streets. She only did the washing of the husband's clothes

224

and caring for the child. Parsons himself never visualised a family outside a "home", on the streets of a city or town, spending its life on the streets vending and scavenging for food. I thought this was a real deconstruction of the Parsonian notion of a nuclear family.

8.5 *Marriage and Lovers discourses under the blankets*

Having established that a number of the married youth had shacks on the fringes or the outskirts of the city, to me they had shelter or a roof over their heads, under which sexual intercourse occurred. I was keen to know if those with totems ever mentioned each other's totem during those encounters. According to Shire (1994:157), during sexual intercourse husband and wife would talk to each other. The woman tended to praise the copulating man profusely by referring to the man's totem in full. Shire refers to this as "lovers discourse under the blankets," and takes the example of the shiri (bird totem), of the *Hungwe* people. Their totem, or masculinity, which is regarded as shameful in every day speech, is a good case in point of the social construction of deviance in that, the street youth's use of vulgar language is regarded as deviant behaviour. Here, we see that adults in dominant society, would use language that is obnoxious during coitus, unacceptable under normal circumstances. Shire (1994:157) says, "However, there is nothing shameful about that language, when it is used to praise *Shiri* men for their sexuality. The sexual organs masked by metaphors in other areas, are openly praised. It is not regarded as obscene or pornography when those men praise themselves as *"Machende eshumba - - muranda wemheche"* (Lion's testicles - - slave of the vagina). Shire goes on to say that although *machende* (testicles) and *mheche* (vagina) are regarded as course words in everyday language, women mention them after sexual intercourse to praise the man, what he calls *"madanha emugudza"* (totemic discourses under the blankets).

In praise of the *ngara* men (porcupine totem), women would say, *"Vakapfura dombo nomuseve rikabuda ropa,"* (those who pierced the rock with an arrow and drew blood). The penis of these men is likened to an arrow, so sharp and so rampant that it penetrates through impossible obstacles, (Shire 1994: 154). The *gumbo* (leg totem) would be praised thus, *"Madyira panze, chitova, waGutu museve, chipazha mongo* (those who eat whilst outside as if referring to testicles, of the penis that ejaculates sweetness into the vagina). I caused much laughter amongst the girls, when I asked them whether they would praise their men after intercourse. It was just a general talk involving a number of girls. I also wanted to know whether after sexual intercourse,

225

they cleaned off the fluids from the penis of their husbands. One of them jokingly said;

"Sekuru ini ndini ndinonaka, handizvo here? Vanobuda rute vazukuru venyu ndivo vangatonditenda" (Uncle, I am the one who is actually sweet, isn't it? Saliva drools from your nephews' mouths during intercourse because of excitement. They should thank the woman and praise her).

The girls burst into laughter as another showing much ignorance of all this said;

"Sekuru mune musikanzwa imi"

(You are naughty uncle), and the girls burst into laughter again. The discussion was punctuated by one who said;

"There is nothing of that sort because we don't know each other's totem on the streets. We don't even ask each other about that".

As to who cleaned the other's genitals, again there was much laughter as one said;

"Ah Sekuru kubata chinhu chemurume, No, hazviite better kunzwa yavamumba mayo" (Ah, uncle I won't handle the penis, I will just feel it when it is in its house meaning the vagina).

The girls said that it was unheard of; to clean the man. They were not aware of such things.

The boys seemed to be aware of such actions, because one of them actually said that they had read vulgar things from wall hangings, sold in the streets on which were written various totems which were sold by vendors. This was a true observation for they are there on the streets with details of how the discourses were to be said. All totemic praises are there. They however said that on the streets, there was no such discourse because they did not consider totems to be important and most of them did not have any totems. I told them that all Zimbabweans had to have a totem. All had totems including the youth on the streets but the unfortunate thing was that no one had told them. The boys laughed about being cleaned after sexual intercourse, with one causing uproarious laughter when he said;

"Handibatwe mboro yangu nemukadzi ini, Kungobudisa, - mubhurugwa straight ndorova pasi." (I don't want a woman to touch my penis, I remove it from the vagina and put it straight i.e. quickly into my pants).

There was more laughter when one of them said;

"Boys *taurayi chokwadi hatina ma* underwear" (Boys say the truth we don't have under pants). We all burst into uncontrollable fits of laughter.

226

8.6 Polygynous relations and Love Portions - and the case of "Small houses"

The girls in marital unions generally were a disgruntled lot. They were bitter that their street husbands were philanderers. One actually said;

"Taneta nekuparikwa nevakomana ava, varume vedu ve mustreet"

(We are tired of these husbands of ours polygamous tendencies). Yet another had said to me;

"Sekuru kunyange ndisina zvakakwana nemwana, akawana mari anoenda ku "small house" dzake somewhere"

(Uncle I don't have enough provisions for myself and the child, yet he goes to other women).

Small house is a Zimbabwean expression, street lingo for a love relationship with a married man. I did realise from this that the street girls really regarded themselves as married. They were no longer just street girls, but wives and mothers who needed to reign-in on their husbands. Generally, the girls or wives were not contended with the treatment they got from their adulterous husbands who regarded them in street lingo as the "bigger house", *vahosi.*

One of the husbands said to me

"Ma Bigger House mudhara haagutsikani, Anonetsa"

(Our real wives of the streets are difficult to please. They are a problem to us). He was referring to the fact that there were quarrels quite often on the streets, as a result of the "wives" jealous. He had gone on to say;

"You see *Sekuru* sometimes you give them money and food, and you go to have fun with others even for two days. When you come back there is real war. She thinks I was at a small house", he said laughing and when I probed as to why he would go for that long, he said;

"Tirivarume ka isu mudhara, heh, handingango fariri muriwo whani ka Big Dhara, murume anochinja usavi"

(I am a man mudhara, heh, I can't have the same relish all the time, real man change the relish), he said laughing heartily I thought here was a clear case of patriarchal thinking and evidently a case of the construction of masculinities, pointing to the unequal power relations prevalent between "husbands" and "wives" on the streets.

The girls on the other hand who were in marital unions, had ways of "fixing" such errant husbands. One of the ways was also cheating by the girls. They would sleep with other men and when I told them it was adultery during a general discussion, one of them had said;

227

"Sekuru yangu ndiyo inobikirwa sadza here iye arere nemumwe mukadzi. Ini handimiriri izvozvo. Maki iyi pahuma kutemwa tichirwa awana ndisipo muna 2004." (Uncle my vagina does not eat *sadza* (a thick maize-meal, Zimbabeans staple food) whilst he is having sex with other women. See; this mark on my forehead, it is a result of a fight with him in 2004).

The other girls roared with laughter as she went on;

"Sometimes we have tried to use love portions from *Mupedzanhamo* and these sometimes do not work. You just waste your money."

Another had said;

"Uncle some of us stay in shacks in bushes. You can't go there alone. You can't go there with another man. We really have problems."

When I probed as to what they do in such instances, there was laughter from the girls as one of them said;

"Sekuru, we are grown ups, we see what to do. Surviving on the streets this far, is not a joke, one has to be street-wise"

Another was more explicit;

"Sekuru sometimes you have sex here on the streets, in some dark place with a poacher or you go to those buildings you were shown in the Kopje, where most of us stay. That is *Sodoma* and *Gomora"*

She said as the others again burst into laughter.

When I expressed fear for their health due to the HIV and AIDS pandemic, the girls seemed unperturbed by the prospect of dying from the disease. One of them emphasised;

"Sekuru, we told you, we know about the disease but the situation on the street forces you to indulge in unprotected sex. As you see we are still quite fit. It seems we are surviving or are we carriers *sekuru*?"

She said as they all laughed. Another married on the streets had also interjected.

"Sekuru on the streets, we are at the mercy of our husbands. Even if we don't sleep with other men, they will still infect us as they sleep all over. So *iwafa wafa sekuru"*

(The weak will die *sekuru*).

The girls (wives mainly), believed that it was fair that they be left to do as they pleased. The boys were very jealous and harassed them all the time, even for no apparent reason especially when they were drunk.

8.7 Conflicts in Street Families

The areas of conflict I identified were over multiple sexual partners, with the wives accusing their husbands of being irresponsible. The husbands would also accuse their wives of cheating with one of the boys saying;

> "Big *Dhara*, these wives of ours are a problem. They make unnecessary demands, although we try to give them what they need in order to survive. They seem not to appreciate *(havagutsikani)*."

Another husband had said;

> "These girls always quarrel with us demanding to do what they want, but who can allow a wife to just roam all over the place like a stray cow? There are hyenas here *mudhara* on the streets", he laughed.

The husbands did realise that their wives were unhappy that they spend all their life on the streets at the bus terminus. One wife had lamented thus;

> "There is noone to tell of the oppressive nature of these husbands of ours. They do what they want and go where they want. We are like prisoners although we sometimes escape. But if you are caught cheating, you can be harmed by these cruel husbands of ours."

The wives also were bitter that the husbands did not allow them to use the various reproductive health technologies.

One of the wives complained bitterly saying;

> "*Sekuru*, these guys have no money but they don't want us to use any contraceptives. It's an area of concern to most of us and is an area of conflict because they oppress us."

The other wives had concurred that they wished they could have contraceptives, which are safe for their health rather than continue to use herbs they were not sure of their side effects. The husbands on the other hand, insisted that the wives had to be at a safe place in the city rather than be on the streets where raids could occur anytime and they risked being removed from the city by municipal authorities. Again this was an area in which the construction of masculinities was quite evident. I also felt, this really was a simulation of the relations between men and women in mainstream society. One of the husbands with reference to the use of contraceptives said;

> "It makes our wives prostitutes. We don't want our wives to use tablets. How will we know that they are not cheating us by having sexual relations with other men? No, Big Dhara, my wife will never use those things."

One might think it's a stupid way of controlling a wife, who after all cheats, but this is how most men in dominant society, who argue against the use of contraceptives think. They might be actually having adulterous affairs with married women, but they don't want their wives to have other sexual partners. To me, what was happening on the street was an eye opener in that, I realised that although people in mainstream society saw the street involved people as different from themselves, in many ways they mirrored relations in dominant society.

There was an interesting case of conflict that included other kin of a husband. The husband who was one of my key informants, had a mother who was a former squatter in Harare. Widowed, she had managed to get a piece of land in *Domboshava*, where she now lives with several of her daughters who have been divorced. I was mainly interested in the issue of conflict in this case. The boy told me of how he had gone to *Domboshava*, to inform his mother that he now had a wife. The mother had been happy and asked him to bring his wife and child to *Domboshava*. He decided to leave the wife there and the child and his intention was to eventually establish his own home there, so that his son could grow up in a good environment. So that he could get a good education, unlike him who had only done Grade four in Epworth. After his father's death, the family had become destitute with no source of livelihood, forcing him to go into the streets. His plans were scuttled when his wife arrived on the streets after three weeks, complaining bitterly because of the ill treatment she got from the mother in law and her daughters. She summarised the problems to me thus;

> "*Sekuru*, it is true that *vamwene* (mother in law) and *muroora* (daughter in law) don't stay well together. They treated me like a slave and sometimes, I would see they were gossiping about me and laughing scornfully. I did not feel safe and I decided to leave. What really irked me was a comment by one of the sisters that, my son resembled me, not them not even their brother. I could not stand such attacks."

The husband went to *Domboshava* and there was a real war with his mother and sisters and from that time none of them went to *Domboshava*. I realised that some of the youth, had relatives with whom they had been in constant communication, although most were really double orphans.

Generally, I learnt that in the event of fights and quarrels between husband and wife, no one would be involved in defusing the conflict as one said;

> "If you go to the police when you are beaten, they will tell you that *magunduru* are a problem,

you must solve your problems alone. So we just get along after our fights."

One husband also said;

"In the street once our quarrel is over, it is over, life goes on, because *hapana wekuchemera, Unochema ukanyarara*" (there is no one to cry to, you cry until you are tired and you stop on your own)

Generally, the couples were getting along very well. I have to be honest, I was impressed by some fathers who would come to the terminus during my presence and talk nicely to their wives, give them food and briefly play with the children, in the case of those who had children. They seemed to love their children, which made me desire to find out what these parents aspirations were for their children.

8.7.1 *Caring for children on the Streets and parental "Great Expectations"*

The children's movements are quite restricted on the streets because it is not like the open spaces found in most residential areas. Generally there were about four or five children at a time depending on the movements of the mothers. One of the mothers actually said;

"We are happy God blessed us with these children. I have two. One who is three and this two month old girl, a boy and a girl. As you can see, they are well dressed all the time. The father tries to provide their needs and I also try whenever I get an opportunity to make money"

She said with a smile as if to imply illicit means of getting money, like cheating the husband from time to time. When I talked to another mother she also said;

"*Sekuru,* it's good to have a child because you know that you have someone to care for you in old age. If God keeps my son and he becomes a man and starts to work maybe he can look after me."

There was no reference to the father. She seemed to think of herself and the son in future and when I probed as to why she was not including the father, she said;

"These men of ours are naughty. You never know if they will still be alive. They are criminals, they are reckless with life. Most of them die in remand prison. You have heard that."

I told her I was aware of three who had died in remand, during the eight months I had been on the streets.

From time to time the husbands would come to see their wives. It was during some of those

231

times that I actually witnessed the fathers having fun time with their children; Like teasing them, making them laugh or caressing them to show their fondness. Some of the times, it was quite touching to see how they expressed their love as they would be giving their children some goodies to eat. These varied, sometimes it would be an orange or an apple or some sadza and stew. My assumptions before going to the field, that the young ones would be in pathetic states of need and being malnourished were not confirmed. Rather the contrary proved to be true, with one mother saying.

"These guys love their children. We can't say they love all the same, because if it is a boy they tend to have special fondness for him than for a girl."

Those who were also there hummed in agreement. I thought those were patriarchal tendencies evident in mainstream society, where if a man does not have a son, the wife will continue to bear children, such that she may end up with a big family, as the wife tried to get a son to please the husband. The girl child has traditionally been seen as second best, to the boy child who traditionally, was the heir to the family estate in the event that the father died. Such thinking however has been dealt a death blow, by the plethora of legislative provisions starting with The Age of Majority Act of 1982, which empowered the girl child and women in general. They are no longer seen as minors at law but socially, there are still problems endemic to patriarchal societies - women and girls are not accorded equal status in communities. I tried to find out on the streets whether the "wives" observations were true. One of the husbands said;

"Big *dhara chokwadi chakanaka mudhoni weboys ndizvo. Gero riri bho but inini I am happy mukadzi wangu akatanga neboys.*" (Big dhara, the truth is that a boy is better. A girl is also a child but I prefer a boy first.)

Another husband also said;

"*Vamwe vanoti mwana mwana vachinyepera vanhu mumoyo vachida boys. Isu vanhu vatema unobva waziva kuti mhuri iripo. Vasikana akawanikwa zvatopera musha wako wafa*".

(Some people don't say the truth in public. They lie to others when deep down they prefer having a son because the family name continues to exist but with a girl it's the end of the family when she marries).

As to their plans for the children, the responses expressed much uncertainty. One of the *mothers said;*

"*Isu sekuru tinotonetseka kuti vana ava vachazoveyi kana vakasadzidza. Sekuru zvinotyisa*

232

kufunga nezvazvo. Baba vacho vaiti tichanotsvaka pekugara ku Epworth kuitira kuti mwana wedu apinde chikoro as isu manje hatina mabirth tose"

(We, uncle, are in a dilemma as to what to do with our children because there is no school on the streets, yet we want them to be educated. The father says we will go to Epworth one of the high density suburbs, to live there so he can go to school but the problem is that both of us have no birth certificates).

In formal school birth certificates will be required and I thought this was a real problem and yet most seemed unperturbed. Most of the street youth don't have any form of identification. The problem is also that, especially with those who were born in squatter camps, they don't have information of the names of their parents. They spent most of their time on the streets as young children and so this I thought, was going to be a new generation without any form of identification.

Another mother was equally worried and said;

"Some of us are like this because we were not able to get good education. I really become afraid to think of a future with uneducated children, who will also grow on the streets. *Sekuru*, your question brings pain in my heart. What do you think I do sekuru?"

She managed to continue though before my response;

"I wish the report you write could bring change for us. We are also human beings and it's not possible not to bear children, when we are having sex. What does Government mean when they don't seem to plan anything proper for us and our children. *Sekuru* please be our ambassador."

Like in past cases, I had to be honest and ensure I never raised the youth's expectations unnecessarily high by making false promises. I told her that my wish was that they also could go through the report, because it was about their lives so they checked if what I had written was a true story of their lives on the streets to which she said;

"I can't read much English."

One of the fathers had this to say about the future plans of the children on the streets;

"Few of us seem to think about this Big Dhara. The truth is I had never seriously thought about this, but as the child grows, I see myself moving off the streets to settle in one of the high density areas, so that my child can go to school."

When I asked him what he expected his son to become he quickly said;

"Lecturer like you, so he can earn lots of money."

I did not want to discourage him by telling him lecturers were getting poor salaries.

Another father had said he wanted his son to become a doctor and the girl child to become a nurse or a teacher. Yet another father said he wanted his son to be a pilot. The mothers too had high expectations with one saying she wanted her daughter to become a President of Zimbabwe, so she could address the problems of the poor. She actually said

"Haangazomboregi kugadzirisa nyaya yehurombo iye akura mahuri. Anotogadzirira vana mai vake upenyu hwakanaka uye hapana angazogara mustreet".

{She would not leave us in this kind of poverty. She will have the poor's problems at heart since she grew in poverty and will be forced to address the plight of the poor on the streets).

When I told the mothers that the government was planning to take them to some homes, one of which was the First Lady of Zimbabwe's Iron Mask Farm, one said;

"They want to take us to farms when their children are in town, *hazviite"* (It does not work) Another had joined thus;

"Kuda kuti itisa chibharo mumafarms avo. Isu tofa tichirimiswa here navana vedu ivo vagere zvakanaka"

(They want us to do forced labour on their farms so they become even richer staying in the city with their children whilst we die in destitution.)

The husband had no kind words for the government in general and such projects;

"We told you this is our work place. We won't move out of the street. We will die here in the city not on a farm Big *Dhara hazviite ngavakanganwe."* (We wont go there)

The others around concurred, saying in order for children to get education they were going to have make-shift shelters in areas close to high density suburbs, from where they will walk into the streets to do their work on the streets whilst their wives were at those homes. The questions really provoked much debate and a lot of emotions directed at the government, the city authorities and society in general. One "sexual poacher", obviously without family commitments, made all present laugh, when he said whilst in a drunken stupor;

"Muchamama vafana. Taikuudzai kuti muchaita sei nevana ava"

(You are going to regret. We used to tell you not to have children in the streets - what are you going to do with these children as they are growing up,)

8.8 Today's Parents, Tomorrow's Grandpas - wither the street generation

As I spent days and some nights with these youth, I wondered whether they were having time to think of themselves in old age and how they will spend their days. One of the boys said and I thought he was right;

> "Big Dhara isu tiri "mazhing-zhong", tiri mafeki, hatisviki 50 years isu tose. Iyezvi vamwe vedu vari kufa nezvakasiyana siyana. Vamwe vanofira ku Reeds (Remand prison), vamwe ne AIDS, vamwe vanorobwa vaba vofa. Ini hangu Big Dhara handifunge nezve kuchembera".

(Dhara we are not as fit as those of your generation. We are dying very young. Some of us just don't think of old age because we don't expect to reach such an age).

'Zhing-Zhong' is street lingo for Chinese merchandise, which flooded the Zimbabwean market from 2000, and is associated with counterfeits, not genuine quality products. Another key informant who has been on the streets most of his life said;

> "Big Dhara on the streets there is no time to think like that, but since you want to know let me say, I hope things will be OK in 40 years time. Ask why Big Dhara".

And I probed as to why and with a smile he said;

> "Ma war vetereni ose ari kupiwa mari mahara anenge afa saka tozopiwa isu mavetereni omu street". (All veterans of Zimbabwe's liberation war who are being given pensions by the government will be dead. We will be given that money as veterans of the streets)

There was an uproarious laughter and some clapped their hands. This was none other than Sekuru Gudo. Some were actually praising him saying Nyamuzihwa - - some Sinyoro --- some Murehwa - - to indicate his claimed multiple totemism.

The girls were also equally uncertain. The girls sentiments were summarised by one who said,

> "Sekuru if wishes were horses, beggars would ride. If I could get money and buy enough stuff to operate a well-stocked vegetable market, I will go and live in the high density suburbs. My problem is cash."

I made them laugh heartily when I asked them why they were not marrying those "mhene", (well-off men), whom they had sexual relations with from time to time and one said,

> "Sekuru most will be married and no one really wants to marry a former street girl sekuru. We are associated with bad things and some of us have no known relatives. Because of traditional

235

beliefs, no sane men will want to live with us, fearing what could happen in the event of our dying".

The youth seemed to be in a quandary as to their well being in old age, with some hoping to graduate or as Muzvidziwa (2004) puts it, "to climb out of poverty", and go to live in the high density areas. It seemed to me just a pipe dream, for the tragic thing which had happened to them, was to have been left on the streets, until they became "husbands" and "wives".

8.9 *Conclusion*

From the above narrative, it is quite evident that the "street family", is a new form of family which is legally constituted, as per the provisions of the Legal Age of Majority Act of 1982. In many ways, it is constituted differently from those families in mainstream society and yet in another sense, it simulates the unequal relations between men and women in dominant society. Differences with the mainstream society family, are mainly that no other kin are involved and no *lobola* is paid because these factors are still important despite the Act cited above. Actually, there is much conflict in dominant society arising, from the Act's implementation. Totemism is very important in mainstream society, which is considered an obsolete idea or practice by the street youth. Courtship in both dominant society and on the streets is still initiated by the men although latest developments in mainstream society, show that women are dating for marriage through both the electronic and print media.

Virginity is not prized in both mainstream society and on the streets and promiscuous relations or adulterous relations tend to prevail in both dominant society and on the streets. Women's movements are quite restricted on the streets by the jealous of the men, who are the "bread-winners", whilst the wives only do the washing of their husbands' clothes. Women or wives have no autonomy on the streets. They don't have any decision making power in all aspects of street life including their reproductive health. It is the street husbands, who dictate how they live and thus the street wives are an abused lot sexually and physically. They are generally provided for, together with the children but the husbands are polygamous in nature, which draws the meagre resources that could have sustained the street family. The story of the street family can aptly be described as a "tragedy of lives," Musengezi and Stounton (2003), as these mainly totemless youth population, is growing as children are born and eventually the government and the city council authorities, will realise that procrastination is a real thief of time. The streets are

236

already dangerous to stroll along at night and even during the day. Already gone are the days of romantic exchanges in the Harare gardens, by those from dominant society, for the possibilities of being mugged or even being murdered by unknown assailants are highly likely. No one can go into the city centre to do window shopping with their wife or their girl friend, for chances of being mugged, embarrassed, robbed or even killed are quite high. This is really the tragedy of procrastinating to resolve this street dwelling problem by society. Society is already paying dearly.

CHAPTER NINE

SEXUAL VIOLENCE AND PHYSICAL ABUSE OF THE STREET GIRLS: A GOOD CASE OF THE CONSTRUCTION OF MASCULINITIES

9.0 *Introduction*

An article in, *The Herald* (of Zimbabwe) of 8 August, Wednesday (2007:1), captures vividly the tone of my discussion below. It was on the front page of *The Herald* and titled, *"Man blows self to death with explosives"*, and briefly read, "The Mining town of Mashava was left in shock, after a man blew himself to death with high powered mining explosives at the weekend, following a heated domestic dispute with his wife, over the discovery of tablets for a sexually transmitted infection in their bedroom."

The unfolding story of violence against street girls of the street will mainly focus on sexual and physical abuse. One has to realize that the purpose, is not to expose the street youth behaviour for condemnation, for worse things could be happening in mainstream society, but rather, to conscientise society of the fact that, in many ways the street youth behaviour, reflects the dominant patriarchal attitudes of men towards women. Men construct myths around their manly or masculine behaviour, shrouded in traditions of antiquity, in order to keep themselves in control of and superior to women. What will be evident is that, the boys regard some traditions as obsolete and yet cultural norms that justify their behaviour, are observed strictly, especially those giving them control of the girls movement and behaviour. Women and girls of the streets, are an otherised lot and the story below clearly shows the relevance of the social constructionist paradigm, in analyzing the sexual and social relations between the boys and the girls on the street.

I will focus at how the boys perceive sexual relations as "fucking", as fixing the girl which to me is some form of violence. This is characterized by force and is not romantic, as evidenced by the sexual metaphors used by men which imply the inflicting of pain on women. Forced sex is rampant which is in legal jargon rape and gang-rape. Girls have no autonomy or any say in such sexual encounters and thus have no power with regards their reproductive health. Fighting and conflicts have arisen on the streets, due to attempts by girls to use the various reproductive health technologies. Girls have no freedom to move as the boys do and if they are discovered to be cheating, which I regard as some form of agency by the girls in order to survive, they are beaten.

To me the girls are a "quarantined" lot, as they are confined to the bus terminus, which in street lingo they call the *"danga"*, that is the base where girls are supposed to spend the day. The boys have freedom to do as they please, because "the street is for men" *(Mustreet ndemevarume vakashinga)*, as boys used to say. Girls, as will be evident in the discussion and narratives below, are bitter that the boys dominate them, exploit them and abuse them.

9.1 *Power differentials as an indicator that, on the streets "anatomy is destiny"*

Boys' low perception of girls in general to me, seemed an important factor in understanding the attitude towards the girls. The boys think in traditional terms as prevails in mainstream society and yet in many ways their behaviour including the vulgar language they use, is anti-tradition. This kind of contradiction in behaviour, justifies my social constructionist conception of the conflict between the boys and the girls. For example, I probed during group discussions why they were not mixing freely with the girls, now that the government of Zimbabwe had legislated for women's empowerment. I had told them that the government's desire was to see men and women being equal in all spheres of life and that is why women, were now a prominent feature even in the uniformed security forces. One of my key informants commanded all the others to keep quiet and said;

"Big dhara some people think we don't know what is happening."

Another had tried to interject saying;

"Be to the point, don't just make us keep quiet",

The others yelled at the latter to keep quiet and the former said, as if to gain assurance of support from others;

"Guys, do you think it's possible to be equal with these girls. I think the government must have better things to do than to waste people's time, talking about women. Women are women naturally. Men are men. Men have a penis and women a vagina. Can these be equal? Who goes on top of the other, *Mudhara anokwira mumwe ndiye mukuru* (Old man he who goes on top of the other is more important).

239

There was uproarious laughter as the others clapped hands and he went on assured of the others support;

"Although we live on the streets it does not mean we are equal with the girls. They can't run, they can't do what we do. We actually feed them and look after them like our children so they must be ruled by us."

Another loquacious drunkard said;

"*Ini handienzaniswe nemunhu ane mhata, hazviite, mhata imhata, mboro imboro.*" (I can't be seen as an equal of one with a vagina when I have a penis.)

I was reminded of the essentialist paradigm which basically argues that due to biology women are inferior to men because another had said;

"*Mustreet mukadzi haasevhaivhe Big dhara. Munoda dhodha sibili.*" (On the streets girls on their own would not survive).

I realized that, generally the boys regarded girls' anatomy as destiny and believed that girls could not challenge the boys in any sphere of life. The one quite evident being that of coitus, where the boys believed penetration was the sign of women's subordination, for the vagina could not penetrate the penis. The debate was so heated that I began to appreciate why the girls were being looked down upon, and that the boys believed in subduing the girls, no wonder why most sexual encounters on the streets were characterized by force and aggression.

On the other hand, the girls were quite bitter about the way boys treated them on the streets with one of my key informants saying, to the laughter of all those girls around;

"*Vanofunga kuti mboro dzavo dzinoshamisa vakomana ivava. Vanozvida zvokuti unodemba kuti chandakaitira musikana. Havatione sevanhu, vanoti harasa* all the time *sekuru. Mustreet hapana anobhadhara* rent (the others laughed again), *ini murume wandinaye haana kunditora kumusha kwangu, ndakauya mustreet ndoga* but *anotoita mhata yangu seyake, chinhu chake, zvinoita here sekuru.*"

(They think their penis is very important, they are very proud and sometimes as a girl I wish I was a boy. They objectify us and harass us all the time. No one pays rent on the streets but they claim to own the street. My husband did not pay *lobola* to my parents and is not the one who brought me onto the streets. He however, claims I am his as if he owns my vagina.)

Another girl had also protested thus;

240

"What is special about being a man. All human beings are important. We are the same. We are going to show these boys one day that they must not abuse us."

I wondered what she meant and she went on;

"One day cross, -- *ticharonga kungobva mustreet kana kungoita strike against them, kuti hatichadi kukwirwa navo, hatichadi mari yavo, hatichadi chikafu chavo sekuru.*"

The others laughed showing it was a grand plan. (She had said that the boys had to be aware that they were not fools as they could organize a big strike on the streets against the abuses by the boys. They could refuse the food, the money and even to have sexual relations with the boys). Yet another girl had made an important observation saying,

"*Isu taneta kuitwa sevasungwa, senhapwa nokuda kwekuti tiri vasikana. Hapana vanhu vanoziva nhamo yatinayo. VeStreets Ahead takaneta kureporter kwavari kurobwa nokurepewa kwatinoitwa mustreet*".

She made others laugh when she said;

"*Vamwe vavo futi vange voda kutorara nesu ikoko*" (We are fed up of being abused yet society ignores us. We made appeals to Streets Ahead, (which is a drop-in-centre where they used to spend the day when they were under 18 years of age but they got no joy and in fact some of the officers there wanted to have sex with them).

When I explored the issue of officers wanting to sleep with them one of them said;

"*Zvakatoitika, mumwe mudhara akabatwa airara nemustreet girl akadzingwa basa.*" (It really happened, that an officer, an old man, was found to be sleeping with street girls and was relieved of his duties).

I was reminded of Chaucer's "*if golde rusite then what will happen to iren*" (If gold rusts then what will happen to iron).

9.2 *Use of Sexual Metaphors as evidence of sadistic tendencies - a form of violence*

Language is an important indicator in the construction of social reality, Berger and Luckmann (1966), because it is through language that important behaviour patterns are communicated.

241

Jensen (1998), for example, explores the use of the word "fucking" and associates it with the American male psyche characterised by denigration of women and their sexuality. The sexual metaphors men use have been described even by Barker (1998), as loaded with notions of masculine superiority, leading to what they refer to as "patriarchal sex." This kind of sexual behaviour, is characterized by the objectification of women, regarding women as sexual objects. Also sexual encounters are perceived as situations to demonstrate virility and superiority over women, which borders on aggressive behaviour. Sex is conceptualized by the boys as occasions to fix girls, who are supposed to bear the consequences for being looked after by the boys.

When I discussed with the boys, how they perceive sexual encounters, I was left with the impression that, this was a form of violence against the girls. One boy said;

"*Ini ndinomekashuwa kuti ndanzwa kunaka kwemari yangu. Ndoda yeshure, kuti ndinyatsochimamisa.*" (The girl has to ensure I get my money's worth from the sexual encounter. I want the "dog style" because that one really fixes her).

There was no element of romance or love in his language but rather, it depicted the nature of "sexual fucking". Fucking can also mean physical abuse like, "I will fuck you" or verbal abuse like "mother fucker." The boys generally used very vulgar language to denigrate the girls. Expressions like "*Ndoda kuchibvarura*" (I want to tear her apart), "I want to really hit the vagina too bad" (*Ndoda kumuridza kutsiva mari yangu. (Ndoda kuchichemedza.*" (I want to make her cry) not with excitement, but this had an element of inflicting pain. As a researcher sometimes, I would get angry with the boys but then I would quickly realize that, that was not my reason for being on the streets; to be an advocate of the girls. I realised that it was my world colliding with that of the youth, making me feel I was more of an "outsider". One of the boys actually described an incident thus;

"*Ndachipa mari yangu chimusikana chimweni mazuva okutanga mustreet, ndakazoita chokubhevhura makumbo kuti ndichisvire chichida kuramba.*" (During my early days on the streets one girl I had bought some goodies, tried to lock her legs and I forced them open and had sex with her).

The girls confirmed that sexual violence against them was quite rampant on the streets with one saying;

242

"Mustreet sekuru hamuna love. Every time *unotoita zvekumanikidzwa. Ukati kwete zvenge wati nhasi ndikwire kakawanda. Vakomana vedu vemustreet sekuru vanongoda zveganyabvu. Bvunzai vasikana, zvinenge zvokukaurisana."* (In the street uncle, there in no love. It is forced sex all the time. If you say today No, it seems as if you have asked for sex several times. These street boys of ours always use force. Ask the other girls, the sexual intercourse is like some form of fixing us.)

Generally, the girls were of the opinion that if they had options they would demand better treatment, but they had no other means of survival on the streets, as their activities were determined by the boys. The boys were in control of the important resource - the street; from where on a daily basis, they got reasonable income, unlike girls who had no other income generating activities, besides selling of sweets and cigarettes. One girl actually said;

"It's only when you are lucky, to sleep with a member of the public who is generous, and some give you lots of money once in a while."

I realized this was some form of agency on the part of the girls. This was a survival strategy despite risking being beaten if caught. One of the girls actually said;

"Ukabatwa usipano (returning to the terminus shade) wotopona nokuti ndange ndaenda kundogeza. Kana wange usiri pa"Danga" unototi pambouya maplain clothes police *iwe uchinge waenda nemhene yako* kushort time."* (If the husband does not find you where he expects you to be, then you say, I had gone to wash clothes and bath, or I had run away from some plain clothes municipal police, though you will be knowing you will have gone for a "short-time" sexual encounter, with some man from the public).

9.3 *"Patriarchal Sex" as objectification of girls - a classic case of sexual violence*

Boys perceive girls as inferior and they objectify them as evidenced above, by the various sexual metaphors they used. I however wanted to get to the bottom of such antiquated notions characteristic of primitive man. The boys used tradition with one saying;

"Mukadzi ukasamurova anofunga kuti haumude. Vakadzi vana mudhara, kubva kare kunyange akadzidza, kunyange akasevenza, anotosvirisa ikoko, handizvo here mudhara?" (if you don't beat your wife she will think you don't love her. Women are like children, even if educated or well employed, they engage in illicit sex, isn't it old man).

I had no answer, we were just the two of us. When I provoked discussion whilst they were gambling about the same issue, I realized that the boys otherise the girls so much using tradition,

243

with one saying;

"They must behave like other women even if we are on the streets. They must keep some distance from men. Men, we hear used to have their space and women theirs, the same mudhara is here on the streets."

When I asked how they treated the girls during sexual intercourse, there was uproarious laughter when one of them said;

"*Tumagaba utwu, kungokwira hatuchina* sound, *mvura dzega, watoite* luck *kuwana adya mushonga wofara*" (These are tins to ejaculate into, usually they are watery in the vulva unless you are lucky to find one who eats herbs to ensure a dry vagina).

I thought this was patriarchal thinking which belonged to pre-colonial times. The word "sound" would imply an object, the vagina as an object together with the body in which it was located being objectified.

The notion of patriarchal sex emanates from the boys perception of girls as inferior, as objects of their gratification. It's not about romance, neither is it about child bearing in most instances, but just about *"FUCKING."* It's just about penetrative sex, in order to ejaculate and also penetrate to show the girl her vagina is inferior and is therefore an indicator of the unequal relations that must prevail between the two sexes. One boy summarized this thus;

"*Mustreet mudhara hapana kunakirana, kungokwira chete nokuti unehavi yekuda mukadzi.*"
(In the street sexual intercourse is just to satisfy a biological need not for enjoyment).

I thought this was like psychological violence perpetrated against the girls of the streets. The girls have no say about their sexual lives on the streets, just as is the case in mainstream society. Women seem to suffer silently. The girls had no words of violence at all as one talkative one said;

"*Sekuru*, it is bad how these boys treat us sexually, like toys. They demand for rear style (dog style). Even if you beg them to get on top they tell you that it is a style of the sick."

The boys really confirmed her observations when one of them said;

"*Mudhara* dog style *ndiyo inovachepesa vasikana ivava.*" (Old man dog style really humiliates these girls).

When I probed as to whether the girls liked it that way, another boy had said;

"*Mukadzi haabvunzwi izvozvo, chake kukwirwa chete sitaira yandinoda*" (A woman has no say as to the sexual position. It's up to me as the man).

I realized that really on the streets girls have no say, no power or autonomy in sexual encounters. To me the boys behaviour in sexual relations was justified through the construction of masculinities, premised on dominant society's relations of inequality between men and women. The boys in many ways exhibited anti-social behaviour and yet when it suited them, and to justify certain behaviour, they pretended to observe societal norms and values.

Boys for example exhibited patriarchal tendency, when they said that girls had no right to refuse sexual intercourse, that it was all pretence. One of them said;

"A girl's No is not true, it is the opposite of what she wants. You just use a bit of force and you will be having sex with her."

The girls expressed outrage at that kind of behaviour with one saying;

"*Wamuudza kuti hazviiti, watodenha zvimwe. Unotovhura makumbo chete. Anotoita zvesimba, nyangwe ukati aiwa anotokuwisira pasi kana ari manheru*" (If you say no, they use force especially at night in our resting bases).

9.4 *Forced Sex or coercive sex as a form of "rape"- A typical case*

The terms are going to be used interchangeably to mean rape. Boys' perception of sex as use of force and girls acceptance of such physical and sexual behaviour as characteristic of men, will not be understood like that in this article. The case below illustrates that, girls don't have anywhere to report the rape cases, and they are being raped all the time and just tolerating the rapists, for they have no protection. This was said by one of the girls. The police will not have anything of that, telling them to resolve their own quarrels and sorting their own problems because; - "mastreet kids you are a problem solve your problems on your own". Also even if the police were to be involved and apply the law to the book, the street boys would easily avoid arrest by moving to the various "bases", some of which are along the Mukuvisi river, and no life-loving police officer would dare go there. They also don't have any form of identity documents.

A key informant's sexual experiences are revealing as a typical case;

245

Ìni sekuru kwandiri vakomana ava havana kusiyana nemhuka dzemusango. Asi mhuka futi hadziite force nerough yavanayo. Iwe unenge watiza nhamo kwawange uchigara zvotoita bad to worse sekuru. Ìni ndakabva kumusha kwedu kuZvishavane ndarepewa nababamukuru, murume watete vangu. Ndasvika MuMasvingo usiku hwekutanga chaihwo ndange ndatova nedambudziko rekusundidzirana nechimwe chimukomana. Usiku hwakatevera ndakaedza kuramba, ndikasunga makumbo asi semhuka inodzinganiswa nembwa ndakaneta akandikwira sekuru, ndaichema asi iye akafunga kuti kunakirwa, akatonyanya kunditsimbirira. (She said sobbing - I calmed her and she continued); Nyaya iyi inondirwadza ini kuti aingondikwira. Ndakabva Masvingo ndokuuya muno. Pandakasvika paMbare musika ndizvo zve zvakaitika, kutondirwirana sendaive ndavada. Usiku hweChitatu ndakarara nevakomana vanenge three vachindivhundutsira kuti tinokunyangarisa. Ndaingochema, sekuru ndinenge ndinomunyeperai. Vakomana ava imhuka chaidzo, imbwa dzinomirira kukwira pabva imwe. Ndichiuya muno mucity, ndaingomanikidzwa zve, vamwe vasikana vachiti ndizvo zvinoitwa mustreet. Isu vasikana tinotokurudzirana kurarwa nokuti vamwe vanenge vasingadi kuzokupa zvokudya zvavo. Mustreet hapana anga nyatsoti mazuva ekutanga airarwa achida, ndezve ginya chete."

(To me these boys are no different from wild animals but even animals don't use force and don't treat their females roughly. It was like coming out of the frying pan into the fire. I had been raped by my paternal aunt's husband. When I got to Masvingo, I was subjected to forced sex despite all my effort to resist, the boys eventually got the better of me as I got tired. It was like dogs chasing an animal which eventually succumbs. I cried but it was of no use, for there was no one to come to my rescue. I eventually left for Harare as I told you last time but it was worse at Mbare bus terminus. The sexual experience was more traumatizing with threats of death. One night I was forced to have sex with three boys. These boys are real dogs, they don't care that you have had sex with one of their own, they also want it. I would cry and they would think it was crying due to excitement and copulate even harder. When I eventually got to the city centre the same forced sex happened and the other girls of the street regarded it as normal behaviour and would encourage you to indulge in such sex. During any girl's first days on the streets boys always use force).

From the narrative, which I cut short of course, it became quite apparent that girls were being raped. Rape is normally regarded as resulting in bruises and injuries, yet even in these instances, where the girl does not scream, a lot of force is still used, that must frighten any civilized person. The girls of the streets repeated these kinds of observations and to cite any others might seem unnecessary repetition. Some of the issues have been referred to in the above pages, but I felt a closer look at the boys behaviour through a specific case would shed more light on the plight of the girl child of the streets. There is no protection whatsoever and as a result the boys who seem quite aware of this state, abuse the girls treating them as they feel like. Physical force and threats are used as in many cases, in rape cases that occur in mainstream society. One can imagine a young girl being shown a knife at night by complete strangers who want her vagina to "fuck". It's quite a painful experience the girls go through. In the above pages, I tried to show the general perception of sex by the boys. Basically, the boys have an essentialist conception of sex taking anatomy to be destiny. It is as if they have a right to demonstrate to the girls, through forced sex, that they are real men hence one can, say rape is associated with the construction of masculinities. The whole experience is about proving superior to the girls.

9.5 *Gang-Rape, an Aborable Form of Sexual Violence*

It is unfortunate that street girls have no protection and despite the fact that, their reproductive health is at risk, no organization has put in place any programme to assist them. In the event of gang-rape one would feel, it would be important to have the girl examined and have her uterus cleaned of the sperms. Street girls are not the only victims who talked about gang-rape. Even women from dominant society are not spared the humiliation, as is evidenced by the case of a middle aged woman who was raped in Harare, right in the city in the late 1990s. This is the tragedy of procrastinating, as society's own marginalized have become a "frankenstein monster." When I talked to some male key informants about this form of sexual behaviour, one said;

"Big dhara mustreet mune mhuka. Vamwe vedu havana kumbogara nevanhu vakuru, vakangobva mumasquatter camp sezvomunoziva, kuti ange akawanda. Saka ivava vakomana havatyi chero kuuraya munhu, chero kupisa, handiti makanzwa vamwe vakapisirana musikana vaviri vakafa. Hapana anogona kuti iwe usadaro sezvamunongonzwa vakomana vachiti, Mugunduru anozvitonga, akauya oga mustreet."(Big *dhara* some of us boys are like wild beasts because as you have already been told, some grew up in squatter camps around the city and got no socialization from any parent for they literally grew up on the streets. These are the boys who can kill or gang-rape without any mercy and no one can stop them for as you have witnessed. *Mangunduru* have no one who controls the other, because each says

247

he came onto the streets on his own and thus no one can control him).

Evidently, there was noone who could claim to be in control and after all, to all the youth anti-social behaviour was the normal way. Another key informant related an incident in which he and four others gang-raped a prostitute. He actually said they did not use any force. This woman came to them on a cold night whilst they sat by a fire, on the fringes of the city. They were drinking opaque beer popularly known as "Skubha" or SCUDS for opaque beer, and she joined them. At about 12 mid-night one of them retired into a plastic shack and she followed him and soon they were having sexual intercourse. He went on;

> "*Mudhara* sugar *gogo ivavo takavakwira* heavy, *tose manje.*" (Old man we really fucked the old woman, all of us).

There seemed not to be any force used as she was drunk but from my own analysis, it was a clear case of gang-rape, for no normal woman can have sex with five men in one night, at the same time. Gang-rape always made me wonder how these youth, could have sex with a single woman without any condoms. The young man actually bragged thus;

> "*Takamuridza mukadzi iyeye* heavy, flesh-to-flesh."(We really fucked her and with no condoms).

He seemed to make a joke out of the incident and when I reminded him of the HIV and AIDS pandemic, he said;

> "Inga *mudhara makaudzwa negen'a kuti isu hatishandise makondomu wani*. Luckily some of us *hatina kubatwa nayo* AIDS *mudhara, tinongori* fit," (You were told old man that we don't use condoms and as you can see some of us look quite fit showing that I have not contracted the disease).

I thought, this was an area the youth needed to be educated about; that looks deceive. One could look fit and yet they could be having the virus in their system.

Girls confirmed that gang-rape was quite prevalent especially when the boys were drunk. One girl actually said;

> "*Kwetinorara sekuru kana zvaitika wotongorega vokukwira nokuti hapana wokuchemera asi vanowanzoita izvozvo vasikana vanyuwani* mustreet."(Where we sleep, even if you cry no one will hear you, the best would be to just let them take turns to have sexual intercourse with

you. Usually it's the new girl on the streets who is humiliated like this).

I had a general discussion with girls during which they showed that most of the forced sex or coercive sex was perceived by the perpetrators as normal because one said somberly.

"*Kwavari zvinotova* funny"(To the boys it's a lot of fun).

The girls were bitter that the boys ill-treated them like that, sexually abusing them and not being sympathetic of their plight, which was the same as theirs. The girls said that no girl ever dared to molest a boy on the streets and yet the opposite was always the norm. They wondered if I could help establish an office on the streets for their protection. I was honest with them that I did not have the capacity but that after my study, should the report be finished, I could give it to policy formulators, so they could see how best to assist them. I told them that, researchers usually only gathered information, and one actually said ;

"Yes its true, you are not the first to come and talk to us. Many others have done this but once they go, they never come back and nothing improves on the streets."

The others laughed and one actually said;

Äre you not going to protect these boys *sekuru* who sexually abuse us?"

I told her the policy makers could be the ones who might not take my findings seriously. To some extend, I thought that she meant that since I was a male researcher, I could try and protect the boys from arrest or reprimands.

9.6 *Statutory Rape on the streets*

According to the Zimbabwe law, having sexual relations with any girl below the age of sixteen, whether by consent is regarded as statutory rape as detailed in the Criminal Law and Codification Reform Act of 2004. Whilst on the streets, listening to the girls sexual experiences, I felt the law was not being fairly administered, for these marginalized girls deserved protection, just like those in mainstream society. All the girls said they had had sex on the streets before the age of sixteen. Some had had sexual intercourse with men from mainstream society also, and I felt that was an area non-governmental organizations lobbying for the protection of the girl child could have lots of advocacy work to do, to protect the vulnerable, otherised girls of the street.

One girl summarized it all;

"*Sekuru. Chero ukati ndichiri mudiki, unoudzwa kuti ndiko kuti ukure".* (Even if you say I am still young the boys tell you that through sex one matures). I was reminded of Shakespeare's Romeo and Juliet in which one of the funny, the characters - nurse said to the young blonde -

249

Juliet - women grow by men) *Hapana wekuudza kana kuchemera. Chero isu vasikana tikaziva mitemo, tinotya kuti tikareporter tinozourawa mustreet nokuti hapana futi zvavanoitwa nemapurisa vanongoti pedzeranai."* (Uncle, even if you tell the boys that you are still young they tell you that sex makes one grow. If we report to the police nothing happens and even if the boys do not dodge the police and are arrested, they will soon be back on the streets and surely the girl will be killed).

The girls generally were unhappy about the sexual abuse on the streets involving even men from society especially the Municipal police, who would not give them anything after having sexual relations with them. Then one girl said;

"Kurara navo nokutya irepu futi sekuru nokuti ini ndinengemumoyo mangu ndisingadi"(Sleeping with them is some form of rape because deep down in my heart I wont be consenting at all).

I had a chance to have some interviews with several young girls below the age of sixteen. The eight I talked to, told me that they had been forced to have sex with the boys, even by their female peers, let alone pressure from the boys who provided for their daily needs. There are many in this age group on the streets today. From the girls stories as well as those of the boys with regards sexual relations with minors on the streets, I want to argue that, this kind of sexual behaviour must be seen as cruel and violent sexual conduct.

9.7 *Sodomy as a form of Sexual Violence*
One male key informer said to me in confidence;

"Big Dhara, what *sekuru Gudo* does is also cruel, especially to young boys. We now know that whenever you see him with small boys and buying them food, it is because he will be sodomising them. I am telling you the truth and if you ask other boys in confidence they will confirm this. Just make sure he does not find out I have told you of his homosexual behaviour, otherwise I will be killed. The boys cannot refuse for they will be forced into accepting anal sex."

Another boy also said during a confidential in-depth interview that, girls also were sodomised by some of the boys on the pretext that they did not want penetrative vaginal sex. He said;

"We know that a number of girls have been forced to have anal sex with some of the rough boys. Not knowing these boys intentions they accept their food or money and they end up having to have dog-style through the anus. *Mudhara* you will not hear a girl who accepts that she has had this kind of sex, with one of us because to the girls it's like being terribly humiliated. After having eaten food, she is told I don't want any other style except anal penetration."

I thought this was very unfair on the unsuspecting girl and a severe blow on the girl's self - esteem. My proposition in this discussion is that, this kind of sex, that might cause emotional instability, could be traumatizing on the part of the girl and hence this is tantamount to violent sexual behaviour. This kind of sexual behaviour, was not much talked about by both boys and girls.

9.8 *Physical abuse - Cases of domestic Violence on the streets*

Fist fights between lovers were common especially on weekends when the boys were often drunk. Emotionally charged verbal altercations, were also quite frequent and most of these emanated from trying to restrain girls movements due to boys suspicions that girls or their wives were cheating them. *The Standard* Newspaper captures the various aspects of domestic violence thus beginning with the definition;

The Standard of 12 August (2007:9) says, it is, any act of physical, sexual, psychological pain, economic deprivation or threat of such abuse against women, men and children by a person intimately connected to them through family relations or acquaintanceship. Domestic Violence refers to any form or all violence that occurs between members of the same family or household. This also applies to boyfriend-girlfriend abuse. The violence results in injury, humiliation, destruction of property and sometimes death. Domestic violence can happen to anyone regardless of race, class, economic status or religion.

Domestic violence can take many forms, and the reader can easily associate these with what is happening on the streets.

Physical Abuse

This form of abuse is visible and includes

* Use of weapons to cause injury. * Being punched, slapped, kicked. * Being assaulted with

251

objects. * Being pushed and shoved. * Attempting to kill/murder.
* Pulling of hair. * Choking.

Sexual abuse.

This can be described as unwanted sexual attention, fondling or rape. Emotional pressure is violation of one's human rights and will be regarded as sexual abuse if one is:

> * Pressuring one to have sex. * Forced to have unpleasant sexual acts. * Prevented from using contraceptives. * Exposing one to STI's or HIV and AIDS or Shown pornographic materials. * Withholding sex to punish.

Psychological/Emotional Abuse.

This form of abuse is very subtle in that there is no physical evidence but it has very damaging effects and very difficult to deal with and it can take the following forms.

* Domination-not allowed to make a point of view.
* Constant criticism. * Humiliation in Public. * Threats. * Use of bad foul language
* Forced spiritual activities. * Restricted freedoms. * Excessive jealousy and asked to account for every movement.

Economic Deprivation.

This is abuse related to economic or monetary issues. It forces the victim to be in a state of continued dependency. This abuse includes:

> * Keeping you short of money for basic family needs. * Making decisions about money without consulting you. * Undermining your attempts to improve your education. * Preventing you from getting a job. * Property grabbing.

One can argue that the various forms of abuse are quite evident on the streets. One wife said to me;

> "*Sekuru*, it is no secret that these boys are very jealous. This is why we are supposed to spend the whole day here. We normally cheat though, especially in times when we know they have much money and will be drinking heavily or when they are locked up in remand. These boys also have "small houses", even here on the streets because there are many bases as you are

now aware. They can go there and spend even a week. Meanwhile I am forced to have sex with the "poachers," who will gladly give me food. The boys know their friends' sexual escapades. When they come back their "spies" tell them about our cheating and then there is noise. I think you heard of two street boys who were burnt to death five years ago with petrol during a fight over a girl. The fights can be quite vicious and the boys don't care what they use. They use broken beer bottles, bricks, stones to harm each other."

Other girls confirmed that they were subjected to physical abuse with one saying,

"*Sekuru*, is it fair for a boy to beat me every now and again saying that I infected him with a sexually transmitted disease. Every now and again whenever he feels like he attacks me. You will see him today, he has a big scar on his forehead after *Sekuru Gudo* hit him with a brick last night for physically harassing me when he was drunk."

When I got to the boys base, I felt pity for the young man, who coincidentally was one of my key participants. Blood was still oozing out slowly from the wound and as I approached the boys one of them said to me;

"*Big Dhara* come and see what *Sekuru Gudo* did last night. He almost killed this poor fellow over a girl at our sleeping base. Is this fair old man but the police are useless, they did not want to hear of it. When he went to report he was told to go away. The police just want to arrest us for nothing."

I had a chance to talk to this boy and briefly he said;

"This is the girl I told you I had sex with, the very first days I came onto the streets and I contracted gonorrhoea and this disease stops and whenever I have sex with another woman it comes again. I will kill her one day," he swore emotionally.

It was quite surprising that he was having sexual relations with other girls and yet would accuse the girl he had sex with seven years ago. I wondered how he could then link this poor girl to his sexually transmitted disease when he was that promiscuous.

I learnt that most cases of physical violence were a result of sexually transmitted infections. These infections I gathered over the fifteen months, were quite common among the street boys. Apart from fights over STIs the boys and girls also fought in the event that a girl was found to be

253

using some contraceptives or any reproductive health technology. The boys don't want to see these on the streets. I thought this was a classic case of the construction of masculinities. The perception that women spread sexually transmitted diseases and not the other way round. I thought it was a case of blaming the victims of the boys' promiscuous behaviour. One of the boys actually referred to a case in which a soldier, once beat one of the girls accusing her of causing him to contract an STI. The boys laughed when their colleague, reminded them of the threats he made to the street husband who later died from tuberculosis. The boys left him to assault the girl, whom the boys said died later of tuberculosis when she was now staying with another man in Epworth, one of the high density residential areas, notorious for all sorts of immoral activities.

Another boy blamed the girls for the fights on the streets saying;

> "*Big Dhara* these girls are a nuisance. They don't decline any men's proposal as long as they see an opportunity to make a "quick buck" (Street lingo for dollars or money). They are always sleeping with men and this is why we are now suffering from STIs that resist treatment. These girls are cruel, they deliberately spread the infections knowing that their vaginas were rotten."

There was uproarious laughter as another said;

> "If I meet Longina I will burn her private parts to ashes for infecting me with a terrible STI. *Big Dhara*, ask these boys, I was only cured when I bought some capsules at the *Mupedzanhamo*. These Nigerian tablets, you know. *Anoshanda Big Dhara, Gavhumende ngaitirege titenge, ivo havana mishonga yacho.* "(Nigerian tablets bought on the open market are effective. The government must not condemn these drugs and yet they have no medicines in their hospitals)".

I learnt that, that girl had actually relocated to Kadoma due to this boy's threats. The boy showed that boys were just consuming tablets bought on the streets, without knowing their negative effects. The excitement shown by the boys during this discussion, proved beyond any reasonable doubt that girls were in real trouble on the streets. The girls were the victims of various forms of violence.

On controlled movements as the cause of fights one girl said to the laughter by the others;

"*Sekuru. Ini mhata yangu haina zita romurume rakanyogwa. Ini ndonzi nomunhu asina kubvisa pfuma kuhama dzangu haufaniri kuenda kwaunoda here sekuru, kudenha ka uku. Ivo vakomana ava vanongoita madiro vachitozviti "mapocha.*" (How can one want to control my movements when they never paid *lobola* to my relatives. The boys do what they want and have sex with many other girls and brag that they are poachers." My vagina has no male's name written on it).

Some other time another girl made others laugh when she said;

"*Isuwo tave mapocha. Vakomana ivava maitiro avo ndiwo akonzera kuti tivachovhese bhasikoro risina mweya.*" (We have also become poachers learning from these boys who have taken us for a ride all along.)

There was laughter and clapping of hands when one married girl said;

"*Nyangwe isu tine nhamo nevarume vedu vanotimanikidza kurara navo nyange tisingadi kunonzi fongora izvozvi. Ukaramba unonzi wange uine chikomba, havanei kuti uri kumwedzi , vana sekuru Gudo vanongokurara.* (Even us with husbands on the streets, are forced to have sex with them. Even if you are menstruating, you will be forced to even have rear entry "dog style).

Yet another with a husband said;

"*Chinobhowha sekuru, chinoitisa hondo, ndechekuti varume vedu ava vemudondo vanotiparika, vanoenda* for some days. *Kana ouya ukati umboramba kuvhura makumbo* (The others burst into laughter) *unorobwa zvisingaite. Vaneudzvanyiriri. Isu tinonzi tisakwirwa nokuti tiri vakadzi vavo. Ivo vanongoita semabhuru emashanga.*"

The others laughed again. (What is boring is that they have small houses and do as they please. A wife is supposed to wait for his coming and should you resist sex, you can be given a severe beating for it. They oppress us and yet they behave like bulls). The word *"vemudondo"* struck me. It, in dominant society, implies illicit relationships that have not been sanctioned by other relatives. A good example will be that of a man and woman who meet in a forest and have sex. Its *"zvemudondo"*. Behaviour that is not acceptable which could lead to children *"vemudondo"* that is illegitimate children.

One of the girls summarized their sentiments when she said, showing her knowledge of current affairs;

"*Iro* Domestic Violence Bill racho ngariuyewo mustreet"; to the applause of the other girls.

(The Domestic Bill needs to apply to those on the streets).

One of them watered down their excitement when she said

"*Magunduru vasikana haazive chinonzi mupurisa musazvinyengera. Tongoramba tichibhimhidzwa nemapenzi aya.*"

(Street boys, girls, don't care about this and don't respect any law as well as the police. They will continue to beat us). This bill was tabled in parliament of Zimbabwe several years ago and has now become an Act of Parliament in 2006.

9.9 Putting the Cart before the Horse:- No Freedom without Resources

As I sat on the pavement many a day, I thought the girls were in a real predicament; on the one hand they could not do without the boys and on the other hand, they have to concede, or mortgage their womanhood to the boys as guarantee for safety and survival. The issue here is of self-autonomy or independence, which is impossible for the girls as long as they are dependent on boys for their survival. No reproductive health programme, will be effective on the streets as long as girls have no autonomy and have no control over their bodies. I thought of the various, legislative provisions effected by the Government of Zimbabwe since independence, to socially and economically empower women. I felt pity for the street girls, who to authorities seemed to be non-existent. Some of these laws are well captured in an UNFPA report of 2000 thus;

Notable legislation that enhance the legal status of women in Zimbabwe

Policy/legislative change	Implications
Sexual Offences Act (201)	•1 Criminalises marital rape •2 Criminalises wilful transmission of HIV and AIDS
Administration of Estates (Amendment) ACT (1997)	•3 Reformed inequitable customary inheritance laws
Constitutional Amendment No. 14 (1996)	•4 Inclusion of gender as one of the grounds upon which discrimination is prohibited •5 Gives equal status to alien spouses of both Zimbabwean males and females
Infanticide Act (1991)	•6 Established the crime of infanticide to replace the murder charge in cases where mothers kill their newly

	born babies taking into consideration circumstances such as post-natal depression, rejection by both boyfriend and parents, etc.
Deeds Registries	•7 Women can register immovable property in their own name Amendment Act (1991) (applied only to urban and rural commercial land but not communal where the majority of African women live)
The Electoral Act (1990)	•8 Enables women to vote in general land by-elections and to stand for election in presidential and Parliamentary elections on equal terms with men.
Finance Act (1998)	•9 Separate taxation for spouses (but husband claims tax exemption on children)
Maintenance Amendment Act (1989)	•10 Requires a negligent non-custodian parent to contribute regularly to maintenance of minor children in the custody of the other parent. •11 An appeal against maintenance order no longer has the effect of suspending enforcement of such an order (1989), thereby frustrating the efforts of many respondents who filed appeals to delay payment thereof •12 The courts are empowered to attach terminal benefits (e.g. pensions) accruing to any person ordered to pay maintenance and who subsequently leaves employment in order to avoid paying it. •13 A woman wishing to claim maintenance from a man living in a different city or area no longer has to follow him to that area to file a maintenance claim against him. She can file her claim from the court nearest to her and the man is the one who will travel to that court for the hearing •14 A woman married under customary law (i.e. without a marriage certificate) is entitled to maintenance from that man after the dissolution of the union (1990)
Deceased person's Family Maintenance Amendment Act (1987)	•15 Establishes the right of a surviving spouse and children - to continue occupying the matrimonial house - use the household goods and effects they were using immediately before the deceased's death - use and enjoy the crops and animals - make it a crime for anyone to interfere with these rights of the deceased's property, thereby reducing the likelihood of property grabbing by opportunistic relatives
Matrimonial Causes Act (1985)	•16 Provides for an equitable distribution of matrimonial assets on divorce •17 Removes the fault principle as a ground for divorce •18 Recognizes the contribution of the housewife as meriting a share of matrimonial assets upon divorce •19 A woman can claim ,maintenance from her ex-spouse anytime after the divorce should there be need for it
Public Service Pensions	•20 Makes provisions for female contributors in Public

(Amendment) Regulations (1985)	Service to contribute to their pension at the same rate as male contributors. (Women can now also contribute to medical schemes in their own right).
Labour Relations Act (1984)	•21 Prohibits employers from discriminating against any prospective employee, in relation to employment, on the grounds of among other things, sex •22 Provides for three months paid maternity leave 75% salary) and emphasized that no employer shall discriminate against any employee on the grounds of race, tribe, place of origin, political opinion, colour, creed or sex in relation to wages, recruitment, promotion, training and retrenchments
Immovable Property (Prevention of Discrimination)Act, 1982	•23 Prohibits discrimination in respect of the sale, lease or disposal of immovable property and the financing or any such sale, lease or disposal on the ground of, among other things, sex.
Legal Age of Majority Act (1982) Now part of the General Laws Amendment Act)	•24 Confers full legal capacity on every Zimbabwean citizen aged 18years and above (before this law African women were rendered as perpetual minors) •25 Capacity for daughter to inherit father's estate •26 Capacity for women including widows to qualify as guardians of minors and to administer an estate •27 Guardians no longer have to sue for seduction damages in the case where the girl is over 18 years.
Minimum Wages Act	•28 Stipulates minimum wages for difficult types of unskilled (1980) occupations. Most women in formal employment are found in the unskilled category •29 Categorizes seasonal worker (tobacco, tea and cotton pickers) as permanent and entitled to pension benefits
Equal Pay Regulations	•30 Equal pay for equal work •31 Half an hour before lunch and half an hour after lunch for breastfeeding

The Gender Policy is an important tool in the effort to improve the status off women in Zimbabwe. In addition Zimbabwe also acceded or ratified several of the United Nations Conventions which include the Convention on the Elimination of All Forms of Discrimination Against women (CEDAW), the United Nations Declaration of Human Rights (UDHR), the African Charter on Human and People's Rights of 1981.

I thought, this plethora of legislative enactments are a noble endeavour in the quest to liberate women from repressive patriarchal attitudes ad tendencies. But the fact that women were economically dependent on men, meant such efforts were like putting a cart before the horse. Without economically empowering women, so they can partake in decision making just as their male counterparts do, on a day to day basis, will mean women cannot make sexual and reproductive health decisions, that ensure their safety. On the streets, the girls are dependent, socially and economically on the boys, such that no HIV and AIDS intervention programme will be successful unless accepted by the boys.

9.10 *Conclusions*

One finds that a comprehensive definition of the nature of violence is quite a difficult exercise, but only suffice to conceptualise it in terms of either sexual or physical violence. Domestic violence, one can argue is more elaborated, in that, it captures a number of behaviours as detailed by *The Standard* newspaper article, cited above. Machera (2004), takes cognisance of the various aspects of the definition referred to above. Within such a context, which evidently is social constructionist and has nothing to do with biology, it is the boys' social construct, that a girl is less human than themselves. To the boys, whose patriarchal behaviour is indisputable, anatomy is destiny, as was believed by the likes of Freud (2001) and Rousseau to mention but a few essentialists. On the streets the girls have no power at all, and thus have no autonomy and decision making, relating to their daily experiences. It is the boys who dominate every aspect of life. One feels they cannot be condemned, for despite being considered in many ways as antisocial by those in dominant society, they simulate the behaviour of the men in mainstream society.

Sex is characterised by force and violence in most cases. The use of aphrodisiacs for full erections is evident of a psyche that is embedded on sadistic notions of men in general, whether in mainstream society or on the streets. Men have a tendency to perceive sexual intercourse as an occasion to fix or inflict pain on a woman. The various sexual metaphors point to this, for most of them are about the objectification and otherisation of women. Women are not thus seen as equal partners in sexual encounters, but as objects from which men must derive joy. The sexual and physical abuse of the girls on the streets, is thus traced back into mainstream society, where such behaviour has been seen as normal and thus not criminalized, since time immemorial, with many a woman wishing they were men. Women, instead of being happy that, biologically, they are different due to nature, have always lamented their denigrated sex or anatomy as a curse, whilst men have seen themselves as the better sex. This, one can argue, is not much different from racism or apartheid.

259

Harassing girls who are regarded as wives also, because they are suspected of cheating is the highest form of hypocrisy on the part of the promiscuous boys of the streets, who go wherever they want. Victorian tendencies are quite evident. The boys have the courage to accuse girls of infecting them with STIs and yet they are so promiscuous, it would be difficult to know which girl had the disease. The girls have to be confined to the *"danga"*, literally meaning a kraal, like cows, only existing to provide sexual pleasure to the superior boys. If the girls are not found there, there is real trouble as they risk being burnt alive, or being killed in cold blood. Chilling cases of physical abuse were related to me, but unfortunately due to space, I just selected a few. In rhetoric, Zimbabwe has some of the best legislative provisions to empower women, so they stop being chattels of men, but in practice, women are still oppressed, otherised and objectified by their male counterparts, both in dominant society and on the streets.

CHAPTER TEN

SUMMARY OF RESEARCH FINDINGS, CONCLUSIONS AND
RECOMMENDATIONS

10.0 *Summary of Findings*

As discussed in the introductory chapter, the main concern of my study was an attempt to fill-in a knowledge gap, in the lived experiences of street involved people especially the youth. Many studies have been carried out but not much had been done in the area of in-depth studies relating to their sexual behaviour patterns and power relations. Most of the cursory studies had focused on the children's survival strategies and such issues as transactional sex. Studies tended to focus on "Street children", rather than street youth. as in my case, those above twenty years of age.

I found the social constructionist theoretical framework to be the most relevant in analysing the social and sexual relations that prevail amongst the street youth. As is quite clear, the qualitative methods of in depth discussions and conversations, yielded most of my data. I also had my own observations as a participant observer. Life story narratives proved an important source of information also. Survey methods would not have helped much in understanding how the youth construct their world.

Evident from the study was the finding that most of the youth were either double or single orphans and had been forced onto the streets due to either sexual or physical abuse or both. The extended family system was exposed as having become weak, due to the effects of colonisation and urbanisation and their accompanying forms of social organisation. Some bereaved children have become destitute due to neglect by members of their extended family network or even due to abuse by their own biological parents.

Once on the streets, the research reveals that, the youth who got there at very tender ages, joined a sub-group already on the streets with a specific identify; I prefer calling it a "quasi-tribe." A group perceived by those in mainstream society as a nuisance, whose trade mark is drunkenness,

261

filth, torn, dirty and smelly clothes, bare footedness and uncombed hair, hostile to members of the public and generally engaging in anti-social activities like stealing, mugging people, harassing especially women and children and fond of obscene, course language.

It was interesting to find out that though these youths are a condemned lot in official circles, by the government and city council officials, to members of the motoring and business communities, they were a necessary evil. The business community had a readily available source of cheap labour power. The youth are also hired by the well to do, to do various chores at their homes.

It emerged from the study that there was animosity between the city officials and the youth, such that the streets had become a battle ground. One member of the public actually talks of the need for a motor bomb to deal with the problem of the street youth once and for all. The youths meanwhile, are adamant that, they were not born by the street, but are on the streets due to problems not of their making. To the youth the street is their home and they will not move an inch. The city officials are realising that procrastination is the thief of time, as the once small boys and girls "of the streets", are now men and women. It is a real "tragedy of lives" on the streets, as the destitute youths now prey on unsuspecting members of the public, instilling fear and causing havoc, with some members of the public referring to them as "young terrorists". Members of the public are no longer feeling safe to be in the streets at night and even during the day. This is the tragedy of procrastinating on the part of the powers that be, as the youth now pose like a "Frankenstein monster", to members of the Harare community as a whole.

Meanwhile boys and girls' relations on the streets, which have not been explored this far, reveal that the street is a resource, where there is a hierarchy of, opportunities. Boys however have appropriated this resource and girls become dependent on the boys for their day to day survival and for their security. The girl's anatomy, is real "destiny" on the streets, where they are otherised; physically and sexually abused by the boys. I say the girls now constitute an "underclass of an underclass". Issues of gender and power relations on the streets and boys' construction of their masculinities, are seen as mirroring the relations between men and women in dominant society. This is quite evident in this book; which delves into issues of power, decision making and autonomy in social, sexual and reproductive health spheres.

On sexual relations between boys and girls, it was quite evident the boys were more knowledgeable and more forthcoming than girls. Boys were found to have a multiplicity of partners and talked freely about it, while girls were not as free to talk about their sexual escapades as did the boys. Even in mainstream society, one finds that girls or women in general, tend to be conservative in expressing their sexuality, despite being quite knowledgeable and experienced. No woman, especially the married ones in dominant society for example, can tell their husband, what sexual position or technique they prefer that night. Women cannot talk about their past love affairs to their husbands, but men can, with much ease. Even if they are not sexually satisfied after a man's ejaculation, they cannot say it. Despite knowledge of the HIV and AIDS epidemic, boys derived much fun from sleeping all over with some bragging that they were sexual "poachers."

The boys sleep with girls of the streets and also with prostitutes from the various pubs they frequently patronise. They engage in "flesh to flesh," casual, sexual intercourse all the time and do not mind having sex with the same woman one after the other. Casual sex is evidenced by the behaviour of the "sexual poacher", who does not need a stable relationship. The girls too, engage in casual sex known as "short-time," in street lingo, once in a while, as they are forced to cheat in order to supplement their food resources. For the girls, sexual relations are not for fun, but for survival and for protection otherwise if they were secure financially and had a sense of security they would not have engaged in risky sex as is the case with boys. The sexual encounters on the streets reveal the following;

- that girls are an otherised and objectified category
- girls do not control any resources at all, they live at the mercy of the boys
- the girls have no power in those sexual encounters and they do not initiate the sexual encounters and do not determine the occurrence and duration of the intercourse
- girls do not determine the sexual position or techniques and have no power to say No, even to the "dog-style" or rear entry, which the boys are fond of.
- Sexual intercourse is exposed as characterised by the boys need to fix or inflict pain on the girls. The girls seem aware of this kind of attitude, but have no power to resist boys sexual demands.
- Sexual encounters are patriarchal in nature, characterised by what some researchers have

263

referred to as "fucking". The boys show that they determine the sexual and reproductive health behaviour to prevail on the streets.

The boys are consistently rough and aggressive or rather violent in sexual encounters which are characterised by force. The girls are objects of boys' sexual gratification as they have to yield. Virginity is none existent, for most girls get to the streets no longer virgins and both boys and girls did not prize it. Totems too, were found not to be of importance, with some claiming that they had no totems, such that to a traditionalist, this is a real religious tragedy, as totems were considered important in linking the living with the dead amongst the Shona and the Ndebele. Today a quasi-tribe of the totemless is fast growing on the streets.

Heterosexual sex was the most prevalent and mainly being casual sex in nature. For those in marital unions, the treatment by the husbands in sexual encounters, was no different from that of encounters with sexual poachers - the dog style was the most prevalent. Homosexual acts were also found to occur, but not very common. Girls engaged in oral sex, whilst boys had anal sex. Masturbation was quite prevalent as some boys did not want penetrative sex. Bestiality was also found to be taking place but rarely, and this involved well to do whites who would be taking some videos. "Ritual sex", as discussed was also found to be taking place, where the sponsoring person, would take the condoms with sperms;-for presumably ritual purposes.

Power and domination of girls is well evidenced by their lack of say on issues relating to their reproductive health. The girls cannot demand safe sex. They are constrained by their material conditions of abject poverty, in that unlike the boys who control the street as a resource; they don't have anything except their vaginas which I regard, as assets for survival. In order to have food, they have to depend on the boys. They buy clothes from the money they are given either by men from dominant society, or by the street boys. The street boys and the other men from society as the girls put it clearly to me; don't want to use condoms or to engage in what is referred to as "plastic sex". The girls are not allowed to use any contraceptives by these boys, and yet most of the boys don't want to have children from sexual encounters. Girls show agency, by buying herbs and herbal concoctions that help them to abort so often. Abortion is the norm, for most of the girls and yet it poses a serious health hazard.

The dry sex girls are forced to practise, is also quite risky in the event of forced penetration, as the lacerations to the vaginal walls, would expose the girl to infection by STIs and even the dreaded HIV and AIDS. The girls have no decision making powers with regards their own bodies, hence the researchers' description of these girls as, of "appropriated bodies and suppressed souls". Those who become pregnant do not visit any clinic and thus risk themselves, to contracting diseases during birth in such unhygienic conditions. The new born babies could also contract diseases. They however were happy to give birth in such filth, saying that they had never had any health problems. The drugs they buy in case of ailments, are also a real hazard to their health as well as the herbs and aphrodisiacs they buy from "street pharmacists", and expired capsules they get from *Mupedzanhamo*. That girls have no autonomy in sexual and reproductive health matters, has been adequately explored in the above narratives.

The research also found out that, on the streets, a new form of family union has been formed. In many ways it differs from the Parsonian notion of the nuclear family. Parsons never visualised of a family living in the open street. These street dwellers do not value such things as virginity, totems and payment of *lobola*. They can't subscribe to the notion of value consensus for theirs is "anti-social behaviour." Be that as it may, one finds that contrary to some views in some circles, that women are dominated by men because of payment of *lobola*, even on the streets where there is no such practice, girls are dominated in every aspect of their lives by their husbands. Their husbands also sexually and physically abuse them. Conflicts are quite prevalent as the boys have other mistresses popularly known as "small houses". The girls or wives are not allowed to go where they want, except to the river to bath and wash. Girls take advantage of this to cheat by having casual sex with other men, who give them money. They provide sexual favours to those from the municipal police, the Zimbabwe Republic Police and soldiers who can also warn them of impending raids by the city council authorities.

In these street family unions, are children and I found out that, they were quite prized. The problem was however about the future of these children. Most parents expressed the wish that their children have a good education, which was impossible as long as they were on the streets. They were also worried that they were getting old and soon they would be grand parents on the streets - a real tragic state to contemplate about. I realised that definitely the book title had captured well the tone of events on the streets. It was really an unfolding tragedy. I felt it was a tragic-comedy, for I would find myself just laughing on my own, as I reminisced on the happenings on the streets. Adulterous affairs were quite prevalent and the cause of many fierce fights on the streets, the classical example being that of the two boys, who were doused with paraffin or petrol and burnt to death alive whilst hiding in a trench.

Violence has actually been shown to be the norm on the streets. Boys generally subject the girls to both sexual and physical violence. Emotionally, psychologically, the girls are an abused, otherised category. An alienated and objectified lot. An "underclass of an underclass," with those relations of inequality being a mirror image of those relations between men and women in dominant society. The perception of sex by the boys has elements of violence and sado-masochistic tendencies. They want to inflict pain and to fix the girls, as evidenced by the various sexual metaphors they use to denigrate the girls and their vaginas, seeing the penis as more superior and meant to give the vagina a good "hiding", which is typical of patriarchal sex, as discussed in chapter nine. Chapter nine also talks of forced sex, rape and gang rape as the girls also point out that, they are always being subjected to violent, aggressive sexual behaviour, which is quite humiliating but they cannot resist it, because they will be beaten. Most of the girls lamented the lack of any form of protection for them on the streets because if they report to the police, they are told to go away because they are a nuisance. They said they had reported to officials at an NGO, and nothing had been done to the culprits. Actually, they reported that some of the officers at this NGO also wanted to sleep with them. On the whole it is shown that legislative provisions alone without material empowerment of women, will not assure equal access to resources and decision making power in relation to sexual and reproductive health issues.

10.1 *Recommendations*

Over the years, due to a negative perception of the problem of street dwelling, efforts by the officials have been to forcibly remove the children and now the street youth. Bourdillon 1994, 1997, Dube 1999 and other researchers have advised for the need of a positive paradigm shift in resolving the problem and it seems the advice has not been heeded to at all. On the other hand, as expressed by one of the officials from the city council in chapter five, the street children have literally been "reinvading" the streets all the time. The authorities must realise that the street does not become pregnant. The youth have come from somewhere, and that, there were good reasons

266

in most cases for their moving onto the streets. For example, a girl was raped by her paternal aunt's husband and physically and psychologically harassed by other kin, and then one asks her to go back to her home without considering the CAUSE or the PUSH FACTORS. I find this to be hypocritical behaviour in that, an official ignores the possible cause of the child's plight and wants to force the child back into the same situation in the name of reintegration and rehabilitation. This kind of behaviour must be abhorred by all peace loving citizens.

The government must come up with a holistic package as I will propose below, to resolving the problem once and for all. The government is a signatory to the Convention on the Rights of the Child of 1989. The presence of these destitute children on the streets, is real proof of government hypocrisy, because these are also children like any child in mainstream society. The street does not become pregnant and we really can justifiably claim that, what is happening on the streets, is really the tragedy of procrastinating on the part of the government.

Girls are being harassed, abused sexually and physically, they are completely a humiliated category with no resource to sustain themselves, despite the existence of numerous NGOs run by some" fat cats", who receive international awards for mainly rhetoric, than practical help to the needy children; - the street children or the street youth. Dealing with the symptoms rather than the causes of the problem, is just procrastination at the peril of all the Harare residents as is already evident. People are being mugged, harassed and losing valuables with some being stabbed with knives by these youth. One cannot talk of the removal of these children today, when they have families and children, when they failed to remove them whilst they were young in the late 80s and in the 90s because they now resist. They have established networks, that involve municipal police. The boys buy beer for these municipal police officers and girls provide sexual favours so they can avert any move by authorities, to remove them from the streets.

These street youth must be involved in the solution-finding process. We must not have this negative perception of the youth as being illiterate and anti-social. The opposite is actually true that, they are no different from all of us, as repeatedly highlighted throughout the story. The sexual reproductive health behaviour and the social relations of inequality between boys and girls, are actually a simulation of what is happening in mainstream society. These children have demonstrated their tenacity in very rough circumstances and of managing to survive in a very

267

hostile environment. Society has something to emulate from these children; the ability to survive any odds. If this could be a learning point for those concerned about the lack of patriotism in the youth, due to the economic melt- down our country is going through today, the survival strategies of the youth, could be a shining example of surviving in a hostile, socio-economic environment. The point I am making is that, harassing and forcing the children off the streets, is not the correct way to deal with the street involved youth. Let us deal with the causes. How do we fill in the gap left by 'the death', of the extended family, which used to cushion members from the adversities of life? The extended family now only exists socially, but not economically and one can say it exists nominally, because the economic needs of a being sustain their social being.

From the research findings one can argue that, those who are married if economically empowered, will move out of the streets. Some street parents were pessimistic of a future on the streets with their children, wishing they could be given some soft loans, so they can get into vegetable vending in the high density suburbs. They would then pay rentals and send their children to school. We must not wish away the problem of street dwelling, as it is growing by the day. The government and all those NGOs that purport to exist for the welfare of vulnerable and orphaned children, need to unite and come up with a rescue package for those who are now adults rather than just pretend that once they become adults on the streets, they must look after themselves. As will be evident below, talking about HIV and AIDS and interventions is nonsense, when these children are in such a circumstance. The youth are not prepared to change their sexual and reproductive health behaviour. I felt that since some of the parents expressed the wish to have their children educated, if financially empowered they could settle off the streets. This could help in reducing the street population and make them develop a positive attitude towards society and life. It is not officials only, who have a negative attitude, for the children also have adopted the self-fulfilling prophecy that, if the cap fits we will wear it, they see themselves as the vagabonds and the criminals.

One problem of course is that of lack of any form of identity, for these youths, for which one feels the government has to issue such registration certificates and forget about the normal requirements, because most are orphans, born on the streets with no knowledge of any relatives. Loans could only be availed to those with such identity documents and then some officers would be assigned the responsibility of monitoring the activities of these youths after settling them in high density suburbs like Epworth, Mbare, and Hopley etcetera. If provided with plastics, they could construct their own shelters. The government is in the process of building a home for orphans at a farm called Iron Mask Farm, a project of the First Lady, Mrs Grace Mugabe. I heard them say on television that, it was for orphans and vulnerable children. I suppose not those on the streets, because from the study, the youth expressed a lot of surprise at such an initiative to remove them from the streets. They will not move from the streets. Again it shows the old type of perception, which is negative and is premised on the principle of getting rid of the youth, seeing them, as a problem, rather than a participatory approach, based on a positive perception of the problem. As long as society does not show compassion for the plight of these youths and regard them in positive light, running battles on the streets are just the beginnings of worse things to come. This is really the tragedy of procrastinating in that, it is now almost twenty years since the first children were noticed on the streets, and due to procrastination on the part of government and city council officials, soon all of us will bear the consequences as the street youth are causing havoc on the streets.

There is need for a holistic approach now to resolve this impasse on the streets between the youth and the authorities. The government should work together with the non-governmental organisations, as well as religious based institutions, to deal with the problem. I need to point out here that, no HIV and AIDS intervention programme will work before the material conditions of these children are improved, and the girl child is empowered economically; to have power over their own lives, to be able to say yes or no to issues relating to their sexual and reproductive health. Government legislates that, an adult is anyone over 18 years. This is taken to imply the individual is able to provide for their own needs, an aspect the Non-Governmental Organisations dealing with children, have mistakenly taken to mean they no longer have any responsibility over such youth. Streets Ahead officials for example, say street youth above 18 years of age, should not come to their premise anymore, for they only welcome those below 18. This group of orphans and vulnerable youth, then becomes an abandoned lot, who have to strategise for survival, for no one seems to care about their welfare. The Government has no programme to cater for their well-being. No religious institution has established lasting relations with the youth, despite the fact that the boys expressed willingness to be trained in various trades like welding, after which they could be given loans to start their own income generating projects.

The youths showed they had knowledge or awareness of the HIV and AIDS pandemic and other STIs. It would be fabricating on my part, if I say the youth had misconceptions, because they knew very well that the disease was mainly transmitted through unprotected, penetrative sex, yet they insisted on such kind of sexual behaviour. They do not want to use any condoms and girls have no power to resist such kind of risky sex, as already pointed out above. Neither do they have any independence to do what they want on the streets. No intervention programme will work if my observations above are not taken on board i.e. involving the children in finding a solution and economically empowering the youth especially the girl child. Their socially acceptable activities, like selling parking discs, cleaning cars and vending, could be properly organised with their involvement and be legally recognised since the government has failed to create employment opportunities, even for the law abiding youth leaving our educational institutions en-masse annually today. We could harness this labour power to the benefit of Harare residents. The motoring and business people are already benefiting from interfacing with these youths in the streets, as discussed in chapter five.

Looking at the youths "on the streets", who come onto the street to work and retire to some home at the end of the day, one feels the same could happen with the homeless street youths. As discussed above, they could be encouraged and assisted to have homes in the residential areas. This strategy can only work especially if government and the city council realise the urgency of reconciling with these children, so that they are prepared to work together with society for a lasting solution. Yes, they know they are dying from HIV and AIDS, but it would be naïve of anyone in their right frame of mind, to sit and think of intervention programmes like, supply of female condoms, to hungry girls, who need food. They will not use them of course. The boys will not listen to that of course. The boys will not tolerate use of condoms. I cannot suggest of any educational programmes for the group, as long as they are struggling to survive, for that would be absolute hypocrisy on my part as a researcher. As mentioned earlier, knowledge of HIV and AIDS does not guarantee change of behaviour. We can end up cooking statistics in that direction in praise of our educational programmes, but on the streets its impossible, for the children will not listen to that at all. If squatter settlements could be recognised, this would be ideal as observed above, to settle these youth and then provide educational programmes on HIV and AIDS, on domestic violence and the need to respect girls and women as equals. Operation Restore Order *(Murambatsvina),* can only be seen as a monumental disaster, that should never have been implemented, for it left many poor people worse off. The government has no resources to build new houses for the poor, so the poor should be encouraged to construct their own simple plastic shelters.

In conclusion, one finds it plausible to argue that, in light of the objectives I set out to address, adequate data was collected to comprehensively address them. The sexual behaviours of the street youths, were well captured during the in-depth interviews, discussions and conversations, as well as the researcher's own observations. The area of sexual behaviour had not been explored in much detail by previous researchers, as well as issues of gender and power dynamics between boys and girls of the streets. There was a yawning knowledge gap in this regard. From chapter five up to chapter nine, the story of the street youth, shows the unequal power relations between boys and girls, and why any HIV and AIDS intervention programme will be irrelevant, unless girls are empowered economically.

It is evident from this narrative that a socio-cultural tragedy is unfolding on the streets of Harare. Evidence also points to the collapse of traditional safety nets and the emergence and growth of a totemless, antisocial quasi-tribe. The physical and sexual violence points also to the tragic nature of the lived experiences of the marginalised, hard to reach group. Government and local authorities as already observed above, have for the past two decades failed to avert this socio-cultural disaster. With the high levels of sexual networking evidenced above, the street has became a breeding ground for sexually transmitted diseases and even the dreaded HIV and AIDS scourge. The study thus sheds light on the risky sexual and reproductive behaviours of the street youth. As research on HIV and AIDS has shown, mostly youth in the 18 – 24 years category, are contracting the disease, to which these youth belong, hence the need to sensitise society of the need to capture this category in its various HIV and AIDS intervention strategies. These children come from society and it is society that is to blame for their state of destitution and absolute poverty. Society must not harass and negatively construct these youth but try to involve them in solution finding as discussed above.

10.2 *Contributions to Theory, Methodology and Social Science Research*
One finds this study to be quite significant in that it focuses on a qualitatively poor category that is hardly theorised. Muzvidziwa (2004) defines qualitative poverty as also referring to social

categories not theorised about such that, there is poverty of knowledge around them as is the case with street youth. Capturing the views of the youth in their mother tongue is also something that needs highlighting. This is evidence of fighting the disease of distorting the world view of research participants. My book is a bit long because I had to use vernacular and then translate to English in order to ensure that the children's views were not distorted. Qualitative studies need to be done in this area so that information about street involved youth is adequately captured rather than depend on cursory studies based on the survey methods. It is important for more studies to be done focussing on power dynamics and the youth's perceptions with regard to various social issues such that the social constructionist paradigm becomes important. It however, is important for researchers to be aware of the fact that the extreme form of social constructionism, that ignores, innate human potential, may lead to gross assumptions about the nature of human behaviour. Rather, middle ground social constructivism becomes more preferable to the evolutionary/essentialist paradigm in helping us understand human sexual behaviour.

Culture in this study, is simply demonstrated as the main explanation of the boys and girls behaviour in social and sexual encounters. The book therefore, contributes to the discourse of the anthropology of sex and gender which Oakley (1995) cited above has emphasised, will rage on for many more years to come. The social construction paradigm does help us to understand the power dynamics prevalent on the streets as well as the sexual behaviour patterns of the street youth. To adequately capture these dynamics, one would have to mainly use qualitative methodologies that allow for the collection of detailed information.

Also evident from this study is the view that social science research must not be concerned with issues relating to the origins of the anthropologist, that is, whether, foreign or indigenous, because the most important issue is to observe the rigours of anthropological enquiry. One has to be concerned about capturing and painting a picture close to the lived experiences of those studied. The researcher has however to acknowledge that what he or she reports is just a partial view for no one can claim, absolute objective reporting hence the notion that reports of anthropologists are like fiction writing. The fiction aspect, cannot be completely ruled out of our findings, especially where one has to translate what respondents say in their native language into another language, distortions are inevitable.

10.3 *Some Possible research areas for the Future*

Studies could still be done in the area of reproductive health technologies. Researchers need to expose the level of abuse of drugs and counterfeit drugs on the streets, and the likely negative consequences, which I could not do. Issues relating to homosexual activities could also be further explored as well as issues of ritual sex to find out the likely uses of sperms. More research needs to be done, in terms of the likely consequences of the youth becoming old on the streets. Aging is already a problem in mainstream society and it will be interesting to really find out how best to cater for these street involved people.

BIBLIOGRAPHY

Abane, H. 2000.

"Towards Research into Wife Buttering in Ghana: Some Methodological Issues." In Oyekanmi, F. (ed.). *Men, Women and Violence.* CODESRIA. Dakar, Senegal.

Adams, R. and
Savran, D. 2002.

"Introduction". In Adams, R. and Savran, D. (eds.). *The Masculinities Reader.* 9-14. Blackwell Publishers. Oxford.

Adleman, J. and
Enguidanos, G. 1996.

Racism in Lives of Women. Park Press. Harrington.

Ahlburg, D., Jensen, E.R.
and Perez, A.E. 1997.

Determinants of Extra- Marital Sex in the Philippines. *Health Transition Review.* Supplement to Vol. 7. 467-481.

Ahleberg, B.M. 1994.

Is there a Distinct African Sexuality? A Critical Response to Caldwells. *Africa 64(2) 220-242.*

Akinnawo, E.O. 1995.

Sexual Networking, STDs and HIV and AIDS Transmission Among Nigerian Police Officers. *Health Transition Review.* Supplement to Volume 5. 113-123.

Akuffo, F.W.B. 1999.

The Relationship Between Development and Culture. The Case of Zambia. *South-South Journal of Culture and Development.* 1(1): 86-101.

Amuyunzu-Nyamongo, M.
Tendo-Wambua, L. 1999

"Barriers to Behaviour Change as Response to STD Including HIV and AIDS: The East African Experience. *Health. Transition Centre.* 1-3.

Anarfi, J. K. and
Antwi, P. 1995.

Street Youth in Accra City, Sexual Networking in a High-risk Environment and its Implications for the Spread of HIV and AIDS," In *Health Transition Review.* Supplement to Volume 5. 131-153.

Anarfi, J. K. 1993.

Sexuality, Migration and AIDS in Ghana. *Health Transition Review.* Supplement to Volume 3. 45-69.

Anarfi, J. K. 1997.

Vulnerability to Sexual Transmitted Disease, Street Children in Accra. *Health Transition Review.* Supplement to Volume 7. 281-307.

Anarfi, J.K. 1999.

Initiating Behavioural Change Among Street-involved Youth: Findings from a Youth Clinic in Accra. *Health Transition Centre.* 81-91. Canberra. Australia.

Anarfi, J.K. and
Awusabo-Asare, K. 1993.

Experimental Research on Sexual Networking in Some Selected Areas of Ghana. In *Health Transition Review.* Volume 3. 29-45.

Angrosno, M.V. and
Mays de Perez, K.A. 2000.

Rethinking Observation; From Method to Context. In Denzin, N. and Lincoln, Y.S. *Handbook of Qualitative Research.* 673- 703. Sage Publications. London.

Armstrong, A. 1988.

Culture and Choice: Lesson from Survivors of Gender Violence in Zimbabwe, Harare. Research Project Report.

Arnfred, S. 2004.

Rethinking Sexualities in Africa; Introduction. In Arnfred, S.(ed.). *Rethinking Sexualities in Africa.* 7-35. Alinquivst and Wiksell Tryckeri. Sweden.

Arnfred, S. 2004 .

African Sexuality/ Sexuality in Africa: Tales and Silences," In Arnfred, S. (ed). *Rethinking Sexualities in Africa.* 59-70 Alinquist and Wiksell Tryckeri AB. Sweden.

Aschwanden, H. 1992.

Symbols of Life: An Analysis of the Consciousness of the Karanga. Mambo Press. Gweru.

Awusabo-Asare,K. and
Anarfi, J.K. 1997.

Postpartum Sexual Abstinence in the Era of AIDS in Ghana. *Health Transition Review.* Supplement to Volume 7. 257-271.

Awusabo-Asare, K. Anarfi,
J.K. and Agyeman, K. 1993.

Women's Control Over Their Sexuality and the Spread of STDs and HIV and AIDS in Ghana. In *Health Transition Review.* Supplement to Vol. 3. 69-85.

Ayisi, E. 1979.

An Introduction to the Study of African Culture. Heinemann Educational books, Ltd. London.

Baker, G. 2000

Urban Girls Empowerment in Especially Difficult Circumstances. Southampton. London.

275

Barker, G. 1993.

Research on AIDS: Knowledge, Attitudes And Practices Among Street Youth. *Child World*. 1993: 20(2-3): 41-2 in http//www.ncbinlmnih.gov/entez/fcgi?

Bammeke, F. 2000.

"Gender Differences in Students Perception and Participation in Violence: A Case Study of the University of Lagos, In Oyekanmi, D. (ed.). Men, Women and Violence .CODESRIA. Dakar, Senegal.

Barnard, J. 1973.

The Future of Marriage. World Publishing Company. New York.

Baron, R.A. and
Bryne, D. 1987.

Social Psychology: Understanding Human Interaction, (5th Ed.). Allyn and Balong. London.

Bart, B.P. and O'Brien,
H.P. (eds.). 1993.

Stopping Rape, Successful Survival Strategies. Teachers College Press. New York.

Baylies, L. and Bujra,
J. (eds.). 2000.

"Responses to the AIDS Epidemic in Tanzania and Zambia," In Baylies, C. and Bujra, J. (eds.). *AIDS, Sexuality and Gender in Africa.*25-29. Routledge. London.

Baylies, C. and Bujra,
J. (eds.). 2000.

"The Struggle Continues: Some Conclusions". In Baylies, C. and Bujra, J. *AIDS, Sexuality and Gender in Africa*. 174-198. Routledge. London.

Beal, E.A. 1995.

"Reflections on Ethnography in Morocco: A Critical Reading of Three Seminal Texts". *Critique of Anthropology*. 15(3).

Beattie, J. 1964.

Other Cultures: Aims Methods and Achievements In Social Anthropology. Cohen and West. London.

Becker, H. 1971.

Sociological Work. Aldie Publications. Chicago.

Becker, H. 2004.

"Efundula: Women's Initiation, Gender and Sexual Identities in Colonial and Past Colonial Northern Namibia," In Anfred, S. (ed.).*Rethinking Sexualities in Africa*. 35-39. Almqvist and Wiksell Tryckeri AB. Sweden.

Berger, L. P. and
Luckmann, T. 1966.

The Social Construction of Reality: A Treatise in the Sociology of Knowledge. Garden City, N.Y: Doubleday.

Bhebhe, M. 2000.

"Colonial Stultification of African Science, Technology and The Abuse of The African Culture" In Chiwome et al. *Indigenous Knowledge and Technology in African and Diaspora communities: Multi Disciplinary Approaches* . Southern African Association for Culture and development studies (SAACDS), Harare.

Birke, L. 1992.

"Transforming Biology," In Crowley, H. and Himmelweit, S. (eds.). *Knowing women; Feminist Knowledge*. 66-78. Polity Press. Devon.

Bjornberg, U. 2004.

Making Agreements and Managing Conflicts: Swedish Dual-Earner Couples in Theory and Practice. *Current Sociology*. 52(1): 33-53.

Bo' Strath 2000.

Europe and the Other and Europe as the Other. http//www.arena UTO. No. 1 events/pages/Bo Strath. Pdf.

Bo Wang, Hertog, S. Meier, A. Lou, C. Gao, E. 2005.

"The Potential of Comprehensive Sex Education in China: Findings from Suburban Shanghai" *International Family Planning Perspectives,* 31(2): 63-73.

Bond, V. and Dover, P. 1997.

Men, Women and The Trouble With Condoms: Problems Associated With Condom Use by Migrant Workers in Rural Zambia. *Heath Transition Review*. Supplement to Vol. 7. 377-393.

Bongo, P. 2002.

Unpublished DPhil Thesis Titled, *'The Politics of Environmental Conservation in Selected off-farm Rural Livelihoods; A Case Study of Commercial Tree Bark Fibre Craft Production by Women in Biriwiri and Nyanyadzi, Zimbabwe.* (Department of Sociology. University of Zimbabwe).

Boroffice, O.B. 1995.

Women's Attitudes To Men's Sexual Behaviour. *Health Transition Review*. Supplement to Volume 5. 68-81.

Bourdillon, M. 1994.

Street Children in Harare. *Africa;* Journal of the International African Institute. 4(4): 516-533.

Bourdillon, M. 1993.   *Where are the ancestors? Changing Culture in Zimbabwe.* University of Zimbabwe Publications. Harare.

Bourdillon, M. 1976.   *The Shona Peoples.* Mambo Press. Gweru.

Bourdieu, P. 1977.   *Outline of a theory of Practice.* Press Syndicate of the Cambridge University. New York.

Boyd, C. 2000.   *Decolonisation.* CODESRIA Books. Dakar.

Bo Wang, 2005.   "The Potential of Comprehensive Sex Education in China; Findings from Suburban Shanghai" in International Family Planning Perspectives; Vol 31, No 2.

Bozongwana, W. 2000.   *Ndebele Religion and Customs.* Mambo Press. Gweru.

Brison, S.L. 1998.   "Surviving Sexual Violence: A Philosophical Perspective." In Baker, R.B. Wininger, K.T. and Elliston, F.A. (eds.). *Philosophy and Sex.* 567-583. Prometheus Books. New York.

Britain, A. and Maynard, M. 1994.   *Sexism, Racism and Oppression.* Blackwell Publications. NewYork.

Budgeon, S. and Roseneil, S. 2004.   Editors Introduction. Beyond the Conventional Family. *Current Sociology.* 52(2): 127-135.

Bullough, D. Dixon, D. and Dixon, J.2004.   Sadism, Masochism and History, or When is Behaviour Sado-Masochistic. In Porter, R. and Teich, M. (eds.). *Sexual Knowledge, Sexual Science; The History of Attitudes to Sexuality.* Cambridge University Press. Cambridge.

Butler, U. and Rizzini, I. 2003.   Young People Living and Working on the Streets of Brazil, Revisiting the Literature. In *Children, Youth and Environments.* 13 (1). Retrieved from http://colorado.edu/journals/cye.

Caldwell, J.C. Orubabye, L.O. and Caldwell, P. 1993.   The Role of Religious Leaders in Changing Sexual Behaviour in Southwest Nigeria in an era of AIDS. *Health Transition Review.* Supplement to Volume 3. 93-121.

Caldwell, J.C. Caldwell, P.
Quiggin, P. 1989.

The Social Context of AIDS in Sub- Saharan Africa.
Population and Development Review. 17 (3): 506-515.

Caldwell, P. 1995.

Prostitution and the Risk of STDs and AIDS in Nigeria and "Thailand. *Health Transition Review*. Supplement to Vol. 5. 167-173.

Campbell, C. 2001.

Going Underground and Going After Women; Masculinity and HIV Transmission Amongst Black Workers on the Gold Mines. In Morrell, R. 2001.*Changing Men in Southern Africa*. 128-275.

Caplan, P. 1987.

Introduction in Caplan, P. (ed.). 1-31. Routledge. London.

Carrigan, T. Connell, B
and Lee, J. 2002.

Toward a New Sociology of Masculinity. In Adams, R. and Savron, D. *The Masculinity Studies Reader*. 99-119. Blackwell. London.

Chambers, E. 2000.

Applied Ethnography. In Denzin, N, and Lincoln, S.Y. *Handbook of Qualitative Research*. Sage Publications. London.

Chavunduka, G.L. 1994.

Traditional Medicine in Modern Zimbabwe. U.Z. Publications. Harare.

Chavunduka, G.L. 1979.

A Shona Urban Court. Mambo Press. Gwelo

Chikowore, J. 2004.

Gender Power Dynamics in Sexual and Reproductive Health: A Qualitative Study in Chiredzi District, Zimbabwe. Uppsala University. Netherlands.

Chiome, E. and
Mguni, Z. 2000.

Indigenous Knowledge and Technology in Africa and Diaspora Communities. Southern Africa Association for Culture and Development Studies. Harare.

Chiome, E. and
Mguni, Z. 2000.

The Traditional Healer in Zimbabwe. *In Chiome, E.M. et al (eds.). Indigenous Knowledge and Technology in Africa and Diasporan Communities*. Southern Africa Association for Culture and Development Studies.

Chiroro, P. Mashu, A. and Muhwava, W. 2002.	*The Zimbabwean Male Psyche With Respect to Reproductive Health, HIV, AIDS and Gender Issues.* Centre for Applied Psychology. University of Zimbabwe. Harare.
Chirwa, Y. 2007.	"Children, Youth and Economic Reforms. An Expedition of the State of Street Children in Zimbabwe". In Maphosa, F. Kujunga, K. and Chingarande, S.D. (eds.). Zimbabwe' Development Experiences Since 1980. Challenges and Prospects for the Future. 76-93. OSSREA. Ethiopia.
Chomutare, G. 2007.	"The State of the National Health System in Zimbabwe and its Interface with the HIV and AIDS Epidemic". In Maphosa, F. Kujinga, K. and Chinganande, S.D. (eds.). Zimbabwe's Development Experiences Since 1980. Challenges and Prospects for the Future. 61-76. OSSREA. Addis Ababa. Ethiopia.
Christians, C.G. 2000.	"Ethics and Politics in Qualitative Research". In Denzin, N. and Lincoln, S.Y. *Handbook of Qualitative Research.* 133-156. Sage Publishers, London.
Cohen, B. and Trussell, J. 1996.	*Preventing and Mitigating AIDS in Sub Saharan Africa; Research and Data Priorities for the Social and Behavioural Sciences.* National Academy Press. Washington.
Cole, J.B. 1995.	Human Rights and the Rights of Anthropologists. *Critique of Anthropology.* 17(3).
C.R.C 1989.	Adopted by the General Assembly of the United Nations on 20 November, 1989.
Cornwall, A. and Lindifarne, N. 1994.	"Dislocating Masculinity: Gender, Power and Anthropology". In Cornwall, A. and Lindifarne, N. (eds.). *Dislocating Masculinity; Comparative Ethnographies.* 11-48. Routledge. London.
Crawford, P. 1994.	"Sexual Knowledge in England 1500-1750". In Peter, R. and Teich, M. (eds.).*Sexual Knowledge, Sexual Science, the History of Attitudes to Sexuality.* Cambridge University Press. Cambridge.
Dachneri, N. and Tarasuk, V. 2002.	Homeless, "Squeegee Kids": Food Insecurity and Daily Survival. *Social Science and Medicine.* 54, 1039-1049.

Daines, C.A. 1999.   *Reflexive Ethnography: A Guide to Researching Selves and Others*. Routledge. New York.

Day, S. 1994.   "What Counts as Rape? Physical Assault and Broken Contracts: Contrasting Views of Rape Among London Sex Workers". In *Harvey*, P. and Gow, P. *Sex and Violence*. 172-190. Routledge. London.

De Beavouirs, S. 1988.   *The Second Sex*. Pan Books. London.

Denzin, N. and   *Handbook of Qualitative Research*. Sage Publications.
Lincoln, Y.S. (eds.). 2000.   London.

Denzin, N.K. and   "Introduction; The Discipline and Practice of
Lincoln, Y.S. 2000.   Qualitative Research". In Denzin, N. and Lincoln, Y.S. *Handbook of Qualitative Research*. 1-30. Sage Publications. London.

DeVenanzi, A. 2003.   Street Children and the Excluded Class. In *International Journal of Comparative Sociology*. 472-492.

Dhlembeu, N. and   Responding to the Orphans and Other Vulnerable
Manyanga, N. 2006.   Children's Crisis, Development of the Zimbabwe National Plan of Action. *Journal of Social Development*. 21(1): 35-50.

Dickens, C. 1993.   *Hard Times*. The Norton Anthropology Edition. London.

Di Stefano, G. and   Demographic Characteristics and Family Life.
Pinnell, A. 2004.   *Current Sociology*. 52(3): 339-371.

The Standard   Domestic Violence Bill,
10 December 2006.

Donal, J. and   *Race, Culture and Difference*. Sage Publications, Ltd.
Rattansi, A. 1992.   London.

281

Douglas, M. 1980.   *Evans-Pritchard.* The Harvester Press Ltd. Sussex.

Drakakis-Smith, D. 1997.   *The Third World City.* Routledge. London.

Dube, L.1997.   AIDS-Risk Patterns and Knowledge of the Disease Among
                           Street Children in Harare. *Journal of Social Development in
                           Africa.* 12(.2). 61-75.

Dube, L. 1999.   *Street Children: A part of Organised Society?* Dphil.
                           Dissertation, Sociology Department, University of
                           Zimbabwe. Harare.

Eiwing, K.P. 1994.   Dreams from a Saint: Anthropological Atheism and the
                           Temptation to Believe. *American Anthropologist.* 9(3).
Ennew, J. 1976.   Examining the Facts in Fieldwork. *Critique of Anthropology.*
                           2 (7): 43-67.

Ennew, J. and   "Introduction: Homes, Places and Spaces in the
Kruger, J. 2003.   Construction of Street Children and Street Youth" *In
                           Children, Youth and Environments.* 13(1). Retrieved from
                           http://colorado.edu/journals/cye

Esner, E. W. 1993.   "Foreword, "Critique *of Anthropology.* 1993.

Evans, D.T. 1993.   *Sexual Citizenship; The Material Construction of Sexualities.*
                           Routledge. London.

Ezeilo, N.J. 2003.   HIV and AIDS Human Rights Litigation and De-
                           Stigmatisation: The African Experience. *CODESRIA
                           BULLETIN* Number 2,3 and 4. 65-70.

Felsman, J.K. 2006.   Orphans and Other Vulnerable Children in Zimbabwe.
                           Journal of Social Development in Africa. 21(1). 6-12.

Feltoe, G. 2004.   *A Guide to the Criminal Law of Zimbabwe.* Legal Resources
                           Foundation. Harare, Zimbabwe.

Field, S. 2001.   "Disappointed Men, Masculine Myths and Hybrid Identities in Windermere". In Morrell, R. (ed.). *Changing Men in Southern Africa.* 211-225.

Foa, P. 1998.   "What's Wrong with Rape?" In Baker, R.B Wininger, J.K. and Ellisten, F.A. (eds.). *Philosophy and Sex* by. 583-594. Prometheus Books. New York.

Fokwang, J. 1999.   The African Youth, Competing Cultures and the Future of Development. *South - South Journal of Development.* 1(1): 44-66.

Fontana, A. and   "The Interview-From Structured to Negotiated
Fray, J.H. 2000.   Question Text". In Denzin, N. and Lincoln, Y.S. *Handbook of Qualitative Research.* 645-673. Sage Publishers. London.

Fortier, A. 1990.   Troubles in the Field; the Use of Personal Experiences as Sources of Knowledge. *Critique of Anthropology.* 16(3).

Foucault, M. 1978.   *History of Sexuality; Volume One.* Penguin Books. London.

Foucault, M. 1998.   "Domain," In Wininger, K.J. and Elliston, F.A. (eds.). *Philosophy and Sex.* 405-413. Prometheus Books, New York.

Fox, J.N. 1993.   *Postmodernism, Sociology and Health.* Open University Press. Buckingham.

Francoeur, R.T. 1994.   *Taking Sides, Clashing Issues in Human Sexuality.* The Dushk in Publishing Groups. Guilford. USA.

Freud, S. 2002   "Some Psychological Consequences of the Anatomical Distinction Between the Sexes". In Adams, R. and Savron, D. (eds). *The Masculinity Studies Reader.* 14-21. Blackwell Publishers. Oxford.

Friedl, E. 1994.   Sex the Invisible. *American Anthropologist.* 96(4).

Gadir, Ali. 1992.   Structural Adjustment Programmes and Poverty Creation; Evidence from Sudan. Eastern Africa Social Science Research Review. VIII. (I): 1-22.

283

GALZ, 1994.   Sexual Orientations and Zimbabwe's New Constitution. *Law
                               Society of Zimbabwe* Magazine, Number 3, 1999.

Gaussette, Q. 2001.   AIDS and Cultural Practices in Africa; The Case of the
                               Tonga (Zambia).*Social Science and Medicine*. 52(4).

Geertz, C. 1984.   "Distinguished Lectures and Antirelativism", in American
                               Anthropologist, Vol 86, 1984.

Gelfand, M. 1999.   *The Genuine Shona*. Mambo Press. Gweru.

Giddens, A. 1984.   *The Constitution of Society*. Polity Press. Cambridge

Gillman, S. 1995.   "White Bodies, Black Bodies Toward Iconograph of Female
                               Sexuality. In Gates, L. *Late 19th Century; Art, Medicine and
                               Literature*. University of Chicago Press. London

Gittins, D. 1985   *The Family in Question*. Macmillan Press. London.

Glauser, B. 1997.   Street Children: Deconstructing a Construct. In *Jones, A. and
                               Prout, A. (eds). Constructing and Reconstructing Childhood:
                               Contemporary Issues in the Sociological Study of childhood.*
                               145-164. Palmer Press. London.

Godwin P &   *"Rhodesians Never Die"*. Oxford University Press.
Hancock, L. 1993.   Oxford.

Godwin, P and   *"Rhodesians Never Die"*. Baobab Books. Harare.
Hancock, L. 1993.

Goffman, E. 1969.   "On Face-Work". In Goffman, E.(ed). *Where the Actions.*
                               Penguin Books. London

Goikochea, P. 1990.   Reaching Boys Who Sell Sex in Peru". In *AIDS WATCH
                               1990:* (11): 2-3 on http//www.ncbinlmnih.gov/entez.

Gomo, E. Jokomo, Z.   Zimbabwe Human Development Report; Redirecting
Mate, R. and   Our Responses to HIV and AIDS. "Towards
Chipika, J. 2003.   Reducing Vulnerability-the Ultimate War for Survival.
                               Produced by Poverty Reduction Forum".

Gordon, A.G. 1982.   Human Sexuality. The C.V. Mosby Compan. London.

Green, G. 2001.   "Female Control of Sexuality: Illusion or Reality: Use of Vaginal Products in South West Uganda". *Social Science and Medicine.* 52(4).

Gregory, J.R. 1984.   The Myth of the Male Ethnographer and the Woman's World. *American Anthropologist.* 86(1).

Guild, C. and   *Women and Philosophy: Toward a Theory Of*
Wartofsky, M.W. 1980.   *Liberation.* Perigee Books.New York.

Halperin, M. 1998.   *"Is there a History of Sexuality". In* Baker, R.B. Wininger, K.J. and Elliston, F.A. (eds.). *Philosophy and Sex.* Prometheus Books. New York.

Halperin, D. 2002.   *"The Democratic Body: Prostitution and Citizenships in Classical Athens".* In Adams, R. and Savron, D. The Masculinity Studies Reader. 66-77. Blackwell. London.

Haram, L. 2004.   "Prostitutes or Modern Women? Negotiating Respectability in Northern Tanzania" In Arnfred, S. (eds.)*Rethinking Sexualities in Africa.* Almqvist and Wiksell Tryckeri. Sweden.

Harris, M. 1993.   *'The Evolution of Human Gender Hierarchies a Trial Formulation".* In Miller, B.D. (ed). Sex and Gender Hierarchies. 57-81. Cambridge University Press. Cambridge.

Harvey, P and   *Sex and Violence: Issues in Representation and*
Gow, P. 1994.   *Experience.* Routledge. London.

Hastrup, K. and
Eelsass, P. 1990.   Anthropological Advocacy; A Contradiction in Terms? *Current Anthropology* .31(3).

Hauser-Schaublin,   *"Blood; Cultural Effectiveness of Biological*
B. 1993.   *Conditions".* In Muller, B. (eds.). Sex and Gender Hierarchies. 83-108. Cambridge University Press. London.

Hauser, R. 1994.

"Kraft-Ebing's Psychological Understanding of Sexual Behaviour". In Porter, R. and Teicry, M. *Sexual Knowledge, Sexual Science. The History of Attitudes to Sexuality.* Cambridge University Press. Cambridge.

Heald. 1995.

The Power of Sex: Reflections on the Caldwells' African Sexuality Thesis. *Africa; Journal of the International African Institute.* 65(4): 489-506.

Heath, S. 2004.

Peer-Shared Households, Quasi Communes and Neo-Tribes. *Current Sociology.* 52(2): 161-181.

Hecht, T. 1998.

At Home in the Street: Street Children of North East Brazil. Cambridge University Press. London.

Helle-Valle, J. 2004.

"Understanding Sexuality in Africa: Diversity and Contextualized Individuality". In Arnfred, S. (ed). *Rethinking African Sexualities.* 195-211. Aimqust and Wiksell Trykeri. Sweden.

Herbst, J. 1990.

State Politics in Zimbabwe. The University of Zimbabwe Publications. Harare.

Higgit et al 2003.

Voices From The Margins: Experiences of Street-involved Youth in Winnipeg. Retrieved from http://colorado.edu/jourals/cye

Huggins, M.K. and
Rodriguez, S. 2004.

Children Working Along Paulista Avenue. *Childhood* 11(4): 495-514.

Hutnyk, J. 1998.

"Clifford's Ethnography". *Critique of Anthropology.* 18(4): 339-379.

Huygens, P. et al 1996.

"Rethinking Methods for the Study of Sexual Behaviour". *Social Science and Medicine.* 42(2): 221-231.

Hyde, J.S. 1998.

Understanding Human Sexuality. McGraw-Hill .New York.

I.M.F. 2001;

The IMF Enhanced Structural Adjustment Facility (ESAF): Is it Working? Retrieved from http://www.imf.org/external/pubs/esaf/ext/omdex/it

Ikamba, L.M. and
Ouedraogo, B.2003.

"High Risk Sexual Behaviour: Knowledge, Attitude and Practice Among Youths at Kithangani Ward, Tanga, Tanzania," on
http//wwwzths.usvdedu/arrow/oldarer/01htm.

Irigoroy, L. 1998.

"This Sex Which Is Not One". In Baker, R.B. Wininger, J.K. and Elliston, F.A. (eds.). *Philosophy and Sex.* Prometheus Books. New York.

Jackson, B. 1998.

Fieldwork. Illin Books. New York.

Jackson, M. 1987.

"Facts of Life" or *The Eroticisation of Women's Oppression? Sexology and the Social Construction of Heterosexuality".* In Caplan, P. (ed.).The Cultural construction of Sexuality. 52-82. Routledge. London.

Jagger, M. 1992.

"Human Biology in Feminist Theory; Sexual Equality Reconsidered". In Crowley, H. and Himmelweit, S. *Knowing Women; Feminist Knowledge.* 78-90. Polity Press. Devon.

Jenkins, C. 1999.

Resistance to Condom Use in a Bangladesh Brothel. *Health Transition Centre.* 211-223. Canberra. Australia.

Jenkins, R. 2002.

Foundations of Sociology. McMillan. New York.

Jensen, R. 1998.

"Patriarchal Sex". In Baker, R.B. Wininger, K.J. and Elliston, F.A. (eds.). *Philosophy and Sex.* 533-549. Prometheus Books. New York.

Johnson, T.M. 2006.

Creating a Foundation of Confidence Rethinking Effective HIV and AIDS Prevention Strategies for Zimbabwe's Orphans. *Journal of Social Development.* 21(1): 50-67.

Jones, S. 1993.

Assaulting Childhood; Children's Experiences of Migrancy and Hostel Life in South Africa. Witwatersrand University Press. Johannesburg.

Kaseke, E.1993.

Juvenile Justice in Zimbabwe. *Journal of Social Development in Africa.*8 (1): 13-19.

Kaseke, E. 2003.

Social Exclusion and Social Sexuality: The Case of Zimbabwe. *Journal of Social Development in Africa.*18 (1): 33-49.

Kayongo-Male, D. &
Onyango, P. 1984.

The Sociology of the African Family. Longman Inc. New York.

Kelly, L. 1998.

Surviving Sexual Violence. Polity Press. Cambridge.

Kelly, G.F. 2004.

Sexuality Today. McGraw-Hill. London.

Kheswa and Wieringa,
S. 2004.

"My Attitude is Mainly, ---A Girl Needs to Walk on
The Aisle: Butch-Famine Subculture in Johannesburg, South Africa". In Morgan, R. and Wieringa, S. (eds). *Tommy Boys Lesbian Men and Ancestral Wives; Female Same Sex Practices in Africa.* 199-231. Gala Publishers. South Africa.

Kimuna, S.R. and
Djamba, Y. 2005.

Wealth and Extra Marital Sex Among Men in
Zambia. *International Family Planning Perspectives.* 31(2): 83-90.

Kimmell, M. 2001.

"Afterword". In Morrell, R. (ed.). *Changing Men in Southern Africa.* 337-341. Zed Books. London.

King, H. 1994.

"Sowing the Field: Greek and Roman Sexology". In Porter, R. and Teich, M. (eds). *Sexual Science, Sexual Knowledge.*

Kolibrie 2005.

Otherisation. Retrieved from
http//comedia.kolibrie.net

Konte-Luke, J.K.
Sewankambo, N. and
Morris, M.1997.

Adolescent Sexual Networking and HIV
Transmission in Rural Uganda," *Health Transition Review.* Supplement to Volume 7. 89-101.

Krotz, E. 1997.

Anthropologies of the South, South, their Rise, their Silencing, their Characteristics. *Critique of Anthropology.* 17(3): 237-253.

Kuper, A. 1991.

"Anthropologists and The History of Anthropology". *Critique of Anthropology.* 11(4).

Kwan, D.J. and Lowe, F.C. 1990.

Acquired Immuno Deficiency Sydrome; A Venereal Disease. *Review, Urologic Clinics of North America.* 19(1): 13-24.

Lagree, J. 2004.

Review Essay: Youth, Families and Global Transformation. *Current-Sociology.* 52(1).

LeBlank, M. et al 1991.

The African Sexual System: Comment on Caldwell et al. *Population and Development Review.* 17(3): 497-505.

Leeds, A. 1987.

Fieldwork, History and Anthropological Epistemology: A Critique of Llobera's Scientism. *Critique of Anthropology.* 7(1).

Levin, I. 2004.

Living Apart Together: A New Family Form. *Current Sociology.* .52(2): 223-241.

Lessie, J. 1994.

"Some Indian Views on Menstruation and Female Sexuality". In Poter, R. and Tich, M. (eds.). *Sexual Knowledge, Sexual Science; The History of Attitudes to Sexuality.* Cambridge University Press. Cambridge.

Lim, L. (ed) 1998.

"Child Prostitution" in The Sex Sector; The Social and Economic Bases of Prostitution in South-East Asia; International Labour Office, Geneva.

Llobera, J.R. 1976.

"The History of Anthropology as a Problem". *Critique of Anthropology.* .2(7).

Louw, R. 2001.

"Mkhumbane and New Traditions of (Un) African Same-Sex Weddings". In Morrell, R. (ed.). *Changing Men in Southern Africa.* 287-297.Zed Books, LTD. London.

M'.Kim, Y. et al 2001.

"Promoting Sexual Responsibility Among Young People in Zimbabwe". Retrieved from http://www.tarsc.org/prog5html

Machera, M. 2000.

"Domestic Violence in Kenya; A Survey of Newspaper Reports". In Oyekanumi, F. (ed.). *Men, Women and Violence.* 25-51. A collection of Papers from CODESRIA Gender Institute, (1997).

Machera, M. 2004.

"Opening a Can of Worms: A Debate of Female Sexuality in the Lecture Theatre". In Arnfred, S. (ed.). *Rethinking African Sexualities.* Almqvist and Wiksell Tryckeri, A.B. Sweden.

Magaisa, I.T. 1999.

Thesis (Unpublished) *"Prostitution in Zimbabwe: A Case Study of Black Female Heterosexual Prostitutes in Harare, Zimbabwe.* Department of Sociology, University of Zimbabwe.

Mann, J. Tarantola, D.J.M. and Netter, T.W.1992.

AIDS In The World. Harvard University Press. U.S.A.

Maphosa, F. 2007.

"Zimbabwe's Post Independence Development Policies: Contradictions and Inconsistencies: An Introduction." In Maphosa, F. and Chingarande, S. (eds.). Zimbabwe's Experiences Since 1980: Challenges and Prospects for the Future. 1-9. OSSREA.

Maphosa, F. 2003.

HIV and AIDS at the Workplace; A Study of Corporate Responses to the HIV and AIDS Pandemic in Zimbabwe. *CODESRIA BULLETIN .* Nos. 2, 3and 4. 56-59.

Marek, J. 1997.

Aspects of Male Circumcision in Sub-Equatorial African Culture History. *Health Transition Review.* Supplement to volume7.337-361.

Margolis, M. 1993.

Helping Street Kids Cope With AIDS. *Network,* 1993 May 13 (4): 28-29 on http://www.ncbl.nlm.nih.gov/entrez

Marima, R. 1993.

Survival Mechanisms and Coping Strategies of Street Children in Harare. (BSc Psyc. Dissertation), Psychology Department, University of Zimbabwe.

Masters, W.H. Johnson and Kologny.1995.

Human Sexuality. Longman. Madrid.

Masunungure, E. and Chimanikire, D.P. 2007.	*"Policy Paradigm Shifts in Zimbabwe: From Statism to 'Rolling Back the State'to Policy Vacillations"*. In Maphosa, E. Kujinga, K. and Chimanikire, S.D. (eds.). Zimbabwe's Development Experiences Since 1980: Challenges and Prospects for the Future. 9-34. OSSREA. Addis Ababa, Ethiopia.
May, L and Strikweda 1998.	"Men in Groups: Collective Responsibility for Rape". In Baker, R.B. (ed.). *Philosophy of Sex.* Prometheus Books. New York.
Mazrul, A. 2004.	"On Gender and Sexuality". In Mazrui, A. and Mutunga, W. (eds.). *Race, Gender Culture Conflict: Debating The African Condition.* African world Press. Asmora, Eritrea.
Mbigi, L. 2000.	In Search of the African Business Renaissance: An African Cultural Perspective. Randburg, South Africa Knowledge Resources.
McFadden, P. 1992.	"Sex, Sexuality and the Problem of AIDS in Africa". *Gender in Southern Africa: Conceptual and Theoretical Issues.* SAPES Books. Harare.
Meekers, D. and Calves, A.E. 1997.	"Main Girlfriends, Girlfriends, Marriage and Money; the Social Context of HIV Risk Behaviour in sub-Saharan Africa". *Health Transition Review.* Volume 7. 361-377.
Mufune, P. 2003.	Social Sciences and HIV and AIDS Policies in Africa. *CODESRIA BULLETIN. Nos. 2, 3 and 4.* 44- 48.
Mires, M. 1986.	*Patriarchy and Accumulation on a World Scale: Women in International Division of Labour.* Zed Books Ltd. London.
Mikim, Y. Kols, A. Nyakauru, R. Marangwanda, C. and Chibatamoto, P. 2004.	Using P.R.A. to Explore School-going Adolescents' View on their Sexual and Reproductive Health-Promoting Sexual Responsibilities Among Young People in Zimbabwe. 1-19. Retrieved from http://www.guttmacher.org/pubs/journals/htm.
Miller, B.D. 1993.	"Preface". In Miller, B.D. (ed.). *Sex and Gender Hierarchies.* 8-15. Cambridge University Press. Cambridge.

Miller, B.D. 1993.

"The Anthropology of Sex and Gender Hierarchies". In Miller, B.D. (ed.). *Sex and Gender Hierarchies.* 3-32. Cambridge University Press. Cambridge.

Miller, J.B. 1996.

Towards a New Psychology of Women. Beacon Press. Boston.

Mitterauter, M. 1994.

"The Customs of the Mangaians: The Problem of Incest in Historical Societies". In Porter, R. and Teich, M. (eds.). *Sexual Attitudes to Sexuality.* Cambridge University Press. Cambridge.

Mohlina, C.R. 1998.

"Is There Risk of AIDS Among Adolescents?" *Bol Asoc Chil Prot Farm,* 1988 January-June; 24(1-6):6-9. On http://www.ncbinlm nih.gov/entrez.

Moore, H. 1994.

"The Problem of Exploring Violence in the Social Sciences". In Harvey, P. and Gow, P. *Sex and Violence.* 138-156. Routledge. London.

Moore, J.H. 1994.

"Putting Anthropology Back Together Again: The Ethnographic Critique of Cladistic Theory". *American Anthropologist.* 96(4).

Moran, R. and Castro, C. 1997.

Street Children and the Inter-American Development Bank: Lessons Learnt from Brazil; Inter-American Bank Discussion Paper, March 13.

Morauta, L. 1979.

Indigenous Anthropology in Papua New Guinea. *Current Anthropology.* 20(3).

Morgan, R. and Wieringa, S. 2004.

"Introduction". In Morgan, R and Wieringa, S. (eds.). *Tommy Boys, Lesbian Men and Ancestral Wives; 'Female Same Sex Practices in Africa.* 309-325. Gala Publishers. South Africa.

Morrell and Ritcher 2006.

'Introduction'. In Morrell, R. and Richter, L. *Baba; Men and Fatherhood in South Africa.* 1-13. HSRC Press. Cape Town.

Morris, B. 1997.

In Defence of Realism and Truth; Critical Reflections on the Anthropological Followers of Heideggerr. *Critique of Anthropology.* 17(3): 313-341.

Mortensen, R. 1994.

"The Transformation of Eve: Women's Bodies, Medicine and Culture in Early Modern England". In Porter, R. and Teich, M. (eds). *Sexual Knowledge, Sexual Science: The History of Sexual Attitudes to 'Sexuality.* Cambridge University Press. Cambridge.

Muehlenhard, L. 1998.

"Is Rape, Sex or Violence? Conceptual Issues and Implications". In *Baker,* R.B. Wininger, K.J. and Elliston, F.A. *Philosophy and Sex.* 621-640. Prometheus Books. New York.

Mupedziswa, 2006.

"Editorial". *Journal of Social Development.* 21(1): 3-4.

Mupemba, K. 1999.

The Zimbabwean HIV Prevention Program for Truck Drivers and Commercial Sex Workers: A Behaviour Change Intervention. *Health Transition Centre.* 33-39. Canberra. Australia.

Murphy, C. and
Ross-Larson,
B. (eds.). 2004.

Human Development Report: Cultural Liberty in Today's Diverse World. I.U.N. Plaza, New York. New York. 10017. U.S.A.

Musengezi, C. and
Staunton, I. (eds) 2003.

A Tragedy of Lives; Women in Prison in Zimbabwe. Weaver Press, Harare.

Mushunje, M.T. 2006.

Child Protection in Zimbabwe, Yesterday, Today and Tomorrow. *Journal of Social Development.* 21(1): 12-35.

Mutsvairo, S.1996.

Introduction to Shona Culture. Eiffel Flats, Juta. Harare.

Muzvidziwa, V.N. 2000.

"Food Vending: Adoption Under Difficult Circumstances". *Journal of Social Development in Africa.* 15(3): 69-93.

Muzvidziwa, V.N. 2002.

HIV and *AIDS* and Orphans in Zimbabwe; *Surviving and Coping Mechanisms.* *Paper Presented at SAPES TRUST Colloquium on HIV* and *AIDS and Socio-Economic Development in Southern Africa,* 22-23 Sept.

Muzvidziwa, V.N. 2005.

*Women Without Borders. Organisation for Social Science Research in Eastern and Southern Africa.*OSSREA. Ethiopia.

Muzvidziwa, V.N. 2004.

Reflections On Ethical Issues; A study of How Urban Women Dealt With Impoverishment. *Nordic Journal of African Studies,* 13(3).

Mwikisa, C.N. 2003.

The Impact and Investment Implications of HIV and AIDS On Human Capital in sub-Saharan Africa. *CODESRIA Bulletin* Nos. 2, 3 and 4. 59-62.

Nag, M. 2001.

Sexual Behaviour in India With Rise of HIV and AIDS Transmission. *Health Transition Review.* Supplement to Volume 5. 293-305.

Nakanaabi, L. Ntozi, J. and Lubaale, L. 1997.

AIDS Mortality in Uganda: Circumstances, Factors and Impact of Death. *Health Transition Review.* Supplement to Volume 7. 207-225.

Narayan, K. 1993.

Essay: How Native is a "Native Anthropologist". America Anthropologist. 5(3).

Nardi, P.M. 2001.

"A Vicarious Sense of Belongings; The Politics of Friendships and Gay Social Movements, Communities and Neighbourhoods". In Whitehead, S.M. and Barrett, F.J. *The Masculinities Reader.* 288-307. Polity. Oxford.

Newton, N. 2001.

Applying Best Practices To Youth Reproductive Health; SEATS Project. Report for USAID.

Nhamo, O. 2002.

Desk Study On Sexual Behaviour and Reproductive Health of Children and Young People in Zimbabwe; Awareness Versus Behaviour Change; HIV Infection and Child Sexual Abuse, The Role of Stigma and Discrimination. Zimbabwe Report.

Njang, I. 2003.

Family Sexuality Reproduction in Africa. *CODESRIA BULLETIN Nos. 2, 3 and 4.* 39-42.

Nkabinde, N. and Morgan, R. 2004.

"This Has Happened Since Ancient Times; Its Something You are Born With; Ancestral Wives Amongst Same Sex Sangomas in South Africa". In Morgan, R. and Wieringa, S. (eds). T*ommy Boys, Lesbian Men and Ancestral Wives, Female Same Sex Practices in Africa.* 231-261. Gala Publishers. South Africa.

294

Ntozi, J. and Kiringa, C. 1997.

HIV and AIDS, Change in Sexual Behaviour and Community Attitudes in Uganda. *Health Transition Review.* Supplement to Volume 7. 157-175.

Nussbaum, N. 1999.

Sex and Social Justice. Oxford University Press. Oxford.

Nyathi, P. 2001.

Traditional Ceremonies of amaNdebele. Mambo Press. Gweru.

Oakley, A. 1985.

Sex, Gender and Society. Gower Publishing Co. Aldershot, England.

Ogbuagu, S. C. and Charles, J.O. 1993.

Survey of Sexual Networking in Calabar. *Health Transition Review.* Supplement to   Volume 3. 105-121.

Oloko, B.A. and Omoboloye, A.O. 1993.

Sexual Networking Among Some Lagos State Adolescent Yoruba Students. *Health Transition Review.* Supplementary issue, Volume.3. 151-159.

Olukoshi, A. and Nyamnjoh, F. 2003.

Editorial. *CODESRIA BULLETIN, Special Issues, 2,3* and 4. P.I.

Omorodion, F. 1993.

'Sexual Networking Among Market Women Benin City. Bendel State, Nigeria.

Ondimu, K.N. 2005.

Risky Sexual Behaviours Among Migrant Tea Workers in Eastern and Southern Africa. OSSREA Addis Ababa, Ethiopia.

Orubuloye, I.O. Oguntemehin, F. and Sadiq, T. 1997.

Women's Role in Reproductive Health Decision Making and Vulnerability to STD and HIV and AIDS in Ekiti, Nigeria. *Health Transition Review. Supplement to Volume 7.* 329-337.

Orubuloye, I.O. Omoniyi, O.P. and Shokunbi, W.A.1995.

Sexual Networking, STDs and HIV and AIDS in Four Urban Goals in Nigeria. *Health Transition Review.* Supplement to Volume 5. 123-131.

Orubuloye, I.O. Coldwell, J. and Coldwell, P.1997.

Men's Sexual Behaviour in Urban and Rural Southwest Nigeria; Its Cultural, Social and Attitudinal

Context. *Health Transition Review*. Supplement to Volume 5. 315-329.

Owunaman, D.O. 1995.   Sexual Networking Among Youth in South-Western Nigeria. *Health Transition Review*. Supplement to Volume.5. 57-67.

Oyekamni, (ed) 2000.   Men, Women and Violence. CODESRIA. Senegal.

Oyeneye, O.Y. and
Kawonise, S. 1993.   Sexual Networking in Ijebu-Ode, Nigeria; An Exploratory Study. *Health Transition Review*, Volume 3. Supplementary issue. 171-185.

Padgug, R. 1998.   "Sexual Matters; On Conceptualising Sexuality in History". In Baker, R.B. Wininger, K.J. and Elliston, F.A. *Philosophy and Sex*. 432-449. Prometheus Books. New York.

Panter-Brick, C. 2003.   Street Children, Human Rights and Public Health; A Critique and Future Directions. *Children, Youth and Environments*. 13(1): 147-171.

Parsons, H. 2004.   "Bleak Future for Zimbabwe's Street Children". In *The Standard (Newspaper) of 20 June*, 2004, Zimbabwe, Harare.

Peil, M. 1977.   *Consensus and Conflict in African Societies*. Longman. London.

Pickup, F. Williams, S.
and Sweetman, C. 2001.   *Ending Violence Against Women*. Oxfam Publication.

Pool, R. 1991.   Post-Modern Ethnography? *Critique of Anthropology*. 11(4).

Porter, R. 1994.   "The Literature on Sexual Advice Before 1800". In Porter, R. and Teich, M. (eds.). *Sexual Knowledge, Sexual Science: The History of Attitudes to Sexuality*. Cambridge University Press. Cambridge.

Porter, R. and Teich,
M. (eds.). 1994.   *Sexual Knowledge, Sexual Science; The History of Attitudes to Sexuality*. Cambridge University Press.

Cambridge.

Powell, G. 2006.

Children in Institutional Care: Lessons From Zimbabwe's Experience. *Journal of Social Development*. 21(1). 130-146.

Prah, K. 1989.

In Search of a Tradition for Social Science Research in Africa for the 1990s. *Eastern Africa Social Science Research Review*. 8(1): 30-41.

Preston-Whyte, E. 1999.

Reproductive Health and the Condom Dilemma: Identifying Situational Barriers to HIV Protection in South Africa. *Health Transition Centre*. 139-157. Canberra. Australia.

Rabe, M.2006.

"Being a Father in a Man's World; The Experience of Goldmine Workers." In Morrell, R. and Richter, L. *Baba: Men and Fatherhood in South Africa*. 250-265. HSRC Press Cape Town.

Rapp, 1993.

"Reproduction and Gender Hierarchy; Amniocentesis in America". In Miller, D.B (ed.). *Sex and Gender Hierarchies*. 108-127. Cambridge University Press. London.

Rennie, E.P. 1993.

Changes in Adolescent Sexuality and the Perception of Virginity in a South-Western Nigerian Village. *Health Transition Review. Supplement to Volume 3*. 121-135.

Ritcher, R. and
Ramphele, M.2006.

"Migrancy, Family Dissolution and Fatherhood". In Morrell and Richter 2006. *Baba: Men and Fatherhood in South Africa*. 73-82. H.S.R.L. Press. Cape Town.

Ritcher, L.M. and
Swart-Kruger, J. 1993.

"AIDS-Risk Among Street Children and Youth: Implication for Intervention". *South African Journal of Psychology*. 25(1).

Ritcher, L.M.,
Swart-Kruger, J.
and Barnes, J. 1997

Conference Paper, Titled *"Street Children and Youth in South Africa: AIDS- Related Knowledge, Attitudes and Behaviour"* (Handout in Department of Sociology Library at the University of Zimbabwe). Harare.

Ritcher, L. and Swart,

"Society Makes Survival A Crime". *Recovery 1* (4).

J. 1996.

Rios, D. 2004.   "Mechanistic Explanations in The Social Sciences".*Current Sociology.* 52(1): 75-91.

Ritzer, G. 1992.   *Modern Social Theory.* McGraw-Hill. New York.

Rizzini, I. 1996.   Street Children: An Excluded Generation in South America. *Childhood.* 3(1): 215-234.

Roseneil, S. & Budgeon,   Cultures of Intimacy and Love Beyond "The Family":
S. 2004.   Personal Life and Social Change in the Early 21st Century. *Current Sociology.* 52(2): 135-161.

Roy, K. 2003.   *"Desire On The Street: Same Sex Behaviour and Perception of Sexuality Among Street Youths of Calcutta"* on http://wiseweb,wits.ac.za/conf2003/roy.doc

Ruiz, J. 1994.   "Street youth in Colombia: Lifestyle, Attitudes and Knowledge". *AIDS Health Prom of Exch.* 1994; 12-4 on http://www.ncbl.nlm.nih.gov/entrez.

Rurevo, R. and   Girls: the Less Visible Street Children of Zimbabwe.
Bourdillon, M. 2003.   *Children, Youth and Environments.* 13(1).

Rwabukwall, C.B. 1992.   Sexual Behaviour and the Acceptability of Condoms to Uganda Males. *Eastern Africa Social Science Research Review.* 8(1): 33-46.

Ryan, J. 1992.   "Psychoanalysis and Women Loving Women". In Crowley, H. and Himmelweit, S. *Knowing Women; Feminism Knowledge.* 170-182. Policy Press. Devon.

Ryan, W.G. and   "Data Management and Analysis Methods". In
Bernard, R.H. 2000.   Denzin, N.Y. and Lincoln, Y.S.(eds.). *Handbook of Qualitative Research.* 769-803. Sage Publications. California.

Sabey, J. 2001.   Cost Effectiveness of the Female Condom in Preventing HIV and STDs in Commercial Sex Workers in Rural South Africa. *Social Science and Medicine.* 52(1).

Sanadjian, M. 1990.

From Participant to Partisan Observation: An Open End. *Critique of Anthropology.* 10(1).

Sauve, S. 2003.

Changing Paradigms for Working With Street Youth: The Experience of Street Kids International. *Children, Youth and 'Environments.* 13(1). Retrieved from http://cye.colorado.edu.

Segal, L. 2001.

"The Belly of the Beast: Sex as Male Domination?" In Whitehead, S.M. and Barrett, F.J. *The Masculinities Readers.* 100-112. Polity. Oxford.

Seidler, V.J. 1987.

"Reason, Desire and Male Sexuality". In Caplan, P. (ed.). *The Cultural Construction of Sexuality.* 82-113. Routledge. London.

Silberchmidt, M. 1999.

"Women Forget That Men Are Masters": Gender Antagonism and Socio-Economic Change in Kisii District in Kenya, NORASKA.

Sesay, A. 2003.

The African Child and Youth and HIV and AIDS: Our Tragedy, Our Future. *CODESRIA Bulletin Nos. 2, 3 and 4.* 42-44.

Shire, C. 1994.

"Men Don't Go to the Moon: Language and Space and Masculinities in Zimbabwe". In Cornwall, A. and Lindifarne, N. (eds.). *Dislocating Masculinities Comparative Ethnographies.* 147-159. Routledge. London.

Simasiku, R. 2004.

"The Problem of Street Children in Kampala City". *Report From the Regional Symposium On Child Research in Southern Africa; Children and Youth Living in Circumstances of Poverty and Marginalization, October.*

Singer, L. 1998.

"Sex and The Logic of Late Capitalism". In Baker, RB Wininger, K.J. and Elliston, F.A. (eds.). *Philosophy and Sex.* 449-476. Prometheus Books. New York.

Stacey, J. 2004.

Cruising to Family land: Gay Hypergamy and Rainbow

Kinship. *Current Sociology.* 2(2): 181-199.

Stake, R.E. 2000.

"Case Studies". In Denzin, N. and Lincoln, S.Y. (eds.). *Handbook of Qualitative Research.* 435-455. Sage Publishers. London.

Stanley L. & Wise, S. 1983.

Breaking Out Again: Feminist Ontology and Epistemology. Routledge. London.

Stein. 1998.

"Essentialism and Constructionism in Sexual Orientation". In Baker, R.B. Wininger, K.J. and Elliston, F.A. (eds.). *Philosophy and Sex.* 383-397. Prometheus Book. New York.

Strathern, M. 1987.

Out of Context; The Persuasive Fictions of Anthropology. *Current Anthropology.* 28(3): 251-283.

Stredwick, R. 2001.

"Epistemological Boundaries and Methodological Conflicts in Post-Modern, Consumer Research. *Working Paper Series* (2001) No. WP001/01, University of Wolverhampton, UK.

Sutherland, J.R. and Sawatsky, K.G. 1996.

Human Factor Decay and Sexual Harassment. *Review of Human Factor Studies.* 11(2): 26-45.

Swart, J. 1990.

Malunde: The Street Children of Hillbrow. Witwatersrand University Press. Johannesburg.

Swart-Kruger, J. and Ritcher, L.M. 1997.

"AIDS Related Knowledge, Attitudes and Behaviour Among, South African Street Youth Reflections on Power, Sexuality and The Autonomous Self, (Handout) in Department of Sociology, Library. University of Zimbabwe.

Tadele, G. 2003.

Surviving On The Streets: Sexuality and HIV and AIDS Among Male Street Youth in Dessie, Ethiopia. CODESRIA Bulletin, No. 2, 3 and 4. 98-106.

Thory, A. 2002.

"We Are Changing Our Sexual Behaviour," on http://sound Westhoot. Com/project 08.htm

Torry, W.I. 1979.

Anthropological Studies in Hazardous Environments: Past Trends and New Horizons. *Current Anthropology.* 20(3): 517-540.

Twa-Twa, J.M. 1997.

The Role of the Environment in the Sexual Activity of School Students in Tororo and Pallisa Districts of Uganda. *Health Transition Review*. Supplement to Volume 7. 67-83.

UNAIDS, 2002.

Children On The Brink-http://www.unaids.org

UNAIDS, 2002.

Orphan Support Programmes –
http://www.unaids.org/best practices/
digest/files/reason for hopeintanzania.hotmail.

UNAIDS, 2003.

December, Monthly Bulletin, *"Telling the Story of Southern Africa"* - Report on Angola titled *"Improving the Quality of Reproductive Health Services For War Affected/Displaced Adolescent Girls and Other Vulnerable Youth in Angola.*

UNFPA Report of August 2001.

"World's Youth Resolve to Lead Anti-HIV and *AIDS Crusades, Promote Responsibility"*. Retrieved from http://www.unfpa.org/news/news.cfm?

UNICEF Report. 2002.

Update on Situational Assessment and Analysis of Children in Zimbabwe. "Hope Never Dries- Up: Facing the Challenges".

UNICEF 2003.

Report On Community Dialogue On Orphans and Vulnerable Children, Roma, Unpublished.

UNICEF 2003.

Report on the State of the World's Children, New York.

Van Onselen, C. 1976.

Chibaro; African Mine Labour in Southern Rhodesia, 1900 – 1933, Pluto Press, London.

Vance, C.S. 1992.

"Social Construction Theory: Problems in the History of Sexuality". In Crowley, H. and Himmelweit, S. *Knowing Women; Feminism and Knowledge*. 132-146. Polity Press. Cornwall.

301

Vance, C.S. 1995.

"Social Construction Theory: Problems in the history of Sexuality". In Anthias, F. and Kelly, M.P. (eds.). *Sociological Debates, Thinking About the Social.* 29-42. Greenwich University Press. Kent.

Vianello, M. 2004.

Gender Differences in Access to and Exercise of Power. *Current Sociology.* 52, (3): 501-519.

Wa Thiongo, N. 2005.

Europe on African Memory; The Challenge Of the Pan Africanist Intellectuals, CODESRIA Books.

Wade, W. 1994.

"Man the Hunter: Gender and Violence in Music and Drinking Contexts in Colombia". In Harvey, P. and Gow, P. *Sex and Violence.* 115-138. Routledge. London.

Weeks, J. 1987.

"Questions of Identity". In Caplan, P. The Cultural Construction of Sexuality. 31-52. Routledge. London.

Weiringa, S. 2004.

"Women Marriages and Other Same Sex Practices; Historical Reflections on African Women's Same Sex Relations." In Morgan, R. and Wieringa, S. (eds). Tommy Boys, Lesbian Men and Ancestral Wives, Female Same Sex Practices in Africa. Gala Publishers. South Africa

Weis, L. Fine, M. Wong, L. and Weseen, S. 2000.

"For Whom? Qualitative Research, Representations and Social Responsibilities". In Denzin, N. and Lincoln, Y.S. (eds.). *Handbook of Qualitative Research.* 107-133. Sage Publishers. London.

Whitehead, S. M and Barrett, F. J. 2001

The Masculinities Reader; Blackwell Publishers, Oxford.

Wilson, F. 2006.

"On Being a Father and Poor in Southern Africa". In Morrell, R. and Richter, L. (eds.). *Baba: Men and Fatherhood in South Africa.* 26-38. HSRC Press. Cape Town.

Wood, K. and Jewkes, R. 2001.

"Violence, Rape and Sexual Coercion: Everyday Love in a South African Township". In Whitehead, S.M. and Barret, F.J. *The Masculinities Reader.* 133-141. Polity. Oxford.

Wood, K. and
Jewkes, R. 2001.

"Dangerous Love; Reflections on Violence Among Xhosa Township Youth". In Morrell, R.(ed.). *Changing Man in South Africa.* 317-337. Zed Books. London.

Zamberia, A.M. 2007.

Stigma and HIV Testing Decisions: A Qualitative Analysis. *LWATI: A Journal of Contemporary Research.* 4: 258-273.

Zamberia, A.M. 2004.

HIV and AIDS in Sub- Saharan Africa: A Social Problem. *UNISWA Research Journal.* 18: 21-37.

Zeitlin 1990.

Ideology and Social Theory- London University Press. London.

Zihlman, A.L. 1993. "Sex Differences and Gender Hierarchies Among Primates: An Evolutionary Perspective". In Muller, D.B. (ed.). *Sex and Gender Hierarchies.* 32-52. Cambridge University Press. London